Hot Gimmick

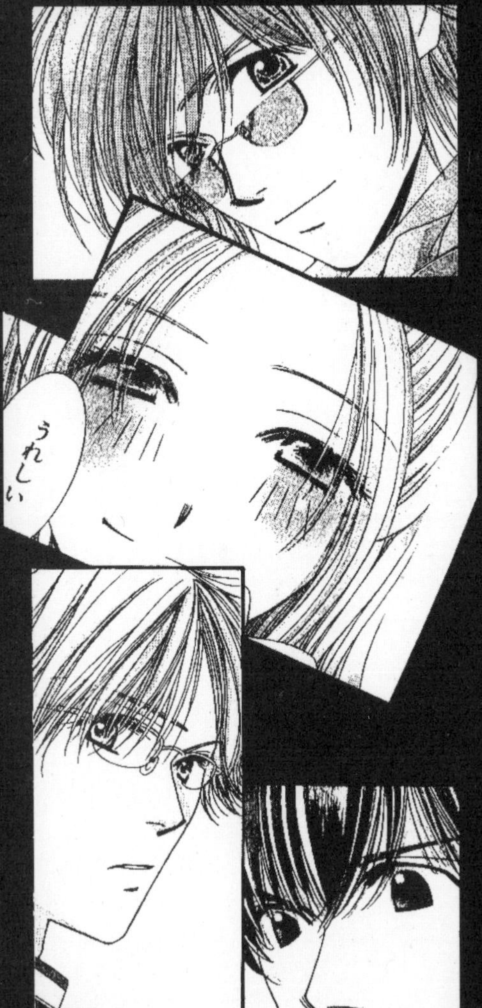
うれしい

vol.2

MIKI AIHARA

HOT GIMMICK
CONTENTS

Chapter 5

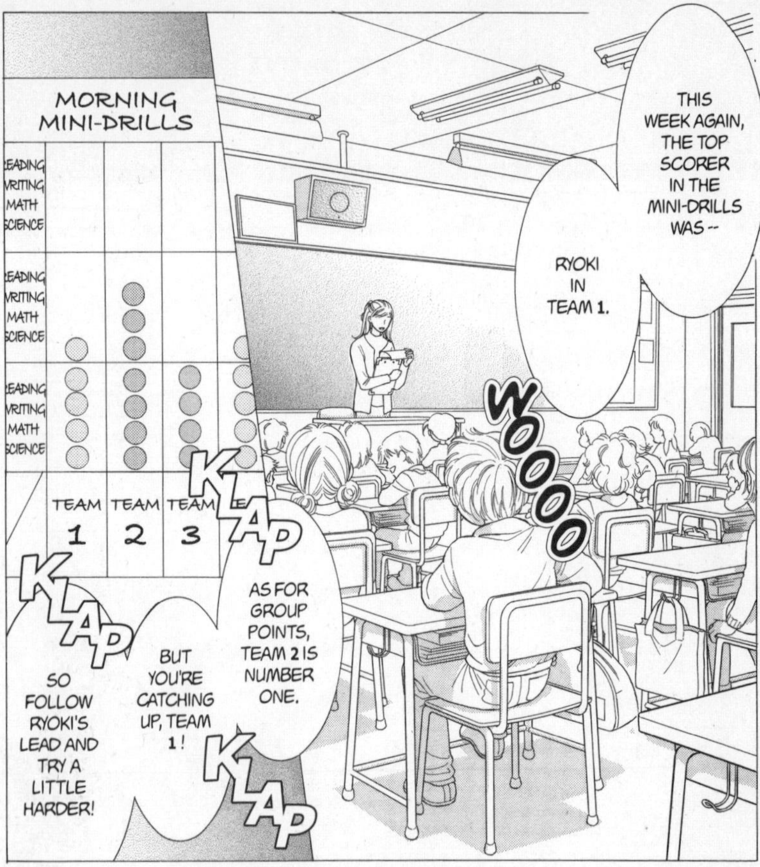
THIS WEEK AGAIN, THE TOP SCORER IN THE MINI-DRILLS WAS --
RYOKI IN TEAM 1.
WOOOOO
MORNING MINI-DRILLS
MATH
SCIENCE
TEAM 1
TEAM 2
TEAM 3
KLAP
AS FOR GROUP POINTS, TEAM 2 IS NUMBER ONE.
KLAP
BUT YOU'RE CATCHING UP, TEAM 1!
KLAP
SO FOLLOW RYOKI'S LEAD AND TRY A LITTLE HARDER!

hot gimmick

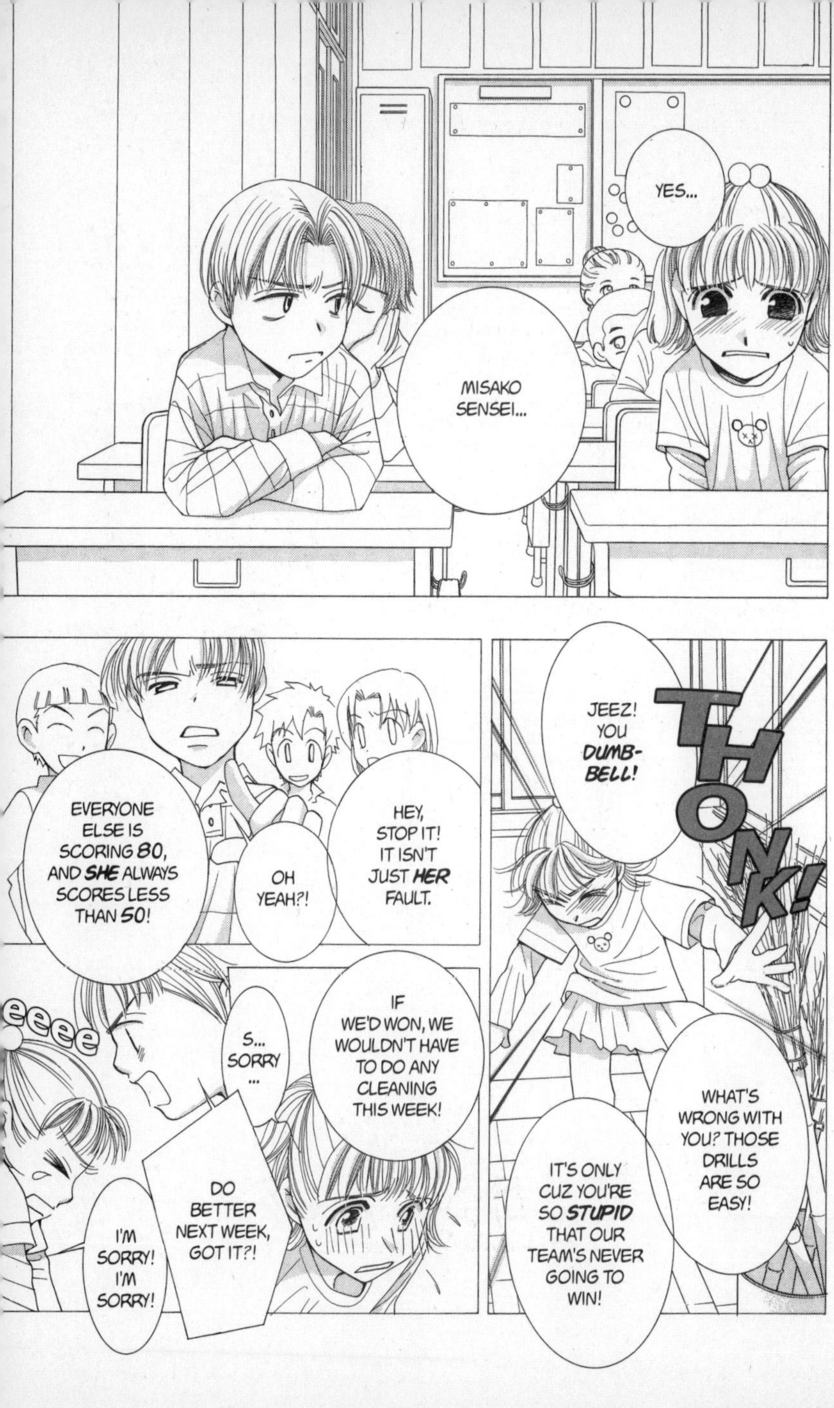
YES...
MISAKO SENSEI...
THONK!
JEEZ! YOU DUMB-BELL!
WHAT'S WRONG WITH YOU? THOSE DRILLS ARE SO EASY!
IT'S ONLY CUZ YOU'RE SO STUPID THAT OUR TEAM'S NEVER GOING TO WIN!
HEY, STOP IT! IT ISN'T JUST HER FAULT.
OH YEAH?!
EVERYONE ELSE IS SCORING 80, AND SHE ALWAYS SCORES LESS THAN 50!
IF WE'D WON, WE WOULDN'T HAVE TO DO ANY CLEANING THIS WEEK!
S... SORRY ...
eeee
DO BETTER NEXT WEEK, GOT IT?!
I'M SORRY! I'M SORRY!

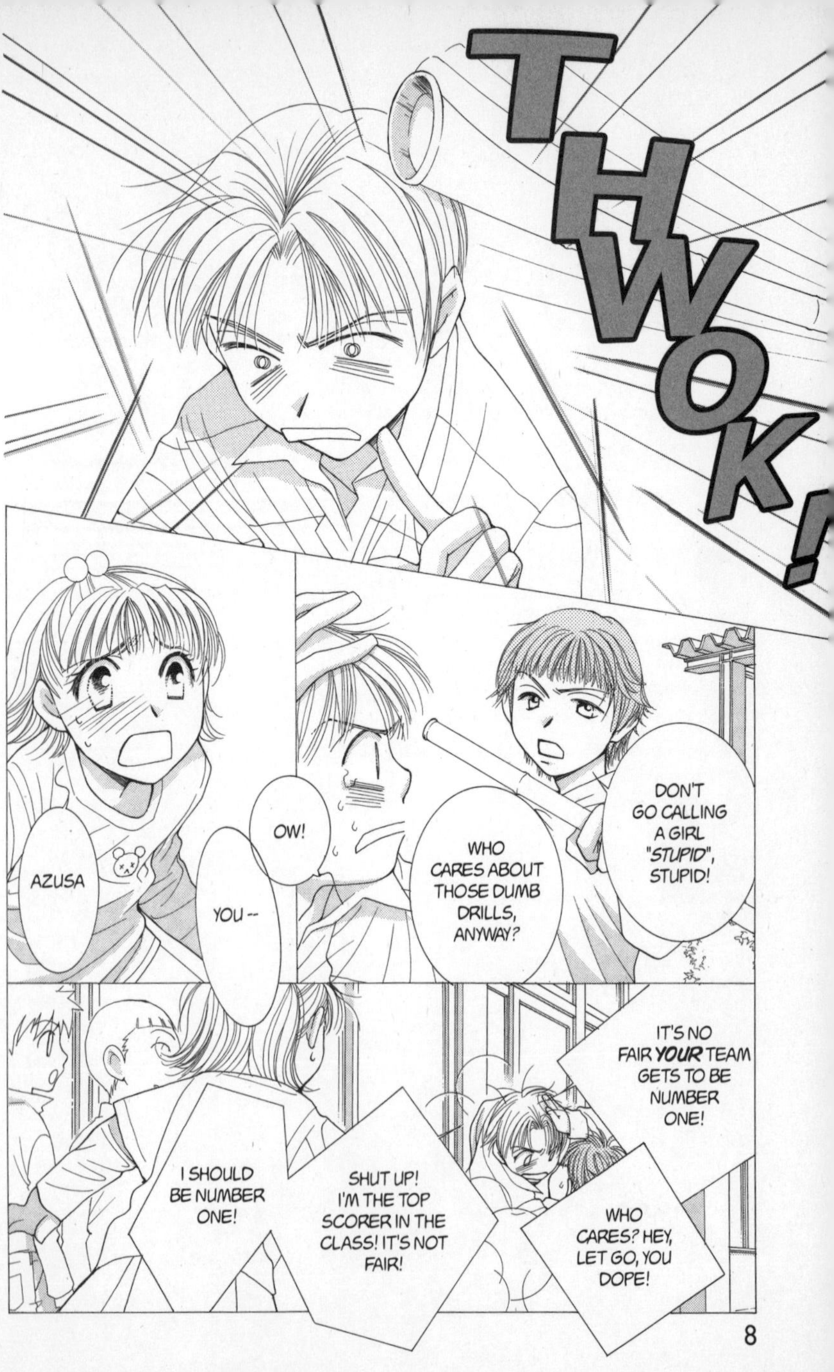
THWOK!
DON'T GO CALLING A GIRL "*STUPID*", STUPID!
WHO CARES ABOUT THOSE DUMB DRILLS, ANYWAY?
OW!
YOU --
AZUSA
IT'S NO FAIR ***YOUR*** TEAM GETS TO BE NUMBER ONE!
WHO CARES? HEY, LET GO, YOU DOPE!
SHUT UP! I'M THE TOP SCORER IN THE CLASS! IT'S NOT FAIR!
I SHOULD BE NUMBER ONE!

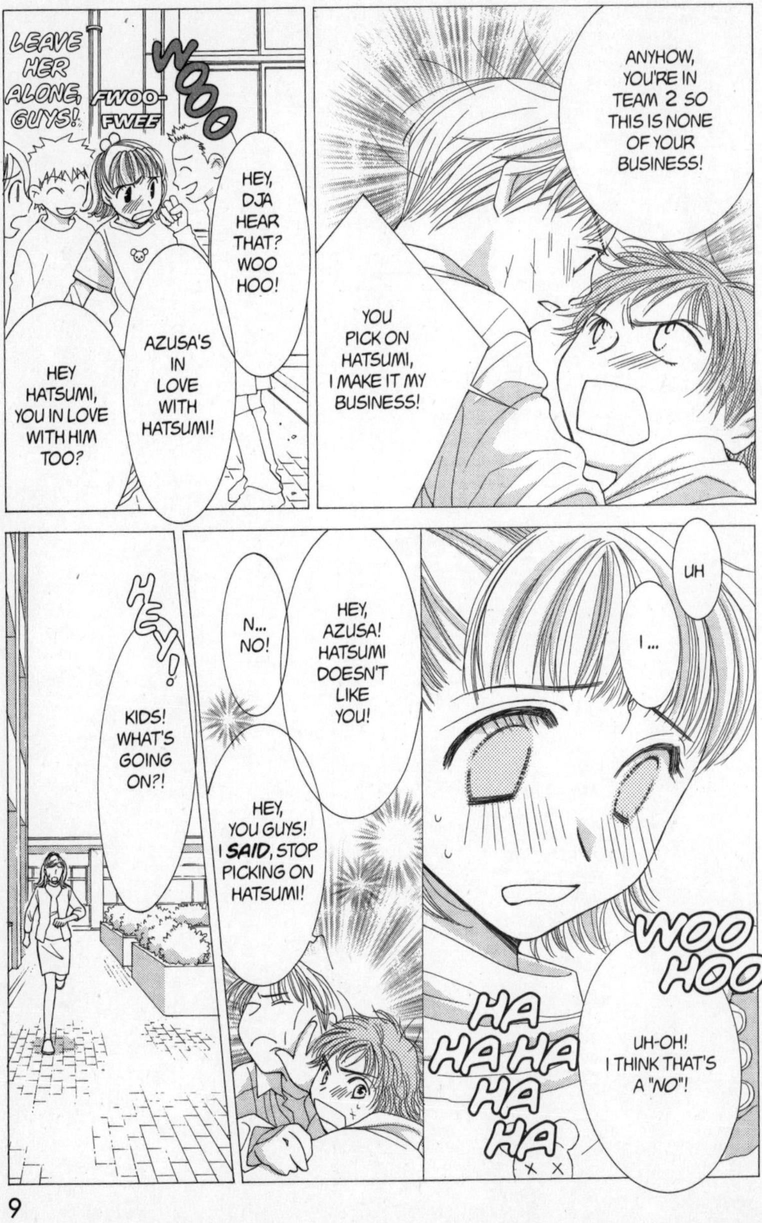
ANYHOW, YOU'RE IN TEAM 2 SO THIS IS NONE OF YOUR BUSINESS!
YOU PICK ON HATSUMI, I MAKE IT MY BUSINESS!
WOOO
HEY, DJA HEAR THAT? WOO HOO!
FWOO-FWEE
LEAVE HER ALONE, GUYS!
AZUSA'S IN LOVE WITH HATSUMI!
HEY HATSUMI, YOU IN LOVE WITH HIM TOO?
UH
I...
WOO HOO
UH-OH! I THINK THAT'S A "NO"!
HA HA HA HA HA HA
HEY, AZUSA! HATSUMI DOESN'T LIKE YOU!
N... NO!
HEY, YOU GUYS! I *SAID*, STOP PICKING ON HATSUMI!
HEY!
KIDS! WHAT'S GOING ON?!

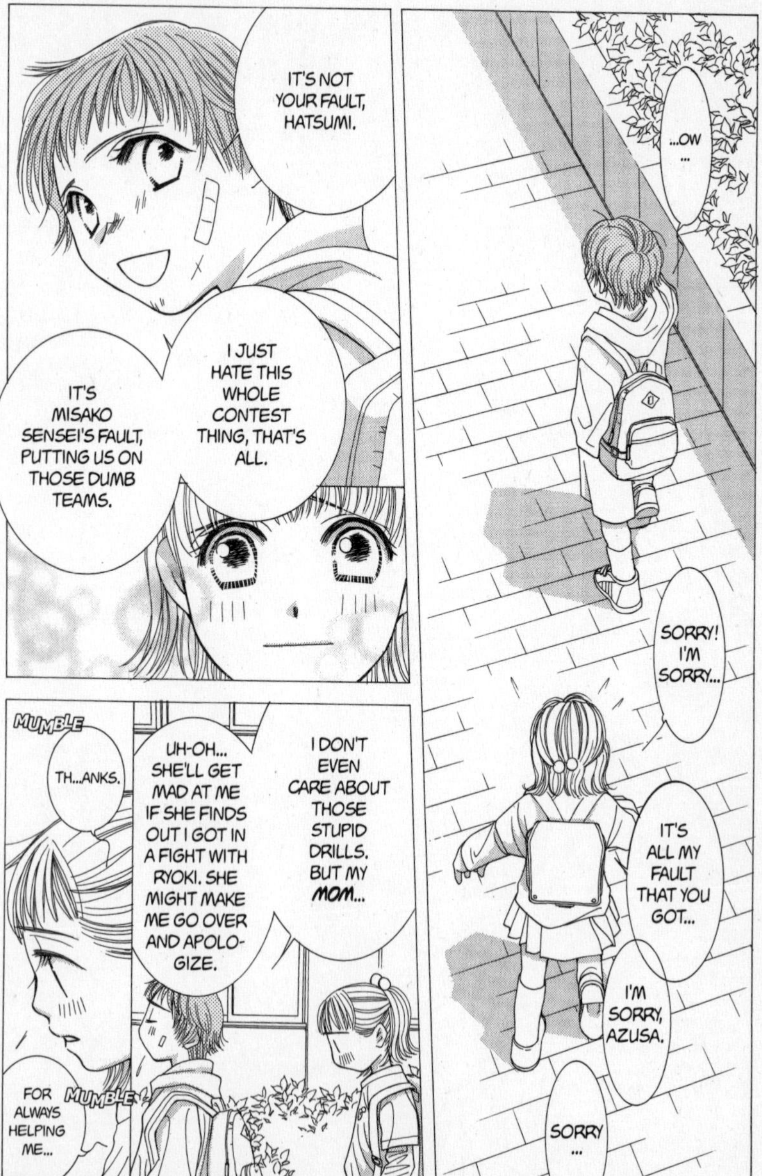
...OW ...
SORRY! I'M SORRY...
IT'S ALL MY FAULT THAT YOU GOT...
I'M SORRY, AZUSA.
SORRY ...
IT'S NOT YOUR FAULT, HATSUMI.
I JUST HATE THIS WHOLE CONTEST THING, THAT'S ALL.
IT'S MISAKO SENSEI'S FAULT, PUTTING US ON THOSE DUMB TEAMS.
I DON'T EVEN CARE ABOUT THOSE STUPID DRILLS. BUT MY *MOM*...
UH-OH... SHE'LL GET MAD AT ME IF SHE FINDS OUT I GOT IN A FIGHT WITH RYOKI. SHE MIGHT MAKE ME GO OVER AND APOLOGIZE.
MUMBLE
TH...ANKS.
FOR ALWAYS HELPING ME...
MUMBLE

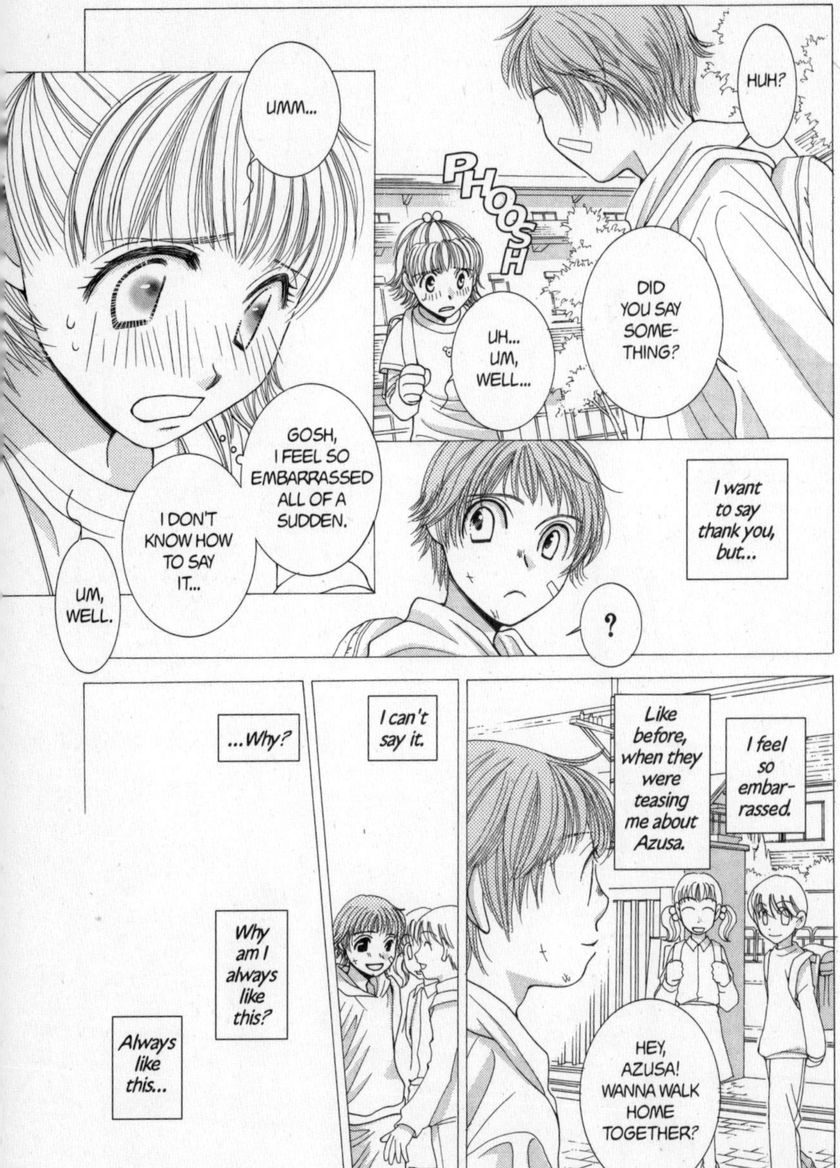
HUH?
PHOOSH
DID YOU SAY SOMETHING?
UH... UM, WELL...
I want to say thank you, but...
?
UMM...
GOSH, I FEEL SO EMBARRASSED ALL OF A SUDDEN.
I DON'T KNOW HOW TO SAY IT...
UM, WELL.
I feel so embarrassed.
Like before, when they were teasing me about Azusa.
HEY, AZUSA! WANNA WALK HOME TOGETHER?
I can't say it.
...Why?
Why am I always like this?
Always like this...

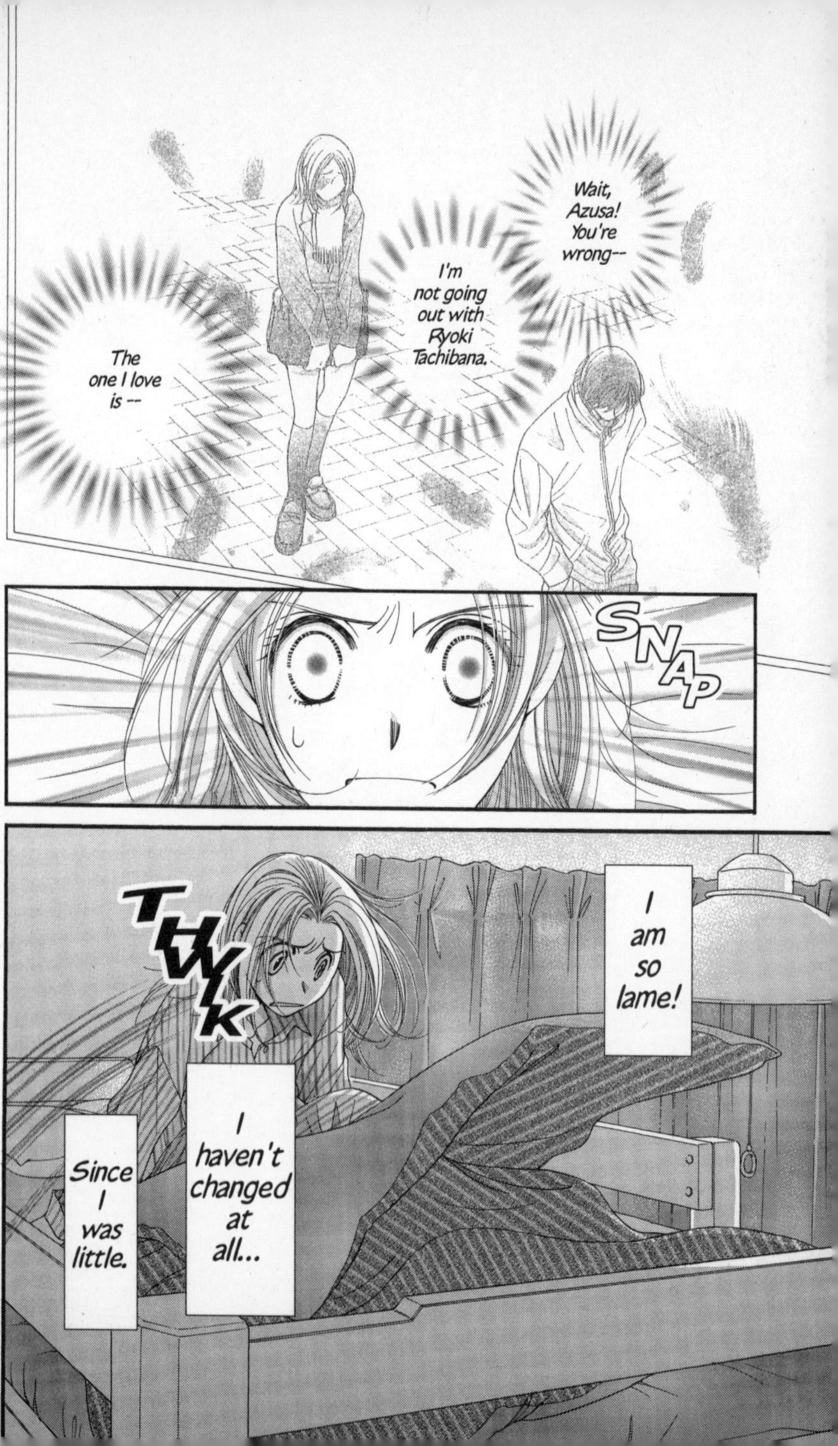
Wait, Azusa! You're wrong--
I'm not going out with Ryoki Tachibana.
The one I love is --
SNAP
I am so lame!
THWK
I haven't changed at all...
Since I was little.

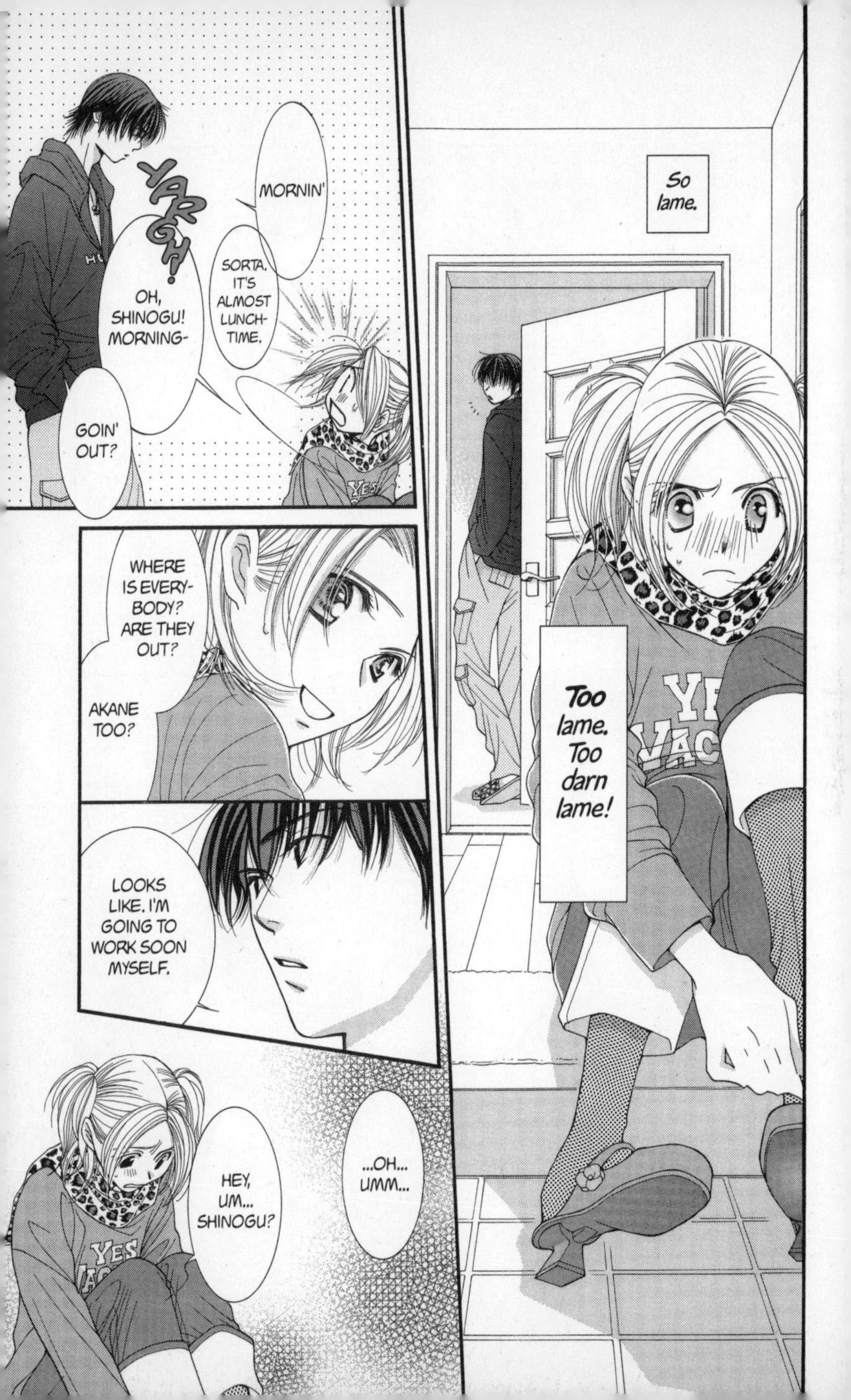
So lame.
Too lame. Too darn lame!
MORNIN'
SORTA. IT'S ALMOST LUNCH-TIME.
YARGH!
OH, SHINOGU! MORNING-
GOIN' OUT?
WHERE IS EVERY-BODY? ARE THEY OUT?
AKANE TOO?
LOOKS LIKE. I'M GOING TO WORK SOON MYSELF.
...OH... UMM...
HEY, UM... SHINOGU?

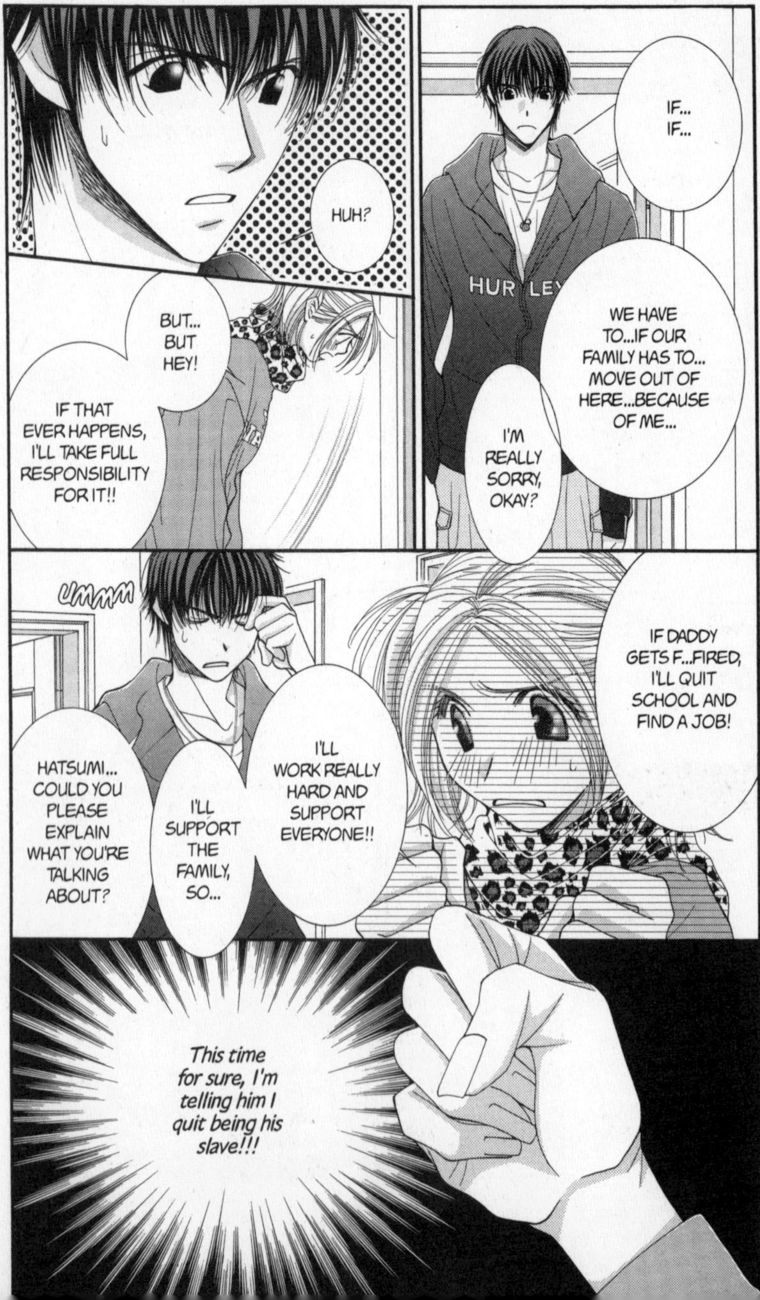
IF... IF...
WE HAVE TO...IF OUR FAMILY HAS TO... MOVE OUT OF HERE...BECAUSE OF ME...
I'M REALLY SORRY, OKAY?
HUH?
BUT... BUT HEY!
IF THAT EVER HAPPENS, I'LL TAKE FULL RESPONSIBILITY FOR IT!!
IF DADDY GETS F...FIRED, I'LL QUIT SCHOOL AND FIND A JOB!
I'LL WORK REALLY HARD AND SUPPORT EVERYONE!!
I'LL SUPPORT THE FAMILY, SO...
UMMM
HATSUMI... COULD YOU PLEASE EXPLAIN WHAT YOU'RE TALKING ABOUT?
This time for sure, I'm telling him I quit being his slave!!!

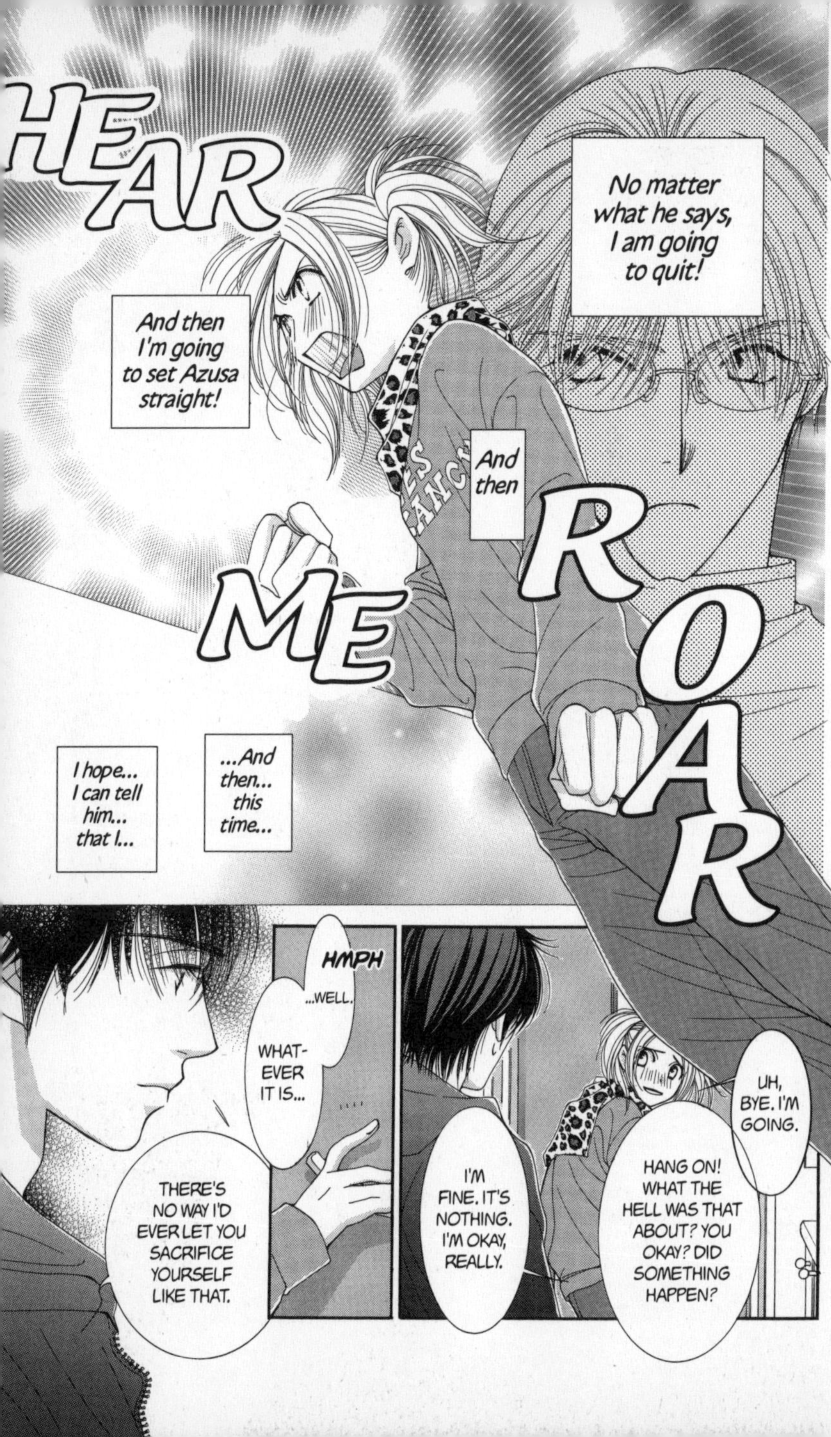
No matter what he says, I am going to quit!
HEAR
And then I'm going to set Azusa straight!
And then
ROAR
ME
...And then... this time...
I hope... I can tell him... that I...
UH, BYE. I'M GOING.
HANG ON! WHAT THE HELL WAS THAT ABOUT? YOU OKAY? DID SOMETHING HAPPEN?
I'M FINE. IT'S NOTHING. I'M OKAY, REALLY.
HMPH
...WELL.
WHAT-EVER IT IS...
....
THERE'S NO WAY I'D EVER LET YOU SACRIFICE YOURSELF LIKE THAT.

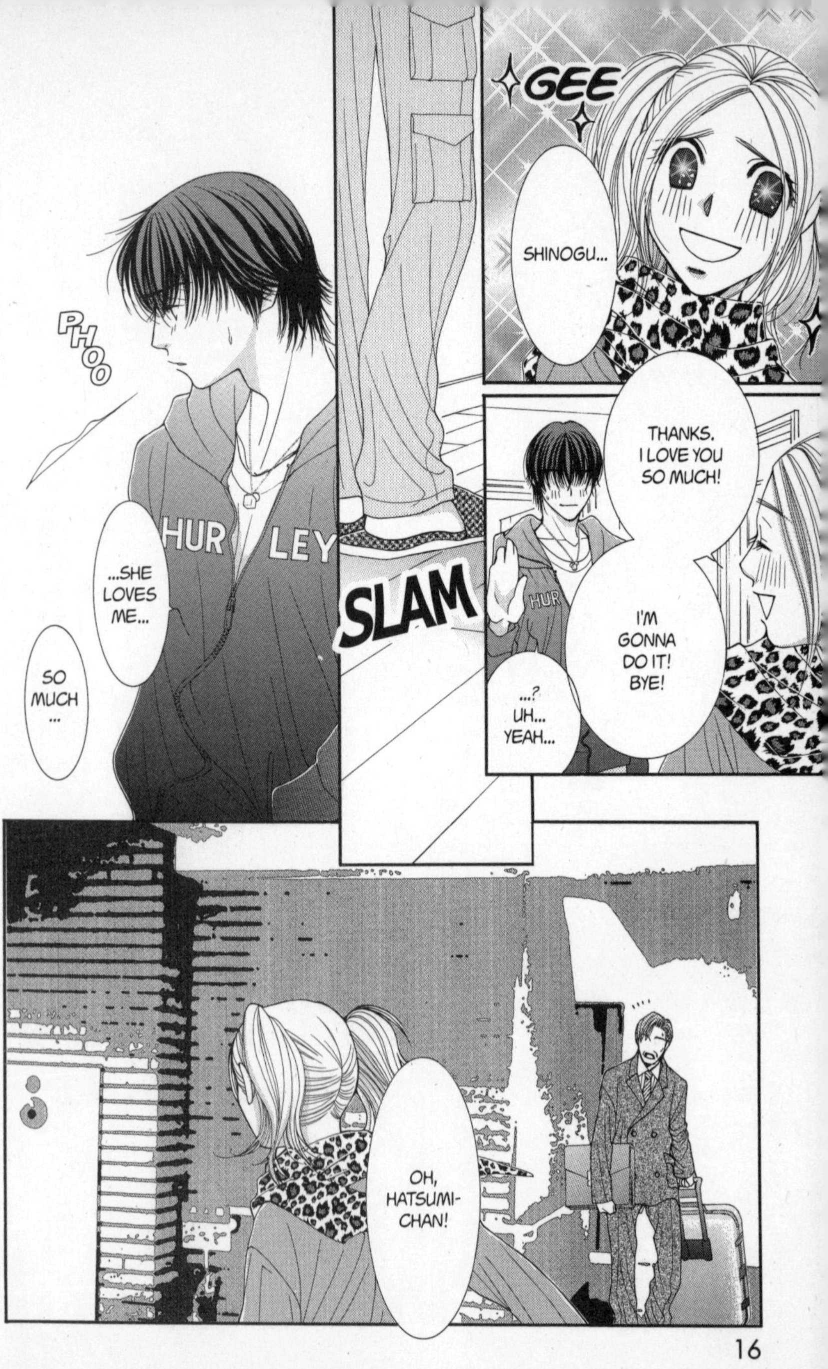
GEE
SHINOGU...
THANKS. I LOVE YOU SO MUCH!
I'M GONNA DO IT! BYE!
...? UH... YEAH...
HUR
SLAM
PHOO
HUR LEY
...SHE LOVES ME...
SO MUCH ...
OH, HATSUMI-CHAN!

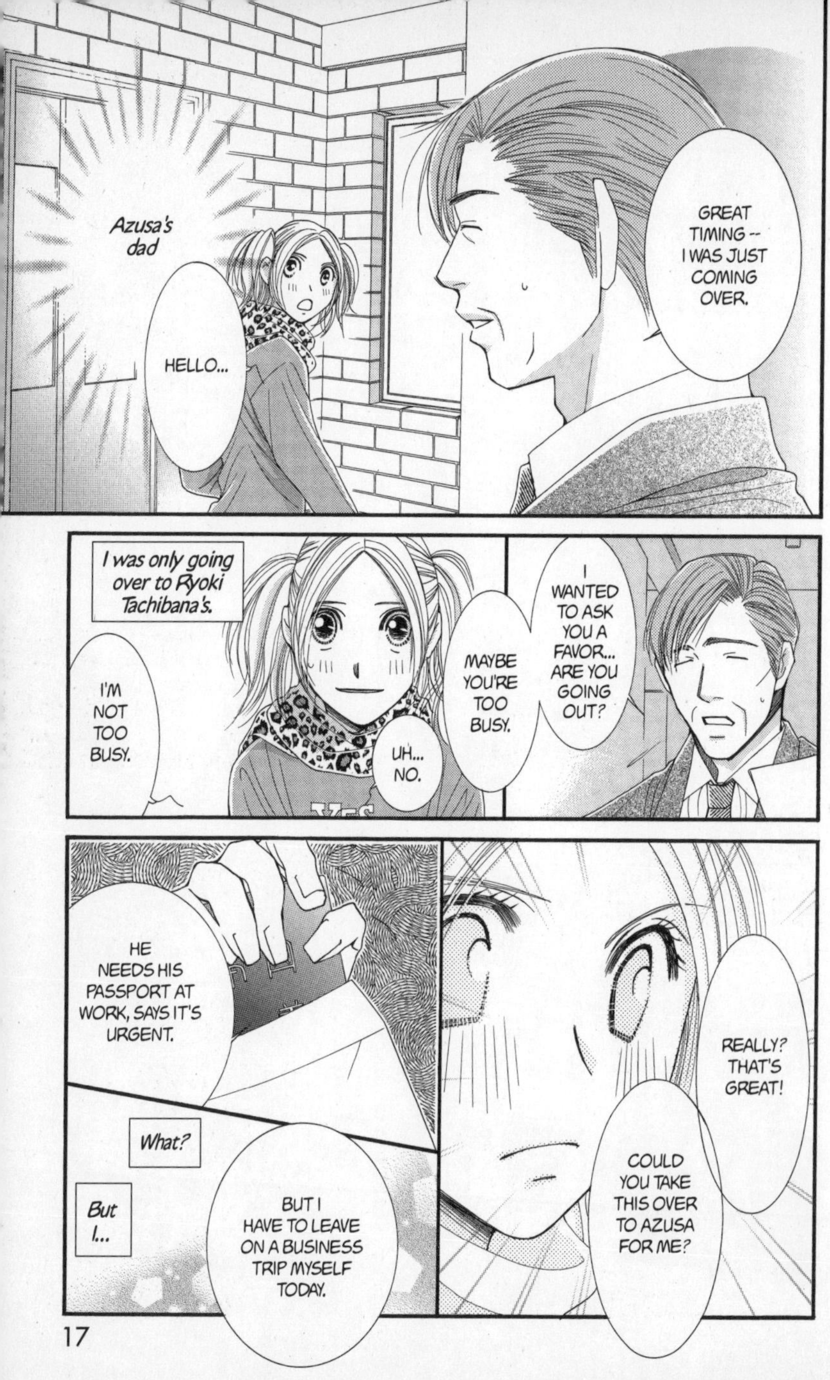
GREAT TIMING -- I WAS JUST COMING OVER.
Azusa's dad
HELLO...
I WANTED TO ASK YOU A FAVOR... ARE YOU GOING OUT?
MAYBE YOU'RE TOO BUSY.
UH... NO.
I was only going over to Ryoki Tachibana's.
I'M NOT TOO BUSY.
REALLY? THAT'S GREAT!
COULD YOU TAKE THIS OVER TO AZUSA FOR ME?
HE NEEDS HIS PASSPORT AT WORK, SAYS IT'S URGENT.
What?
BUT I HAVE TO LEAVE ON A BUSINESS TRIP MYSELF TODAY.
But I...

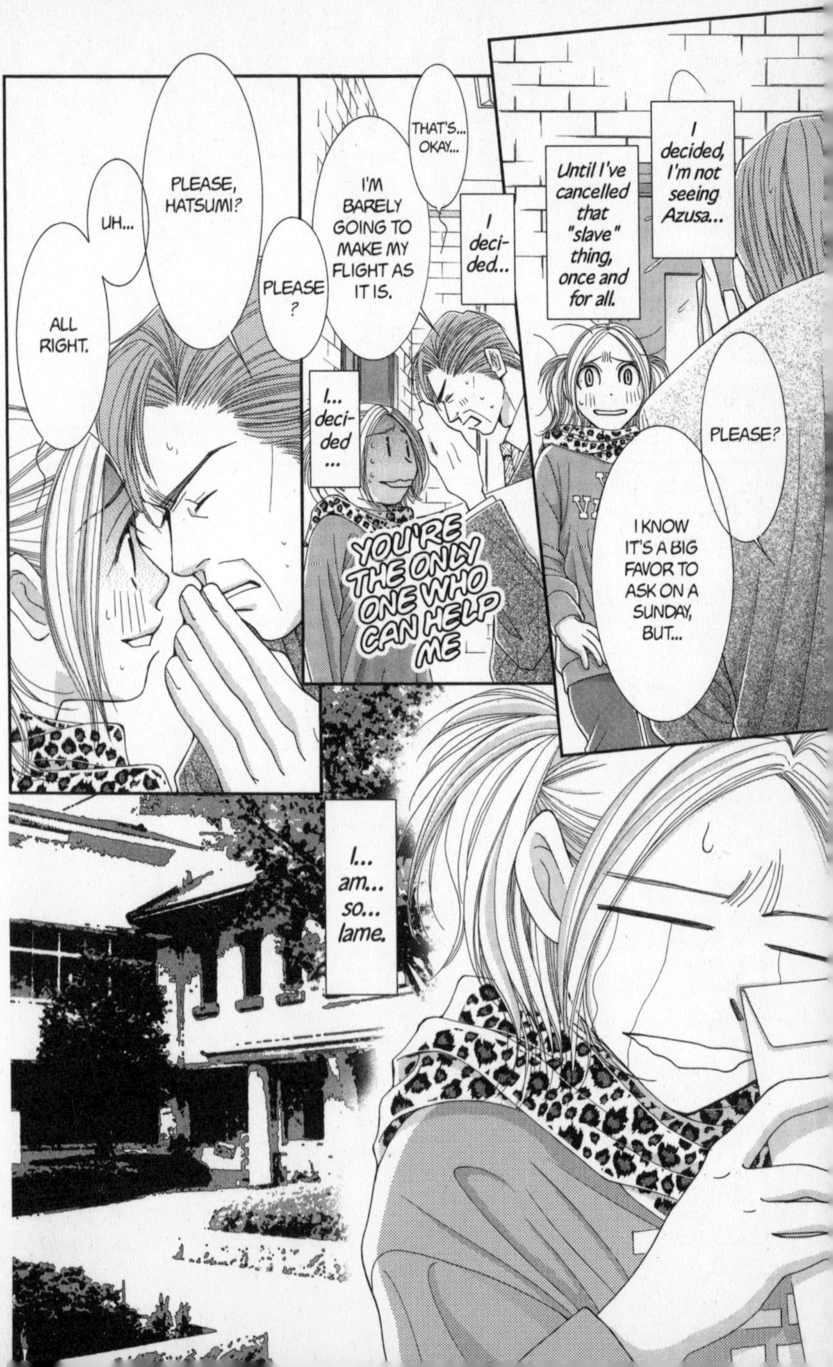
I decided, I'm not seeing Azusa...
Until I've cancelled that "slave" thing, once and for all.
PLEASE?
I KNOW IT'S A BIG FAVOR TO ASK ON A SUNDAY, BUT...
I decided...
THAT'S... OKAY...
I'M BARELY GOING TO MAKE MY FLIGHT AS IT IS.
PLEASE?
I... decided...
YOU'RE THE ONLY ONE WHO CAN HELP ME
PLEASE, HATSUMI?
UH...
ALL RIGHT.
I... am... so... lame.

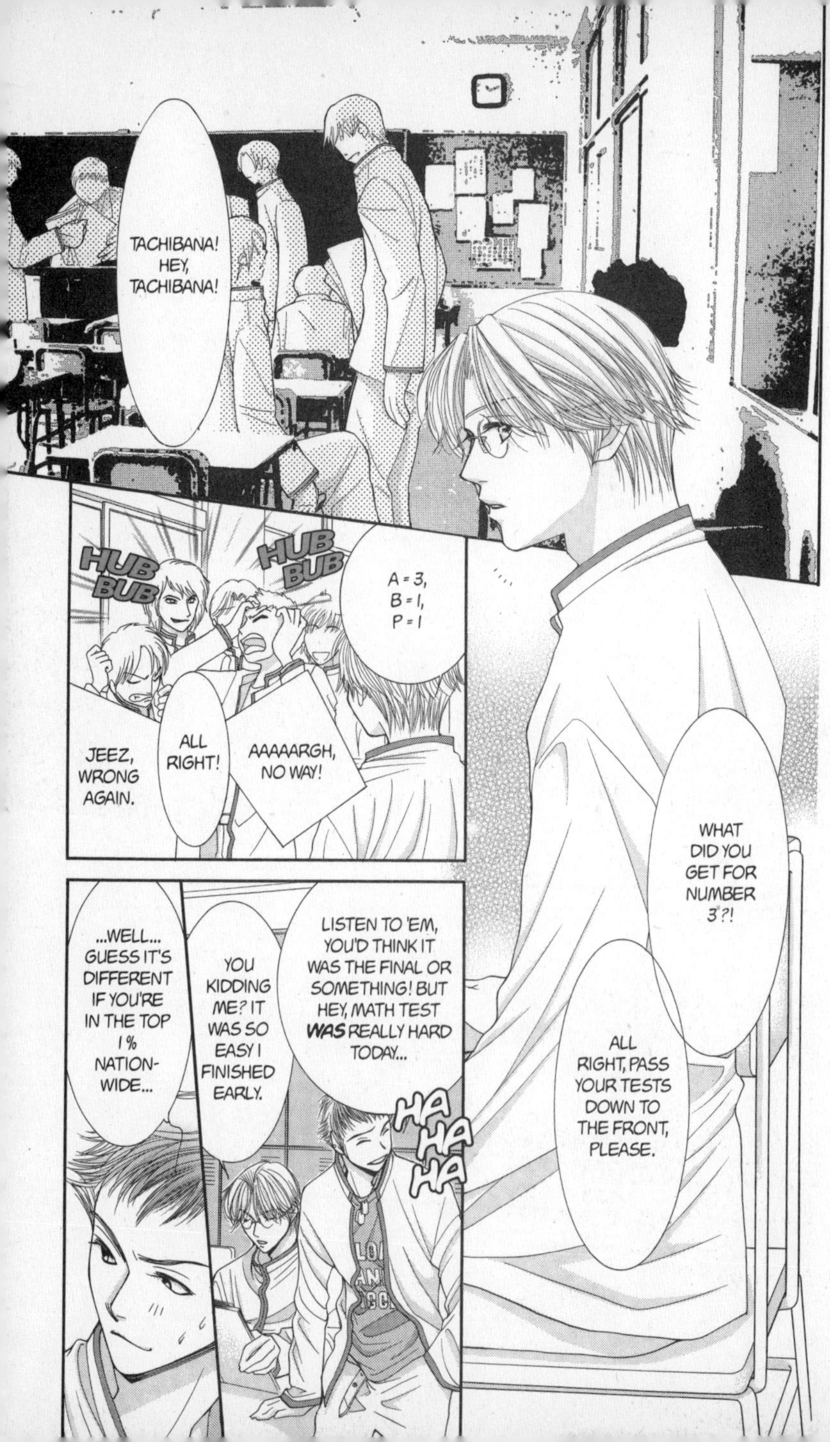
TACHIBANA! HEY, TACHIBANA!
...
WHAT DID YOU GET FOR NUMBER 3?!
ALL RIGHT, PASS YOUR TESTS DOWN TO THE FRONT, PLEASE.
HUB BUB
A = 3, B = 1, P = 1
HUB BUB
AAAAARGH, NO WAY!
ALL RIGHT!
JEEZ, WRONG AGAIN.
LISTEN TO 'EM, YOU'D THINK IT WAS THE FINAL OR SOMETHING! BUT HEY, MATH TEST WAS REALLY HARD TODAY...
HA HA HA
YOU KIDDING ME? IT WAS SO EASY I FINISHED EARLY.
...WELL... GUESS IT'S DIFFERENT IF YOU'RE IN THE TOP 1% NATION-WIDE...

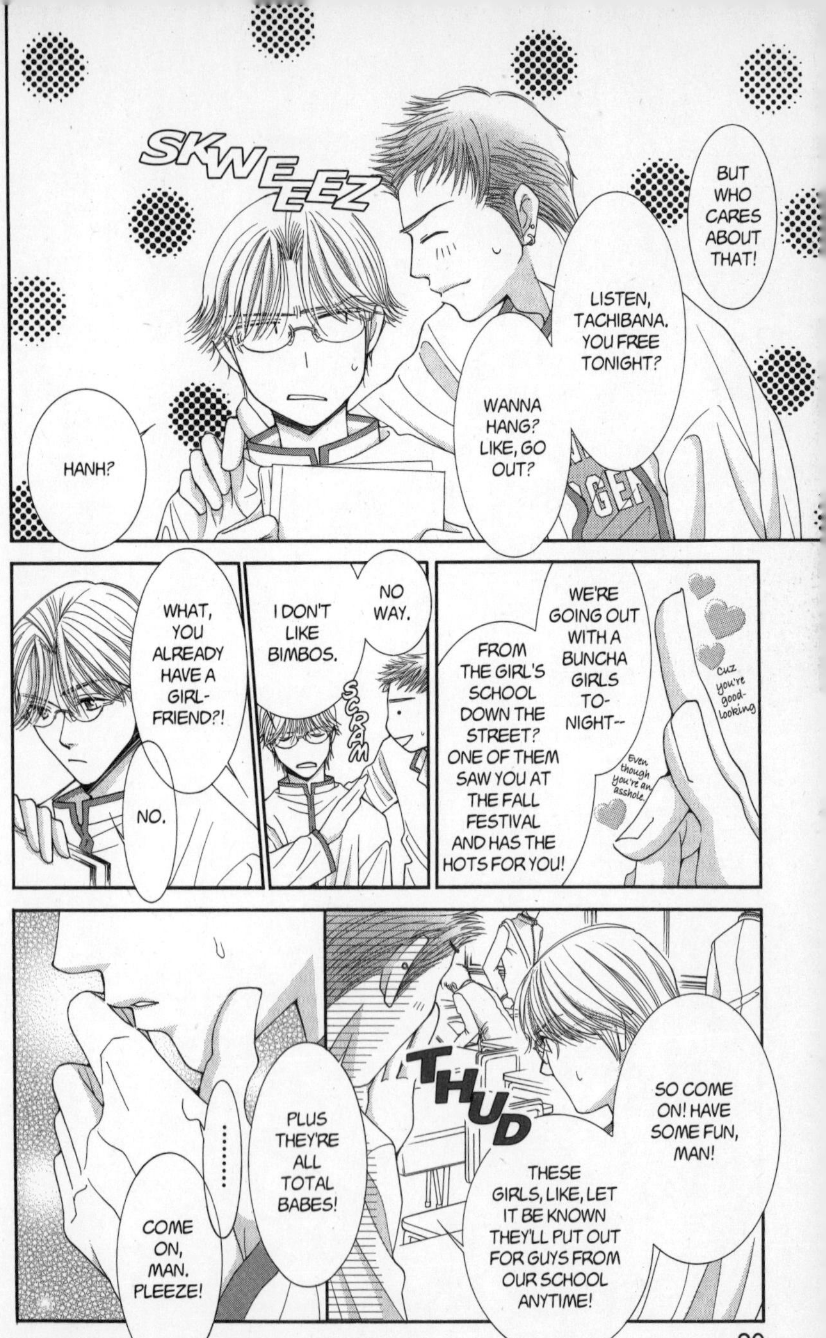
BUT WHO CARES ABOUT THAT!
LISTEN, TACHIBANA. YOU FREE TONIGHT?
WANNA HANG? LIKE, GO OUT?
SKWEEEZ
HANH?
WE'RE GOING OUT WITH A BUNCHA GIRLS TO-NIGHT--
FROM THE GIRL'S SCHOOL DOWN THE STREET? ONE OF THEM SAW YOU AT THE FALL FESTIVAL AND HAS THE HOTS FOR YOU!
Cuz you're good-looking
Even though you're an asshole.
NO WAY.
I DON'T LIKE BIMBOS.
SCRAM
WHAT, YOU ALREADY HAVE A GIRL-FRIEND?!
NO.
SO COME ON! HAVE SOME FUN, MAN!
THESE GIRLS, LIKE, LET IT BE KNOWN THEY'LL PUT OUT FOR GUYS FROM OUR SCHOOL ANYTIME!
THUD
PLUS THEY'RE ALL TOTAL BABES!
......
COME ON, MAN. PLEEZE!

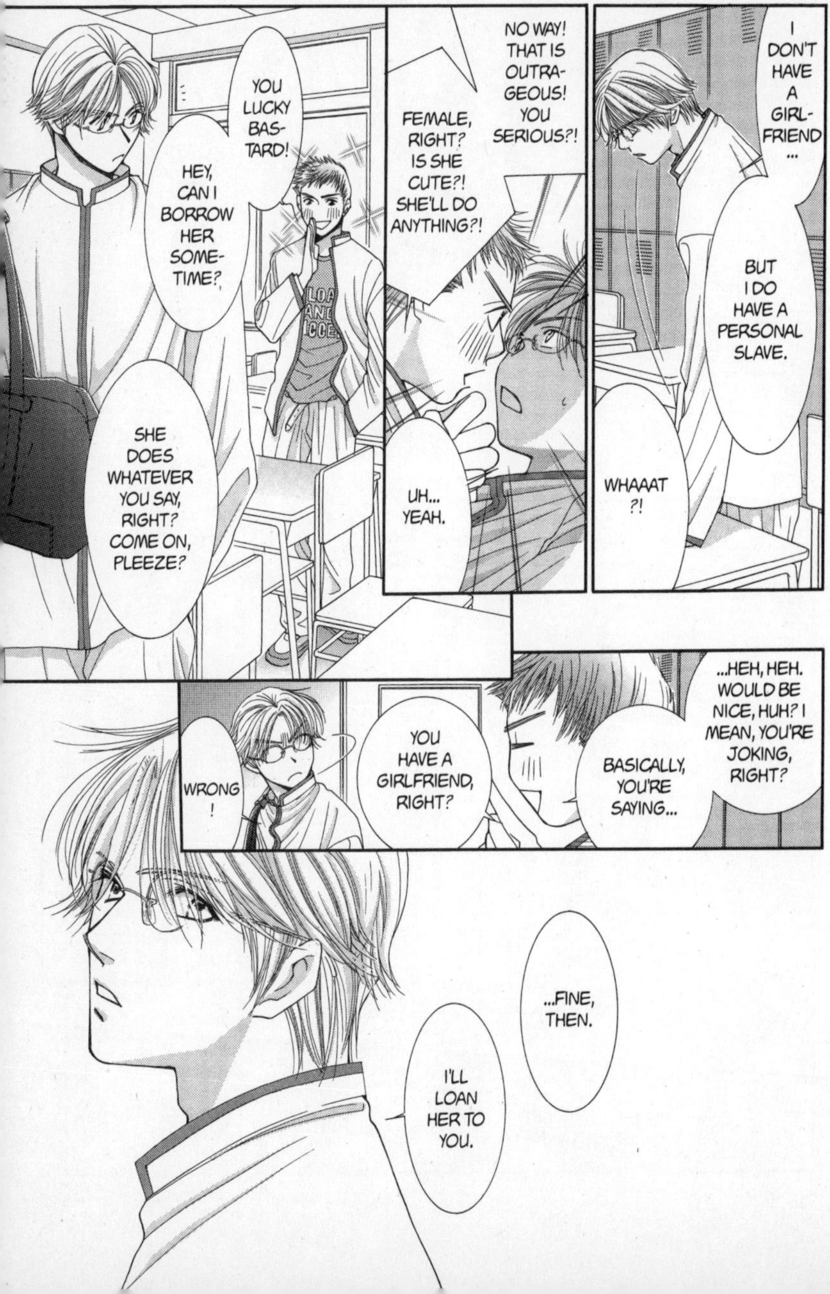
I DON'T HAVE A GIRLFRIEND...
BUT I DO HAVE A PERSONAL SLAVE.
WHAAAT?!
NO WAY! THAT IS OUTRAGEOUS! YOU SERIOUS?!
FEMALE, RIGHT? IS SHE CUTE?! SHE'LL DO ANYTHING?!
UH... YEAH.
YOU LUCKY BASTARD!
HEY, CAN I BORROW HER SOMETIME?
SHE DOES WHATEVER YOU SAY, RIGHT? COME ON, PLEEZE?
...HEH, HEH. WOULD BE NICE, HUH? I MEAN, YOU'RE JOKING, RIGHT?
BASICALLY, YOU'RE SAYING...
YOU HAVE A GIRLFRIEND, RIGHT?
WRONG!
...FINE, THEN.
I'LL LOAN HER TO YOU.

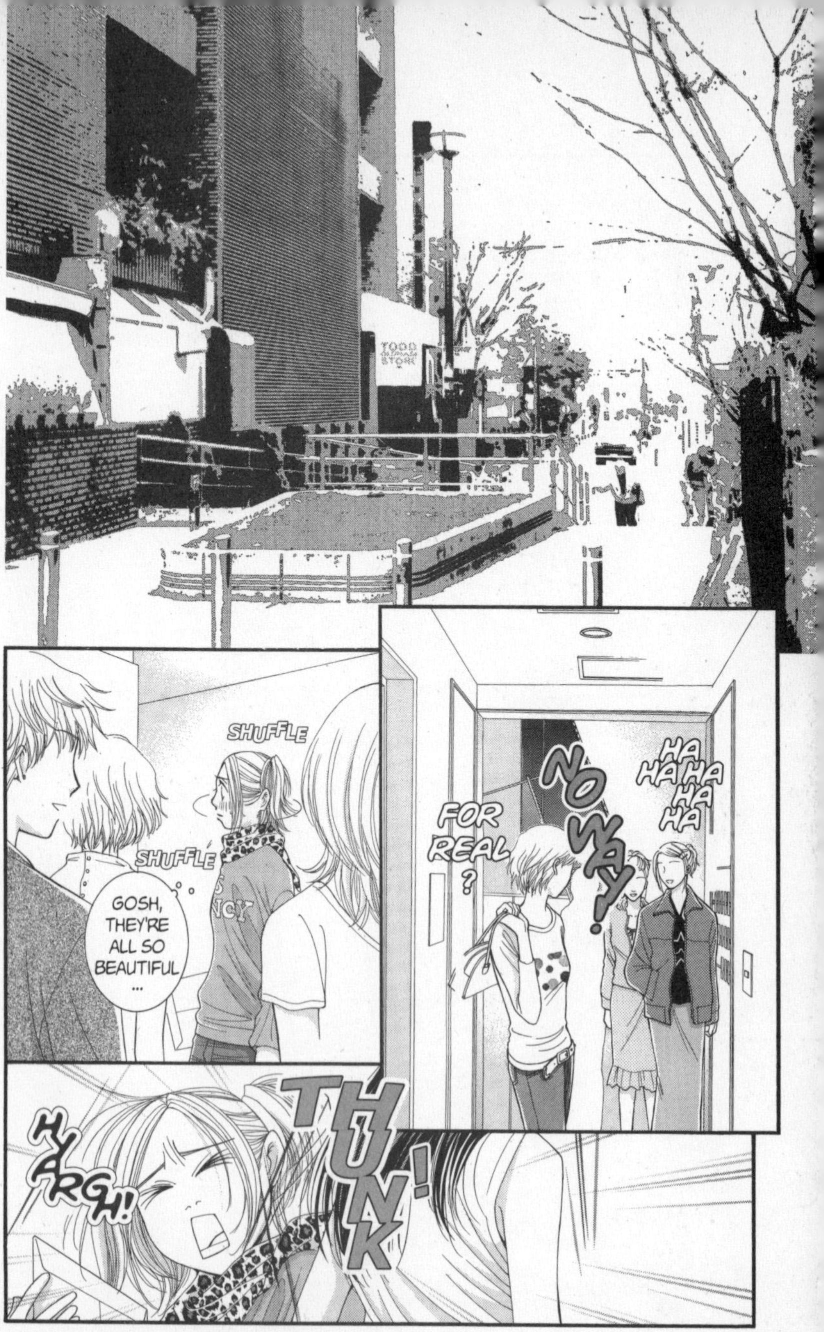
HA HA HA HA HA
NO WAY!
FOR REAL?
SHUFFLE
SHUFFLE
GOSH, THEY'RE ALL SO BEAUTIFUL...
THUNK!
HYARGH!

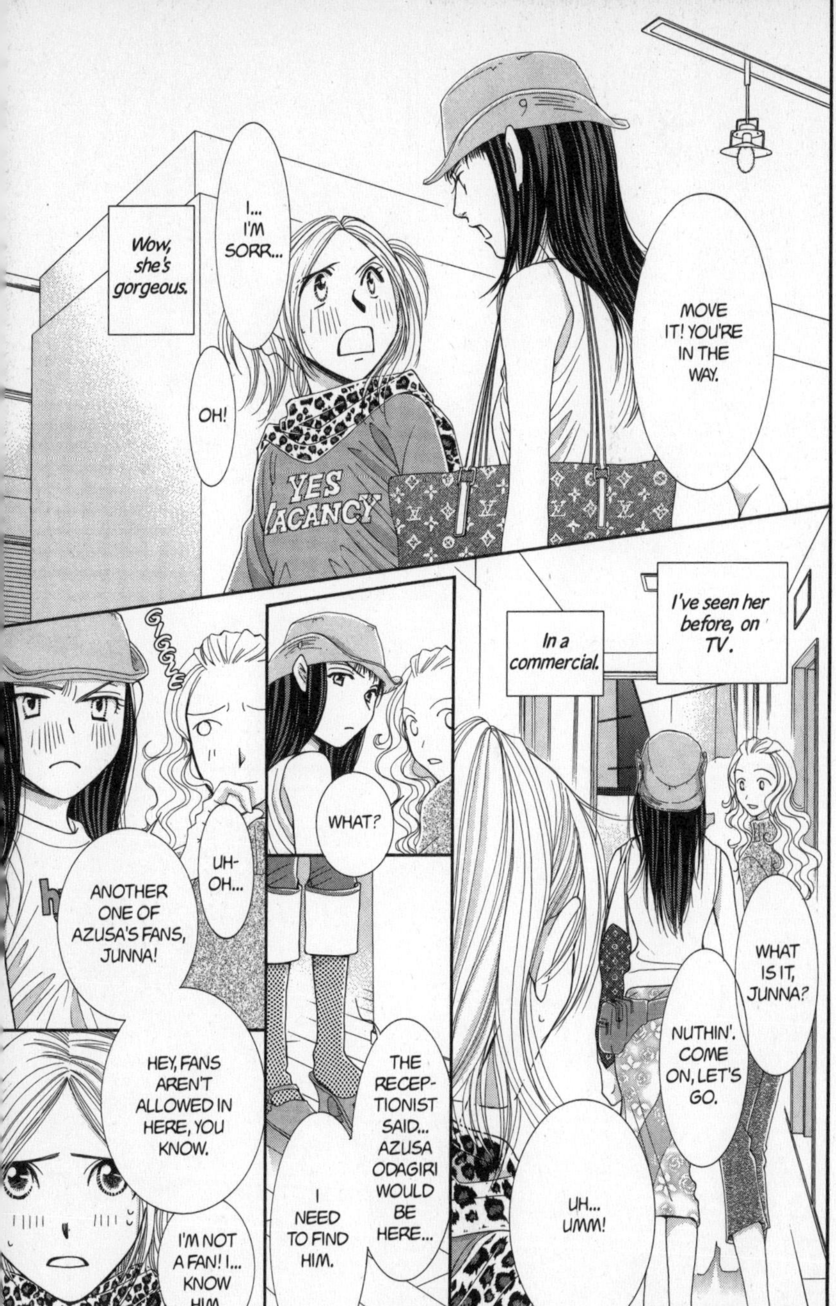
MOVE IT! YOU'RE IN THE WAY.
OH!
I... I'M SORR...
Wow, she's gorgeous.
I've seen her before, on TV.
In a commercial.
WHAT IS IT, JUNNA?
NUTHIN'. COME ON, LET'S GO.
UH... UMM!
WHAT?
GIGGLE
UH-OH...
ANOTHER ONE OF AZUSA'S FANS, JUNNA!
HEY, FANS AREN'T ALLOWED IN HERE, YOU KNOW.
I'M NOT A FAN! I... KNOW HIM.
THE RECEPTIONIST SAID... AZUSA ODAGIRI WOULD BE HERE...
I NEED TO FIND HIM.

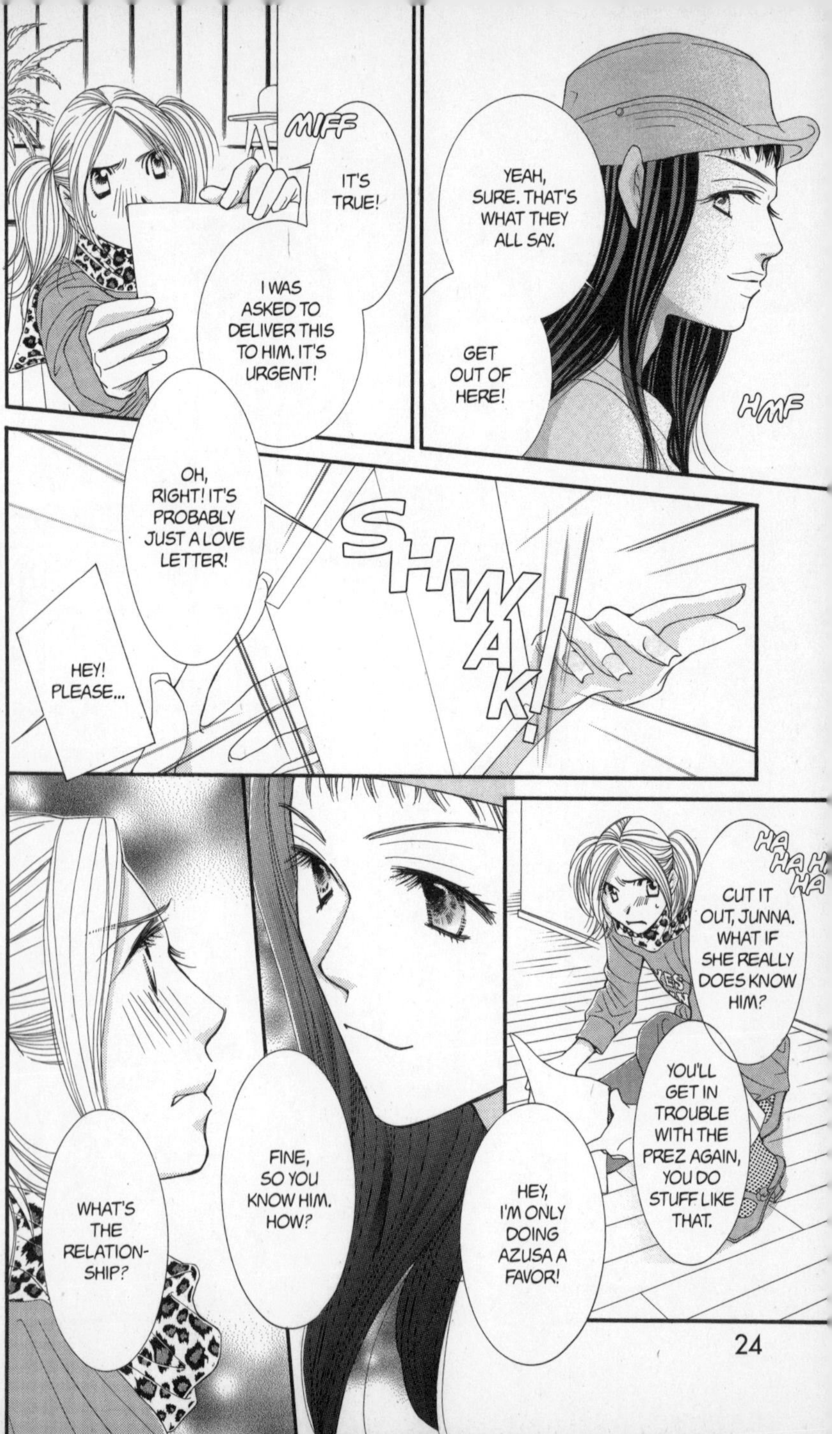
YEAH, SURE. THAT'S WHAT THEY ALL SAY.
GET OUT OF HERE!
HMF
MIFF
IT'S TRUE!
I WAS ASKED TO DELIVER THIS TO HIM. IT'S URGENT!
SHWAK!
OH, RIGHT! IT'S PROBABLY JUST A LOVE LETTER!
HEY! PLEASE...
HA HA HA HA
CUT IT OUT, JUNNA. WHAT IF SHE REALLY DOES KNOW HIM?
YOU'LL GET IN TROUBLE WITH THE PREZ AGAIN, YOU DO STUFF LIKE THAT.
HEY, I'M ONLY DOING AZUSA A FAVOR!
FINE, SO YOU KNOW HIM. HOW?
WHAT'S THE RELATION-SHIP?

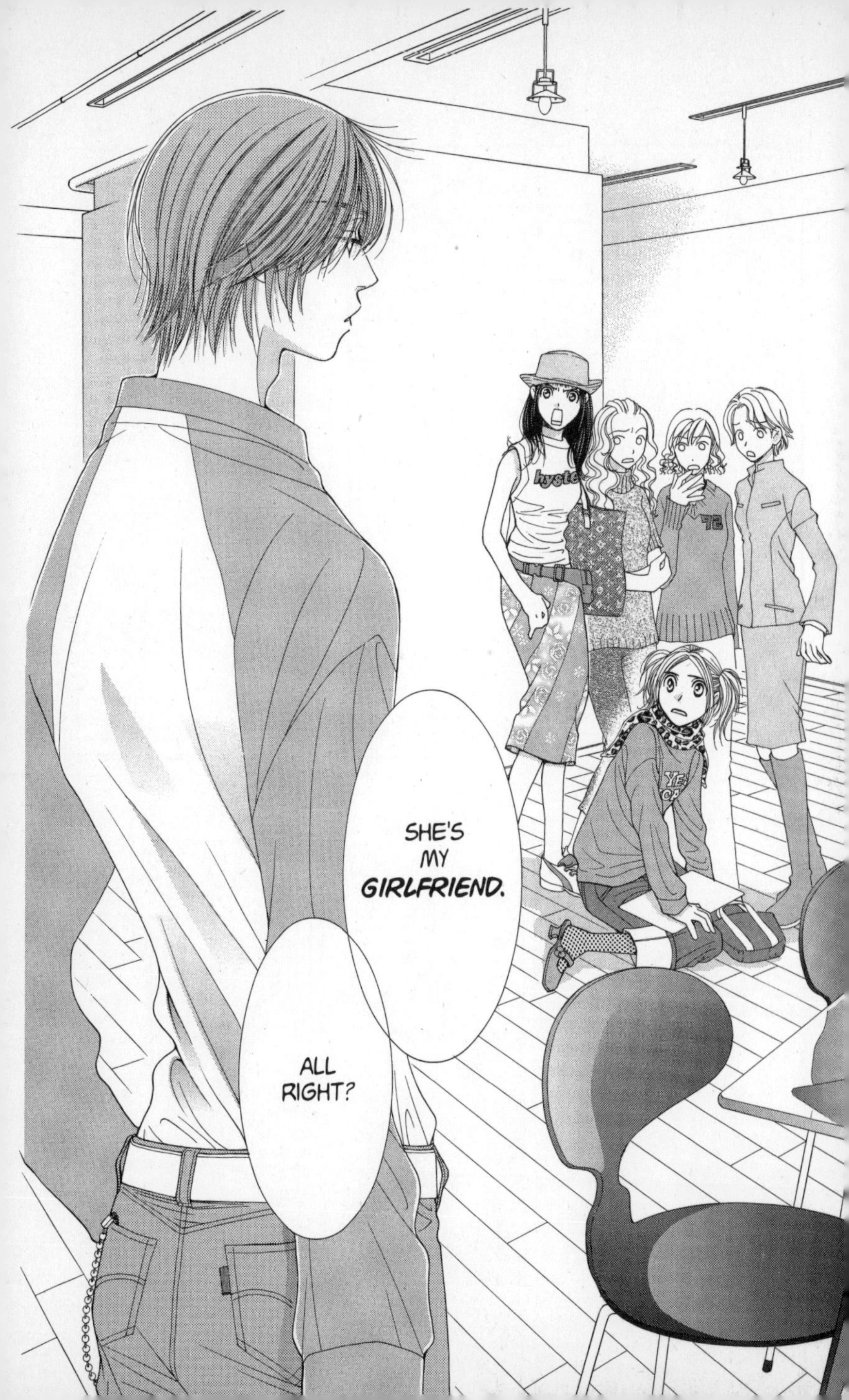
SHE'S MY **GIRLFRIEND.**
ALL RIGHT?

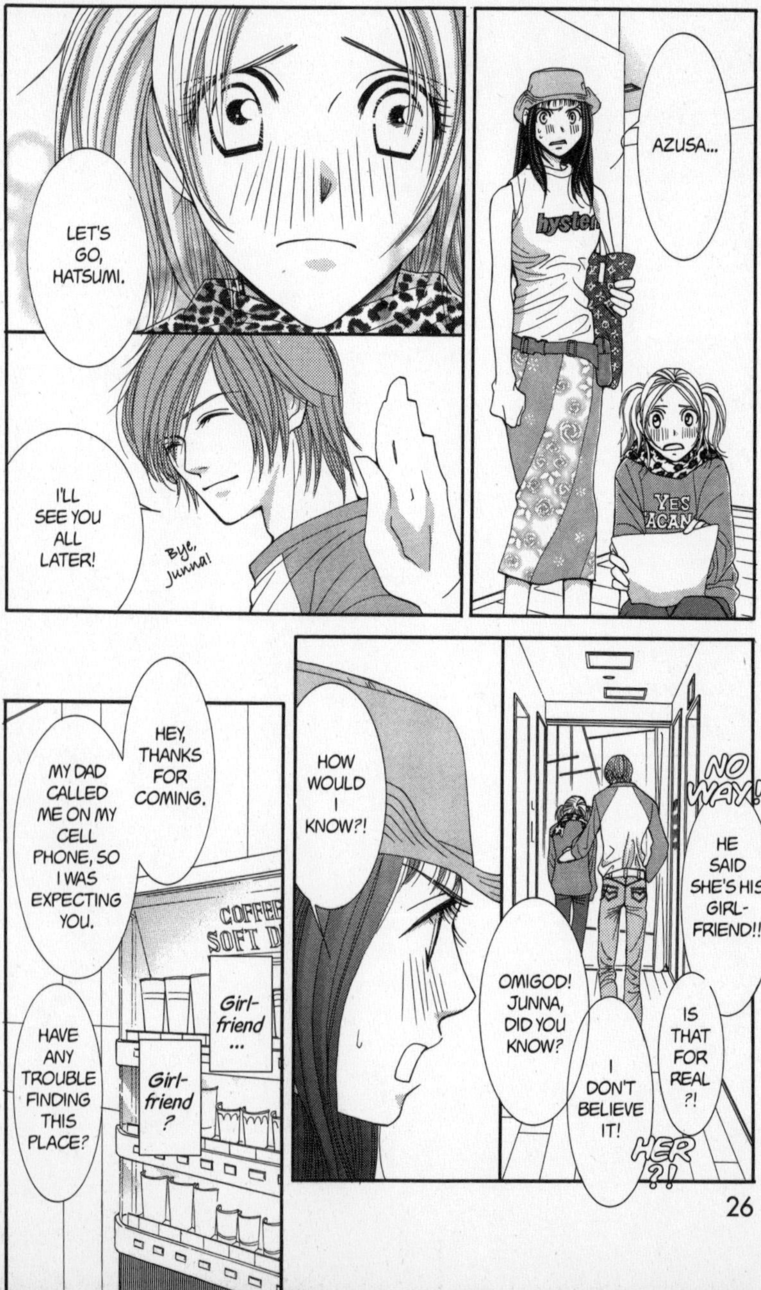
AZUSA...
LET'S GO, HATSUMI.
I'LL SEE YOU ALL LATER!
Bye, Junna!
NO WAY!
HE SAID SHE'S HIS GIRL-FRIEND!!
IS THAT FOR REAL?!
OMIGOD! JUNNA, DID YOU KNOW?
I DON'T BELIEVE IT!
HER?!
HOW WOULD I KNOW?!
HEY, THANKS FOR COMING.
MY DAD CALLED ME ON MY CELL PHONE, SO I WAS EXPECTING YOU.
Girl-friend...
Girl-friend?
HAVE ANY TROUBLE FINDING THIS PLACE?

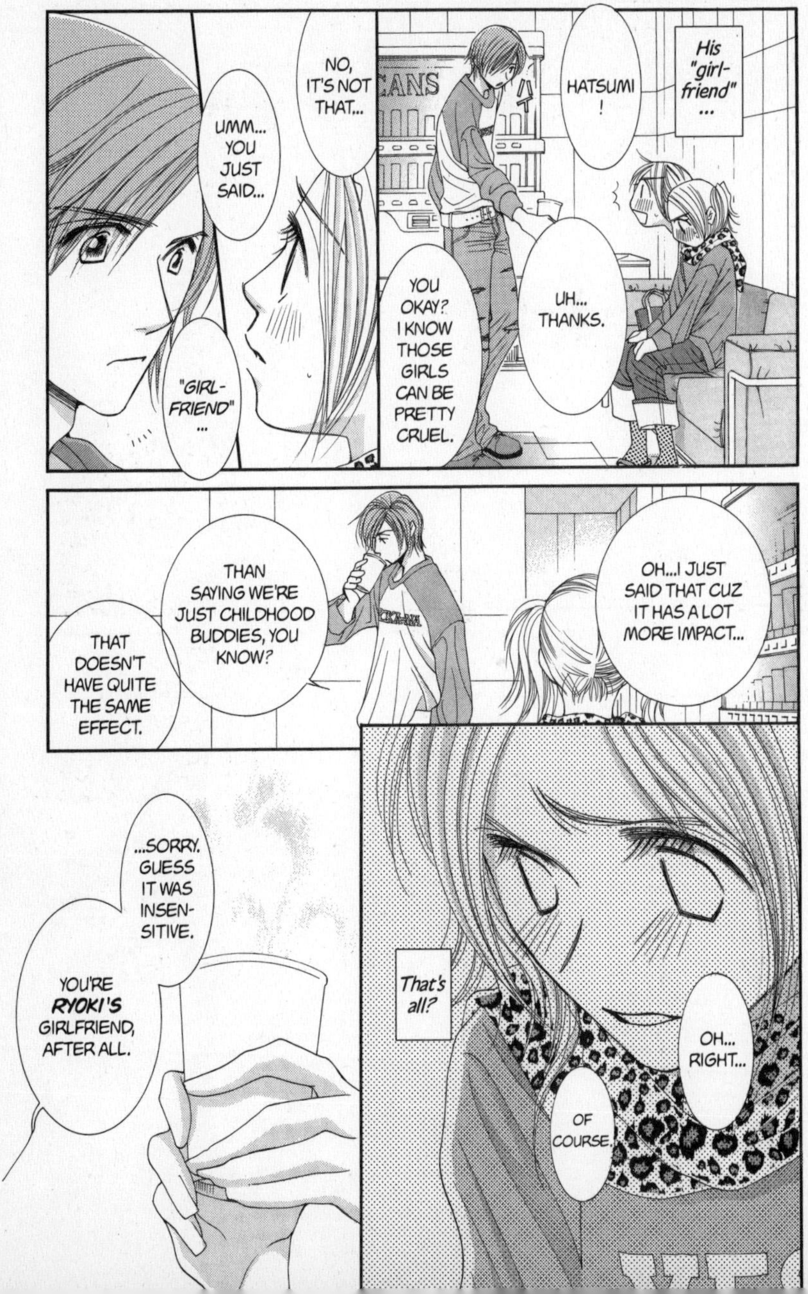
His "girl-friend"...
HATSUMI!
UH... THANKS.
YOU OKAY? I KNOW THOSE GIRLS CAN BE PRETTY CRUEL.
NO, IT'S NOT THAT...
UMM... YOU JUST SAID...
"GIRL-FRIEND"...
OH...I JUST SAID THAT CUZ IT HAS A LOT MORE IMPACT...
THAN SAYING WE'RE JUST CHILDHOOD BUDDIES, YOU KNOW?
THAT DOESN'T HAVE QUITE THE SAME EFFECT.
OH... RIGHT...
OF COURSE.
That's all?
...SORRY. GUESS IT WAS INSEN-SITIVE.
YOU'RE **RYOKI'S** GIRLFRIEND, AFTER ALL.

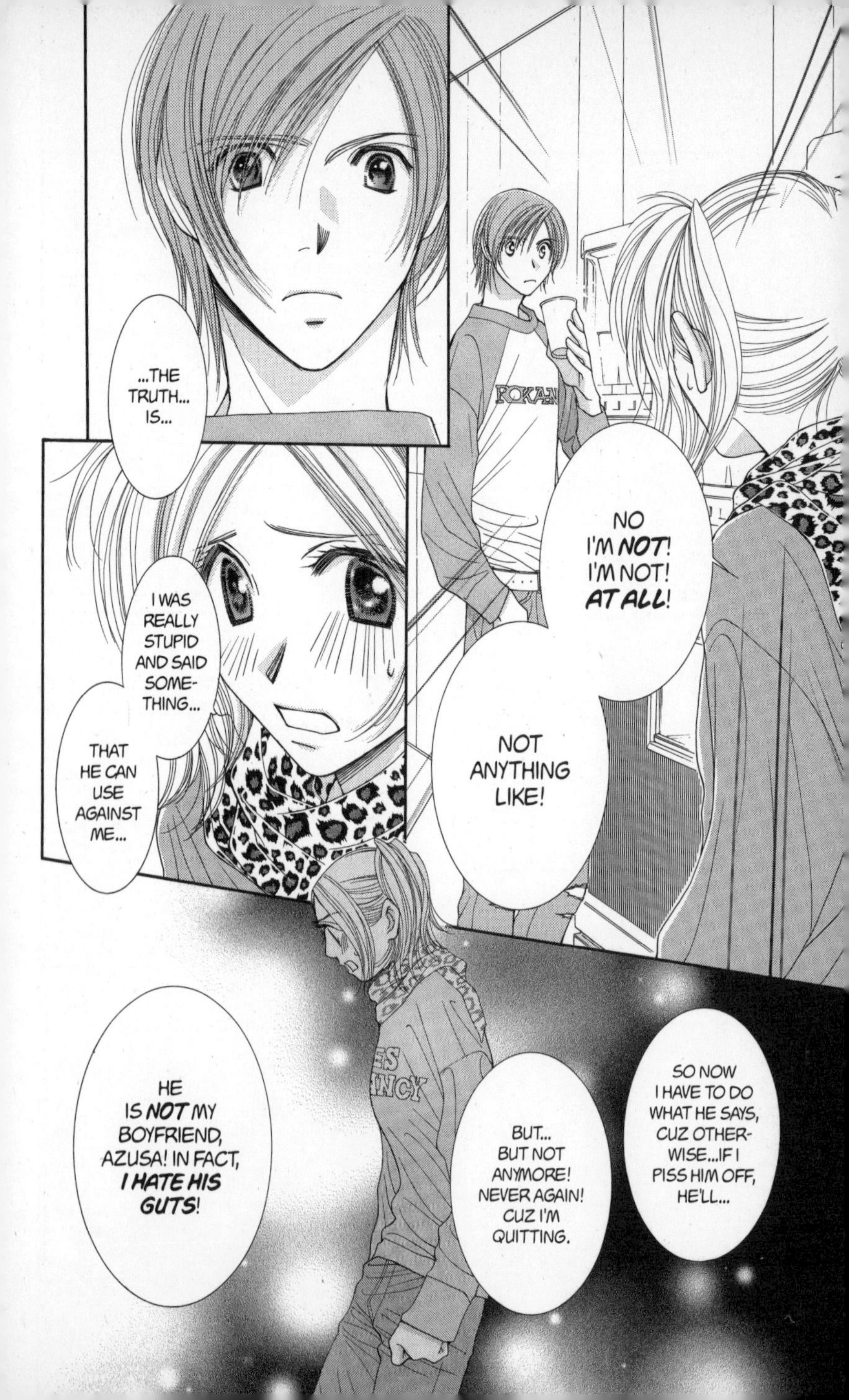
NO I'M **NOT**! I'M NOT! ***AT ALL***!
NOT ANYTHING LIKE!
...THE TRUTH... IS...
I WAS REALLY STUPID AND SAID SOME-THING...
THAT HE CAN USE AGAINST ME...
SO NOW I HAVE TO DO WHAT HE SAYS, CUZ OTHER-WISE...IF I PISS HIM OFF, HE'LL...
BUT... BUT NOT ANYMORE! NEVER AGAIN! CUZ I'M QUITTING.
HE IS ***NOT*** MY BOYFRIEND, AZUSA! IN FACT, ***I HATE HIS GUTS***!

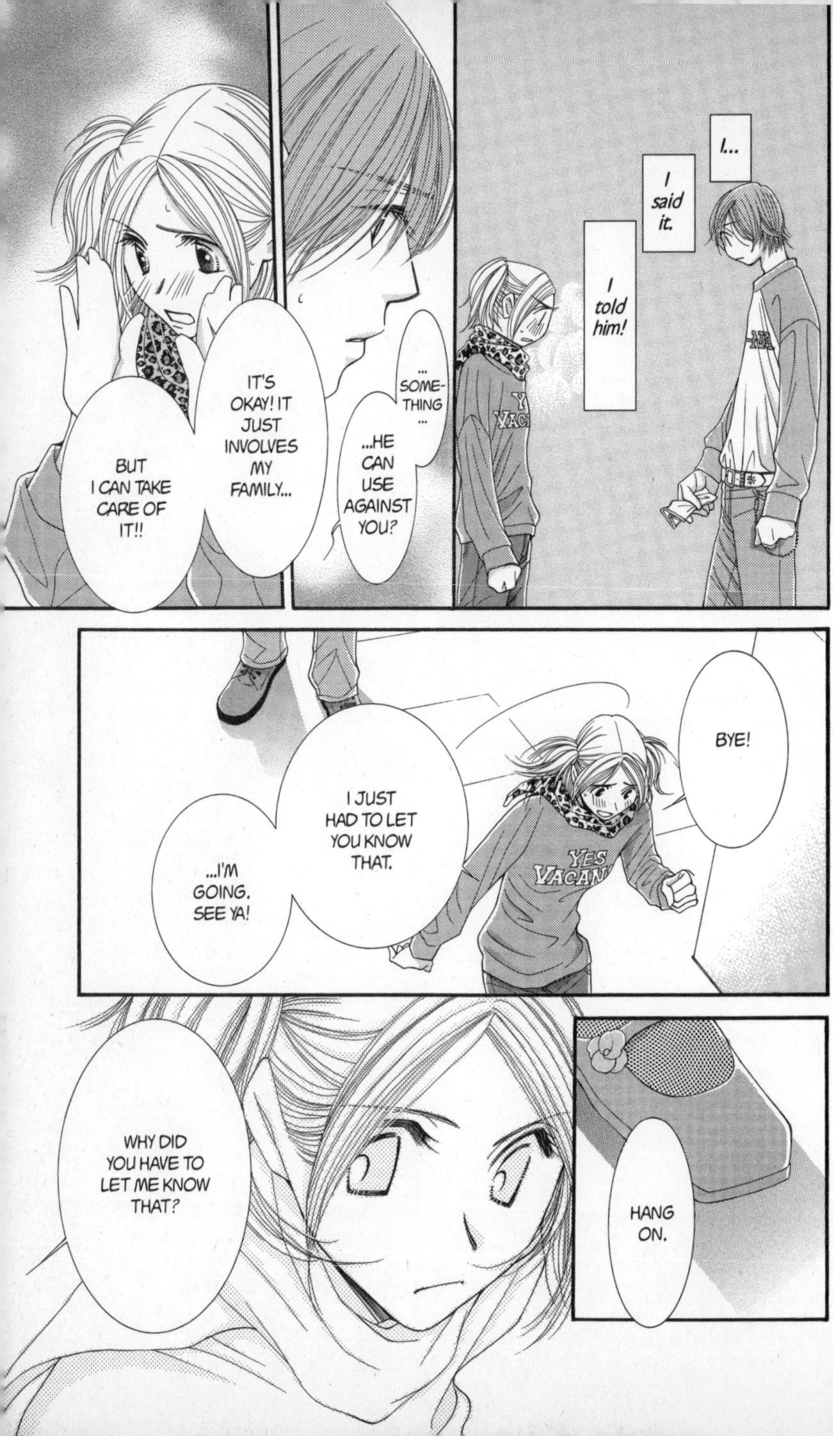
I...
I said it.
I told him!
...SOMETHING...
...HE CAN USE AGAINST YOU?
IT'S OKAY! IT JUST INVOLVES MY FAMILY...
BUT I CAN TAKE CARE OF IT!!
BYE!
I JUST HAD TO LET YOU KNOW THAT.
...I'M GOING. SEE YA!
HANG ON.
WHY DID YOU HAVE TO LET ME KNOW THAT?

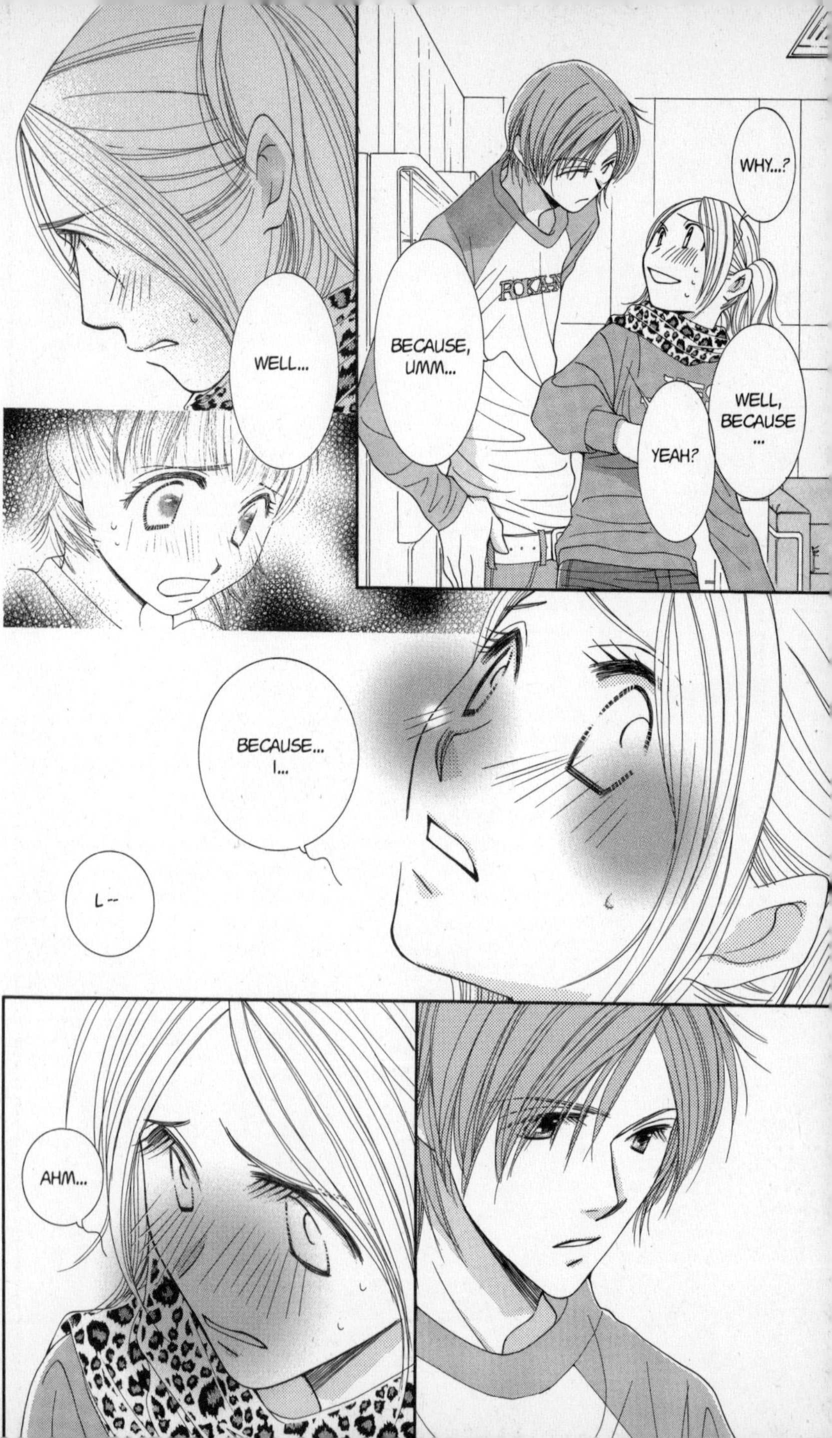
WHY...?
WELL, BECAUSE ...
YEAH?
BECAUSE, UMM...
WELL...
BECAUSE... I...
L --
AHM...

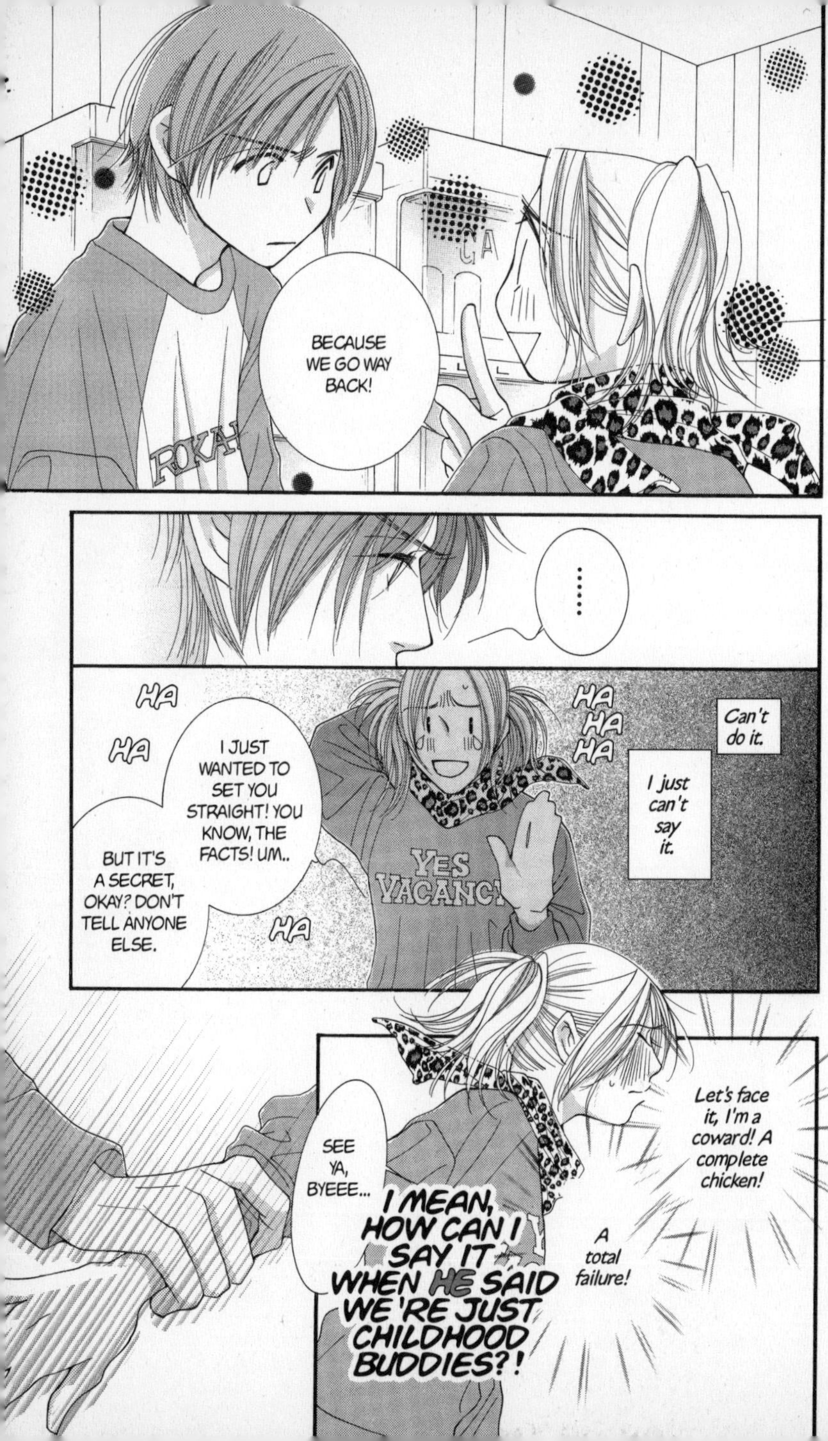
BECAUSE WE GO WAY BACK!
......
Can't do it.
I just can't say it.
HA HA HA
I JUST WANTED TO SET YOU STRAIGHT! YOU KNOW, THE FACTS! UM..
HA
HA
BUT IT'S A SECRET, OKAY? DON'T TELL ANYONE ELSE.
HA
Let's face it, I'm a coward! A complete chicken!
A total failure!
I MEAN, HOW CAN I SAY IT WHEN HE SAID WE'RE JUST CHILDHOOD BUDDIES?!
SEE YA, BYEEE...

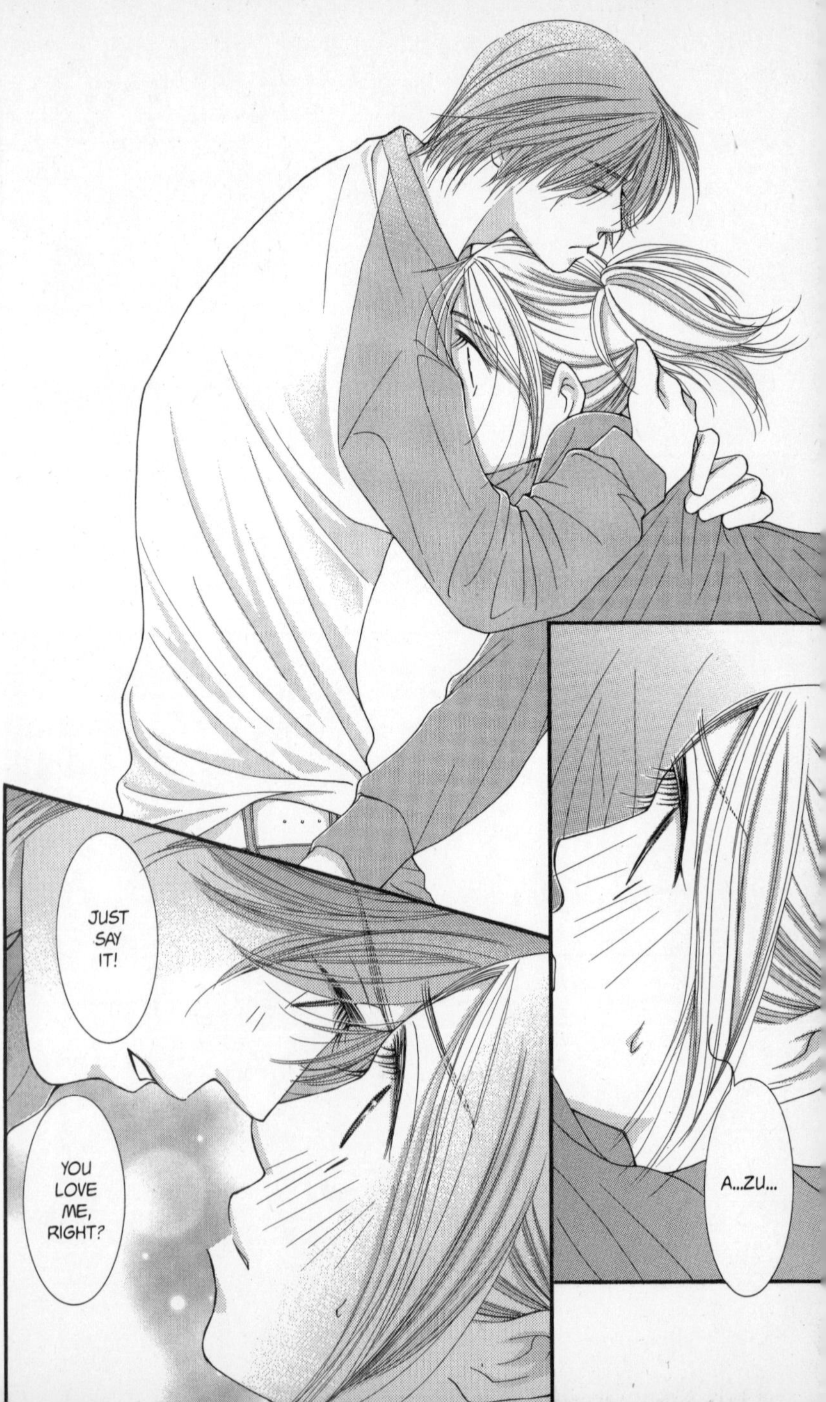
A...ZU...
JUST SAY IT!
YOU LOVE ME, RIGHT?

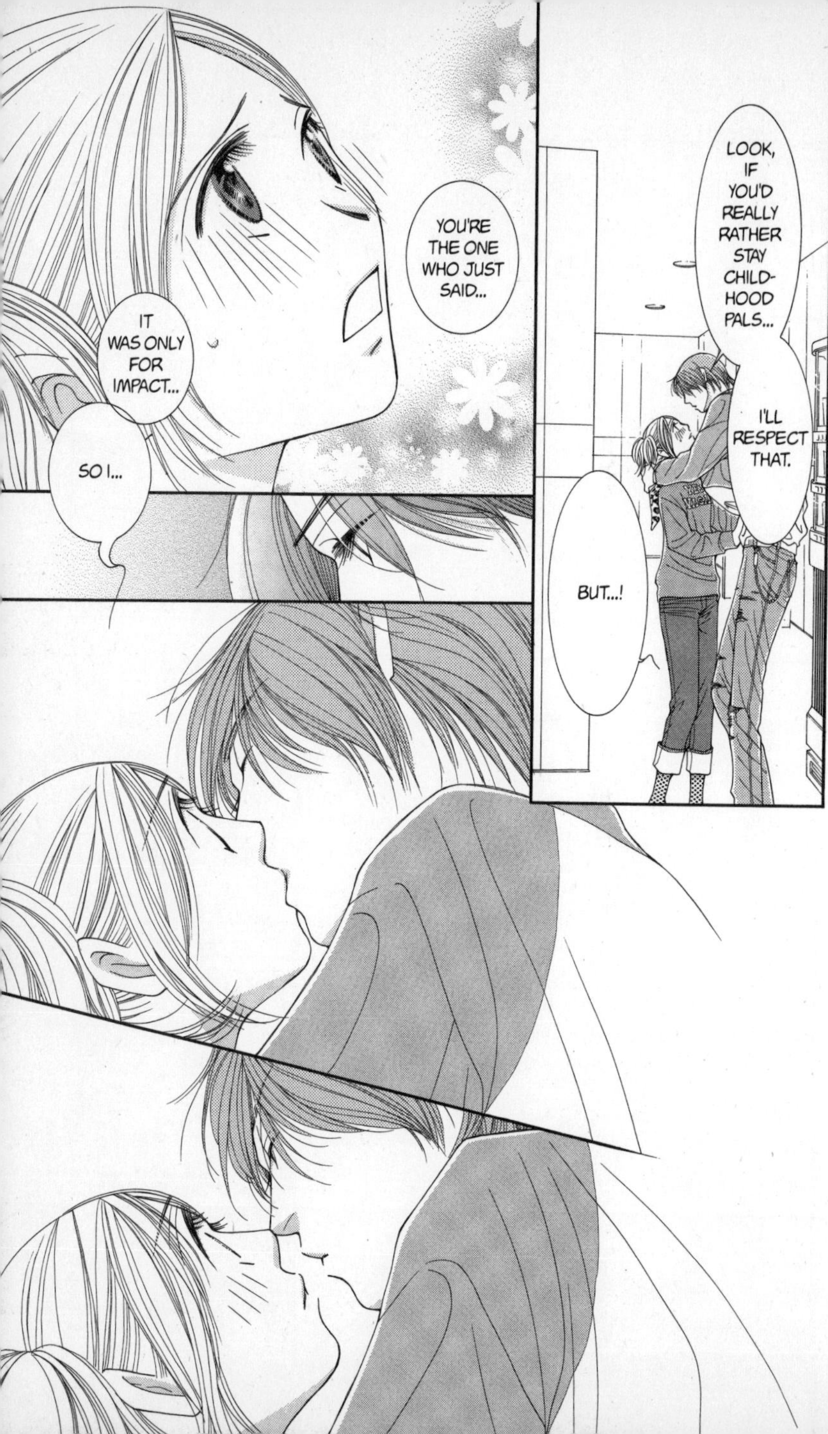
LOOK, IF YOU'D REALLY RATHER STAY CHILD-HOOD PALS...
I'LL RESPECT THAT.
BUT...!
YOU'RE THE ONE WHO JUST SAID...
IT WAS ONLY FOR IMPACT...
SO I...

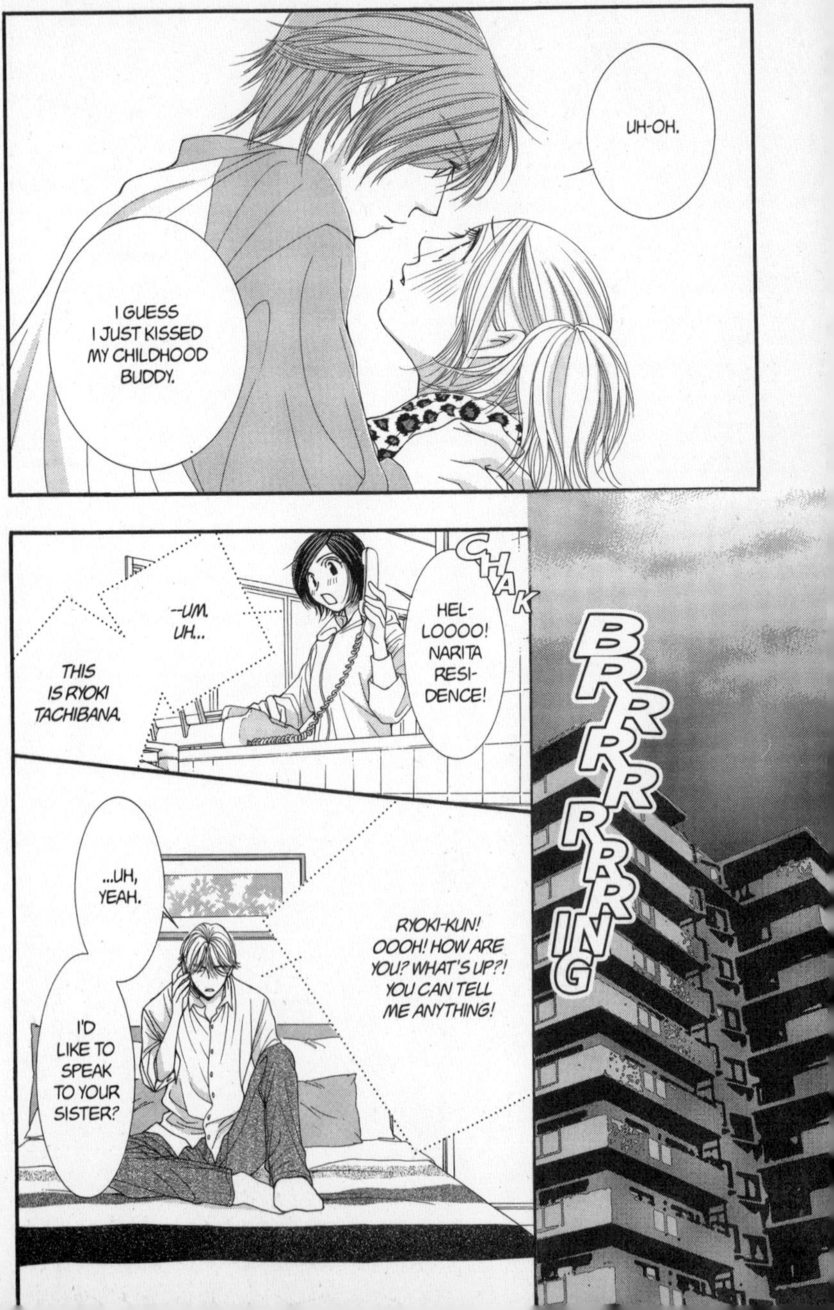
UH-OH.
I GUESS I JUST KISSED MY CHILDHOOD BUDDY.
BRRRRRRRING
CHAK
HEL-LOOOO! NARITA RESI-DENCE!
--UM. UH...
THIS IS RYOKI TACHIBANA.
RYOKI-KUN! OOOH! HOW ARE YOU? WHAT'S UP?! YOU CAN TELL ME ANYTHING!
...UH, YEAH.
I'D LIKE TO SPEAK TO YOUR SISTER?

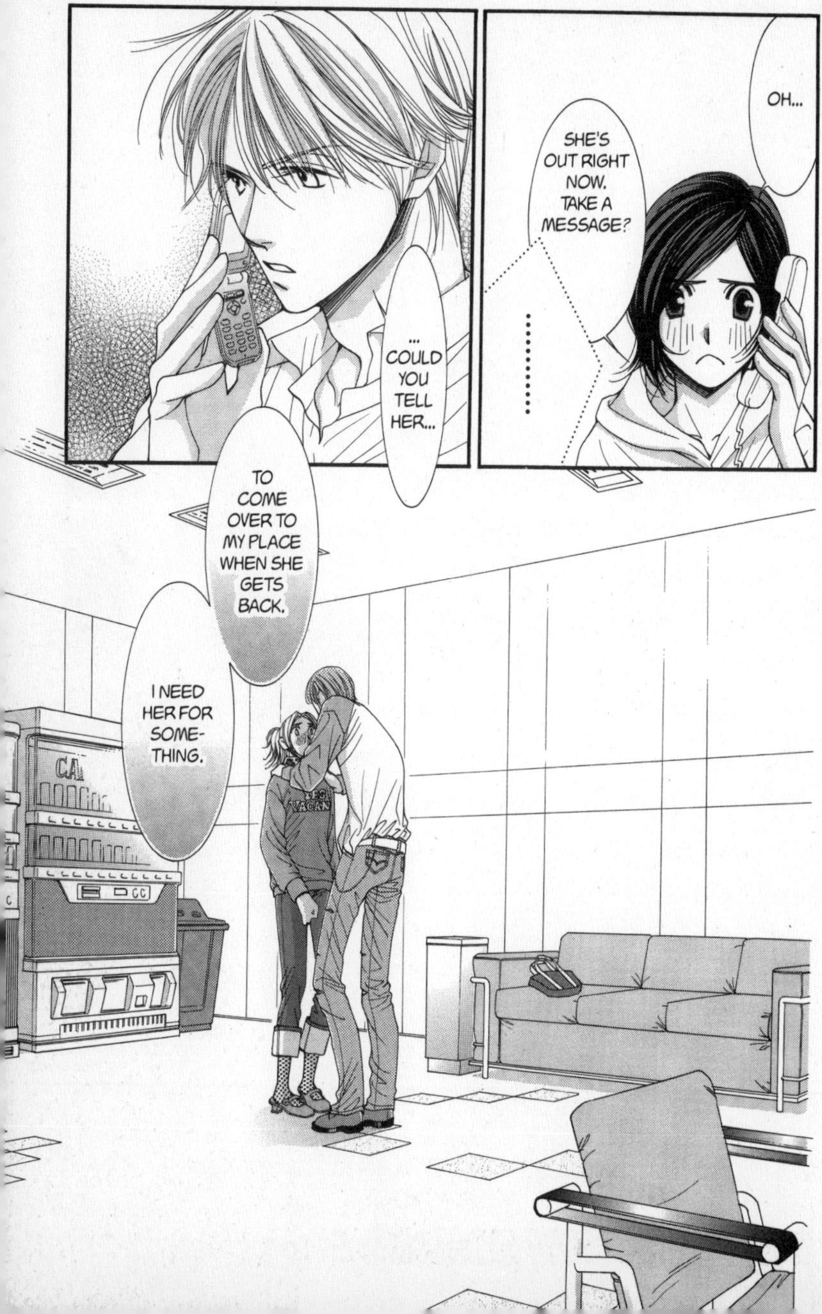
OH...
SHE'S OUT RIGHT NOW. TAKE A MESSAGE?
....
...COULD YOU TELL HER...
TO COME OVER TO MY PLACE WHEN SHE GETS BACK.
I NEED HER FOR SOME-THING.

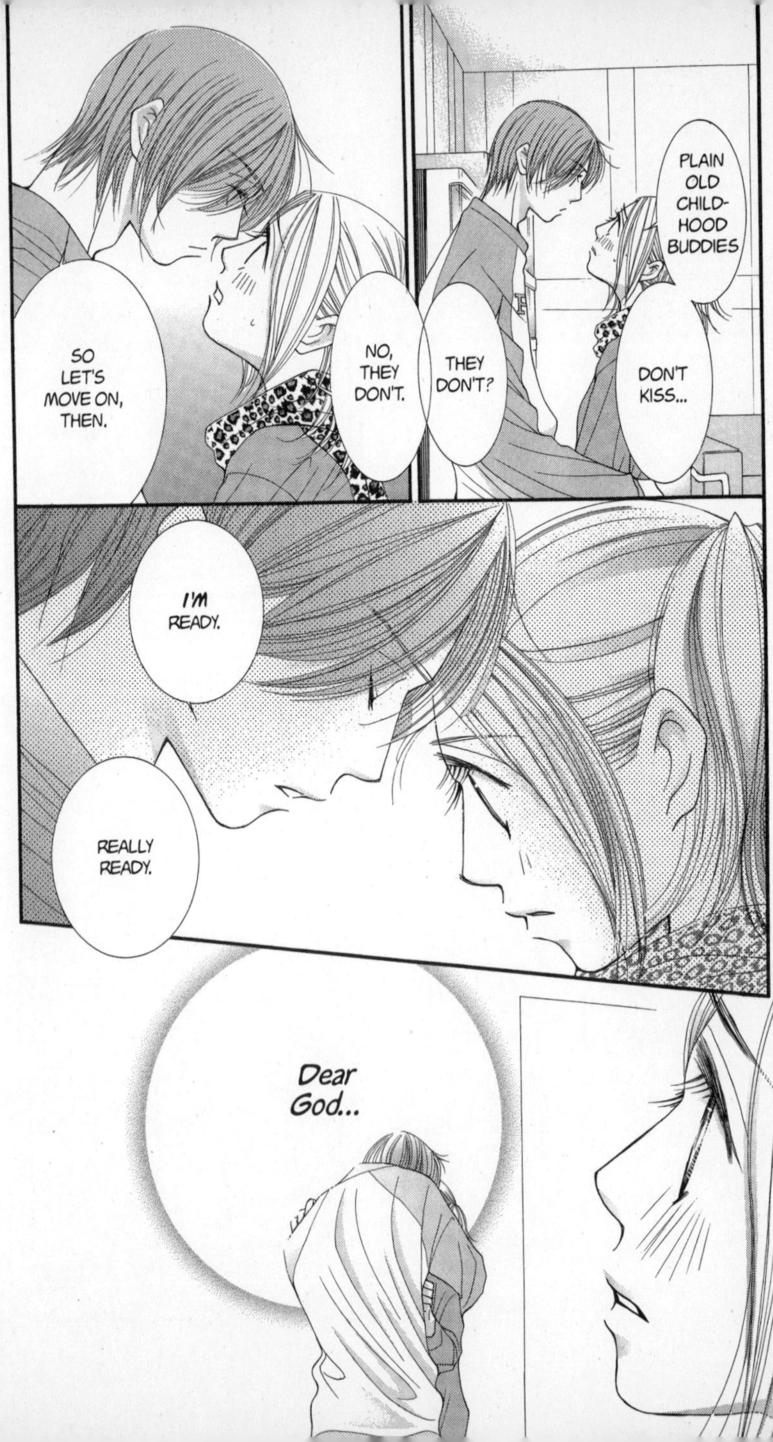
PLAIN OLD CHILD-HOOD BUDDIES
DON'T KISS...
THEY DON'T?
NO, THEY DON'T.
SO LET'S MOVE ON, THEN.
I'M READY.
REALLY READY.
Dear God...

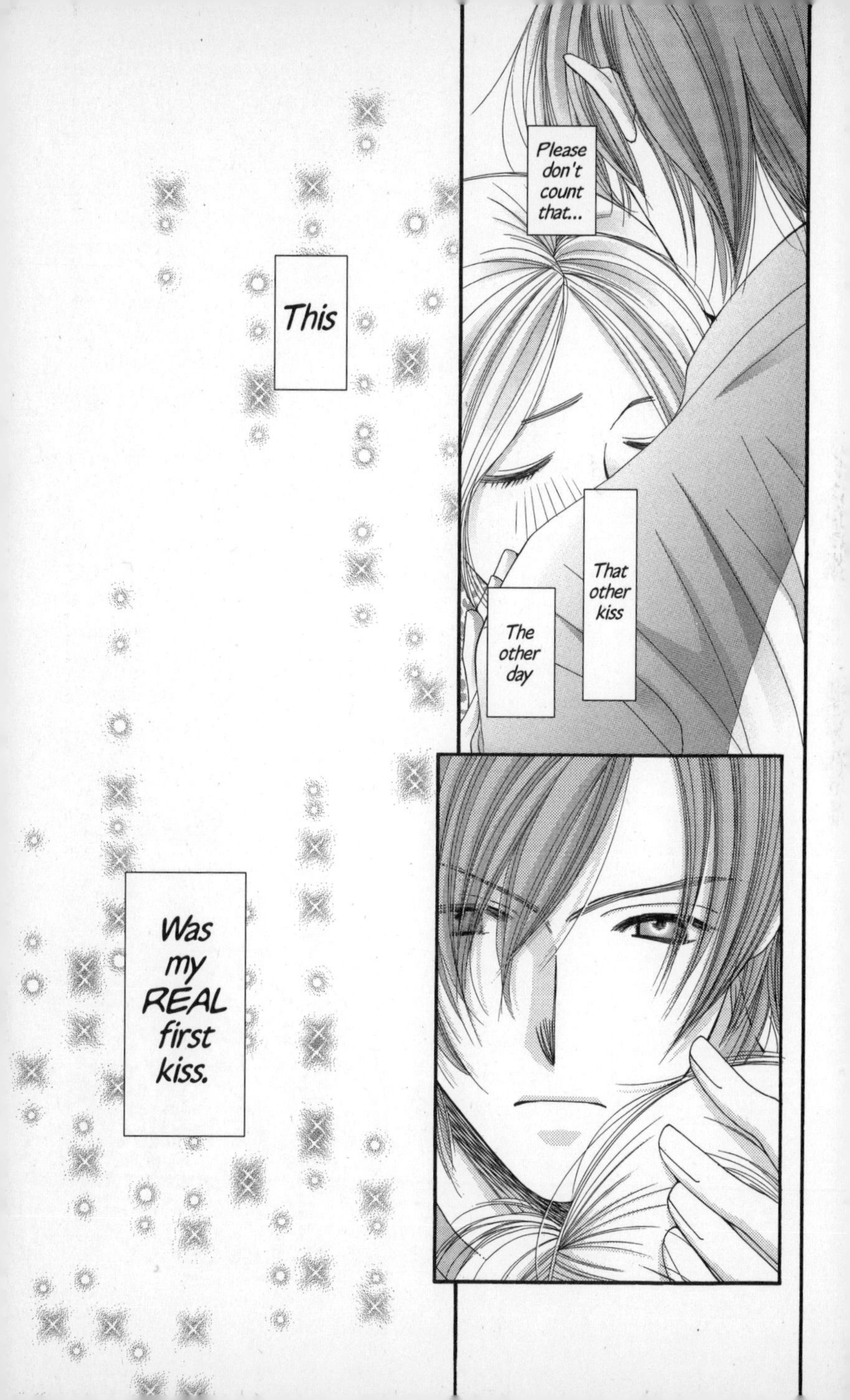
Please don't count that...
That other kiss
The other day
This
Was my REAL first kiss.

Chapter 6

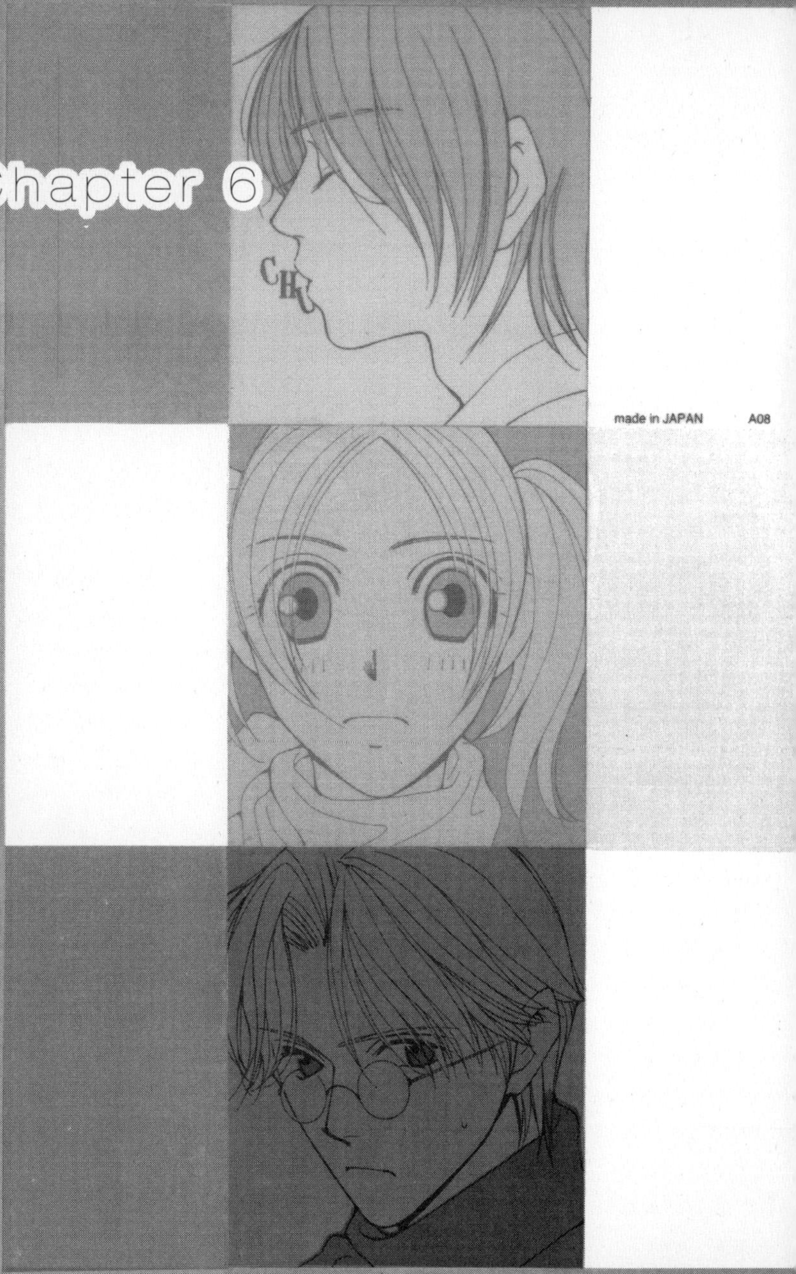
CHU
made in JAPAN A08

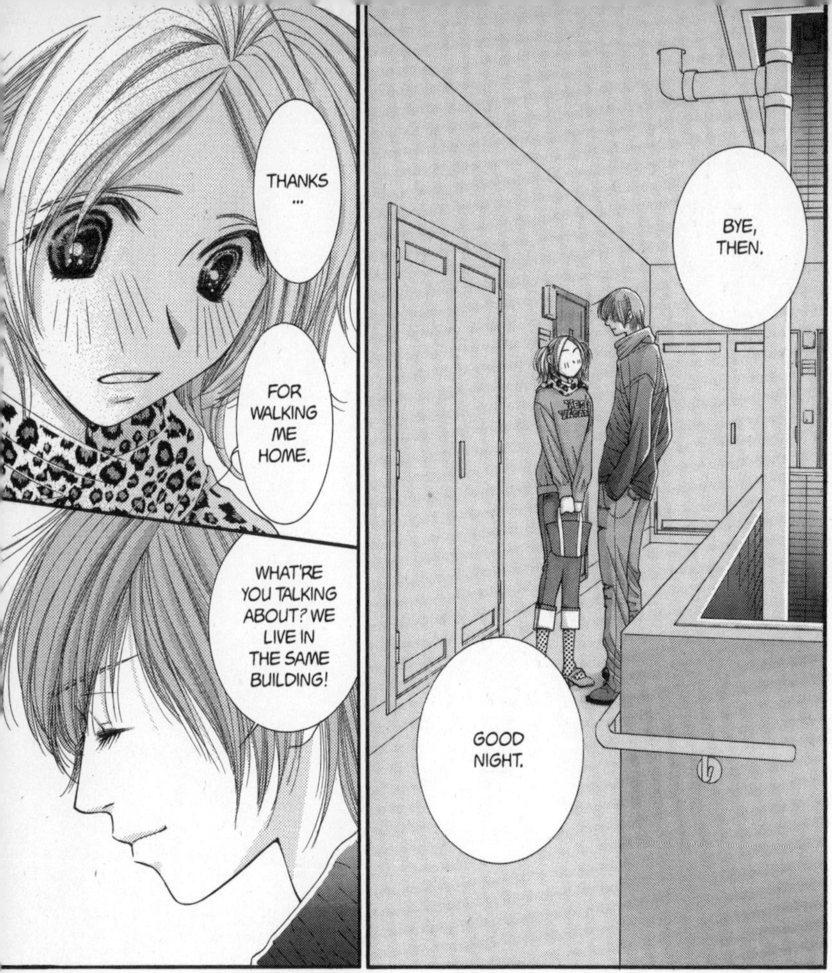
BYE, THEN.
GOOD NIGHT.
THANKS ...
FOR WALKING ME HOME.
WHAT'RE YOU TALKING ABOUT? WE LIVE IN THE SAME BUILDING!

hot gimmick

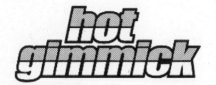

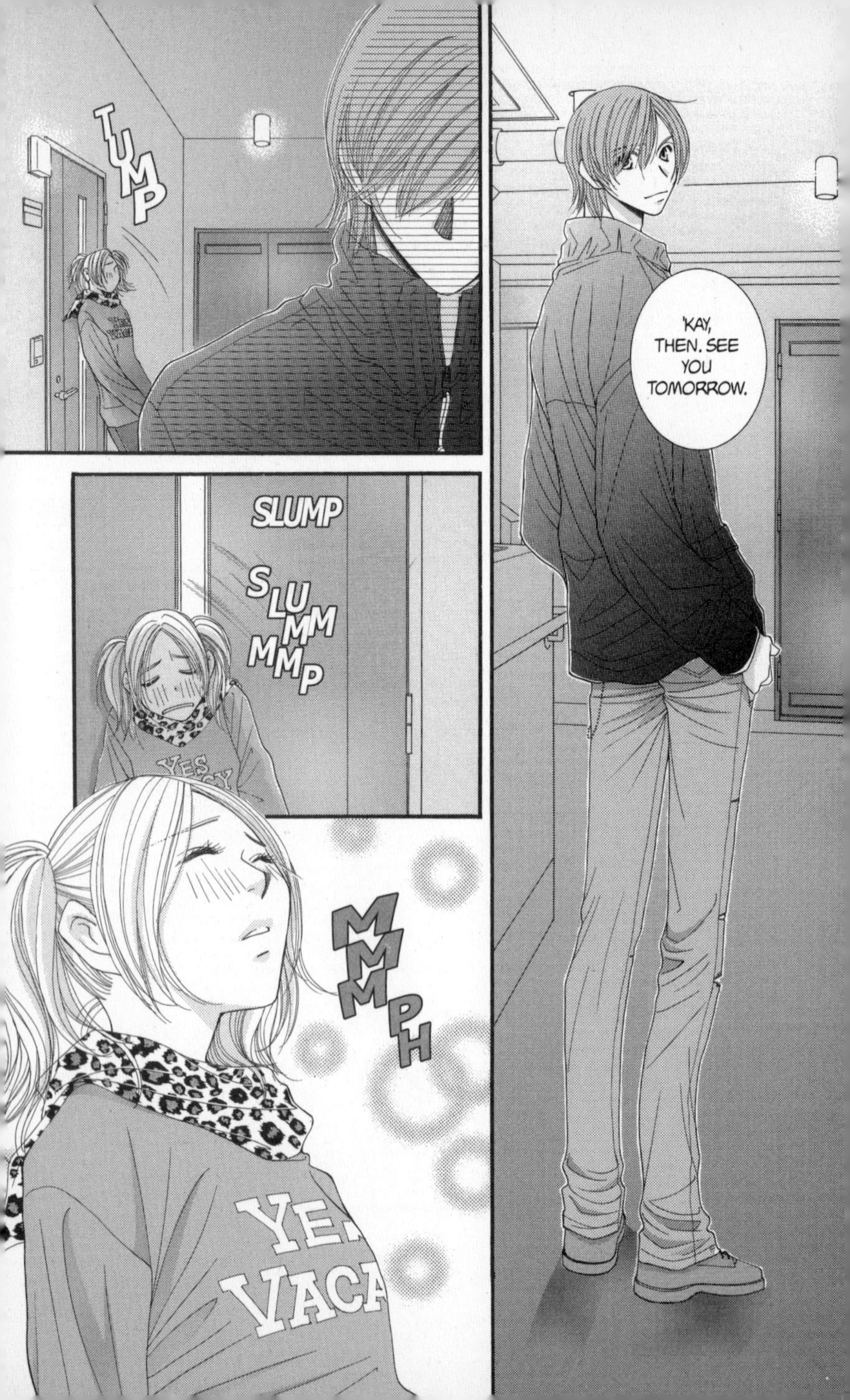
'KAY, THEN. SEE YOU TOMORROW.
TUMP
SLUMP
SLUMM
MMMP
MMMPH

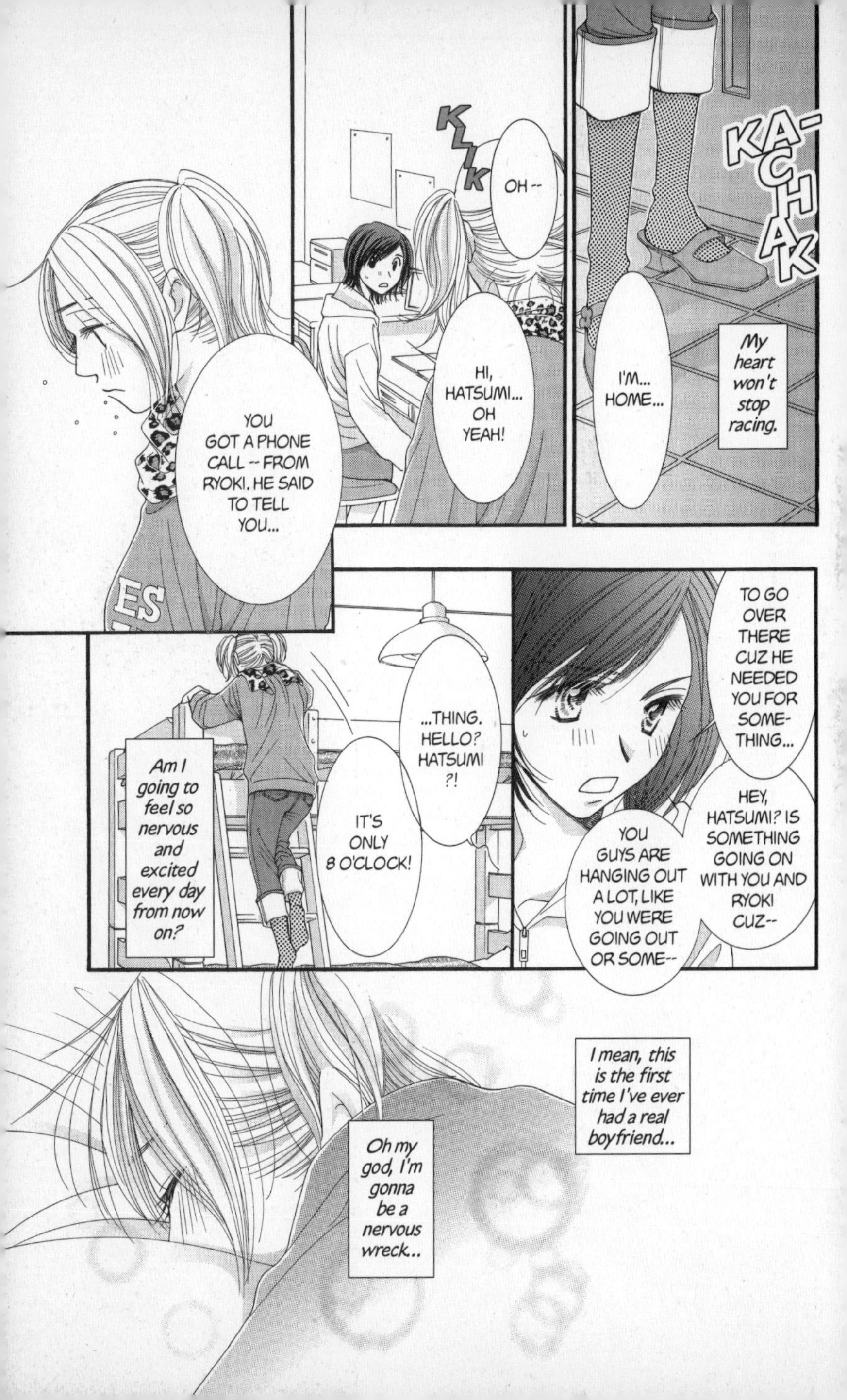
KA-CHAK
I'M... HOME...
My heart won't stop racing.
KLIK
OH --
HI, HATSUMI... OH YEAH!
YOU GOT A PHONE CALL -- FROM RYOKI. HE SAID TO TELL YOU...
TO GO OVER THERE CUZ HE NEEDED YOU FOR SOME-THING...
HEY, HATSUMI? IS SOMETHING GOING ON WITH YOU AND RYOKI CUZ--
YOU GUYS ARE HANGING OUT A LOT, LIKE YOU WERE GOING OUT OR SOME--
...THING. HELLO? HATSUMI ?!
IT'S ONLY 8 O'CLOCK!
Am I going to feel so nervous and excited every day from now on?
I mean, this is the first time I've ever had a real boyfriend...
Oh my god, I'm gonna be a nervous wreck...

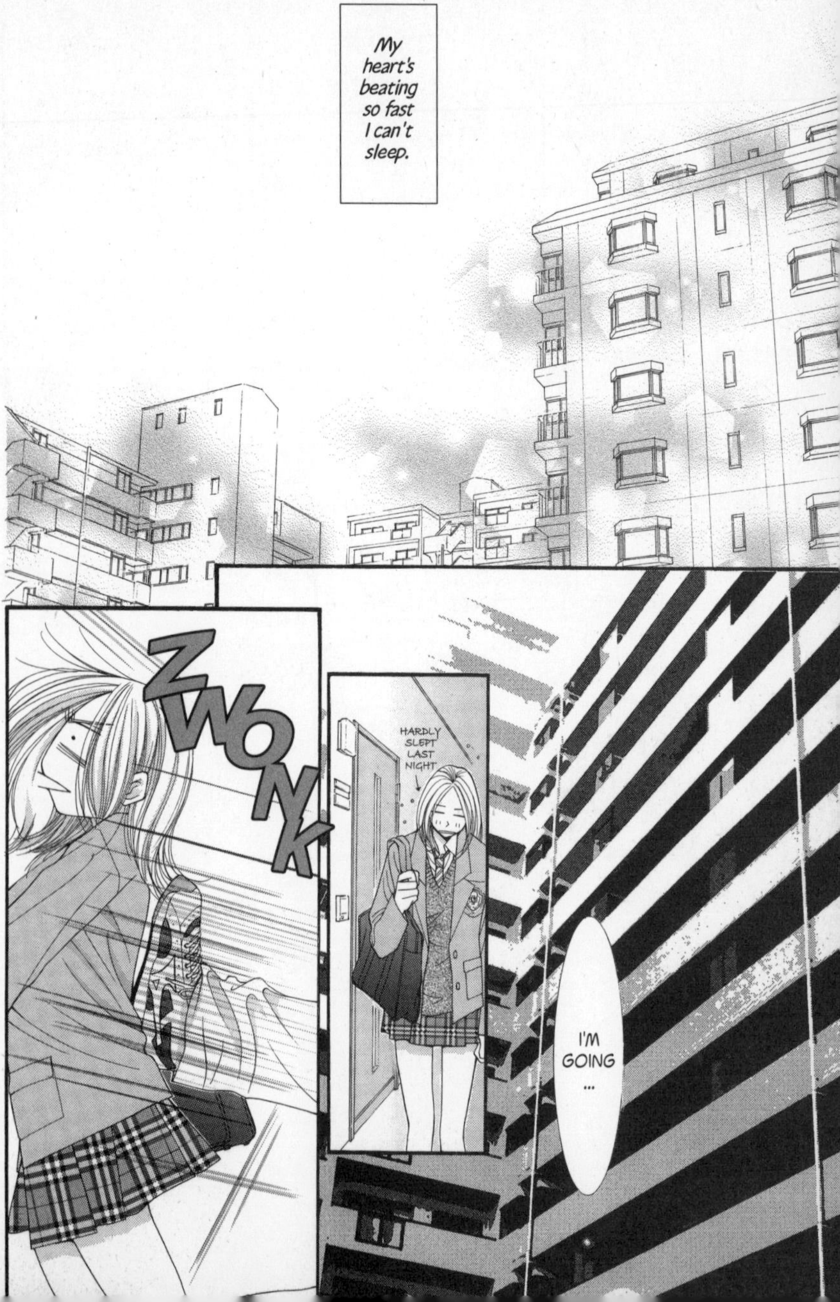
My heart's beating so fast I can't sleep.
HARDLY SLEPT LAST NIGHT
I'M GOING ...
ZWONK

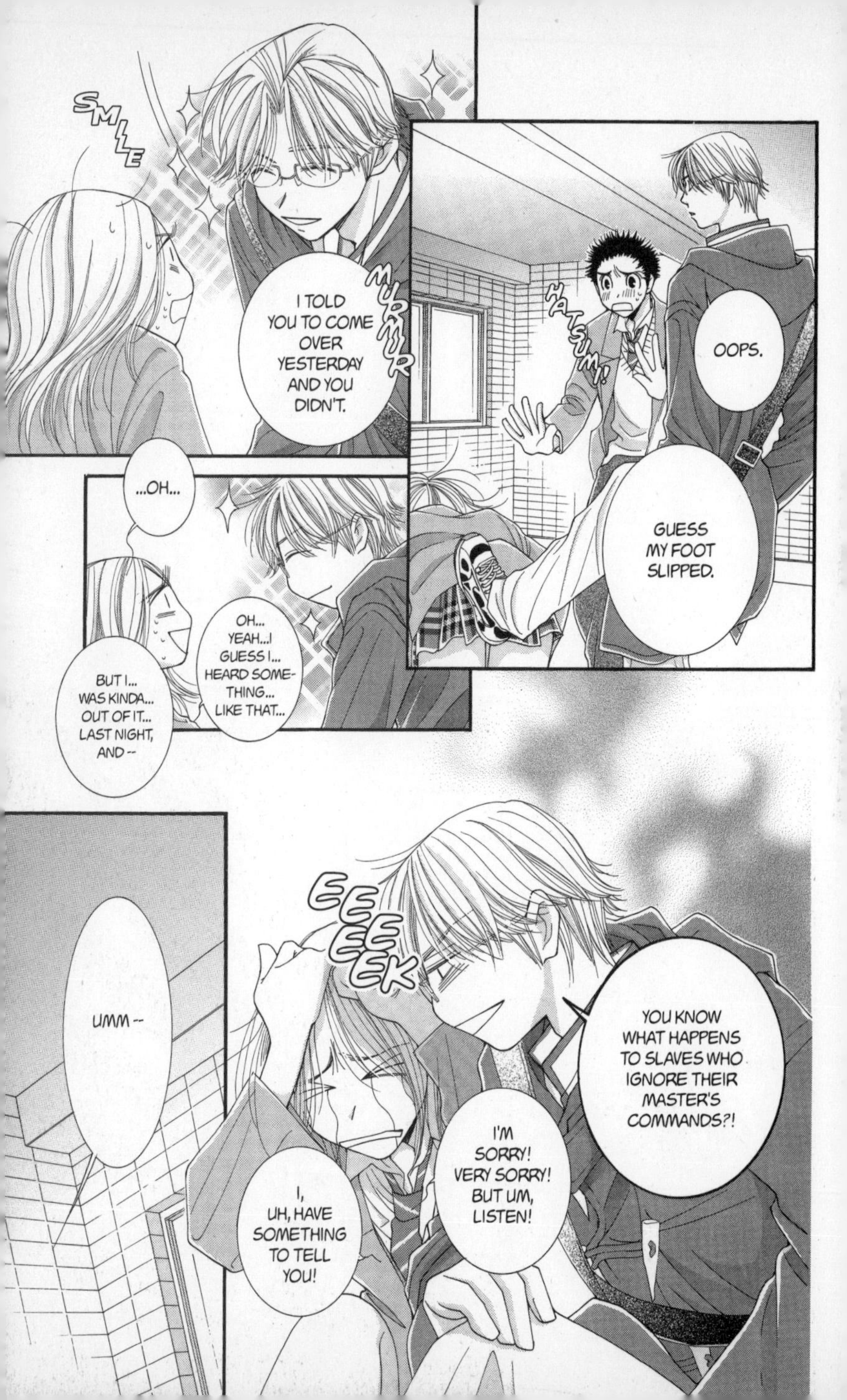
HATSUMI!
OOPS.
GUESS MY FOOT SLIPPED.
SMILE
MURMUR
I TOLD YOU TO COME OVER YESTERDAY AND YOU DIDN'T.
...OH...
OH... YEAH...I GUESS I... HEARD SOME-THING... LIKE THAT...
BUT I... WAS KINDA... OUT OF IT... LAST NIGHT, AND --
EEEEEK
YOU KNOW WHAT HAPPENS TO SLAVES WHO IGNORE THEIR MASTER'S COMMANDS?!
I'M SORRY! VERY SORRY! BUT UM, LISTEN!
I, UH, HAVE SOMETHING TO TELL YOU!
UMM --

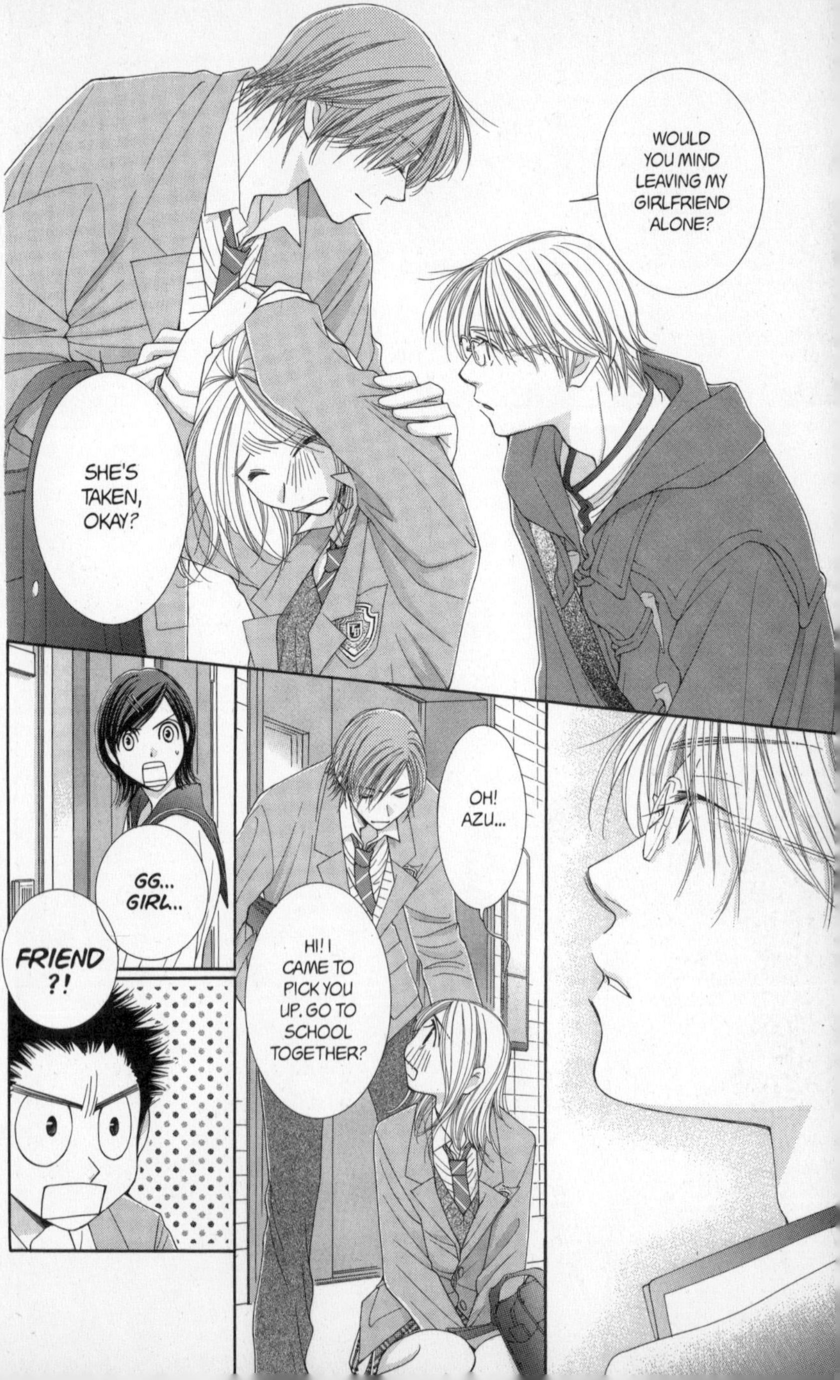
WOULD YOU MIND LEAVING MY GIRLFRIEND ALONE?
SHE'S TAKEN, OKAY?
OH! AZU...
HI! I CAME TO PICK YOU UP. GO TO SCHOOL TOGETHER?
GG... GIRL...
FRIEND ?!

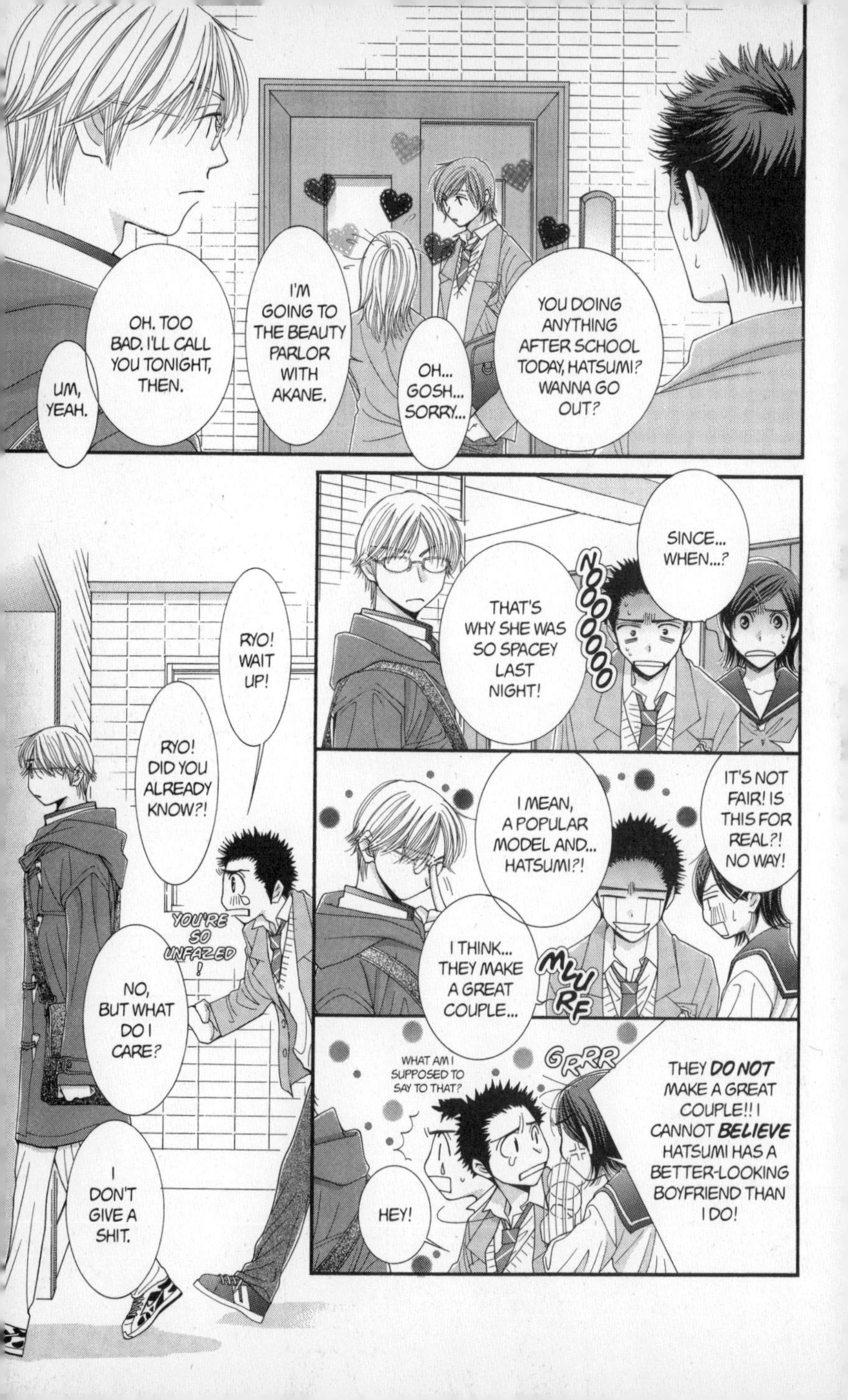
YOU DOING ANYTHING AFTER SCHOOL TODAY, HATSUMI? WANNA GO OUT?
OH... GOSH... SORRY...
I'M GOING TO THE BEAUTY PARLOR WITH AKANE.
OH. TOO BAD. I'LL CALL YOU TONIGHT, THEN.
UM, YEAH.
SINCE... WHEN...?
NOOOOOOO
THAT'S WHY SHE WAS SO SPACEY LAST NIGHT!
IT'S NOT FAIR! IS THIS FOR REAL?! NO WAY!
I MEAN, A POPULAR MODEL AND... HATSUMI?!
I THINK... THEY MAKE A GREAT COUPLE...
MLURF
THEY **DO NOT** MAKE A GREAT COUPLE!! I CANNOT **BELIEVE** HATSUMI HAS A BETTER-LOOKING BOYFRIEND THAN I DO!
GRRR
WHAT AM I SUPPOSED TO SAY TO THAT?
HEY!
RYO! WAIT UP!
RYO! DID YOU ALREADY KNOW?!
YOU'RE SO UNFAZED!
NO, BUT WHAT DO I CARE?
I DON'T GIVE A SHIT.

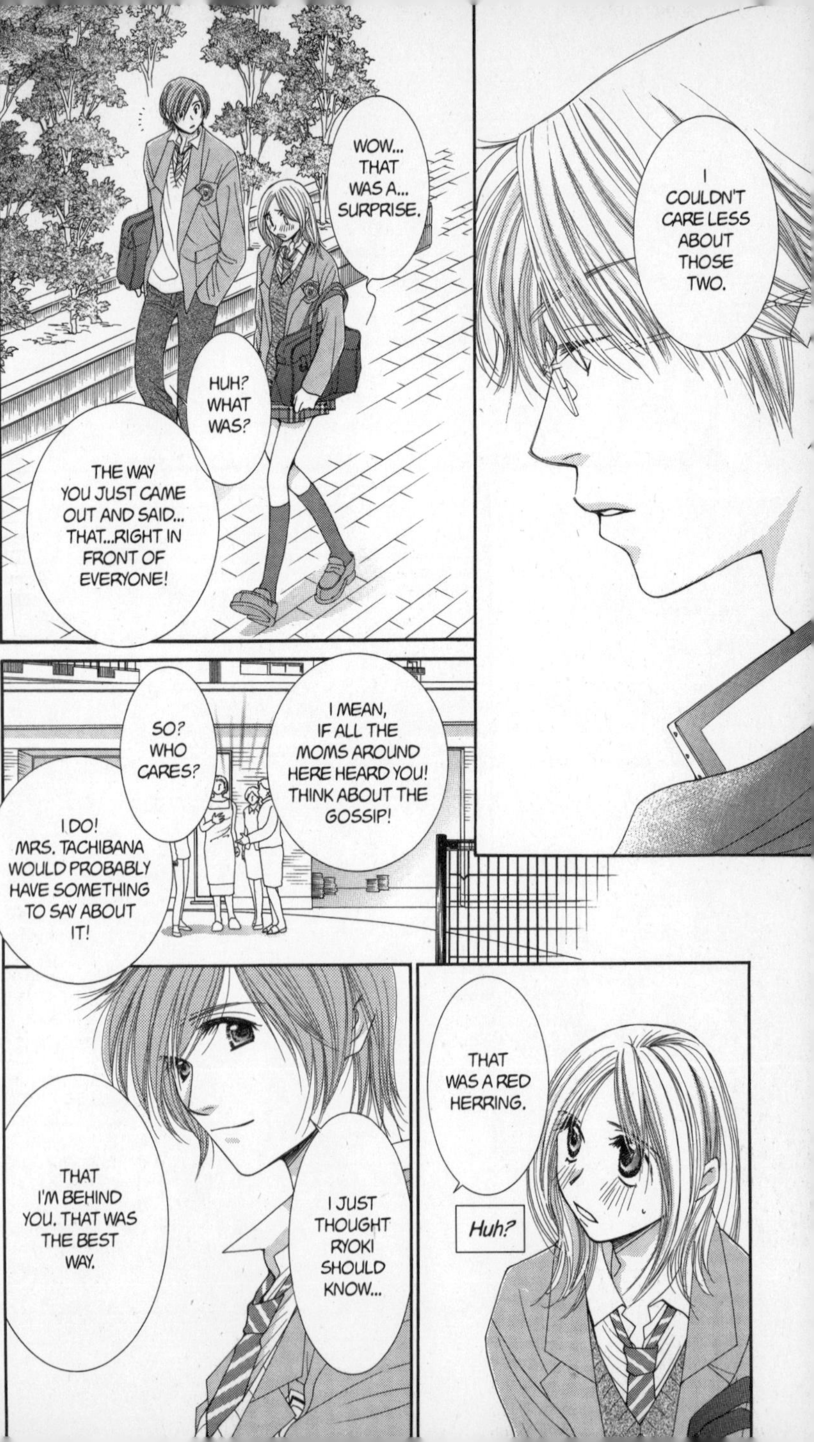
I COULDN'T CARE LESS ABOUT THOSE TWO.
WOW... THAT WAS A... SURPRISE.
HUH? WHAT WAS?
THE WAY YOU JUST CAME OUT AND SAID... THAT...RIGHT IN FRONT OF EVERYONE!
I MEAN, IF ALL THE MOMS AROUND HERE HEARD YOU! THINK ABOUT THE GOSSIP!
SO? WHO CARES?
I DO! MRS. TACHIBANA WOULD PROBABLY HAVE SOMETHING TO SAY ABOUT IT!
THAT WAS A RED HERRING.
Huh?
I JUST THOUGHT RYOKI SHOULD KNOW...
THAT I'M BEHIND YOU. THAT WAS THE BEST WAY.

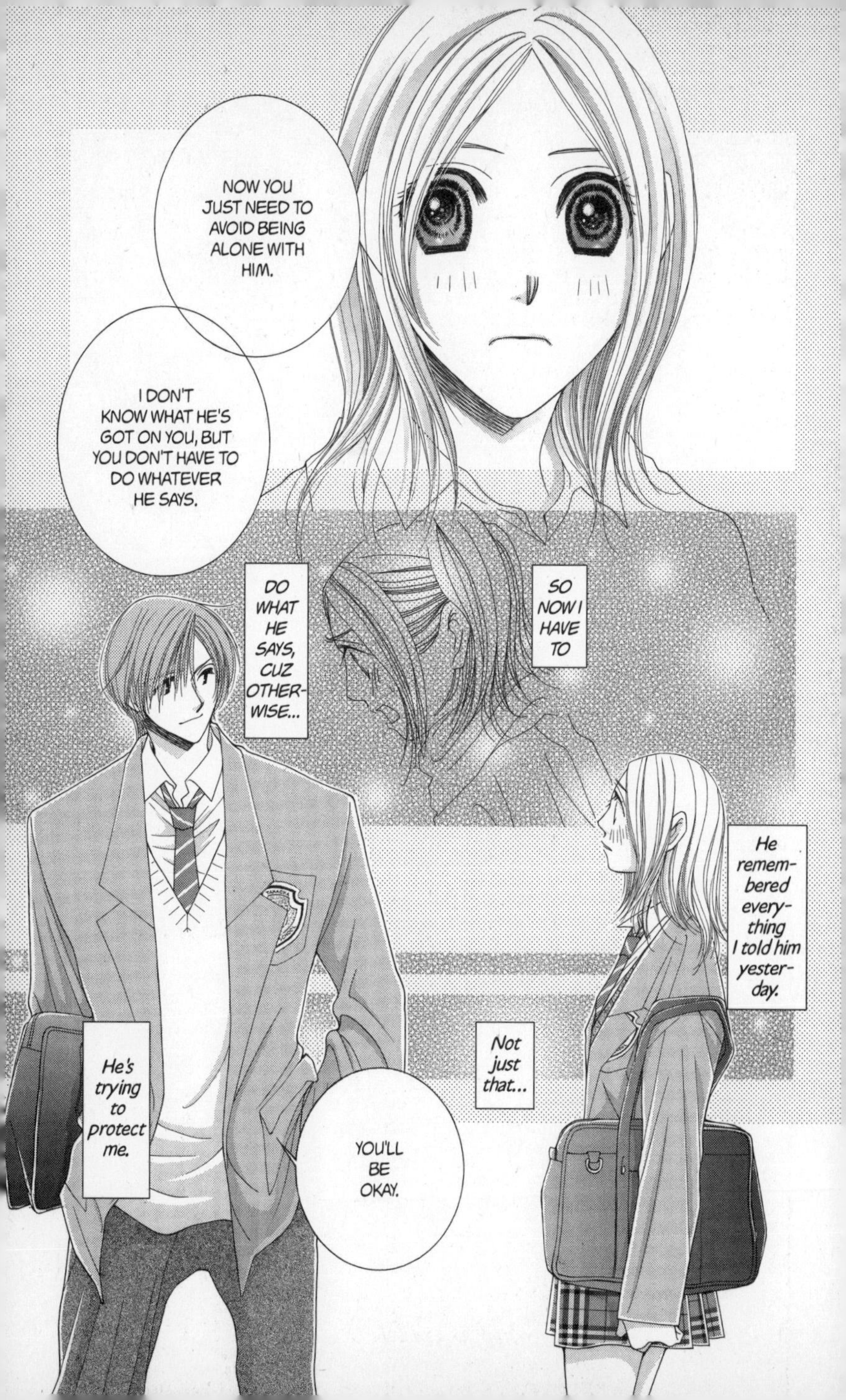
NOW YOU JUST NEED TO AVOID BEING ALONE WITH HIM.
I DON'T KNOW WHAT HE'S GOT ON YOU, BUT YOU DON'T HAVE TO DO WHATEVER HE SAYS.
SO NOW I HAVE TO
DO WHAT HE SAYS, CUZ OTHERWISE...
He remembered everything I told him yesterday.
Not just that...
He's trying to protect me.
YOU'LL BE OKAY.

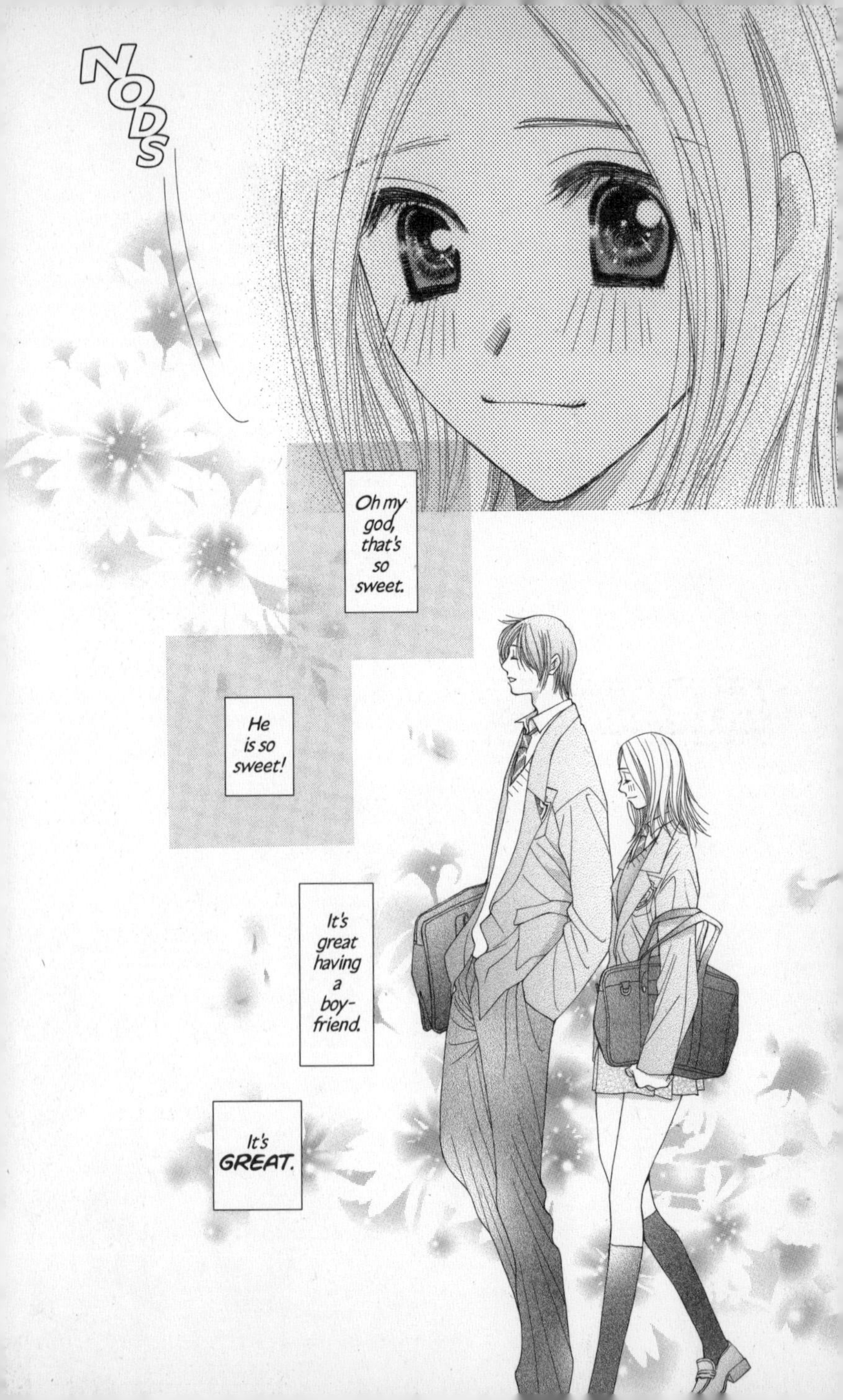
NODS
Oh my god, that's so sweet.
He is so sweet!
It's great having a boy-friend.
It's GREAT.

hotgimmick

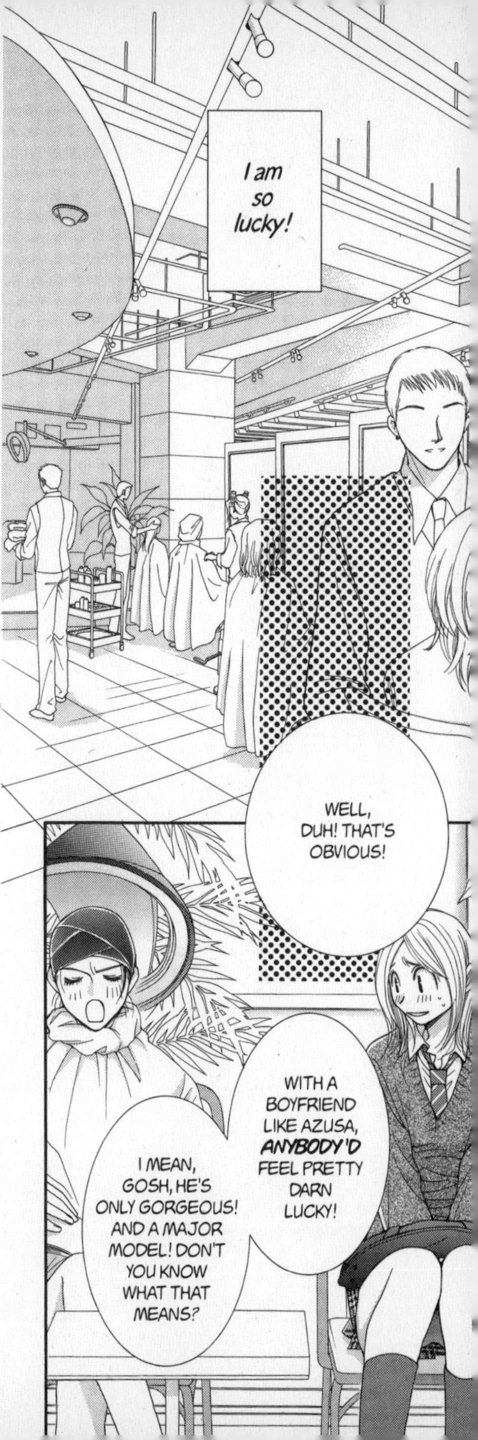
I am so lucky!
WELL, DUH! THAT'S OBVIOUS!
WITH A BOYFRIEND LIKE AZUSA, ANYBODY'D FEEL PRETTY DARN LUCKY!
I MEAN, GOSH, HE'S ONLY GORGEOUS! AND A MAJOR MODEL! DON'T YOU KNOW WHAT THAT MEANS?

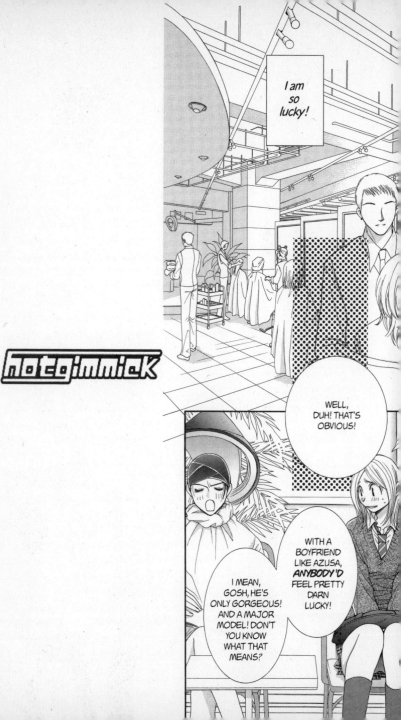

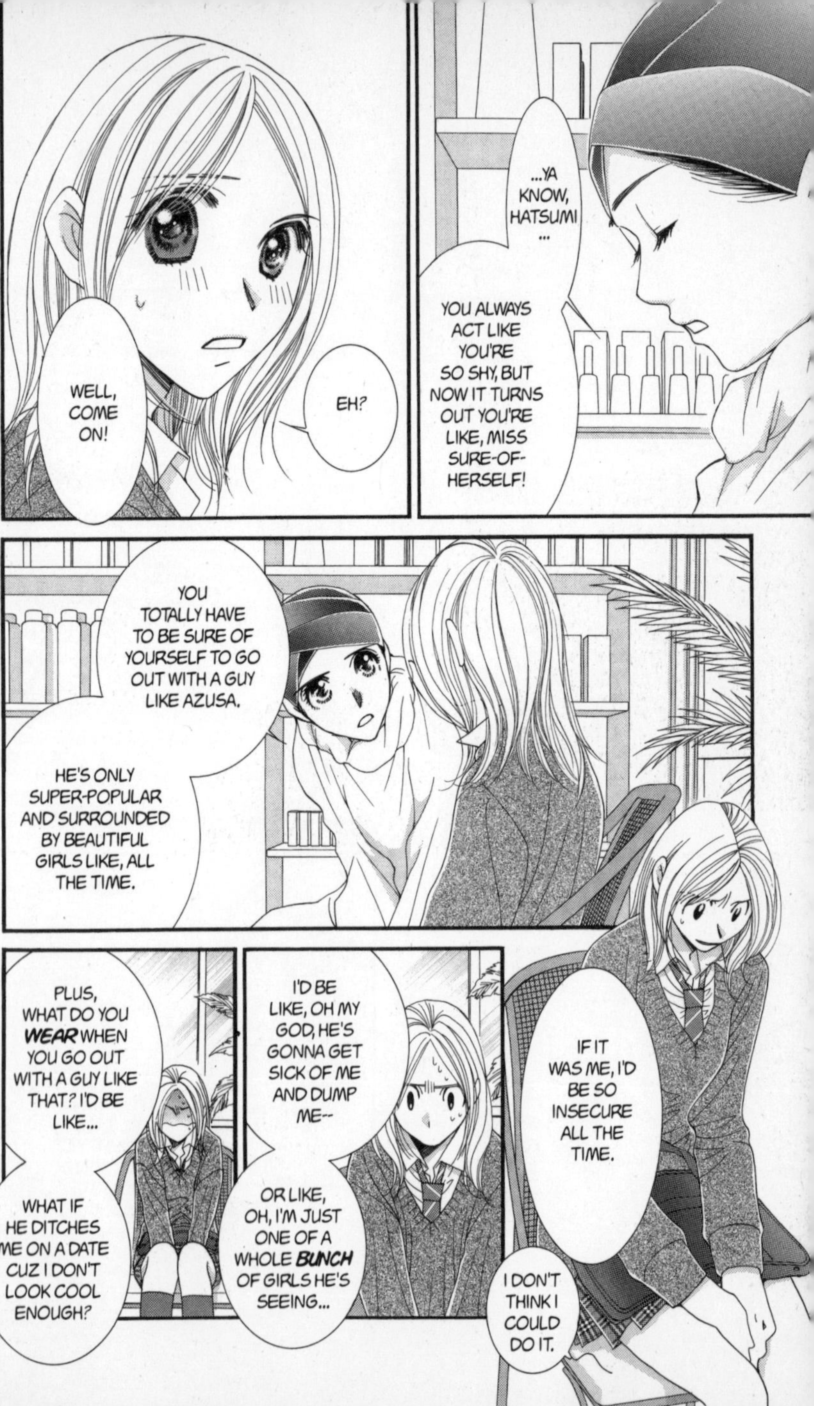
...YA KNOW, HATSUMI ...
YOU ALWAYS ACT LIKE YOU'RE SO SHY, BUT NOW IT TURNS OUT YOU'RE LIKE, MISS SURE-OF-HERSELF!
EH?
WELL, COME ON!
YOU TOTALLY HAVE TO BE SURE OF YOURSELF TO GO OUT WITH A GUY LIKE AZUSA.
HE'S ONLY SUPER-POPULAR AND SURROUNDED BY BEAUTIFUL GIRLS LIKE, ALL THE TIME.
IF IT WAS ME, I'D BE SO INSECURE ALL THE TIME.
I DON'T THINK I COULD DO IT.
I'D BE LIKE, OH MY GOD, HE'S GONNA GET SICK OF ME AND DUMP ME--
OR LIKE, OH, I'M JUST ONE OF A WHOLE BUNCH OF GIRLS HE'S SEEING...
PLUS, WHAT DO YOU WEAR WHEN YOU GO OUT WITH A GUY LIKE THAT? I'D BE LIKE...
WHAT IF HE DITCHES ME ON A DATE CUZ I DON'T LOOK COOL ENOUGH?

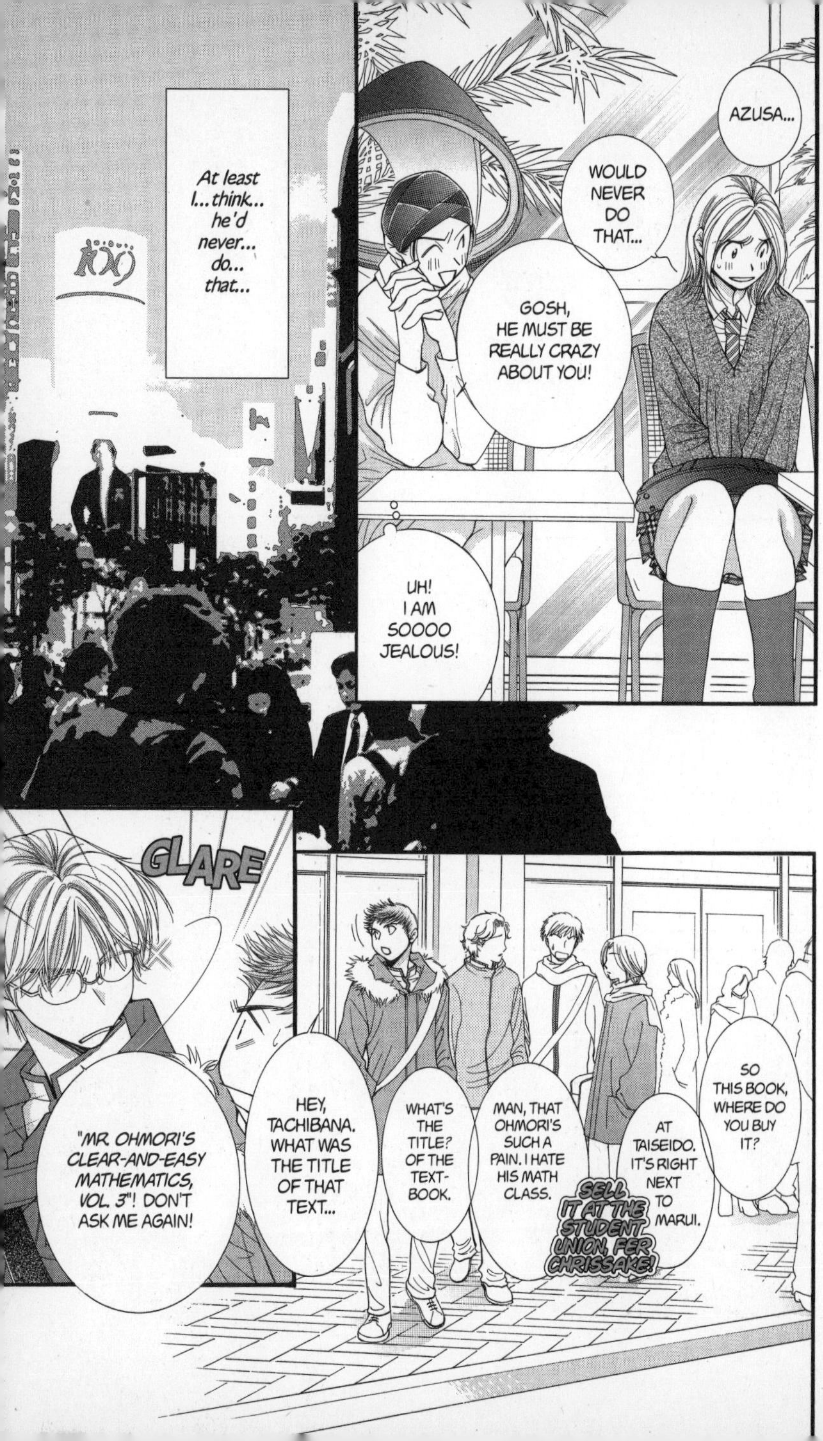
AZUSA...
WOULD NEVER DO THAT...
GOSH, HE MUST BE REALLY CRAZY ABOUT YOU!
UH! I AM SOOOO JEALOUS!
At least I...think... he'd never... do... that...
SO THIS BOOK, WHERE DO YOU BUY IT?
AT TAISEIDO. IT'S RIGHT NEXT TO MARUI.
SELL IT AT THE STUDENT UNION, FER CHRISSAKE!
MAN, THAT OHMORI'S SUCH A PAIN. I HATE HIS MATH CLASS.
WHAT'S THE TITLE? OF THE TEXT-BOOK.
HEY, TACHIBANA. WHAT WAS THE TITLE OF THAT TEXT...
GLARE
"MR. OHMORI'S CLEAR-AND-EASY MATHEMATICS, VOL. 3"! DON'T ASK ME AGAIN!

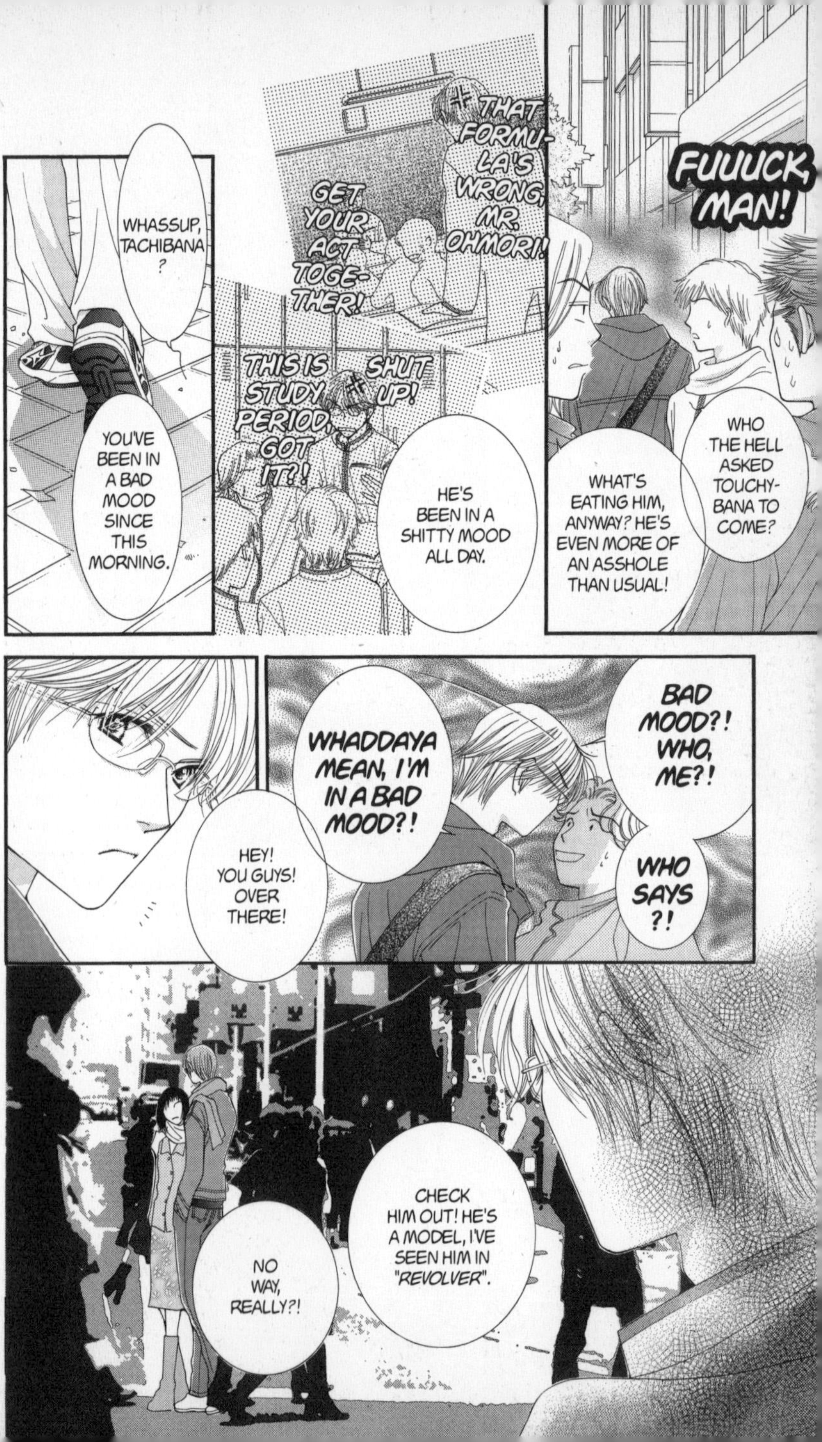
FUUUCK, MAN!
WHO THE HELL ASKED TOUCHY-BANA TO COME?
WHAT'S EATING HIM, ANYWAY? HE'S EVEN MORE OF AN ASSHOLE THAN USUAL!
THAT FORMU-LA'S WRONG, MR. OHMORI!
GET YOUR ACT TOGE-THER!
SHUT UP!
THIS IS STUDY PERIOD, GOT IT?!
HE'S BEEN IN A SHITTY MOOD ALL DAY.
WHASSUP, TACHIBANA?
YOU'VE BEEN IN A BAD MOOD SINCE THIS MORNING.
BAD MOOD?! WHO, ME?!
WHO SAYS?!
WHADDAYA MEAN, I'M IN A BAD MOOD?!
HEY! YOU GUYS! OVER THERE!
CHECK HIM OUT! HE'S A MODEL, I'VE SEEN HIM IN "REVOLVER".
NO WAY, REALLY?!

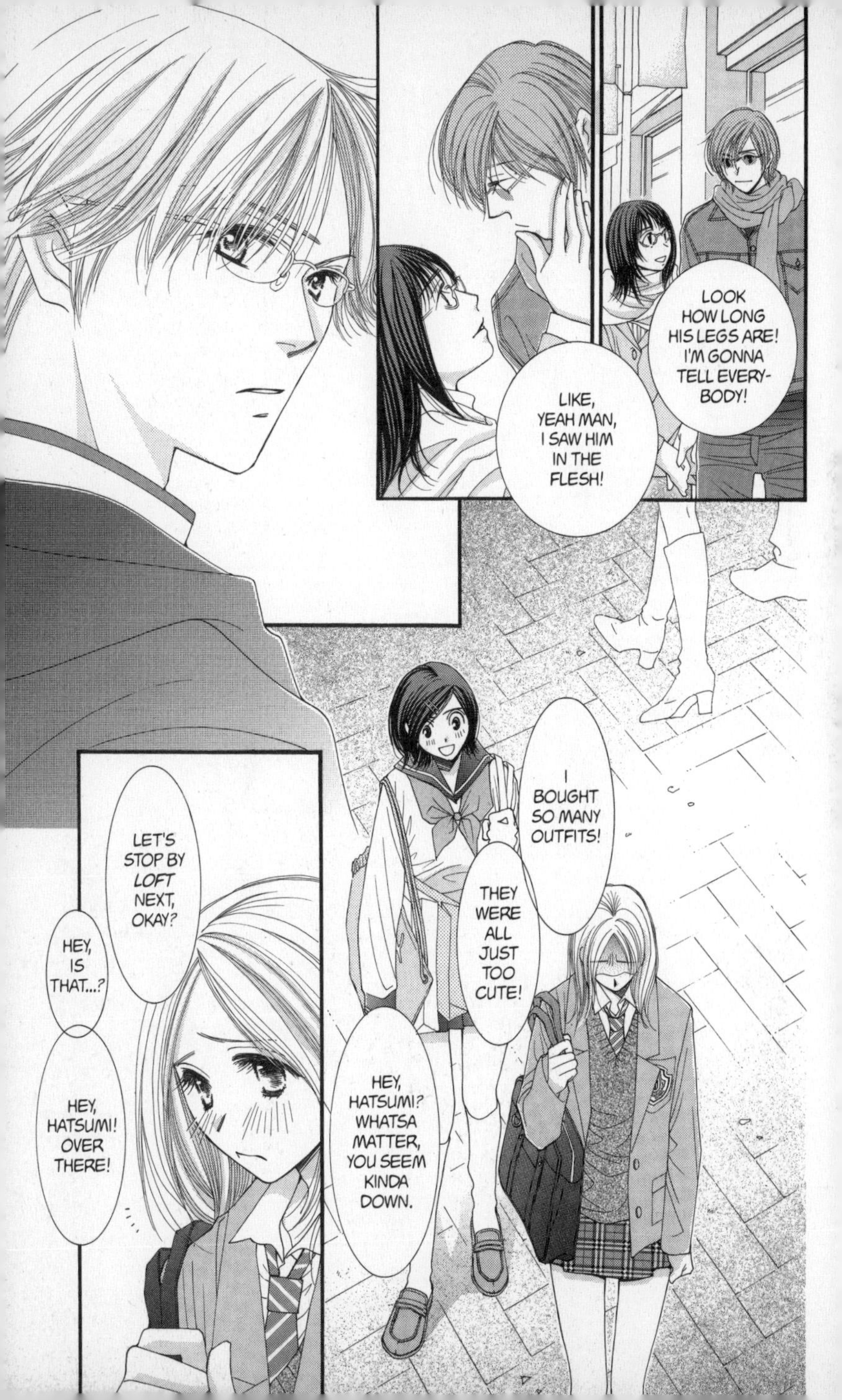
LOOK HOW LONG HIS LEGS ARE! I'M GONNA TELL EVERY-BODY!
LIKE, YEAH MAN, I SAW HIM IN THE FLESH!
I BOUGHT SO MANY OUTFITS!
THEY WERE ALL JUST TOO CUTE!
HEY, HATSUMI? WHATSA MATTER, YOU SEEM KINDA DOWN.
LET'S STOP BY *LOFT* NEXT, OKAY?
HEY, IS THAT...?
HEY, HATSUMI! OVER THERE!

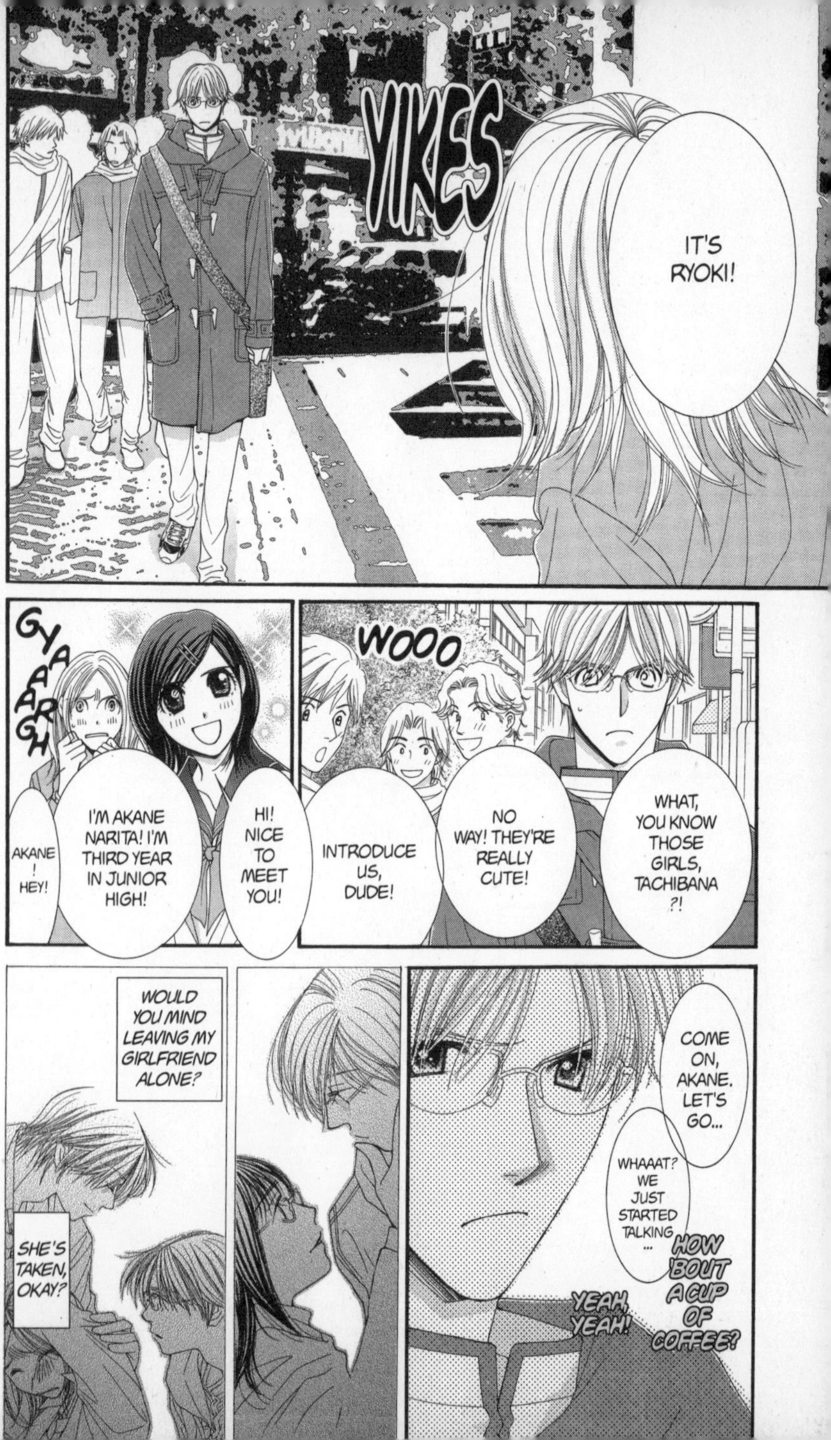
IT'S RYOKI!
YIKES
WHAT, YOU KNOW THOSE GIRLS, TACHIBANA?!
NO WAY! THEY'RE REALLY CUTE!
WOOO
INTRODUCE US, DUDE!
HI! NICE TO MEET YOU!
I'M AKANE NARITA! I'M THIRD YEAR IN JUNIOR HIGH!
GYAAARGH
AKANE! HEY!
COME ON, AKANE. LET'S GO...
WHAAAT? WE JUST STARTED TALKING...
HOW BOUT A CUP OF COFFEE?
YEAH, YEAH!
WOULD YOU MIND LEAVING MY GIRLFRIEND ALONE?
SHE'S TAKEN, OKAY?

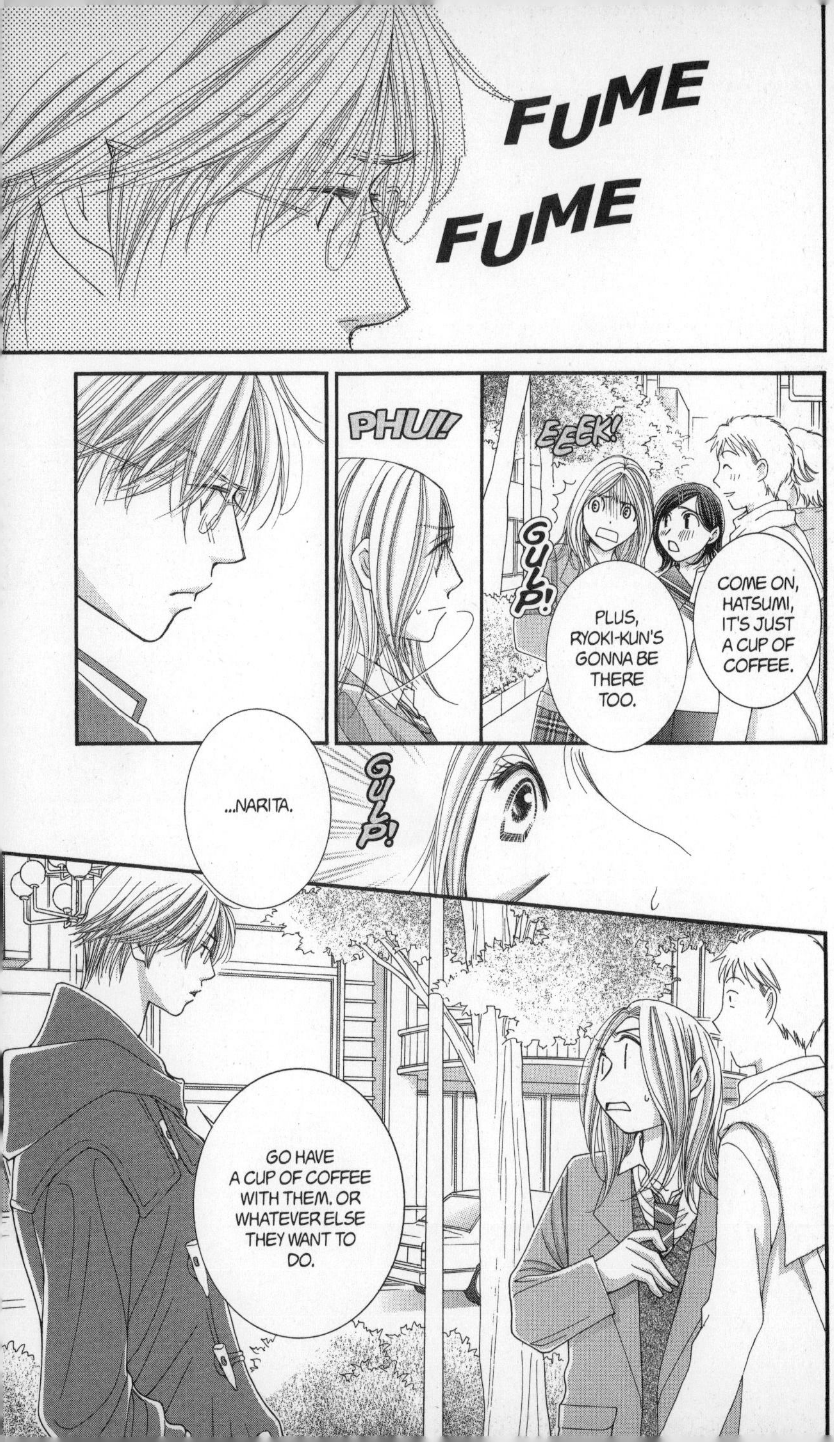
FUME
FUME
EEEK!
COME ON, HATSUMI, IT'S JUST A CUP OF COFFEE.
GULP!
PLUS, RYOKI-KUN'S GONNA BE THERE TOO.
PHUI!
GULP!
...NARITA.
GO HAVE A CUP OF COFFEE WITH THEM. OR WHATEVER ELSE THEY WANT TO DO.

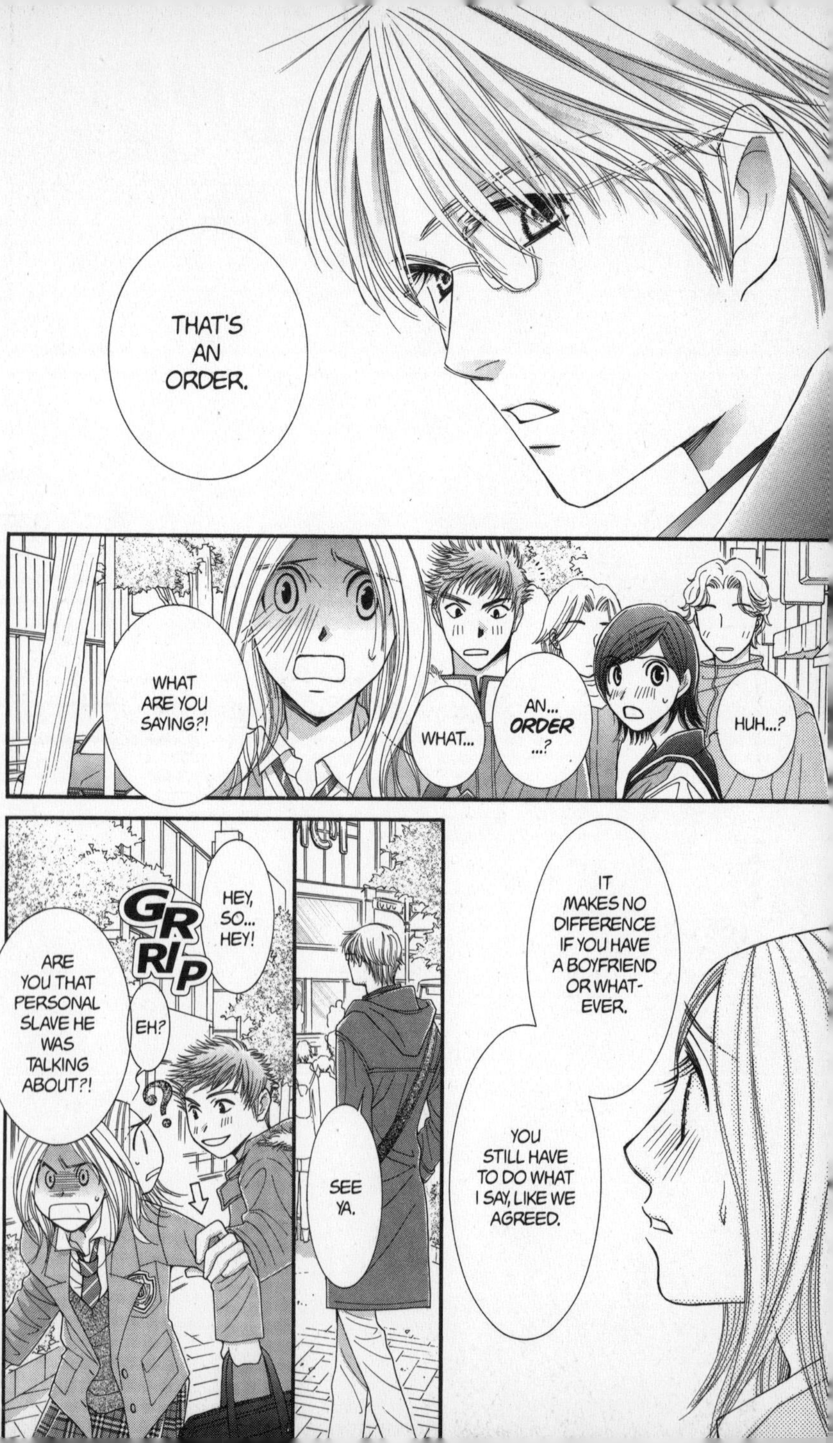
THAT'S AN ORDER.
HUH...?
AN... ORDER ...?
WHAT...
WHAT ARE YOU SAYING?!
IT MAKES NO DIFFERENCE IF YOU HAVE A BOYFRIEND OR WHAT-EVER.
YOU STILL HAVE TO DO WHAT I SAY, LIKE WE AGREED.
SEE YA.
HEY, SO... HEY!
GRRIP
EH?
ARE YOU THAT PERSONAL SLAVE HE WAS TALKING ABOUT?!

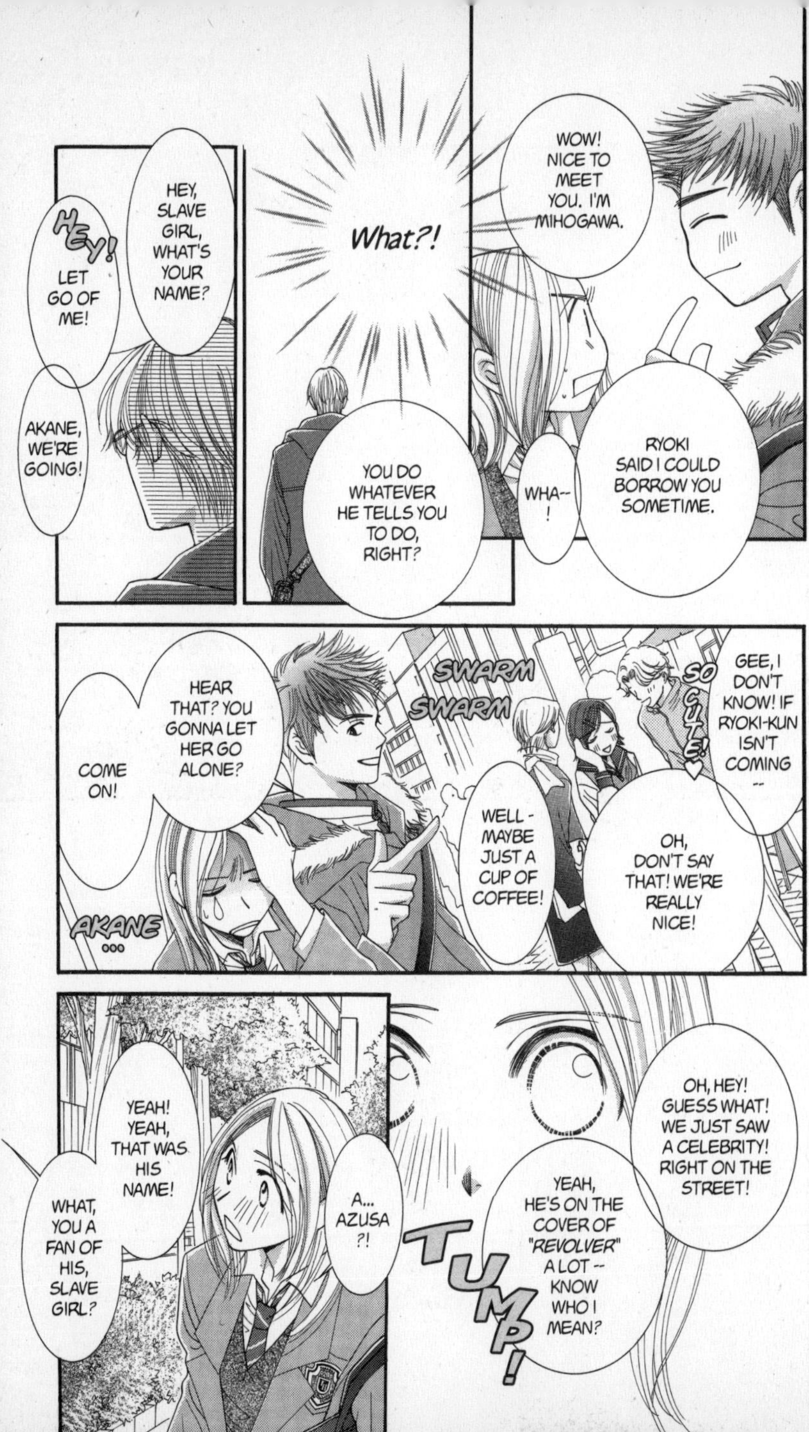
WOW! NICE TO MEET YOU. I'M MIHOGAWA.
RYOKI SAID I COULD BORROW YOU SOMETIME.
WHA-- !
What?!
YOU DO WHATEVER HE TELLS YOU TO DO, RIGHT?
HEY, SLAVE GIRL, WHAT'S YOUR NAME?
HEY! LET GO OF ME!
AKANE, WE'RE GOING!
GEE, I DON'T KNOW! IF RYOKI-KUN ISN'T COMING --
SO CUTE!
OH, DON'T SAY THAT! WE'RE REALLY NICE!
WELL - MAYBE JUST A CUP OF COFFEE!
SWARM
SWARM
HEAR THAT? YOU GONNA LET HER GO ALONE?
COME ON!
AKANE ...
OH, HEY! GUESS WHAT! WE JUST SAW A CELEBRITY! RIGHT ON THE STREET!
YEAH, HE'S ON THE COVER OF "REVOLVER" A LOT -- KNOW WHO I MEAN?
TUMP!
A... AZUSA ?!
YEAH! YEAH, THAT WAS HIS NAME!
WHAT, YOU A FAN OF HIS, SLAVE GIRL?

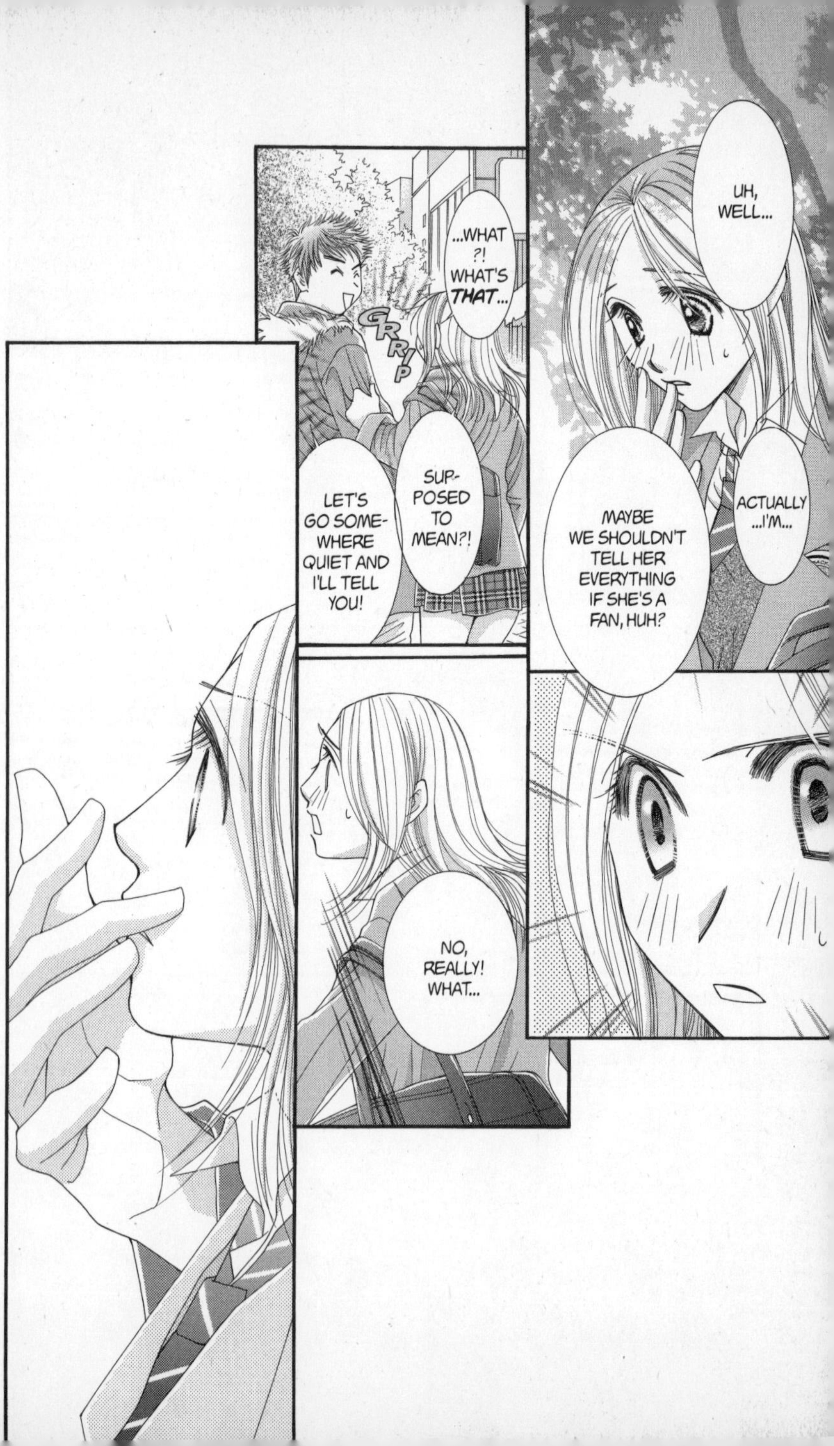
UH, WELL...
ACTUALLY ...I'M...
...WHAT?! WHAT'S THAT...
GRRIP
SUP-POSED TO MEAN?!
LET'S GO SOME-WHERE QUIET AND I'LL TELL YOU!
MAYBE WE SHOULDN'T TELL HER EVERYTHING IF SHE'S A FAN, HUH?
NO, REALLY! WHAT...

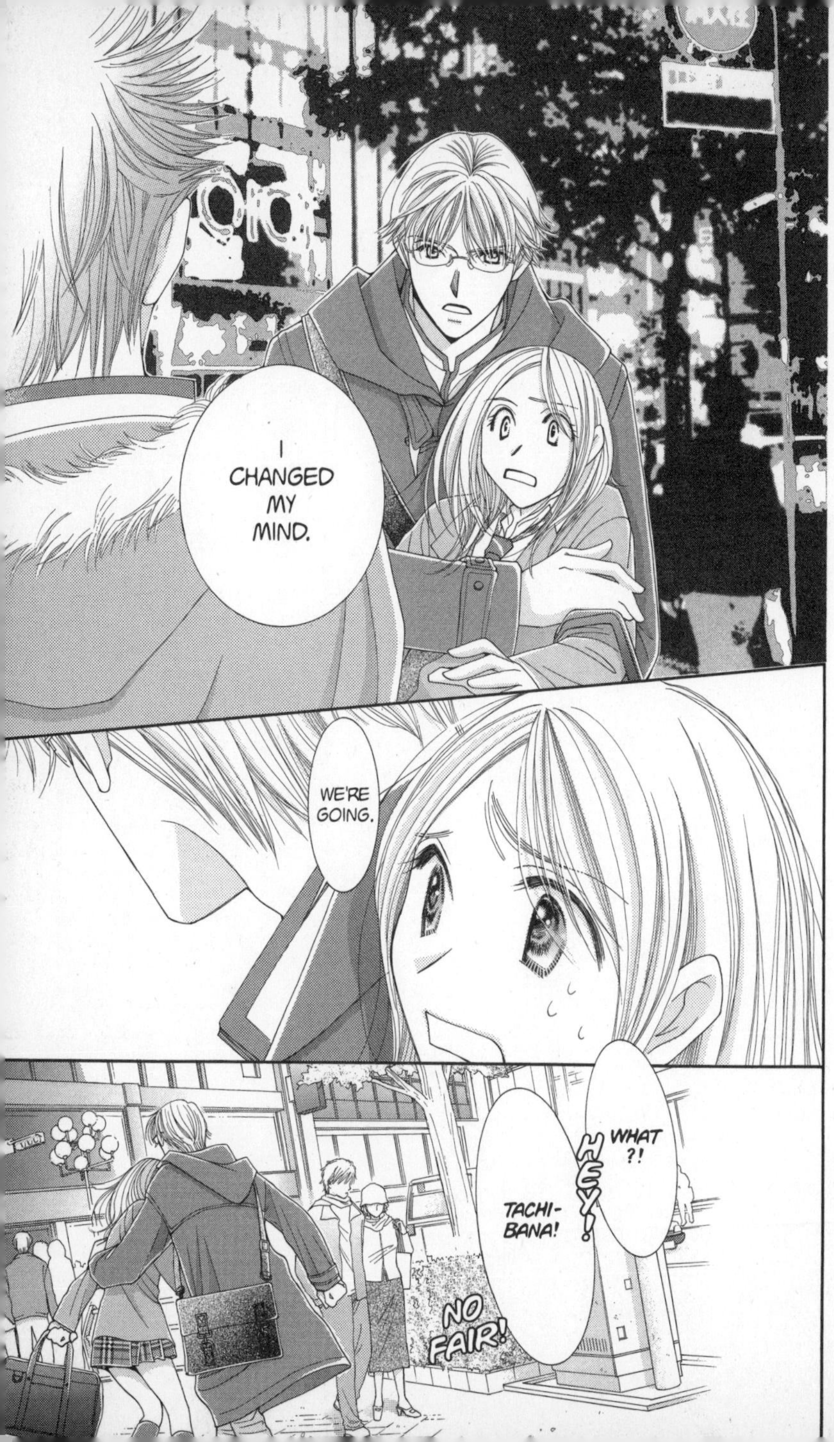
I CHANGED MY MIND.
WE'RE GOING.
WHAT ?!
HEY!
TACHI-BANA!
NO FAIR!

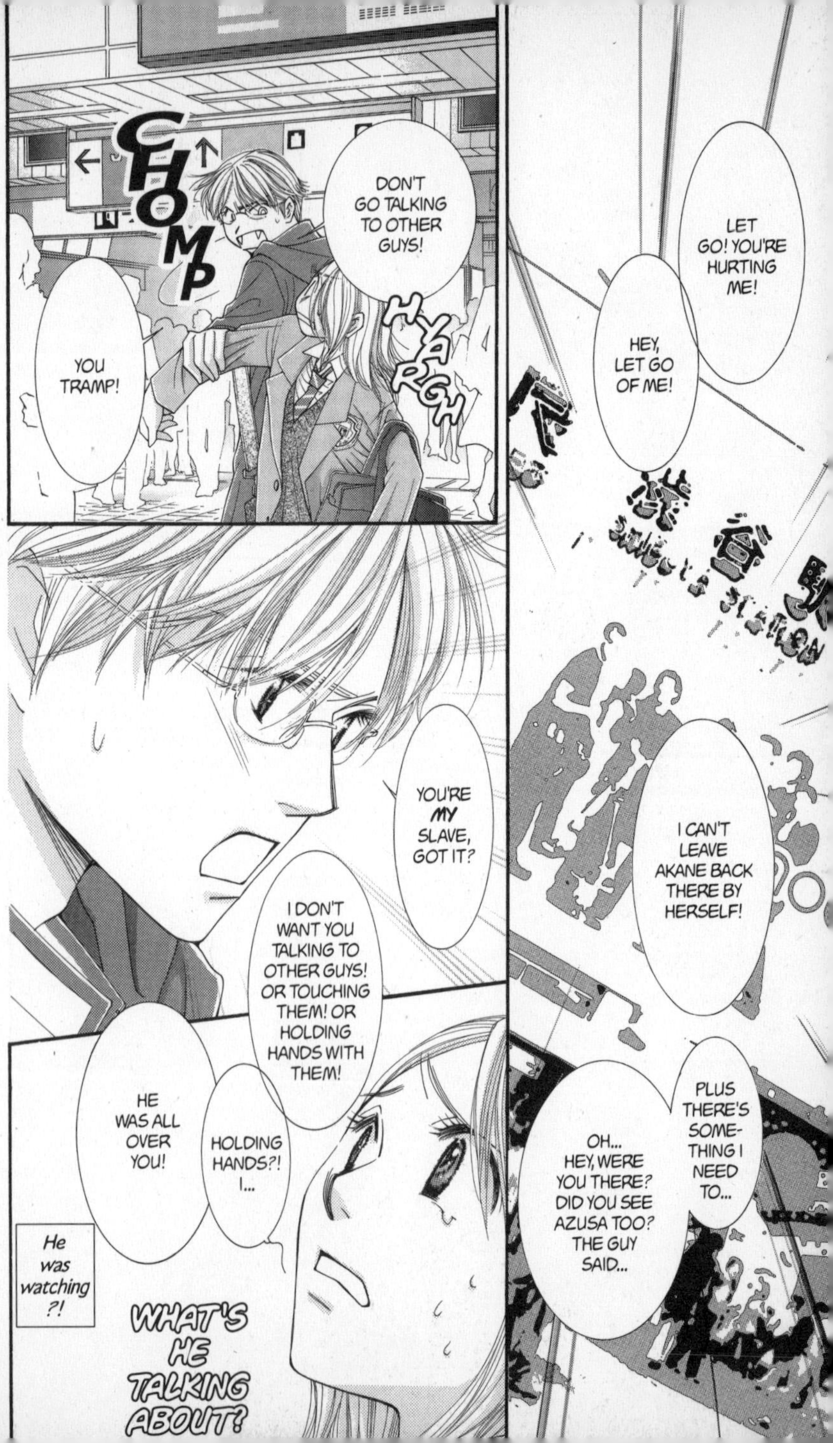
LET GO! YOU'RE HURTING ME!
HEY, LET GO OF ME!
I CAN'T LEAVE AKANE BACK THERE BY HERSELF!
PLUS THERE'S SOME-THING I NEED TO...
OH... HEY, WERE YOU THERE? DID YOU SEE AZUSA TOO? THE GUY SAID...
DON'T GO TALKING TO OTHER GUYS!
CHOMP
HYARGH
YOU TRAMP!
YOU'RE MY SLAVE, GOT IT?
I DON'T WANT YOU TALKING TO OTHER GUYS! OR TOUCHING THEM! OR HOLDING HANDS WITH THEM!
HOLDING HANDS?! I...
HE WAS ALL OVER YOU!
He was watching?!
WHAT'S HE TALKING ABOUT?!

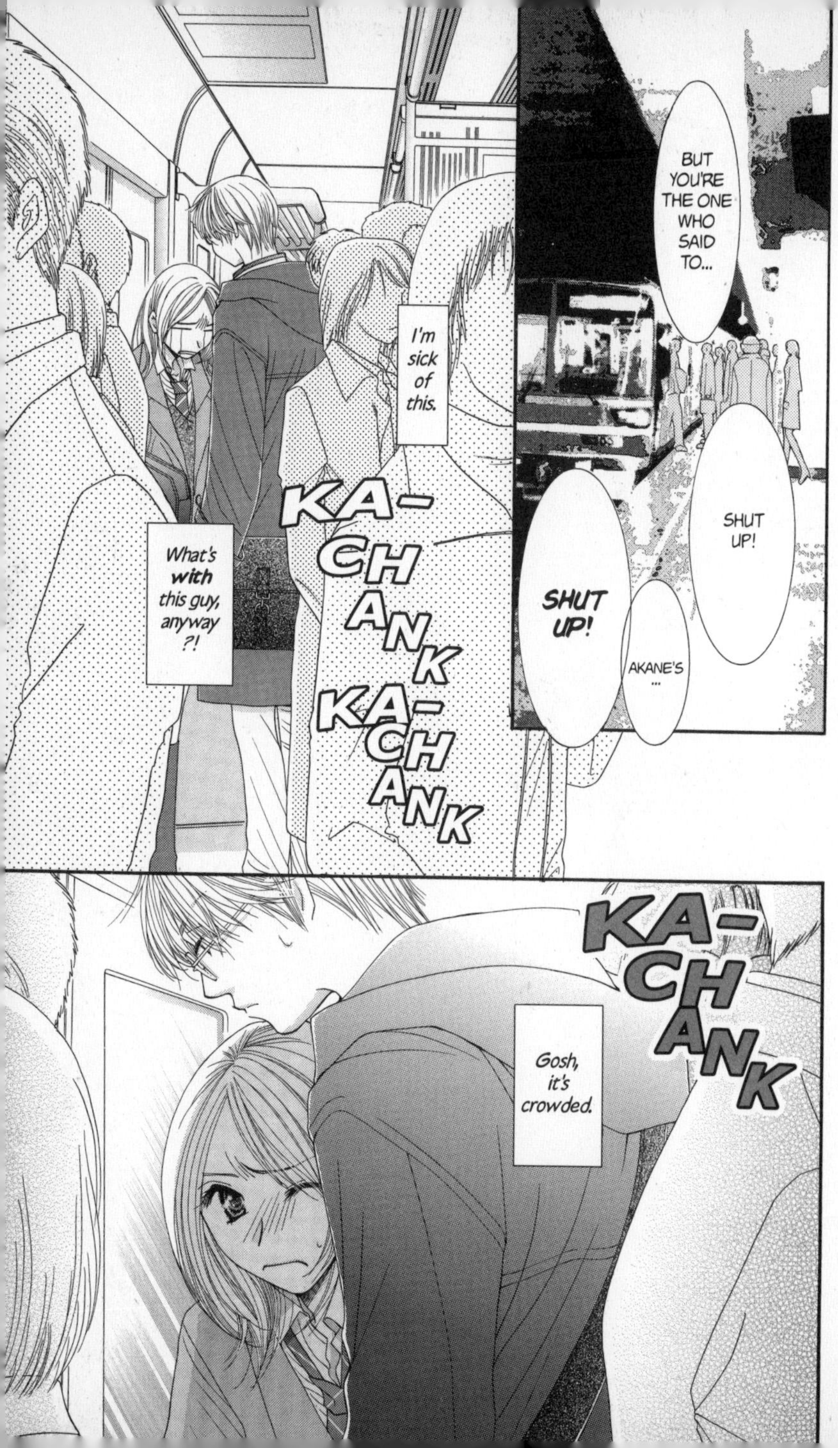
BUT YOU'RE THE ONE WHO SAID TO...
SHUT UP!
AKANE'S ...
SHUT UP!
I'm sick of this.
KA-CHANK
KA-CHANK
What's with this guy, anyway?!
KA-CHANK
Gosh, it's crowded.

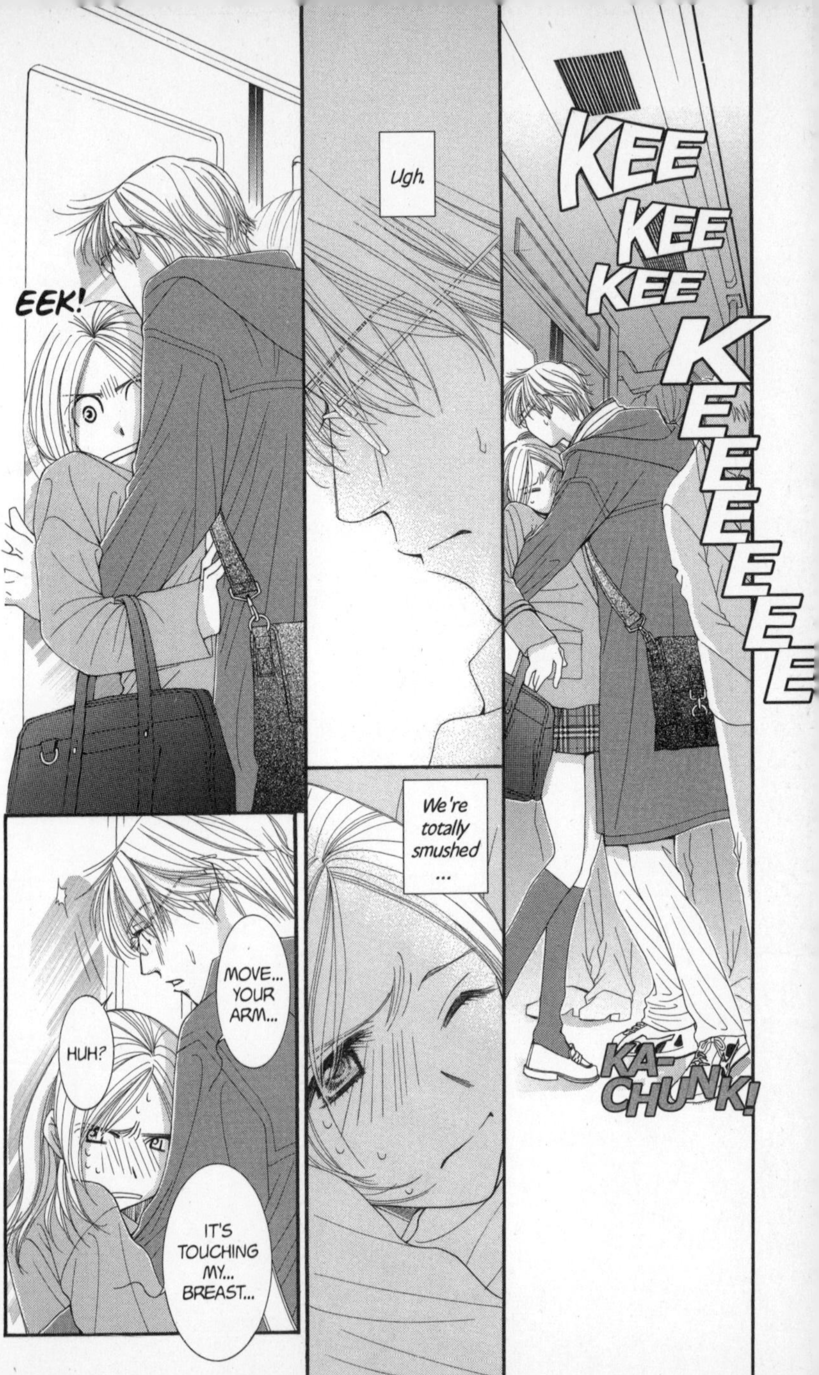
KEE KEE KEE KEEEEEEE
KA-CHUNK!
Ugh.
EEK!
We're totally smushed ...
MOVE... YOUR ARM...
HUH?
IT'S TOUCHING MY... BREAST...

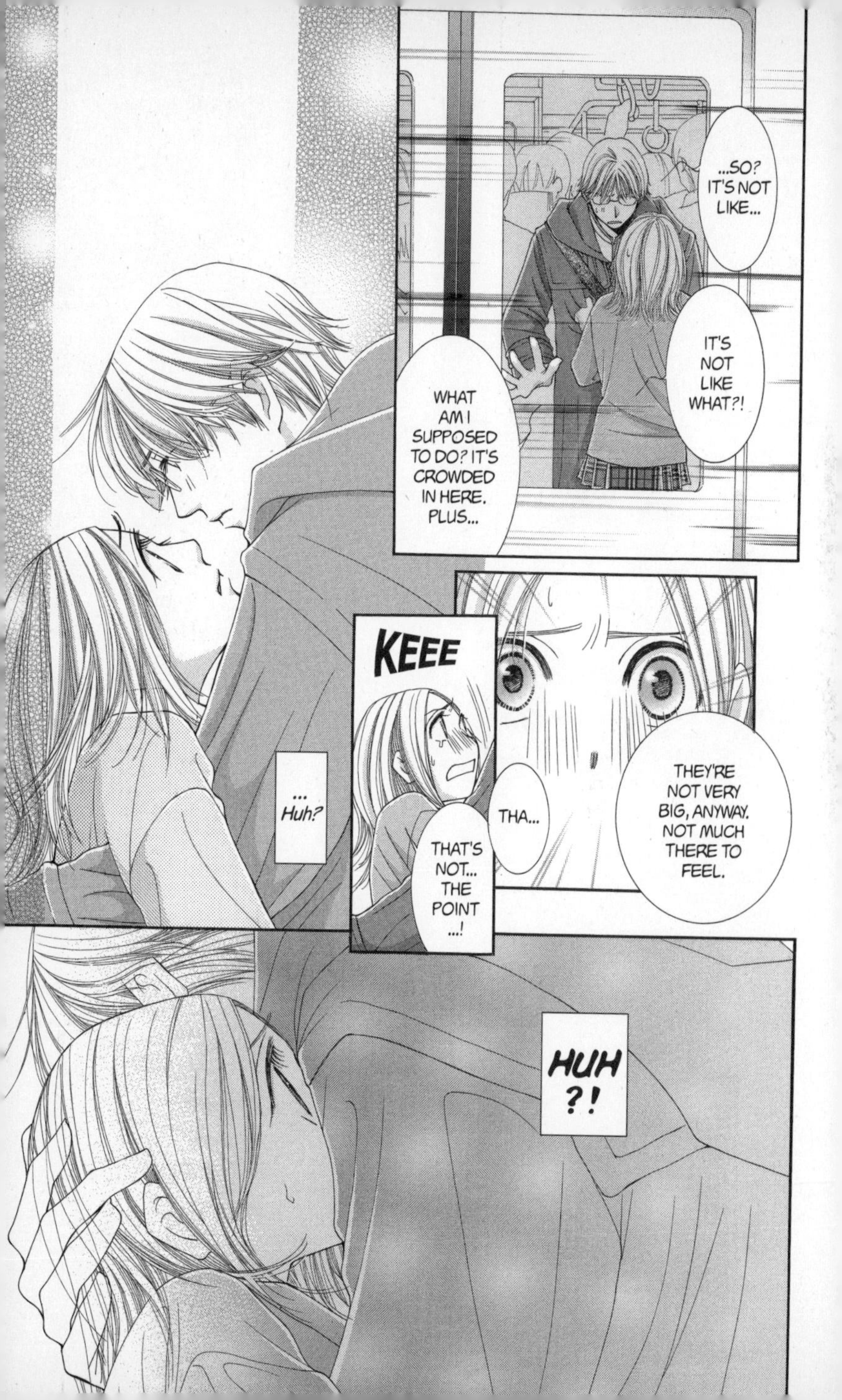
...SO? IT'S NOT LIKE...
IT'S NOT LIKE WHAT?!
WHAT AM I SUPPOSED TO DO? IT'S CROWDED IN HERE. PLUS...
THEY'RE NOT VERY BIG, ANYWAY. NOT MUCH THERE TO FEEL.
THA...
KEEE
THAT'S NOT... THE POINT ...!
... Huh?
HUH ?!

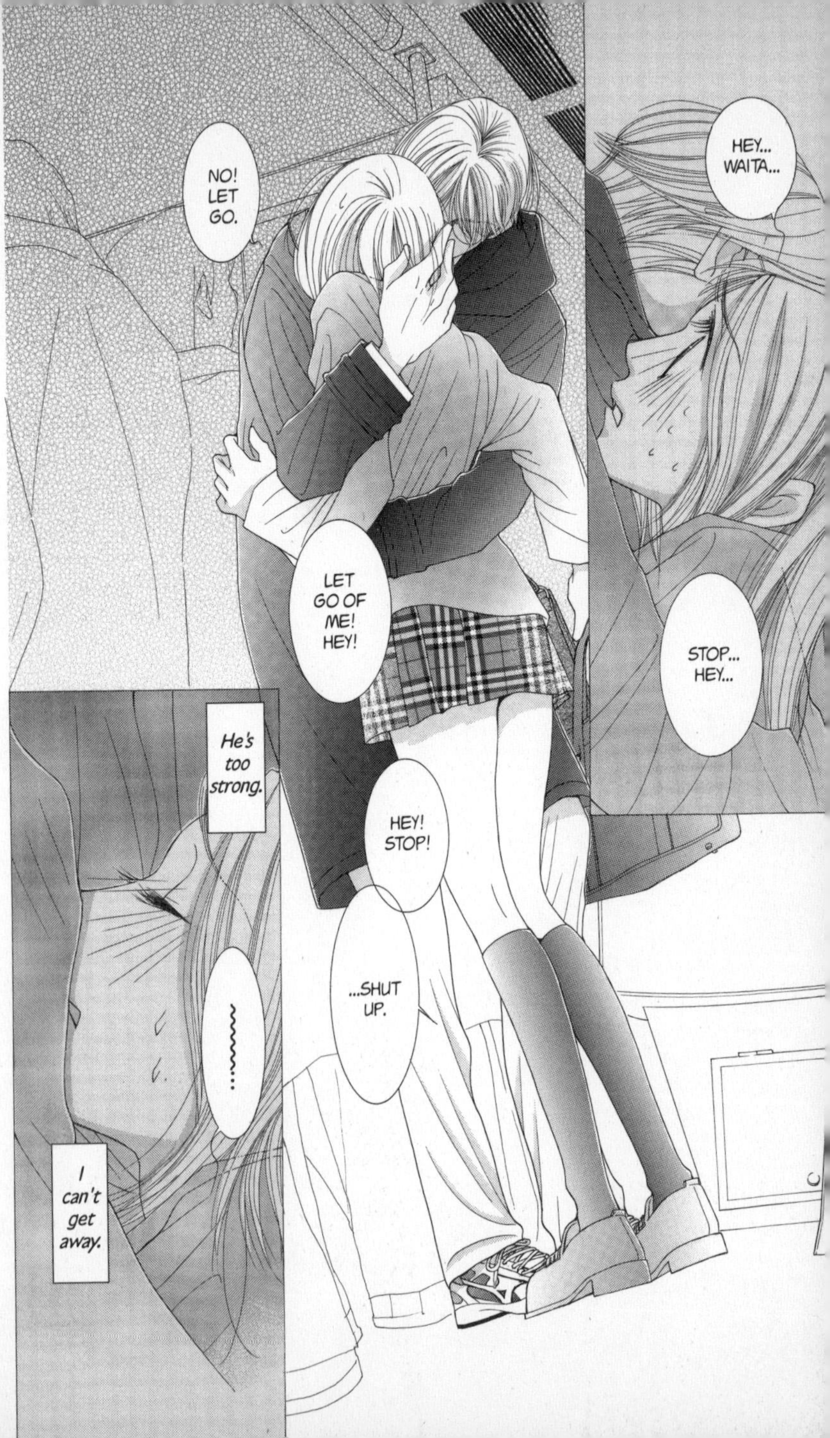
HEY... WAITA...
STOP... HEY...
NO! LET GO.
LET GO OF ME! HEY!
HEY! STOP!
...SHUT UP.
He's too strong.
~~~~~...
I can't get away.
~~~~~

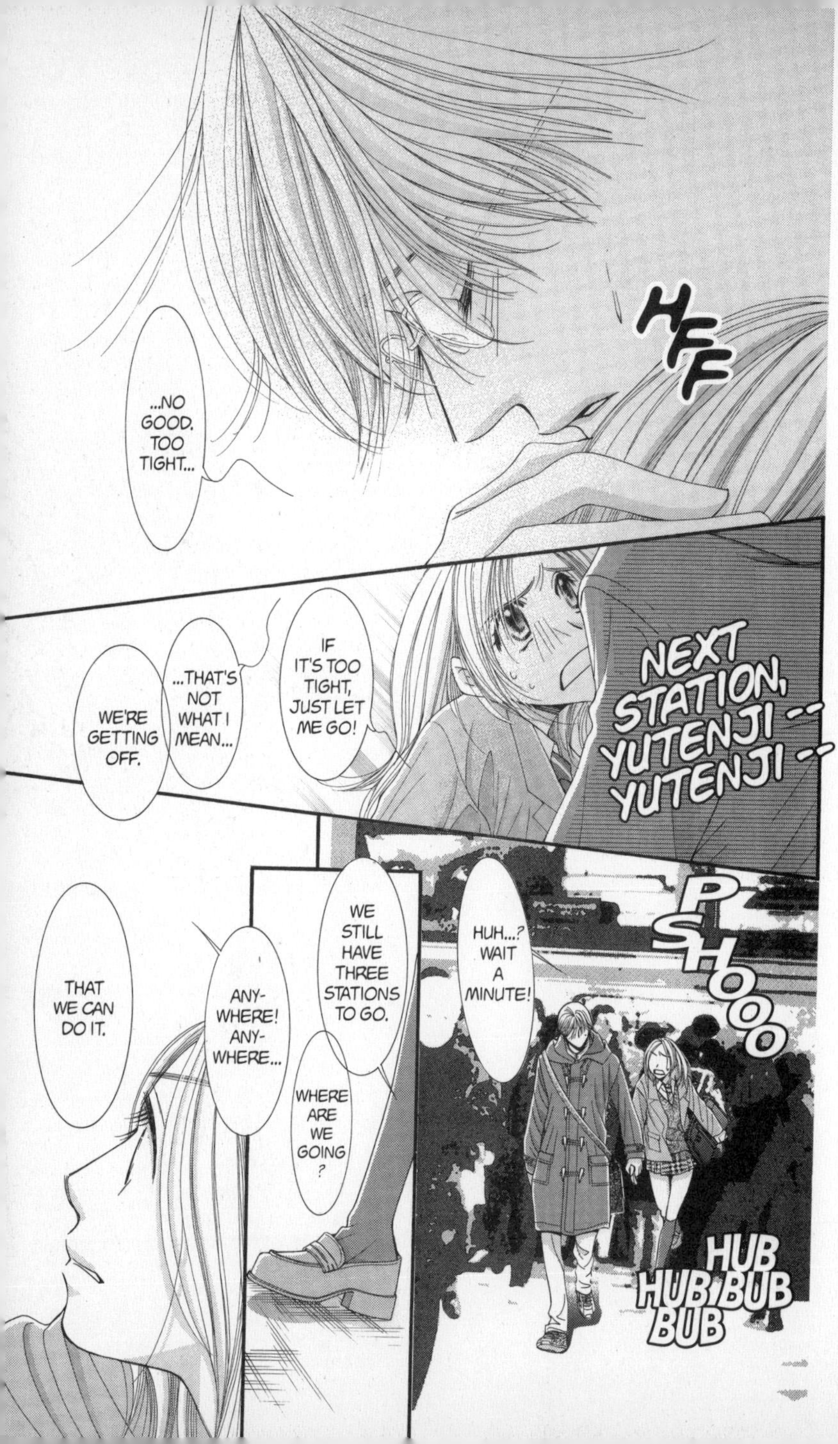
HFF
...NO GOOD. TOO TIGHT...
NEXT STATION, YUTENJI -- YUTENJI --
IF IT'S TOO TIGHT, JUST LET ME GO!
...THAT'S NOT WHAT I MEAN...
WE'RE GETTING OFF.
PSHOOO
HUH...? WAIT A MINUTE!
WE STILL HAVE THREE STATIONS TO GO.
WHERE ARE WE GOING?
HUB HUB BUB BUB
ANY-WHERE! ANY-WHERE...
THAT WE CAN DO IT.

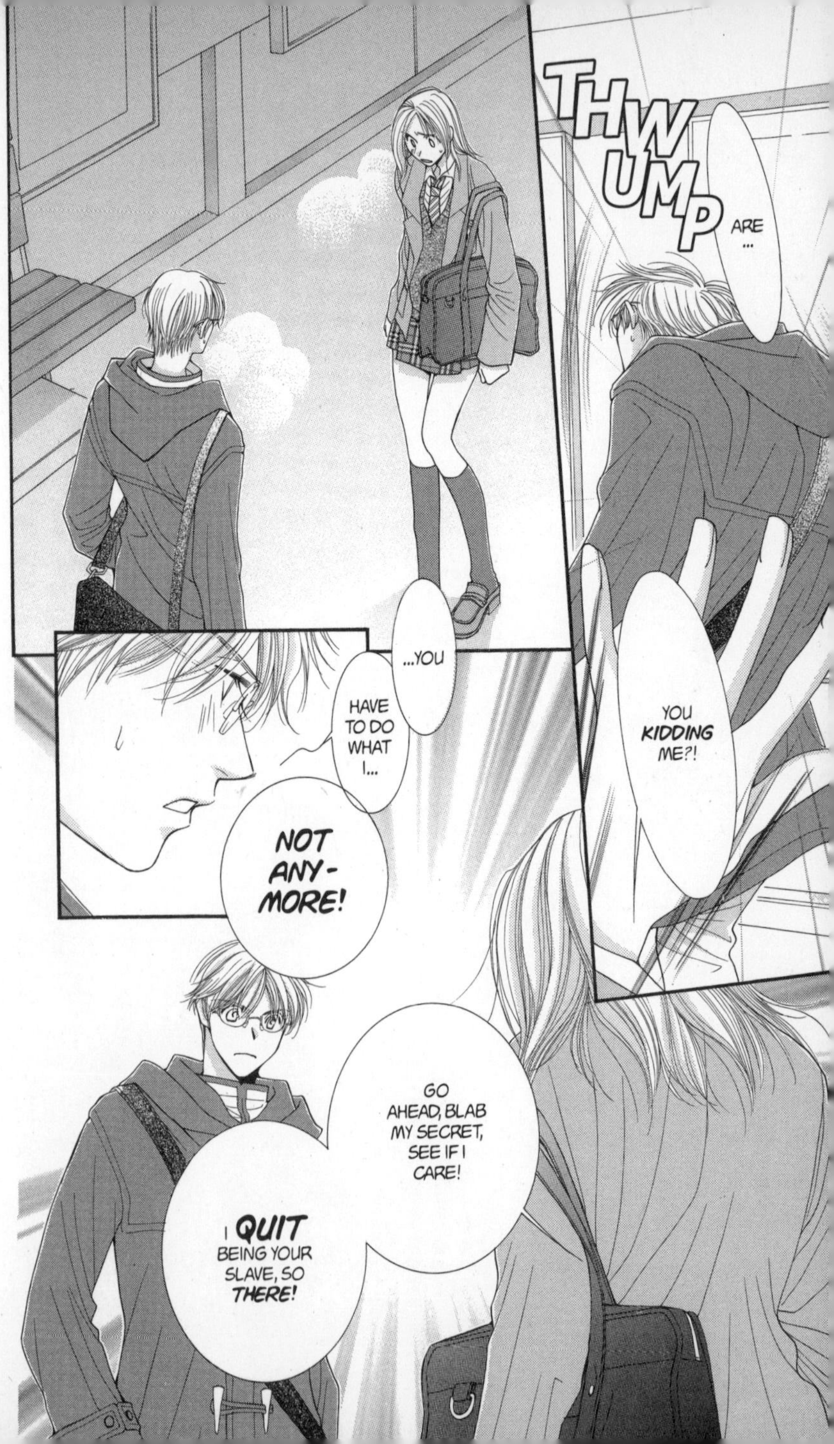
THWUMP
ARE ...
YOU KIDDING ME?!
...YOU
HAVE TO DO WHAT I...
NOT ANY-MORE!
GO AHEAD, BLAB MY SECRET, SEE IF I CARE!
I QUIT BEING YOUR SLAVE, SO THERE!

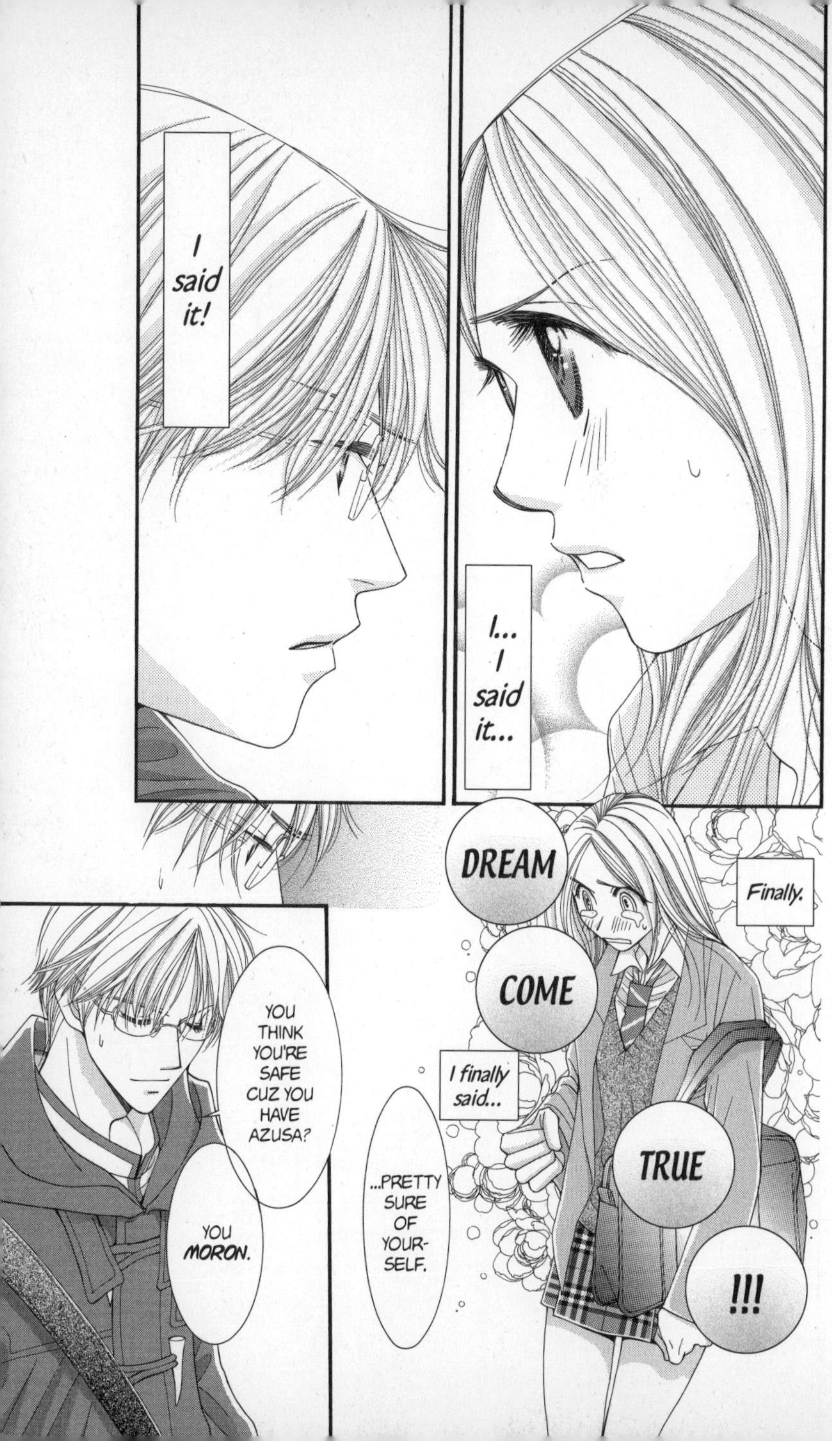
I... I said it...
I said it!
Finally.
DREAM
COME
I finally said...
TRUE
!!!
...PRETTY SURE OF YOURSELF.
YOU THINK YOU'RE SAFE CUZ YOU HAVE AZUSA?
YOU MORON.

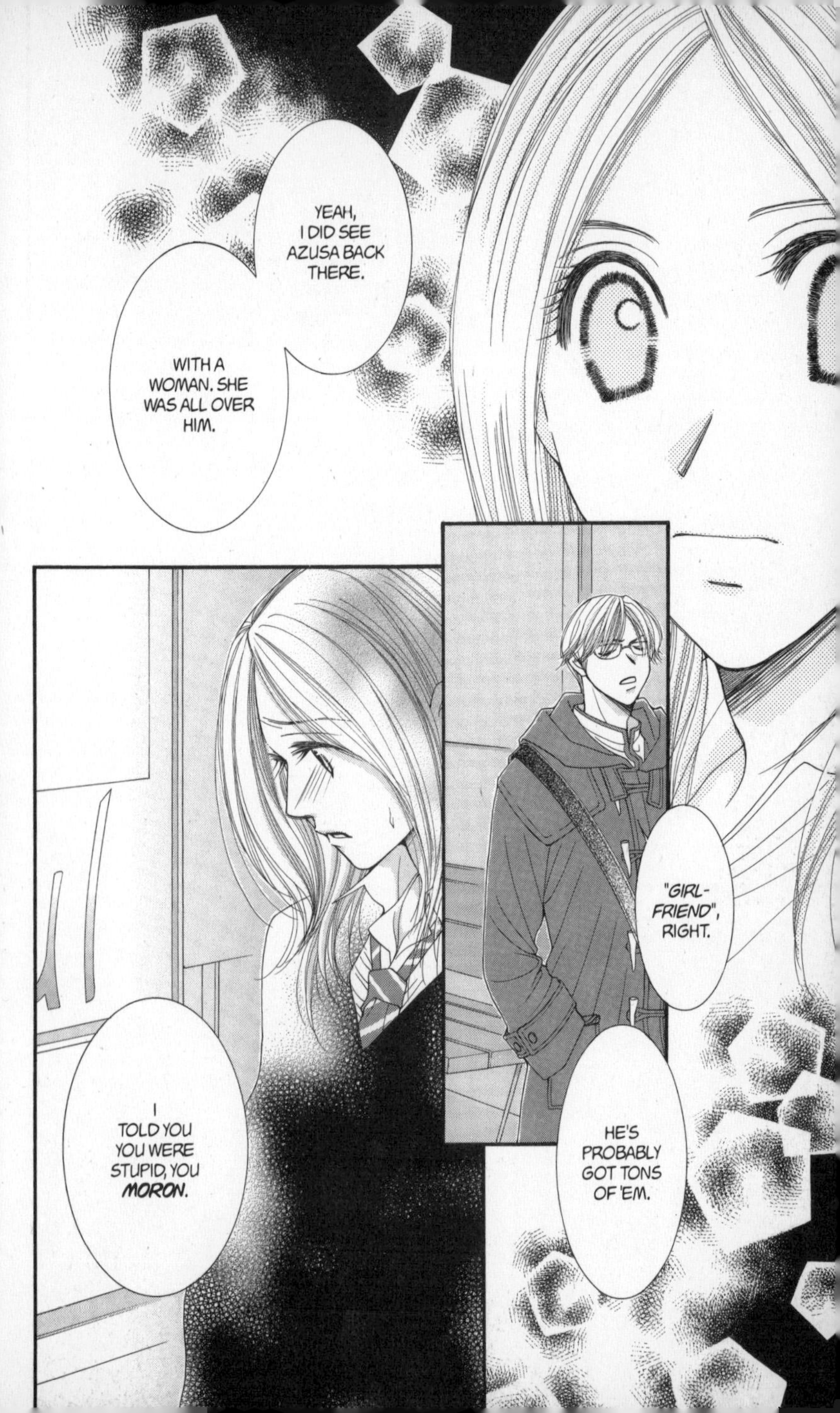
YEAH, I DID SEE AZUSA BACK THERE.
WITH A WOMAN. SHE WAS ALL OVER HIM.
"GIRL-FRIEND", RIGHT.
HE'S PROBABLY GOT TONS OF 'EM.
I TOLD YOU YOU WERE STUPID, YOU **MORON**.

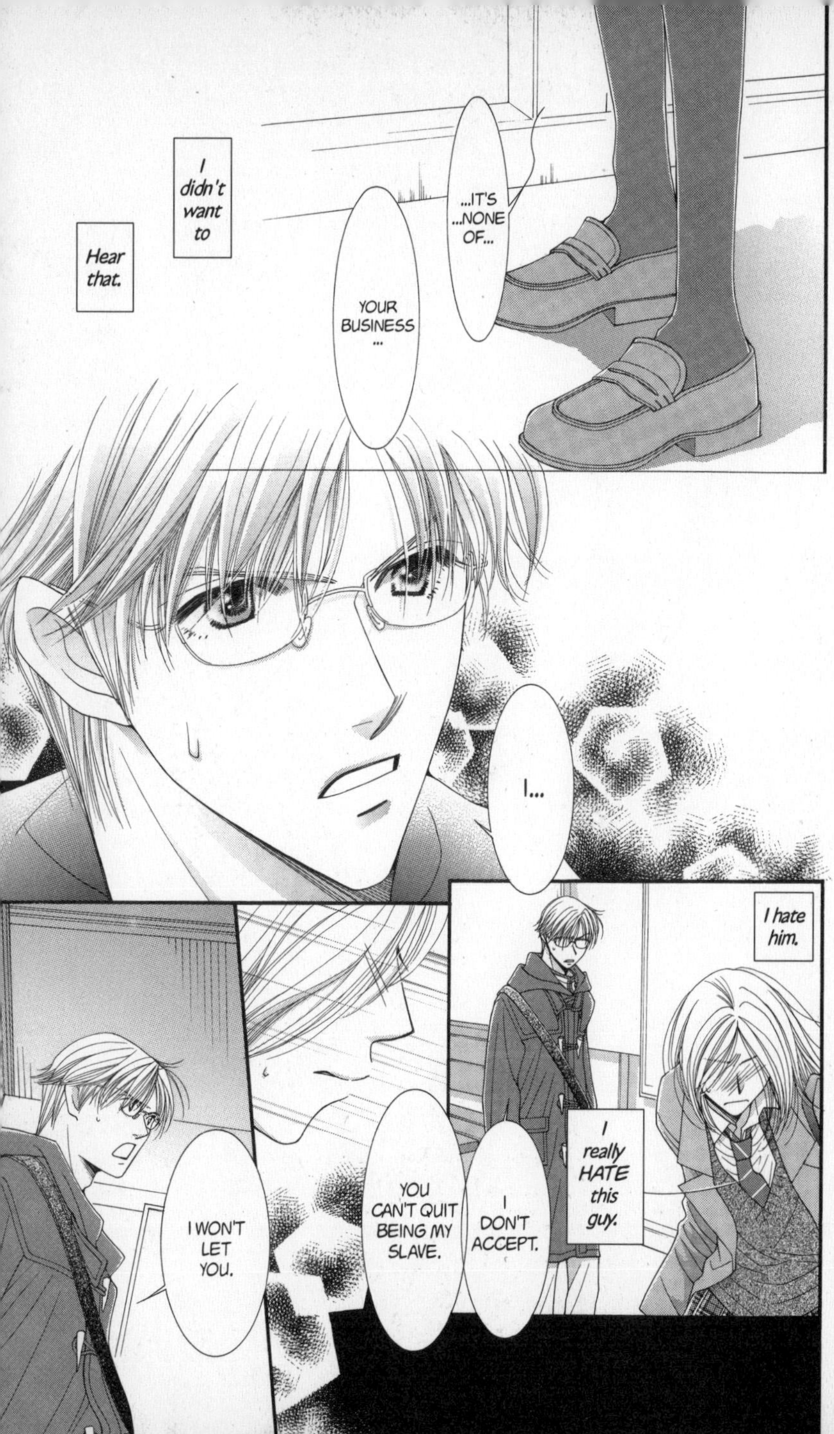
...IT'S ...NONE OF...
YOUR BUSINESS ...
I didn't want to
Hear that.
I...
I hate him.
I really HATE this guy.
I DON'T ACCEPT.
YOU CAN'T QUIT BEING MY SLAVE.
I WON'T LET YOU.

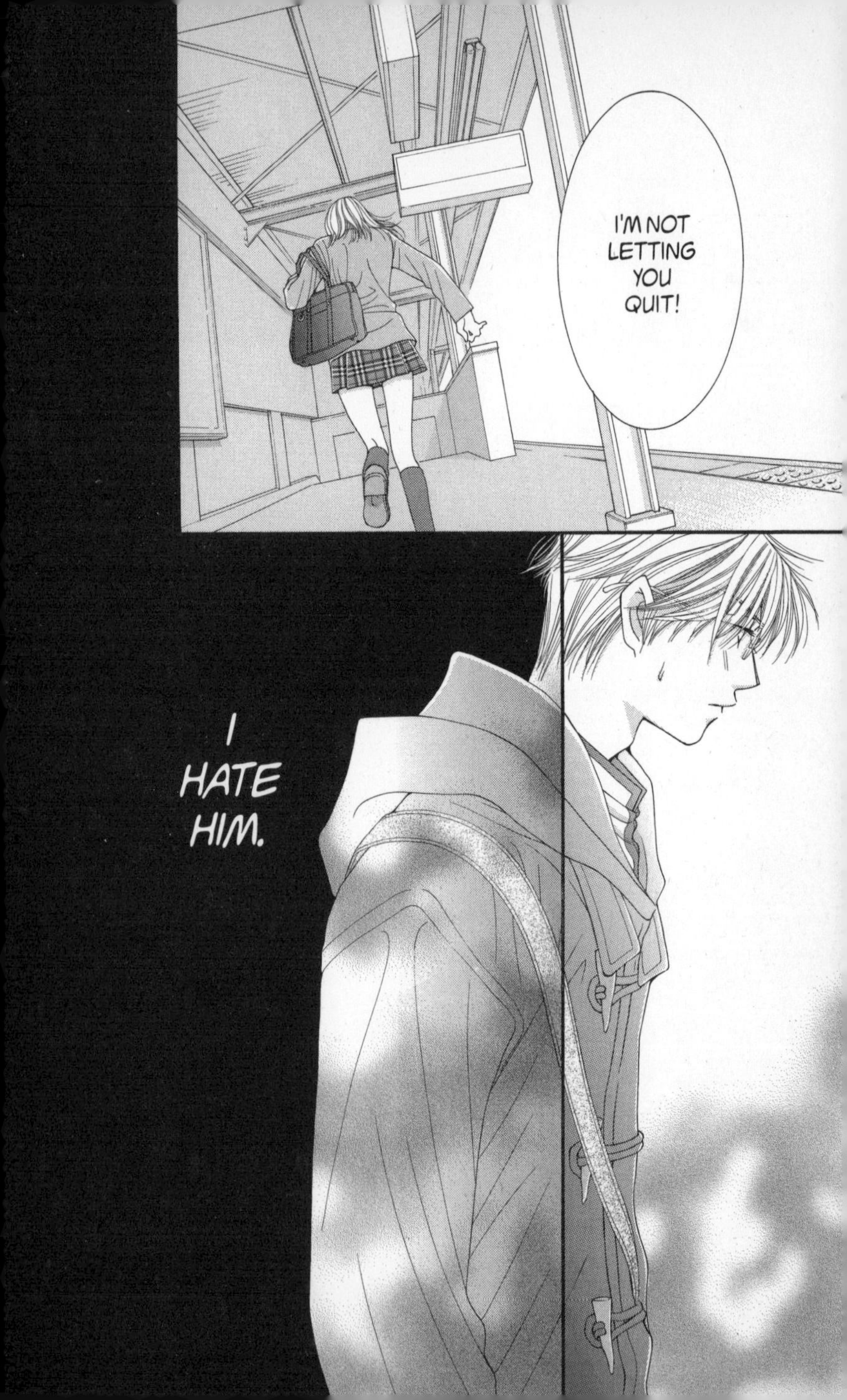
I'M NOT LETTING YOU QUIT!
I HATE HIM.

Chapter 7

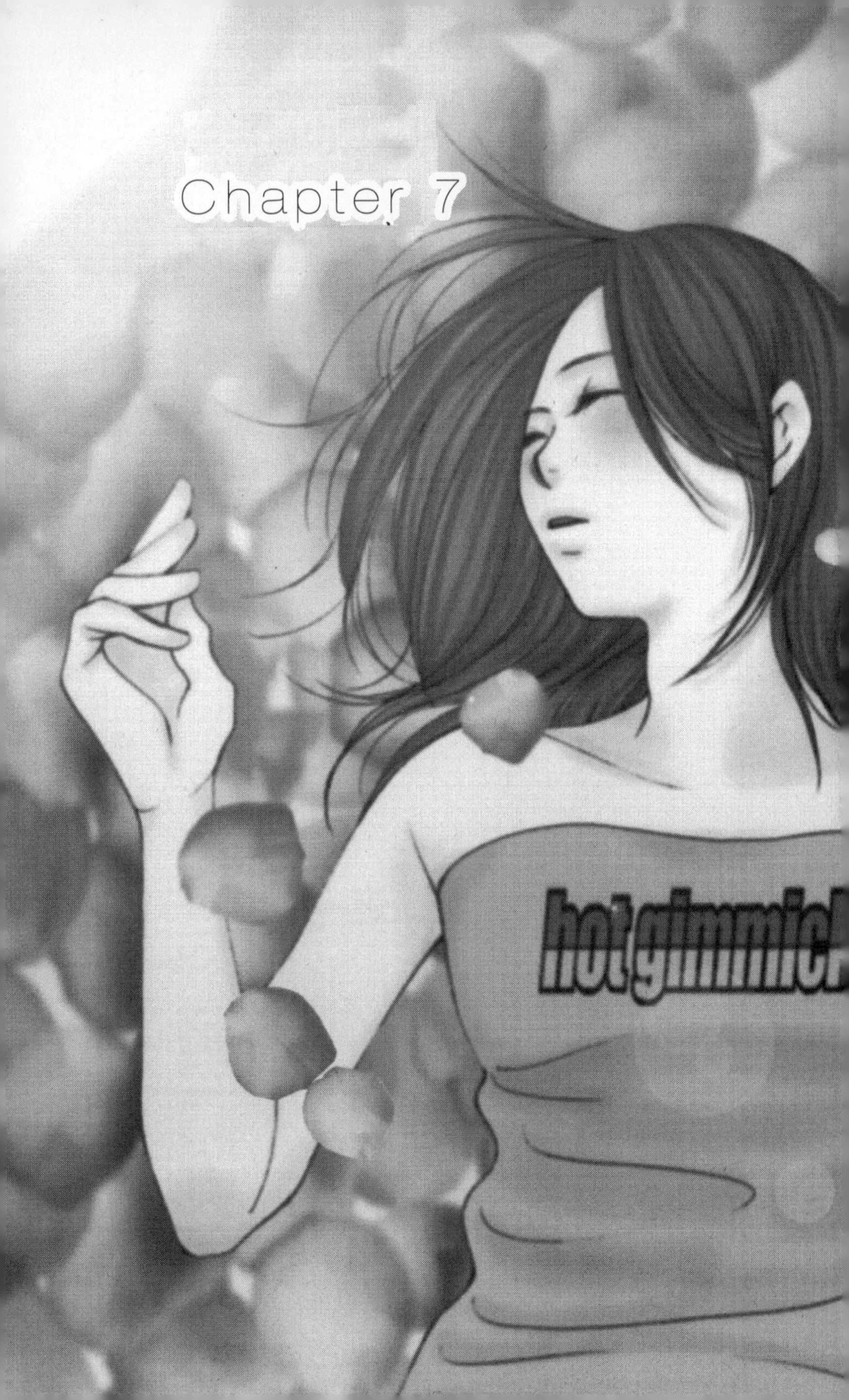
hot gimmic

KLIK!

hot gimmick

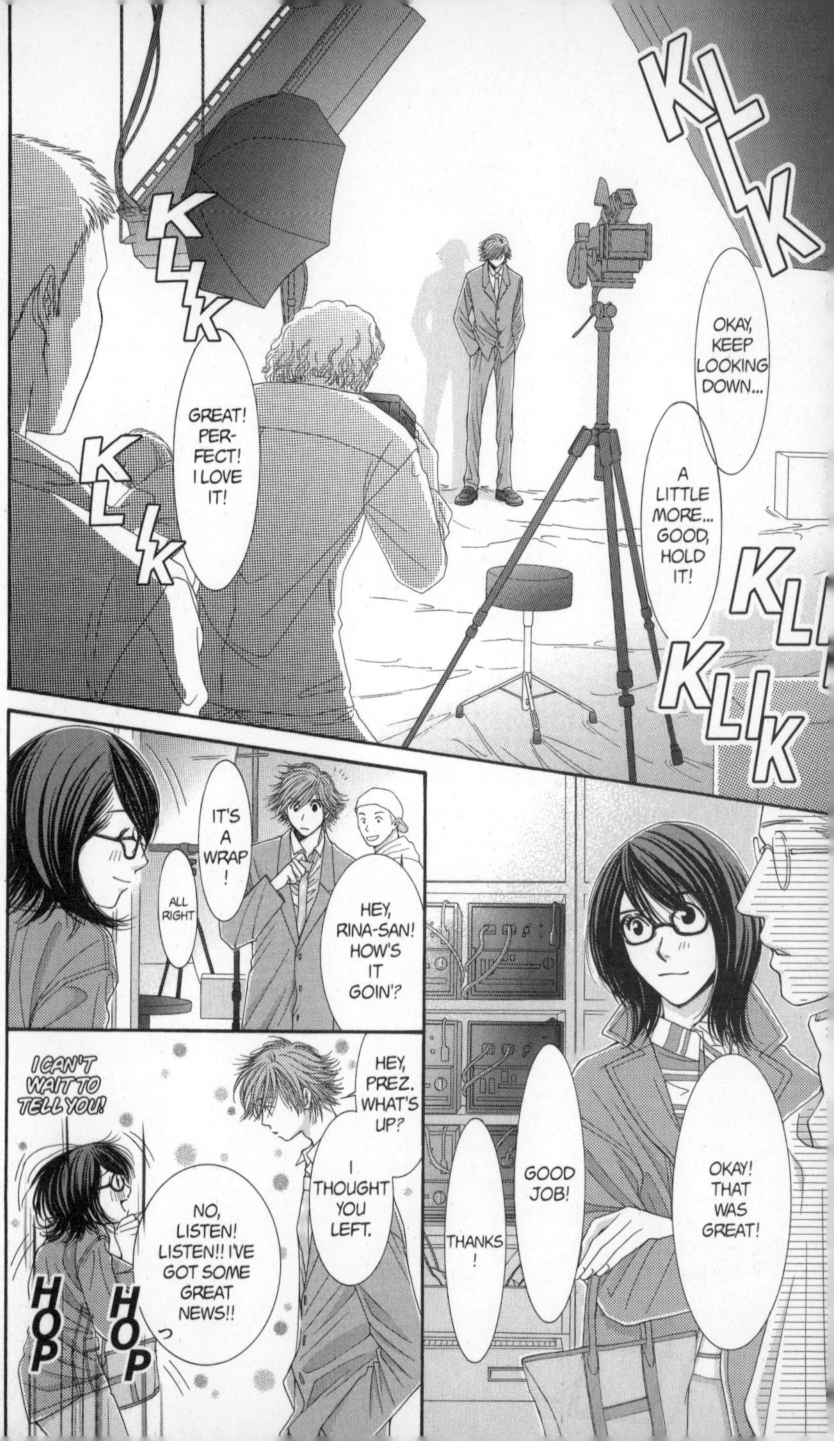
KLIK
OKAY, KEEP LOOKING DOWN...
A LITTLE MORE... GOOD, HOLD IT!
KLIK
KLIK
KLIK
GREAT! PER-FECT! I LOVE IT!
KLIK
KLIK
OKAY! THAT WAS GREAT!
GOOD JOB!
THANKS!
IT'S A WRAP!
ALL RIGHT
HEY, RINA-SAN! HOW'S IT GOIN'?
HEY, PREZ. WHAT'S UP?
I THOUGHT YOU LEFT.
NO, LISTEN! LISTEN!! I'VE GOT SOME GREAT NEWS!!
I CAN'T WAIT TO TELL YOU!
HOP
HOP

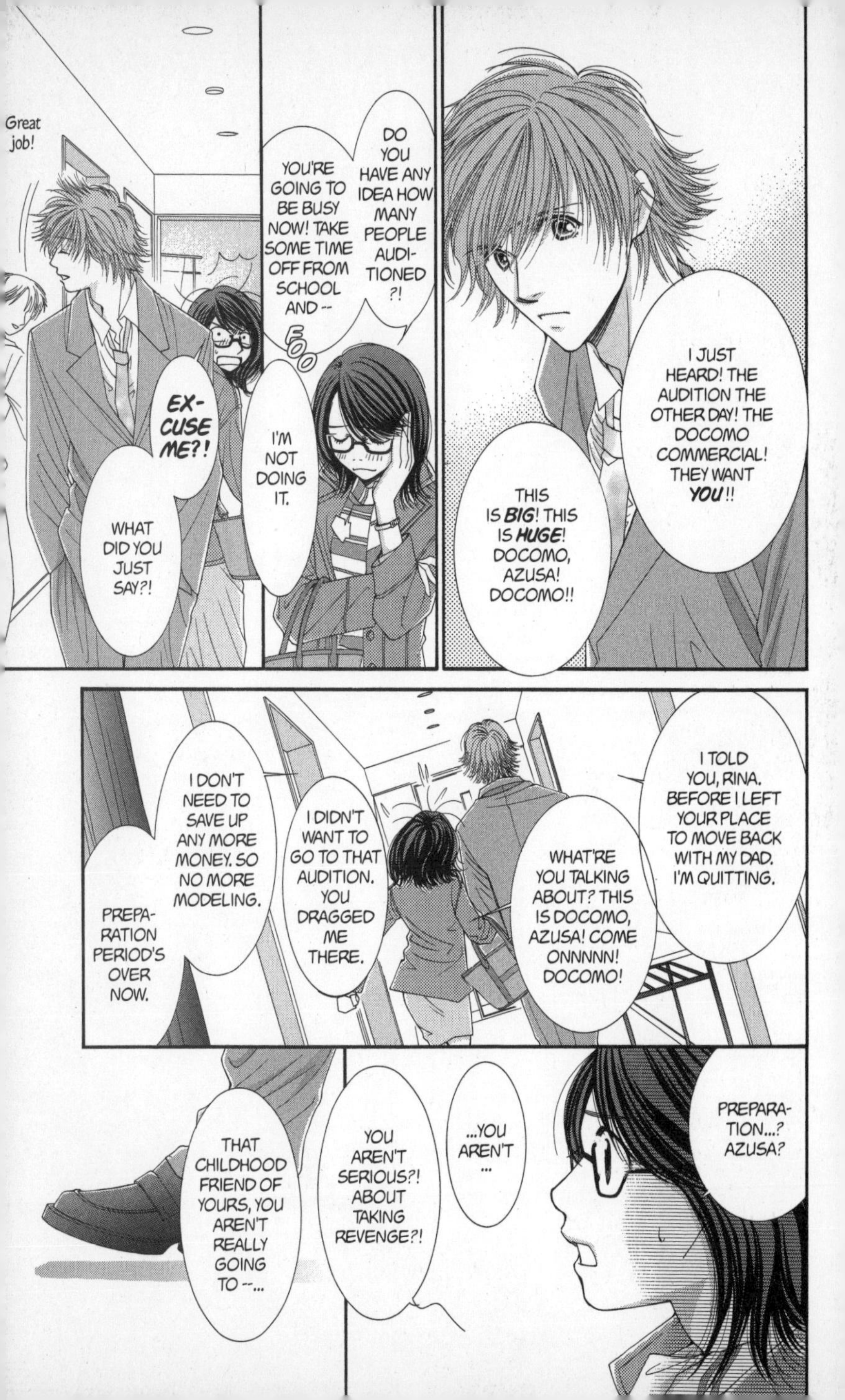
I JUST HEARD! THE AUDITION THE OTHER DAY! THE DOCOMO COMMERCIAL! THEY WANT **YOU**!!
THIS IS **BIG**! THIS IS **HUGE**! DOCOMO, AZUSA! DOCOMO!!
DO YOU HAVE ANY IDEA HOW MANY PEOPLE AUDITIONED ?!
YOU'RE GOING TO BE BUSY NOW! TAKE SOME TIME OFF FROM SCHOOL AND --
FOO
I'M NOT DOING IT.
Great job!
EXCUSE ME?!
WHAT DID YOU JUST SAY?!
I TOLD YOU, RINA. BEFORE I LEFT YOUR PLACE TO MOVE BACK WITH MY DAD. I'M QUITTING.
WHAT'RE YOU TALKING ABOUT? THIS IS DOCOMO, AZUSA! COME ONNNNN! DOCOMO!
I DIDN'T WANT TO GO TO THAT AUDITION. YOU DRAGGED ME THERE.
I DON'T NEED TO SAVE UP ANY MORE MONEY. SO NO MORE MODELING.
PREPARATION PERIOD'S OVER NOW.
PREPARATION...? AZUSA?
...YOU AREN'T ...
YOU AREN'T SERIOUS?! ABOUT TAKING REVENGE?!
THAT CHILDHOOD FRIEND OF YOURS, YOU AREN'T REALLY GOING TO --...

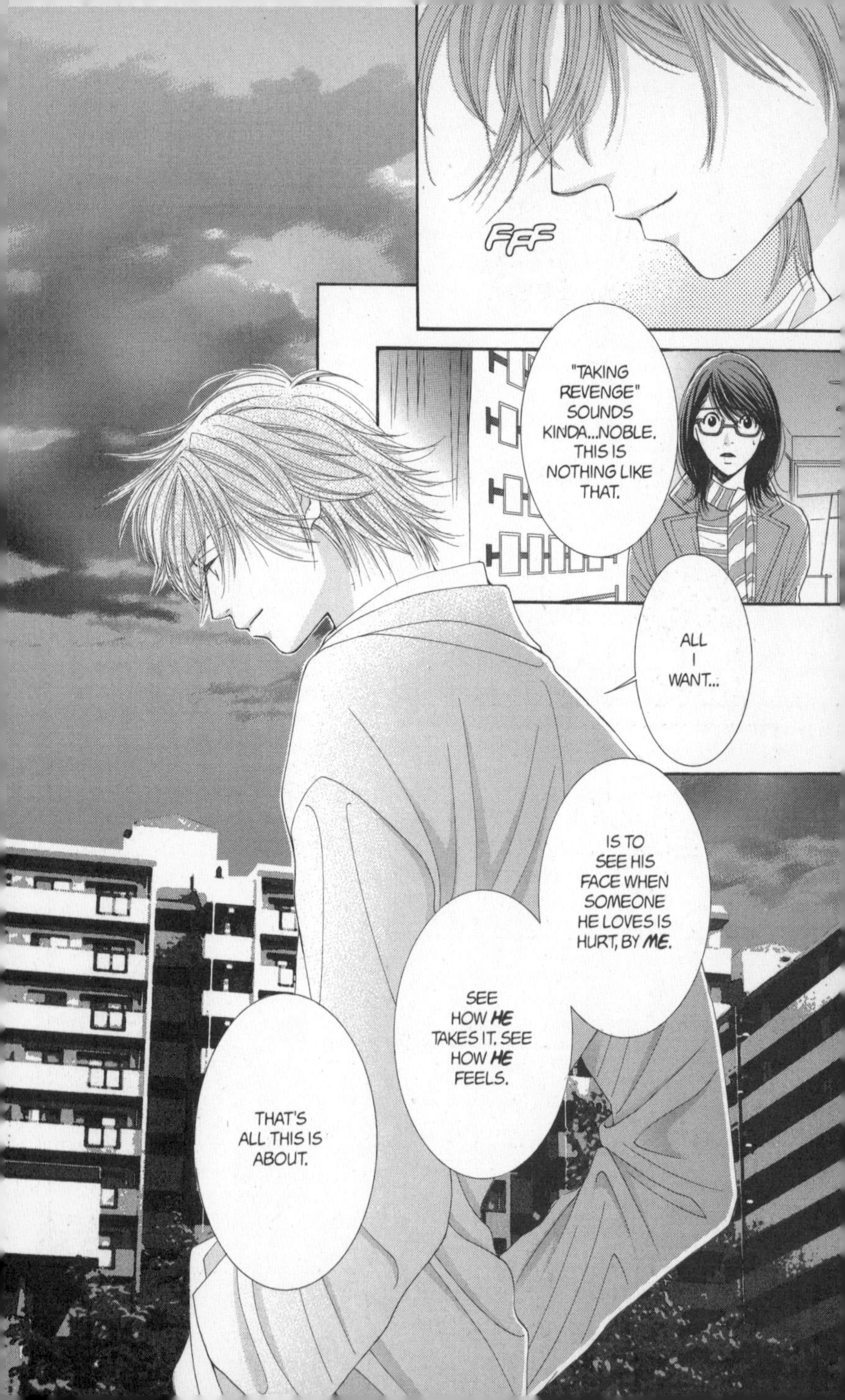
FFF
"TAKING REVENGE" SOUNDS KINDA...NOBLE. THIS IS NOTHING LIKE THAT.
ALL I WANT...
IS TO SEE HIS FACE WHEN SOMEONE HE LOVES IS HURT, BY ME.
SEE HOW HE TAKES IT. SEE HOW HE FEELS.
THAT'S ALL THIS IS ABOUT.

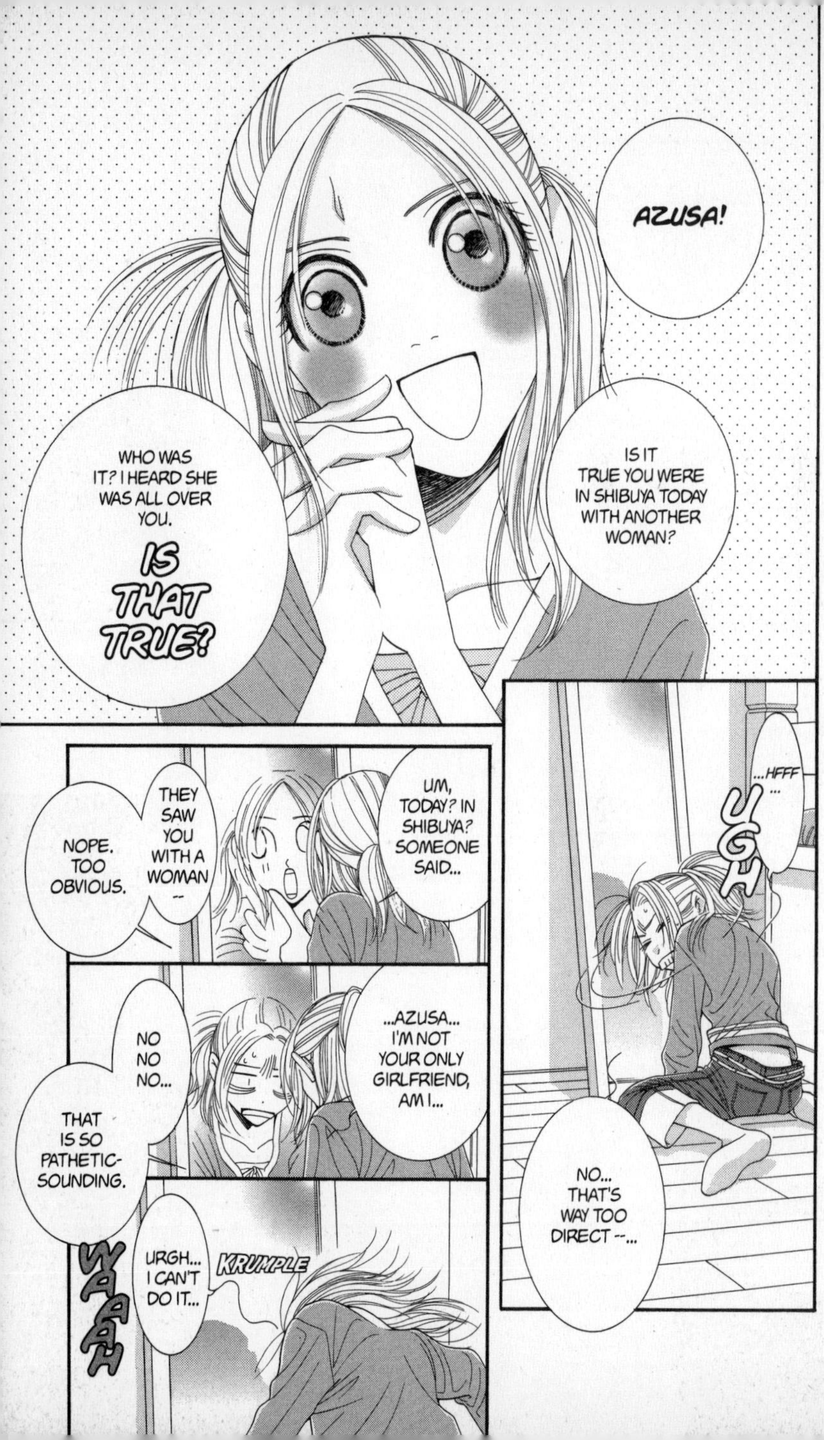
AZUSA!
IS IT TRUE YOU WERE IN SHIBUYA TODAY WITH ANOTHER WOMAN?
WHO WAS IT? I HEARD SHE WAS ALL OVER YOU. IS THAT TRUE?
...HFFF ...
UGH
NO... THAT'S WAY TOO DIRECT --...
UM, TODAY? IN SHIBUYA? SOMEONE SAID...
THEY SAW YOU WITH A WOMAN --
NOPE. TOO OBVIOUS.
...AZUSA... I'M NOT YOUR ONLY GIRLFRIEND, AM I...
NO NO NO...
THAT IS SO PATHETIC-SOUNDING.
KRUMPLE
URGH... I CAN'T DO IT...
WAAAH

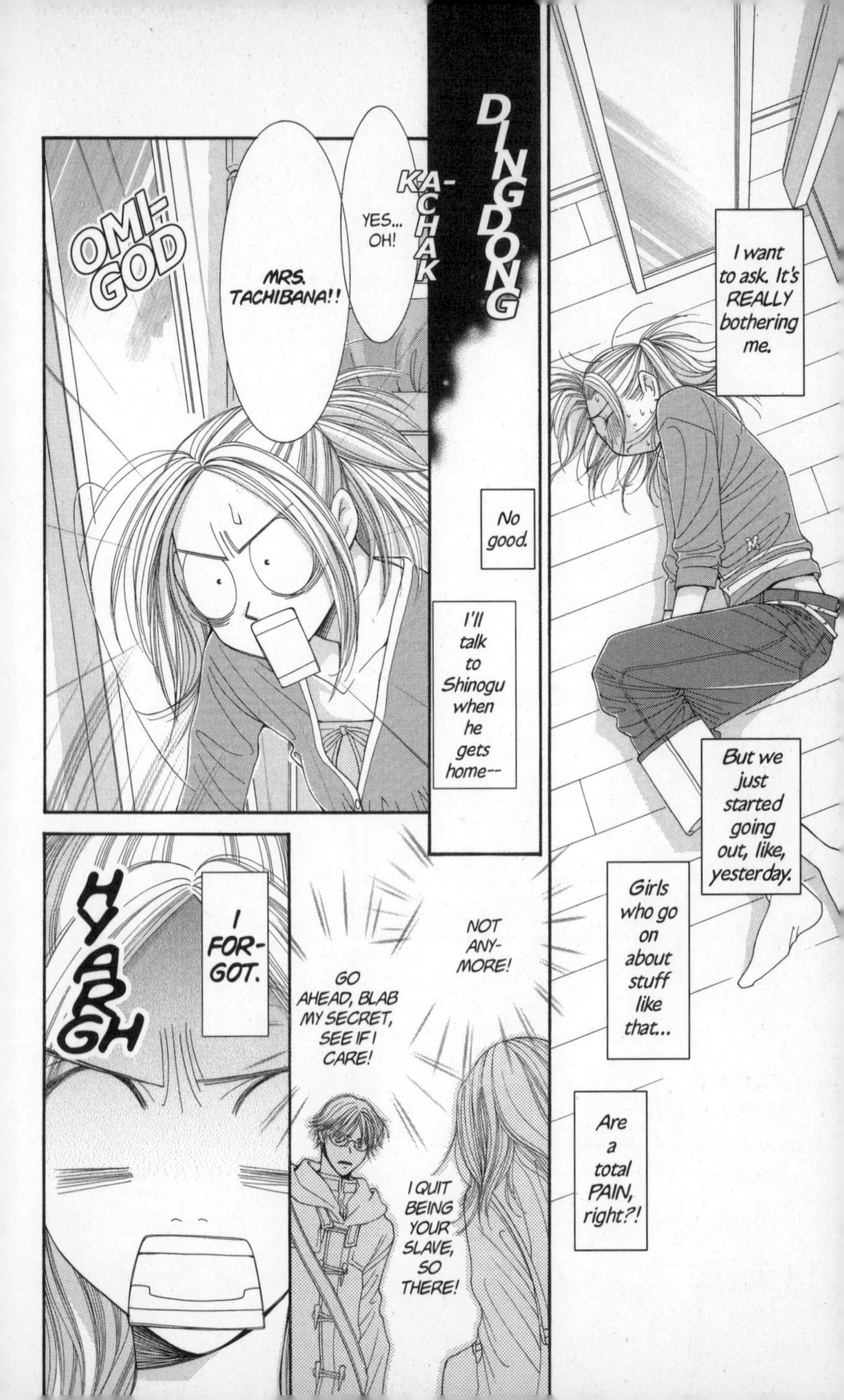
I want to ask. It's REALLY bothering me.
But we just started going out, like, yesterday.
Girls who go on about stuff like that...
Are a total PAIN, right?!
No good.
I'll talk to Shinogu when he gets home--
DINGDONG
KA-CHAK
YES... OH!
MRS. TACHIBANA!!
OMI-GOD
I FOR-GOT.
NOT ANY-MORE!
GO AHEAD, BLAB MY SECRET, SEE IF I CARE!
I QUIT BEING YOUR SLAVE, SO THERE!
HYARGH

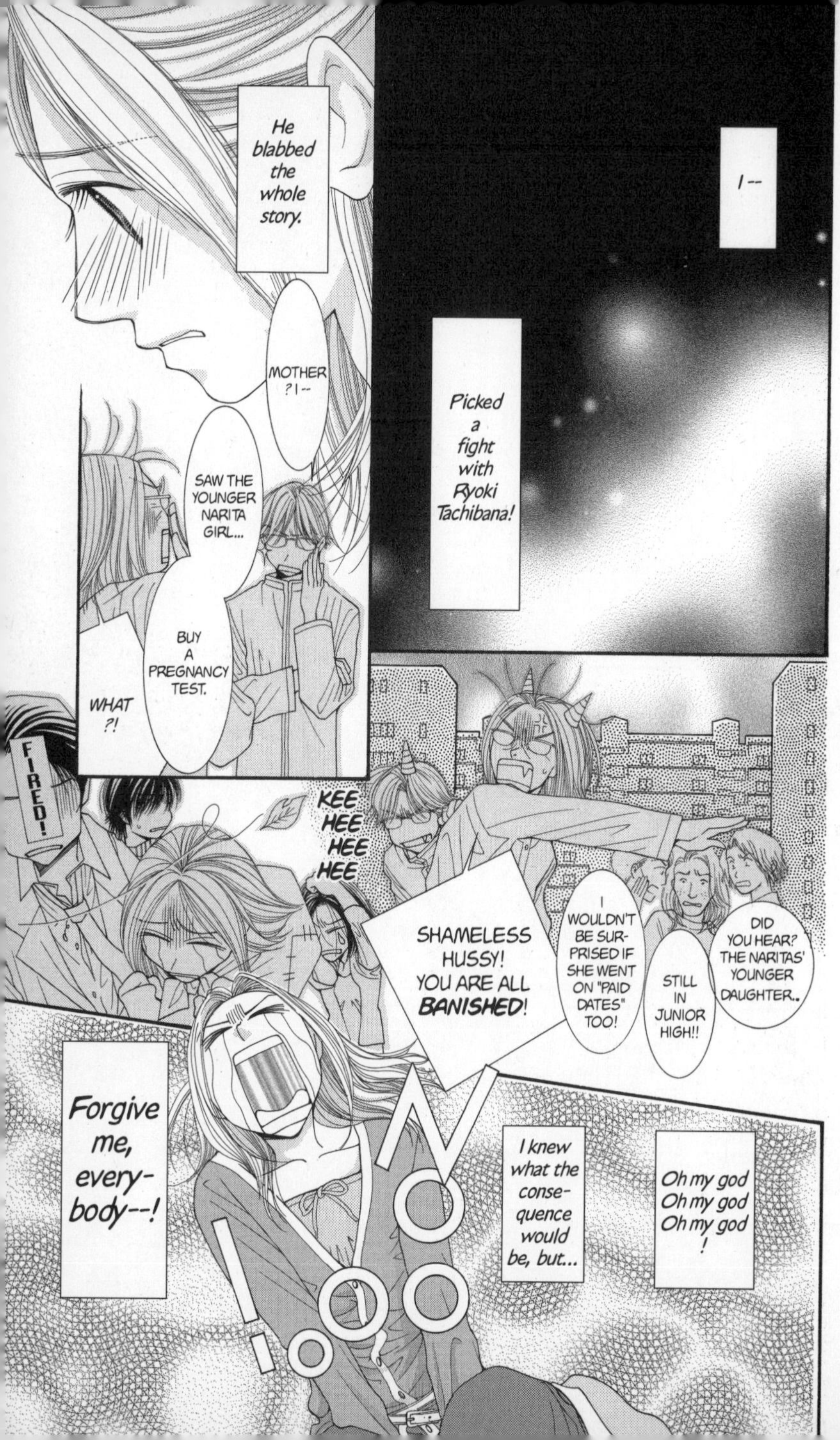
I--
Picked a fight with Ryoki Tachibana!
He blabbed the whole story.
MOTHER?! I--
SAW THE YOUNGER NARITA GIRL...
BUY A PREGNANCY TEST.
WHAT?!
DID YOU HEAR? THE NARITAS' YOUNGER DAUGHTER..
STILL IN JUNIOR HIGH!!
I WOULDN'T BE SURPRISED IF SHE WENT ON "PAID DATES" TOO!
SHAMELESS HUSSY! YOU ARE ALL BANISHED!
KEE HEE HEE HEE
FIRED!
Oh my god Oh my god Oh my god!
I knew what the consequence would be, but...
NOOO!
Forgive me, everybody--!

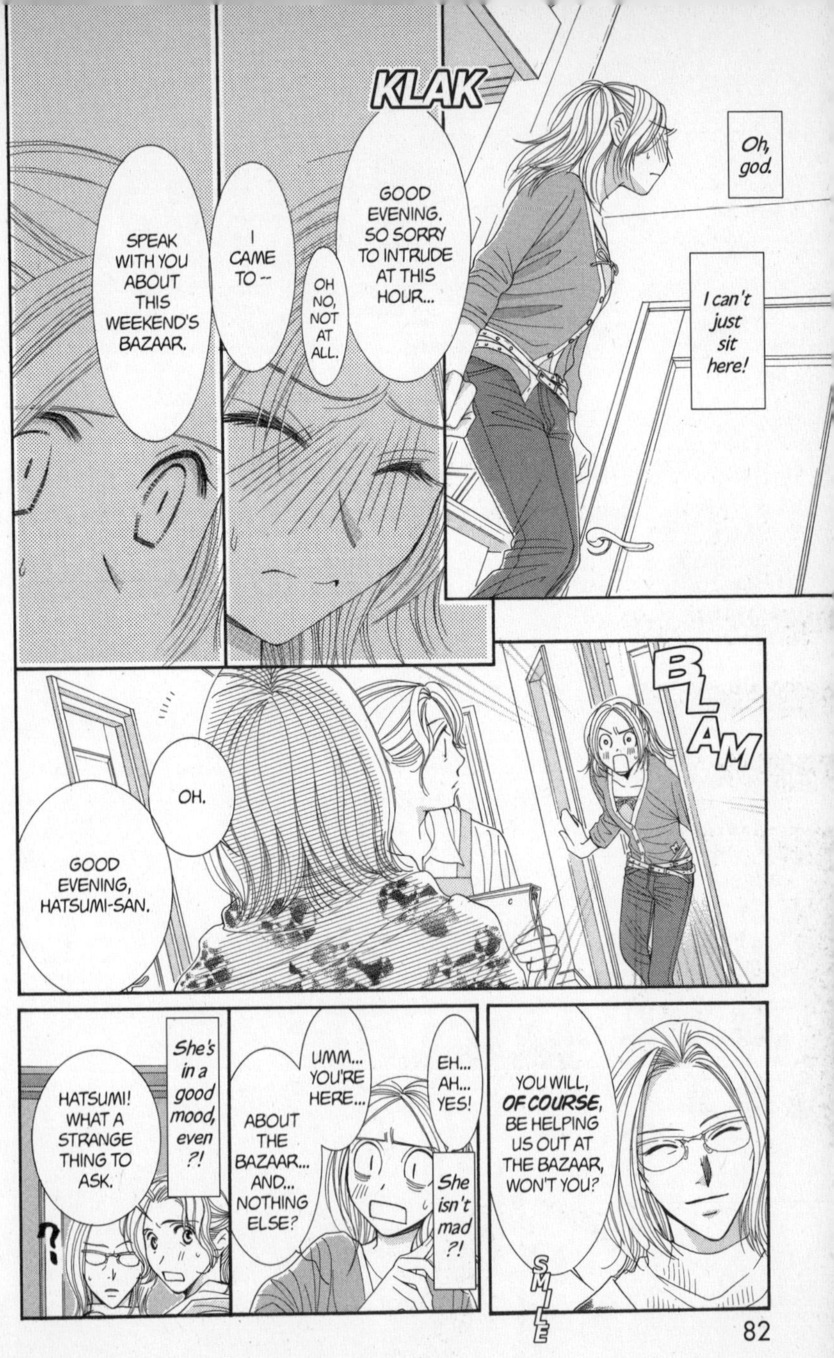
KLAK
Oh, god.
I can't just sit here!
GOOD EVENING. SO SORRY TO INTRUDE AT THIS HOUR...
OH NO, NOT AT ALL.
I CAME TO --
SPEAK WITH YOU ABOUT THIS WEEKEND'S BAZAAR.
BLAM
OH.
GOOD EVENING, HATSUMI-SAN.
YOU WILL, OF COURSE, BE HELPING US OUT AT THE BAZAAR, WON'T YOU?
SMILE
EH... AH... YES!
UMM... YOU'RE HERE...
ABOUT THE BAZAAR... AND... NOTHING ELSE?
She isn't mad?!
She's in a good mood, even?!
HATSUMI! WHAT A STRANGE THING TO ASK.
?!

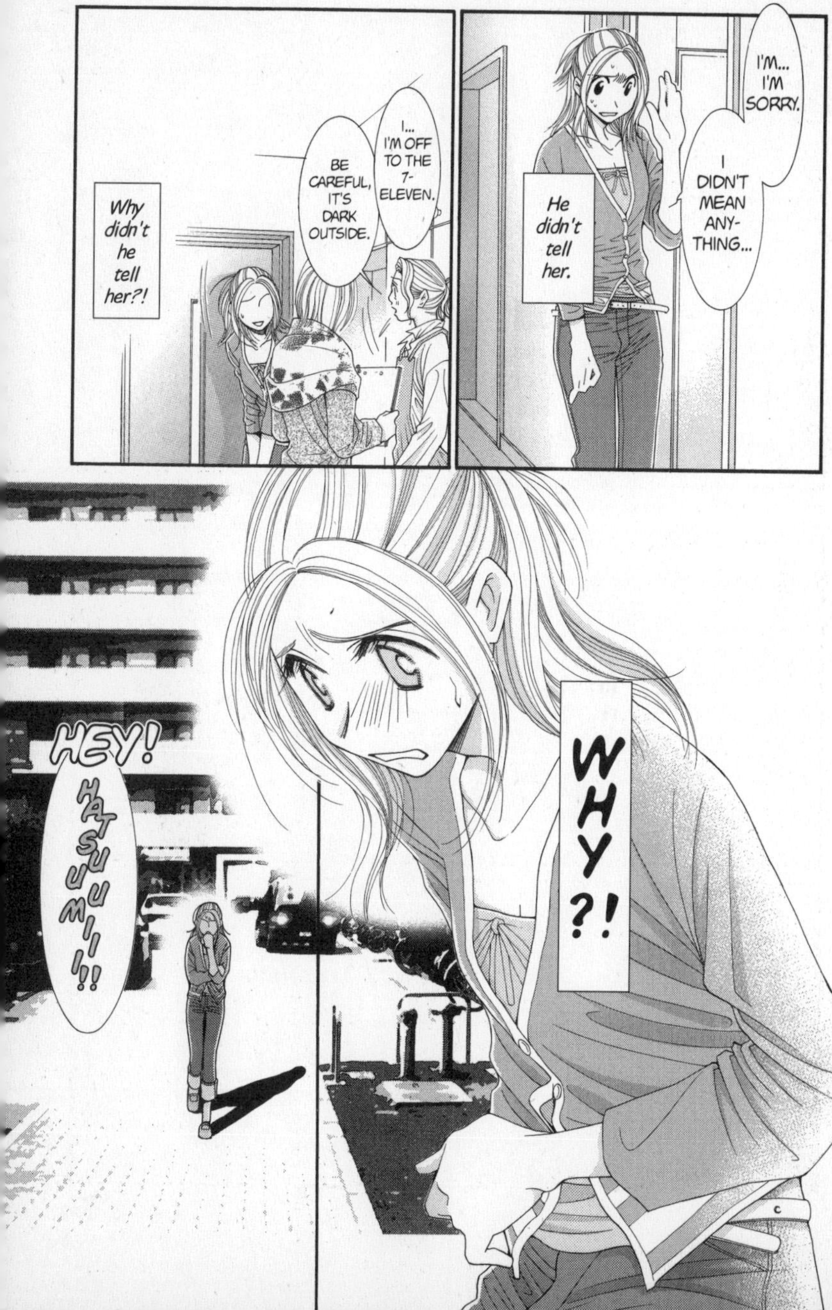
I'M... I'M SORRY.
I DIDN'T MEAN ANYTHING...
He didn't tell her.
I... I'M OFF TO THE 7-ELEVEN.
BE CAREFUL, IT'S DARK OUTSIDE.
Why didn't he tell her?!
WHY?!
HEY!
HATSUUMIII!!

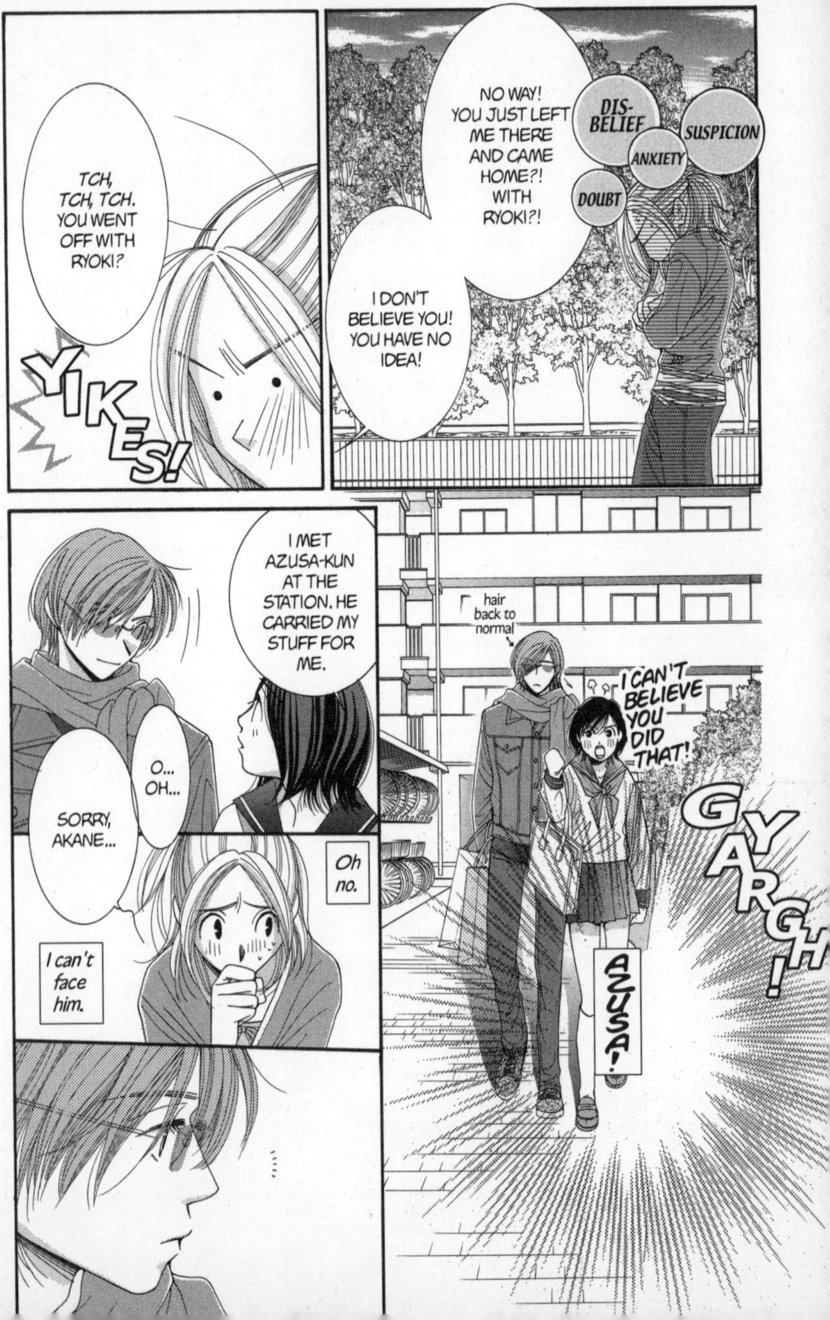
NO WAY! YOU JUST LEFT ME THERE AND CAME HOME?! WITH RYOKI?!
DIS-BELIEF
SUSPICION
ANXIETY
DOUBT
I DON'T BELIEVE YOU! YOU HAVE NO IDEA!
TCH, TCH, TCH. YOU WENT OFF WITH RYOKI?
YIKES!
hair back to normal
I CAN'T BELIEVE YOU DID THAT!
GYARGH!
AZUSA!
I MET AZUSA-KUN AT THE STATION. HE CARRIED MY STUFF FOR ME.
O... OH...
SORRY, AKANE...
Oh no.
I can't face him.

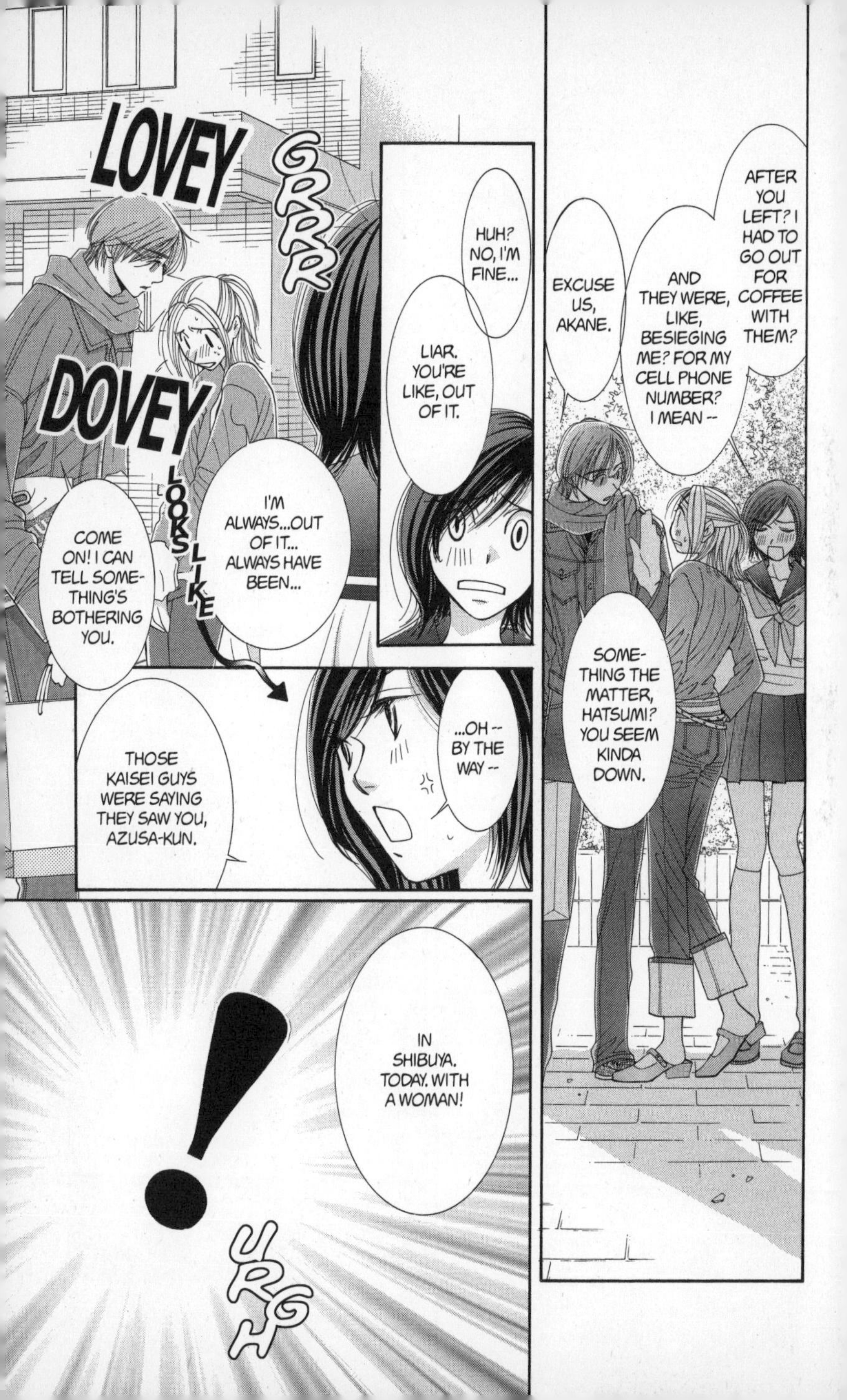
AFTER YOU LEFT? I HAD TO GO OUT FOR COFFEE WITH THEM?
AND THEY WERE, LIKE, BESIEGING ME? FOR MY CELL PHONE NUMBER? I MEAN --
EXCUSE US, AKANE.
SOME-THING THE MATTER, HATSUMI? YOU SEEM KINDA DOWN.
HUH? NO, I'M FINE...
LIAR. YOU'RE LIKE, OUT OF IT.
GRRR
LOVEY
DOVEY
LOOKS LIKE
I'M ALWAYS...OUT OF IT... ALWAYS HAVE BEEN...
COME ON! I CAN TELL SOME-THING'S BOTHERING YOU.
...OH -- BY THE WAY --
THOSE KAISEI GUYS WERE SAYING THEY SAW YOU, AZUSA-KUN.
IN SHIBUYA. TODAY. WITH A WOMAN!
!
URGH

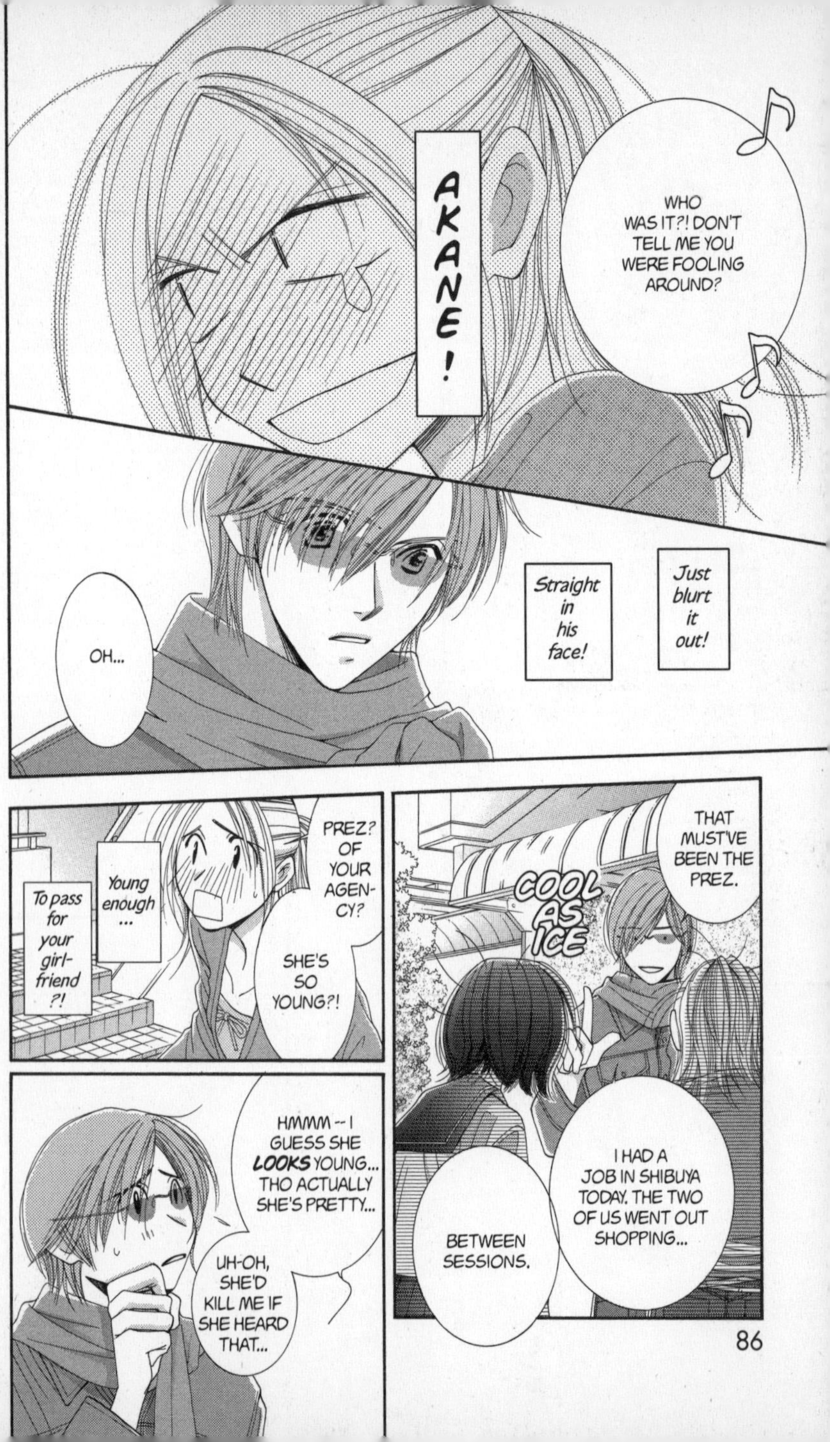

WHO WAS IT?! DON'T TELL ME YOU WERE FOOLING AROUND?
AKANE!
Just blurt it out!
Straight in his face!
OH...
THAT MUST'VE BEEN THE PREZ.
COOL AS ICE
I HAD A JOB IN SHIBUYA TODAY. THE TWO OF US WENT OUT SHOPPING...
BETWEEN SESSIONS.
PREZ? OF YOUR AGENCY?
SHE'S SO YOUNG?!
Young enough...
To pass for your girlfriend?!
HMMM -- I GUESS SHE **LOOKS** YOUNG... THO ACTUALLY SHE'S PRETTY...
UH-OH, SHE'D KILL ME IF SHE HEARD THAT...

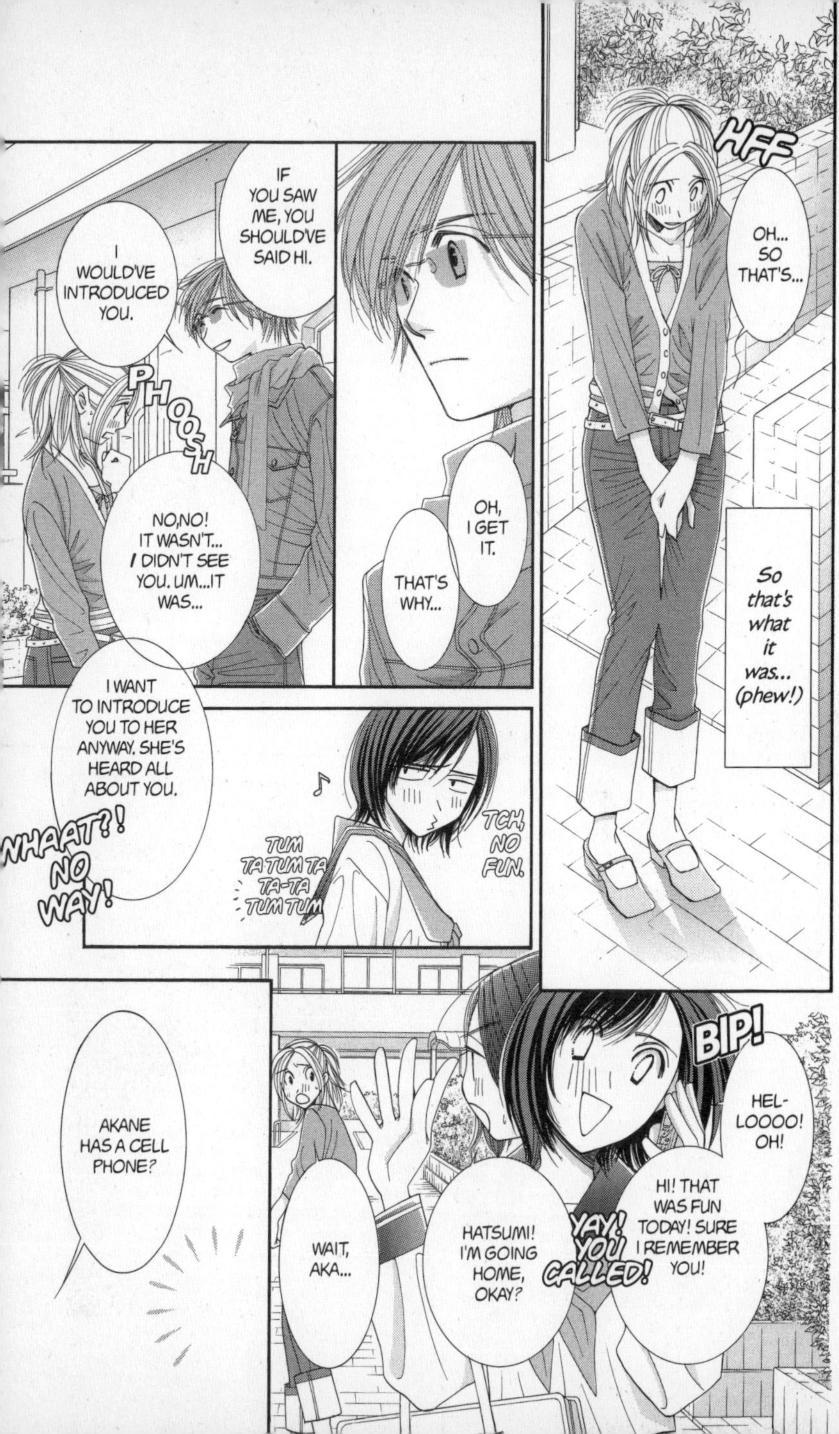
HFF
OH... SO THAT'S...
So that's what it was... (phew!)
OH, I GET IT.
THAT'S WHY...
IF YOU SAW ME, YOU SHOULD'VE SAID HI.
I WOULD'VE INTRODUCED YOU.
PHOOSH
NO,NO! IT WASN'T... I DIDN'T SEE YOU. UM...IT WAS...
I WANT TO INTRODUCE YOU TO HER ANYWAY. SHE'S HEARD ALL ABOUT YOU.
NHAAT?! NO WAY!
TCH, NO FUN.
TUM TA TUM TA TA-TA TUM TUM
BIP!
HEL-LOOOO! OH!
HI! THAT WAS FUN TODAY! SURE I REMEMBER YOU!
YAY! YOU CALLED!
HATSUMI! I'M GOING HOME, OKAY?
WAIT, AKA...
AKANE HAS A CELL PHONE?

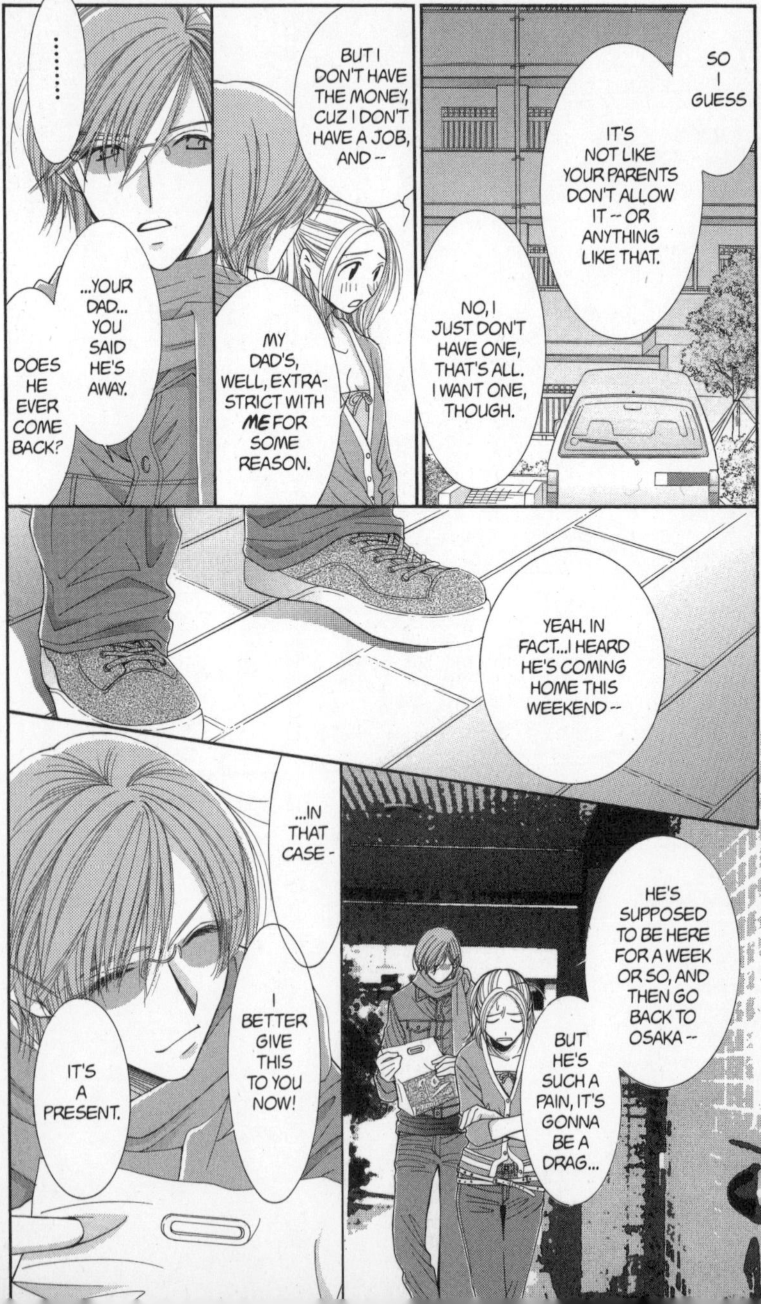
SO I GUESS
IT'S NOT LIKE YOUR PARENTS DON'T ALLOW IT -- OR ANYTHING LIKE THAT.
NO, I JUST DON'T HAVE ONE, THAT'S ALL. I WANT ONE, THOUGH.
BUT I DON'T HAVE THE MONEY, CUZ I DON'T HAVE A JOB, AND --
MY DAD'S, WELL, EXTRA-STRICT WITH *ME* FOR SOME REASON.
......
...YOUR DAD... YOU SAID HE'S AWAY.
DOES HE EVER COME BACK?
YEAH. IN FACT...I HEARD HE'S COMING HOME THIS WEEKEND --
HE'S SUPPOSED TO BE HERE FOR A WEEK OR SO, AND THEN GO BACK TO OSAKA --
BUT HE'S SUCH A PAIN, IT'S GONNA BE A DRAG...
...IN THAT CASE -
I BETTER GIVE THIS TO YOU NOW!
IT'S A PRESENT.

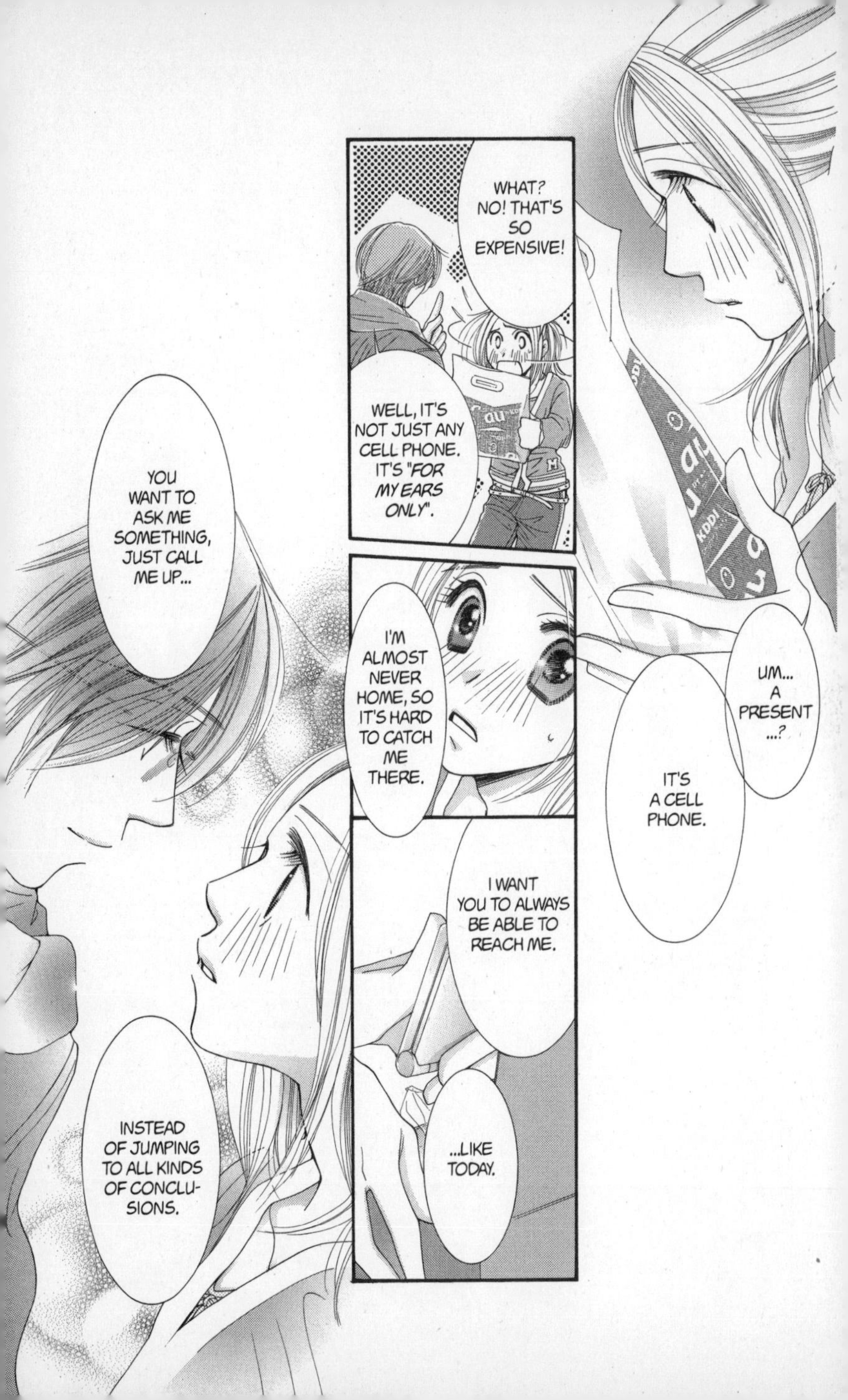
UM... A PRESENT ...?
IT'S A CELL PHONE.
WHAT? NO! THAT'S SO EXPENSIVE!
WELL, IT'S NOT JUST ANY CELL PHONE. IT'S "*FOR MY EARS ONLY*".
I'M ALMOST NEVER HOME, SO IT'S HARD TO CATCH ME THERE.
I WANT YOU TO ALWAYS BE ABLE TO REACH ME.
...LIKE TODAY.
YOU WANT TO ASK ME SOMETHING, JUST CALL ME UP...
INSTEAD OF JUMPING TO ALL KINDS OF CONCLU-SIONS.

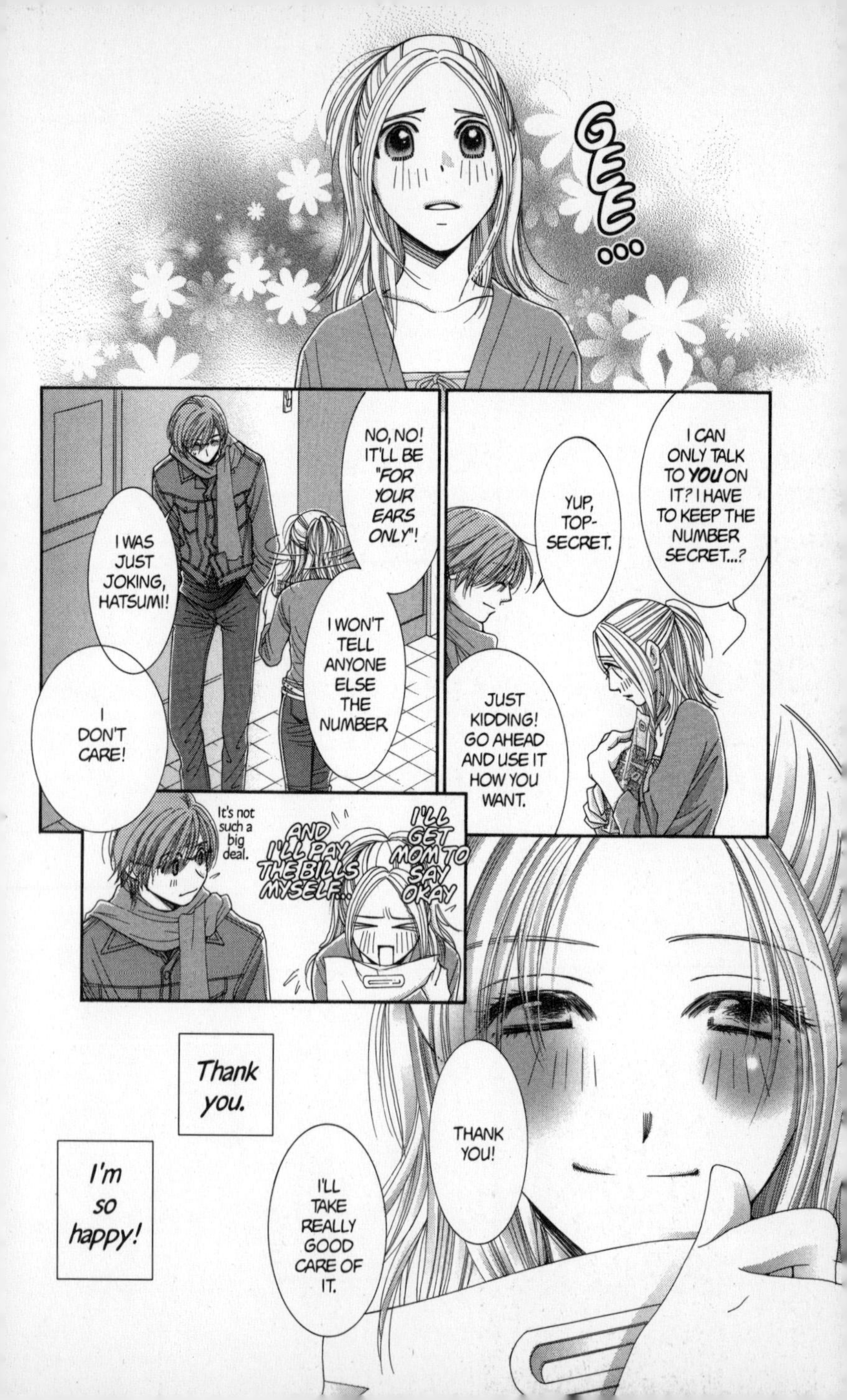
GEE...
I CAN ONLY TALK TO *YOU* ON IT? I HAVE TO KEEP THE NUMBER SECRET...?
YUP, TOP-SECRET.
JUST KIDDING! GO AHEAD AND USE IT HOW YOU WANT.
NO, NO! IT'LL BE "FOR YOUR EARS ONLY"!
I WON'T TELL ANYONE ELSE THE NUMBER
I WAS JUST JOKING, HATSUMI!
I DON'T CARE!
I'LL GET MOM TO SAY OKAY
AND I'LL PAY THE BILLS MYSELF...
It's not such a big deal.
THANK YOU!
I'LL TAKE REALLY GOOD CARE OF IT.
Thank you.
I'm so happy!

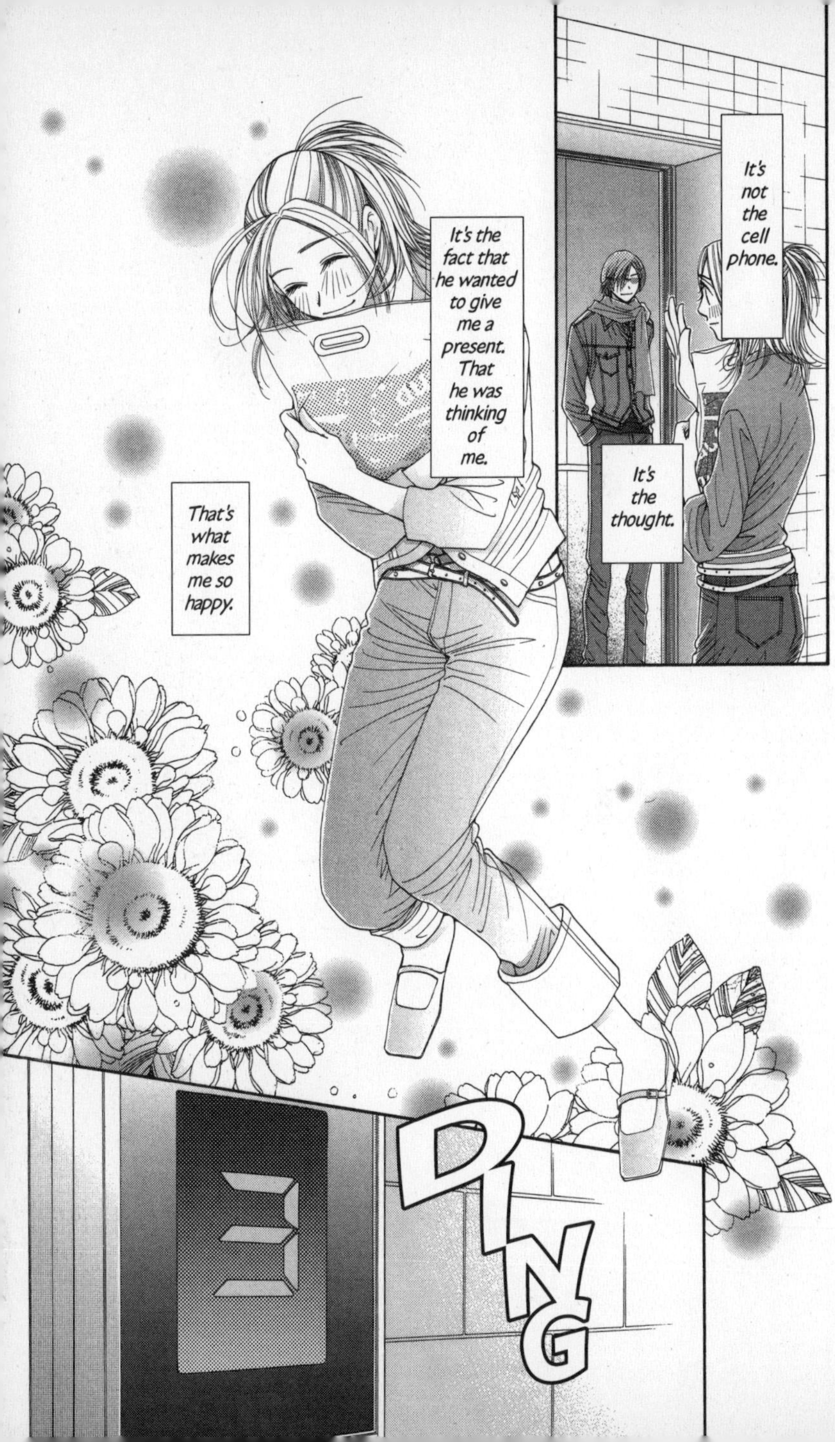
It's not the cell phone.
It's the thought.
It's the fact that he wanted to give me a present. That he was thinking of me.
That's what makes me so happy.
DING

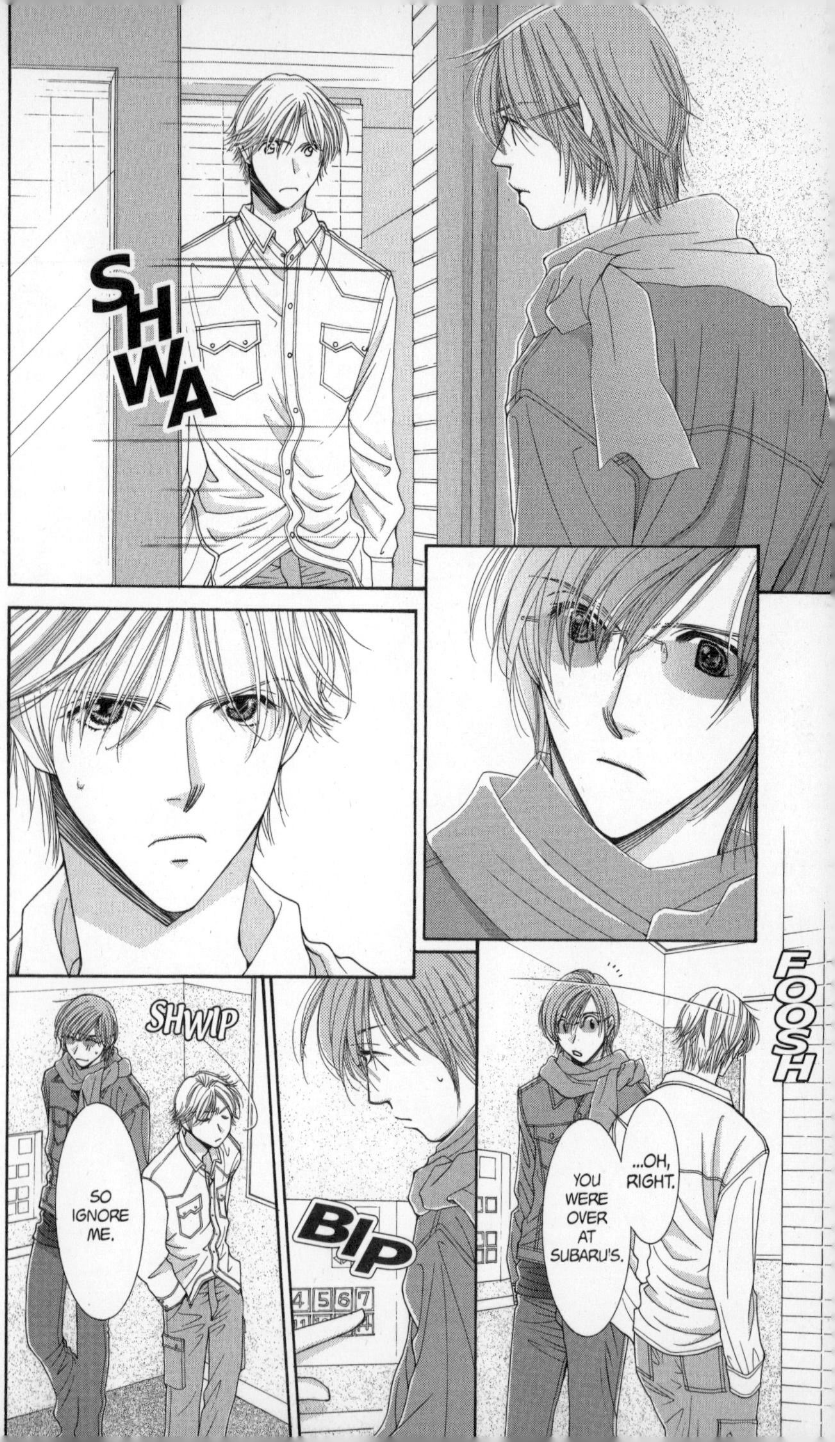
SHWA
FOOSH
...OH, RIGHT.
YOU WERE OVER AT SUBARU'S.
BIP
SHWIP
SO IGNORE ME.

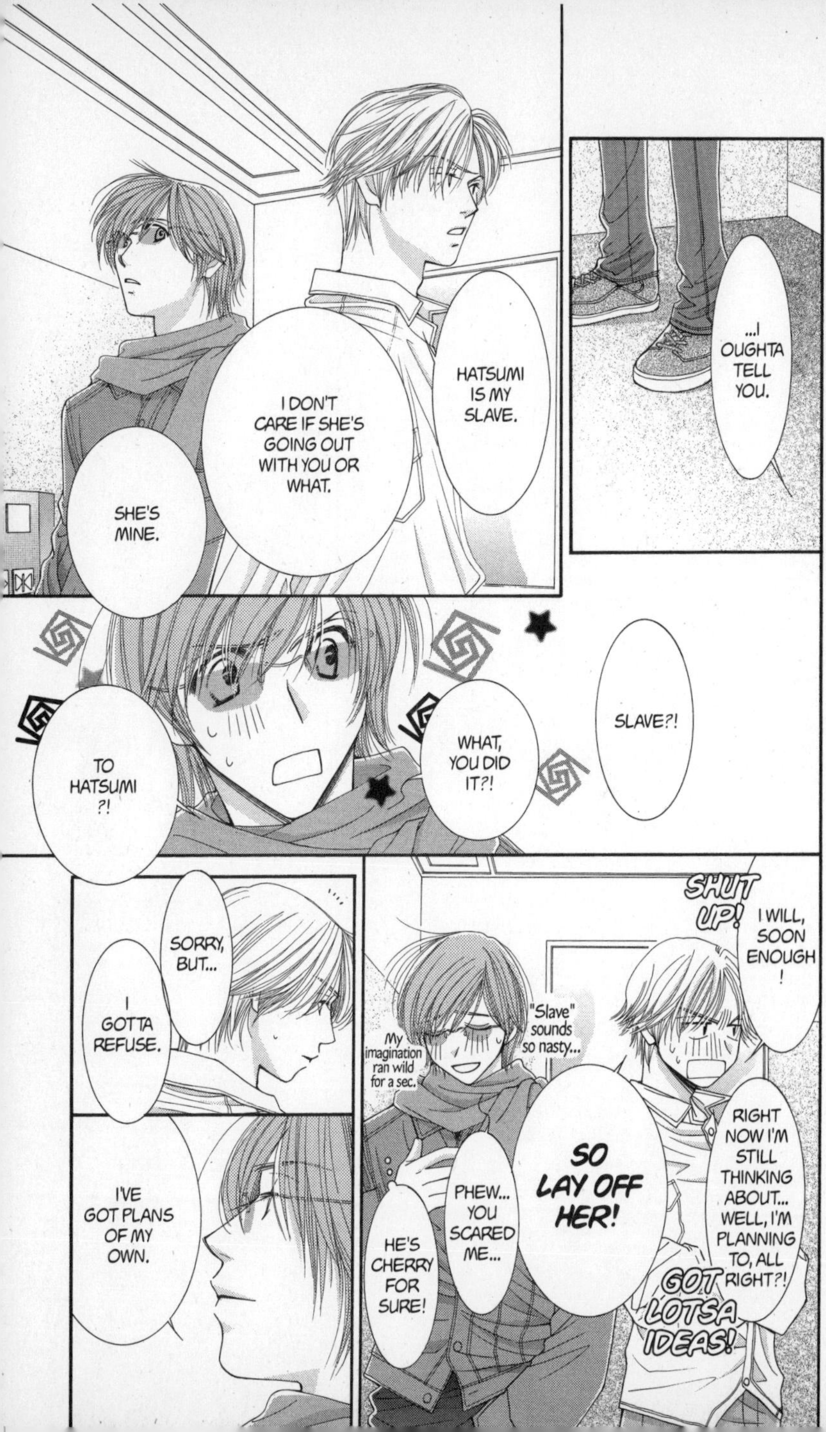
...I OUGHTA TELL YOU.
HATSUMI IS MY SLAVE.
I DON'T CARE IF SHE'S GOING OUT WITH YOU OR WHAT.
SHE'S MINE.
SLAVE?!
WHAT, YOU DID IT?!
TO HATSUMI ?!
SHUT UP!
I WILL, SOON ENOUGH !
RIGHT NOW I'M STILL THINKING ABOUT... WELL, I'M PLANNING TO, ALL RIGHT?!
GOT LOTSA IDEAS!
SO LAY OFF HER!
"Slave" sounds so nasty...
My imagination ran wild for a sec.
PHEW... YOU SCARED ME...
HE'S CHERRY FOR SURE!
SORRY, BUT...
I GOTTA REFUSE.
I'VE GOT PLANS OF MY OWN.

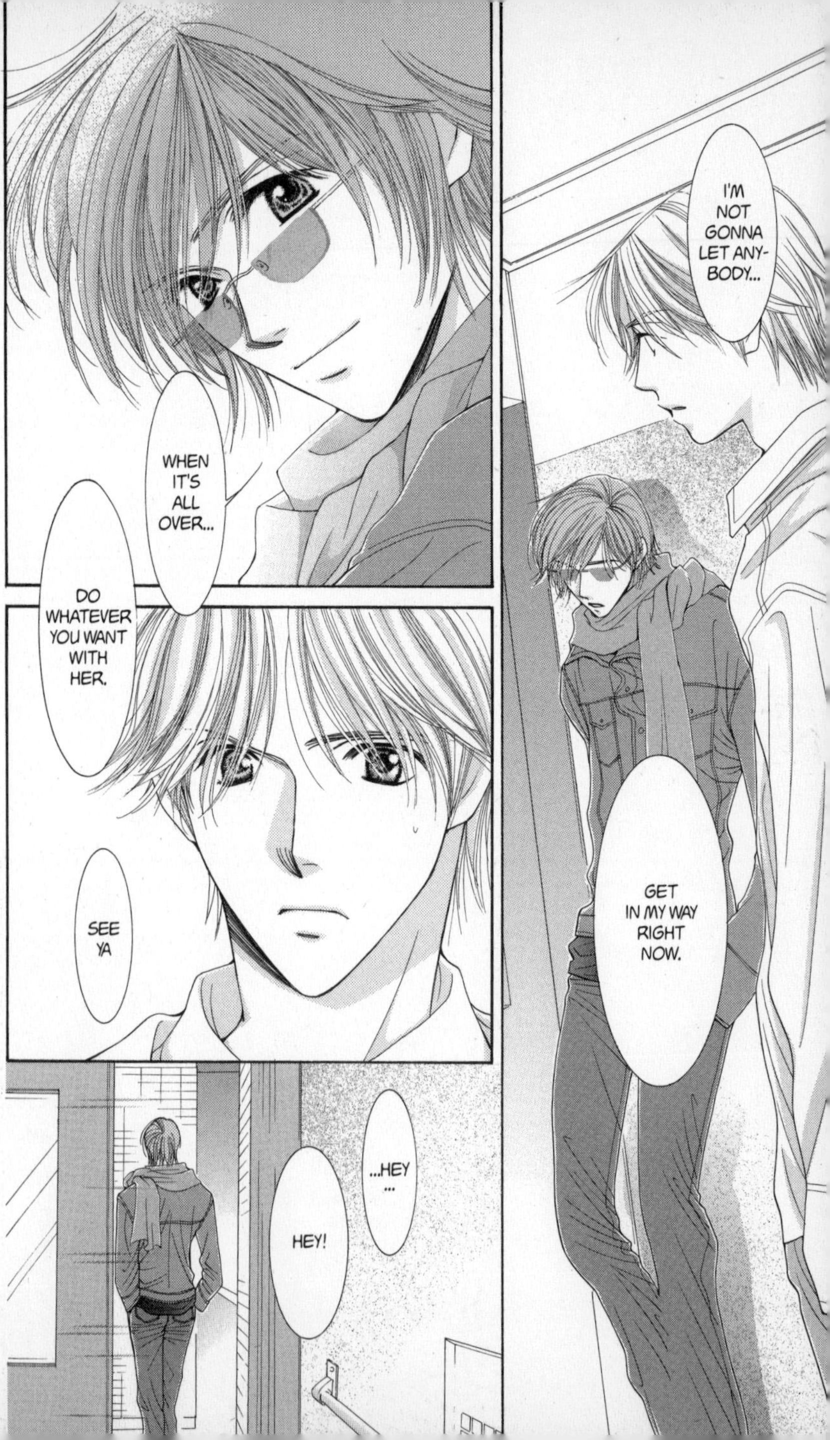
I'M NOT GONNA LET ANY-BODY...
GET IN MY WAY RIGHT NOW.
WHEN IT'S ALL OVER...
DO WHATEVER YOU WANT WITH HER.
SEE YA
...HEY ...
HEY!

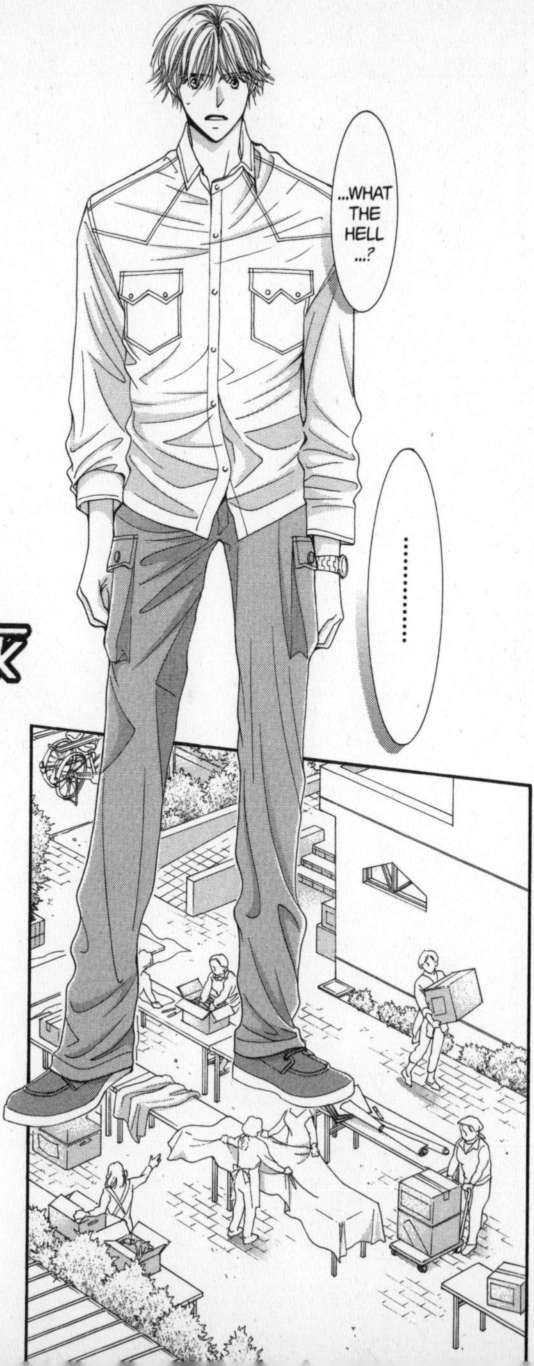
...WHAT THE HELL ...?
....

hotgimmick

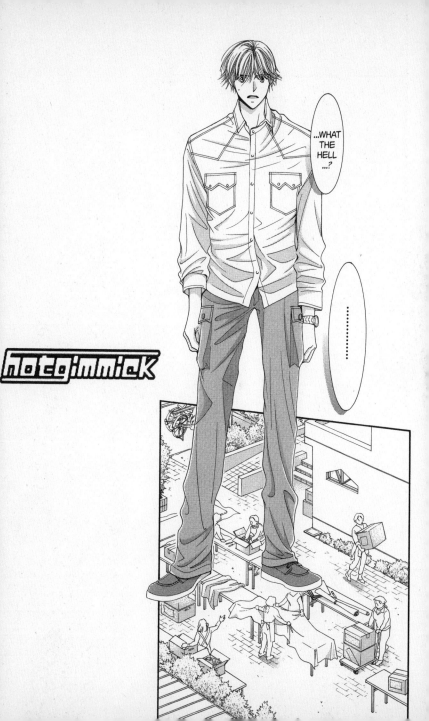

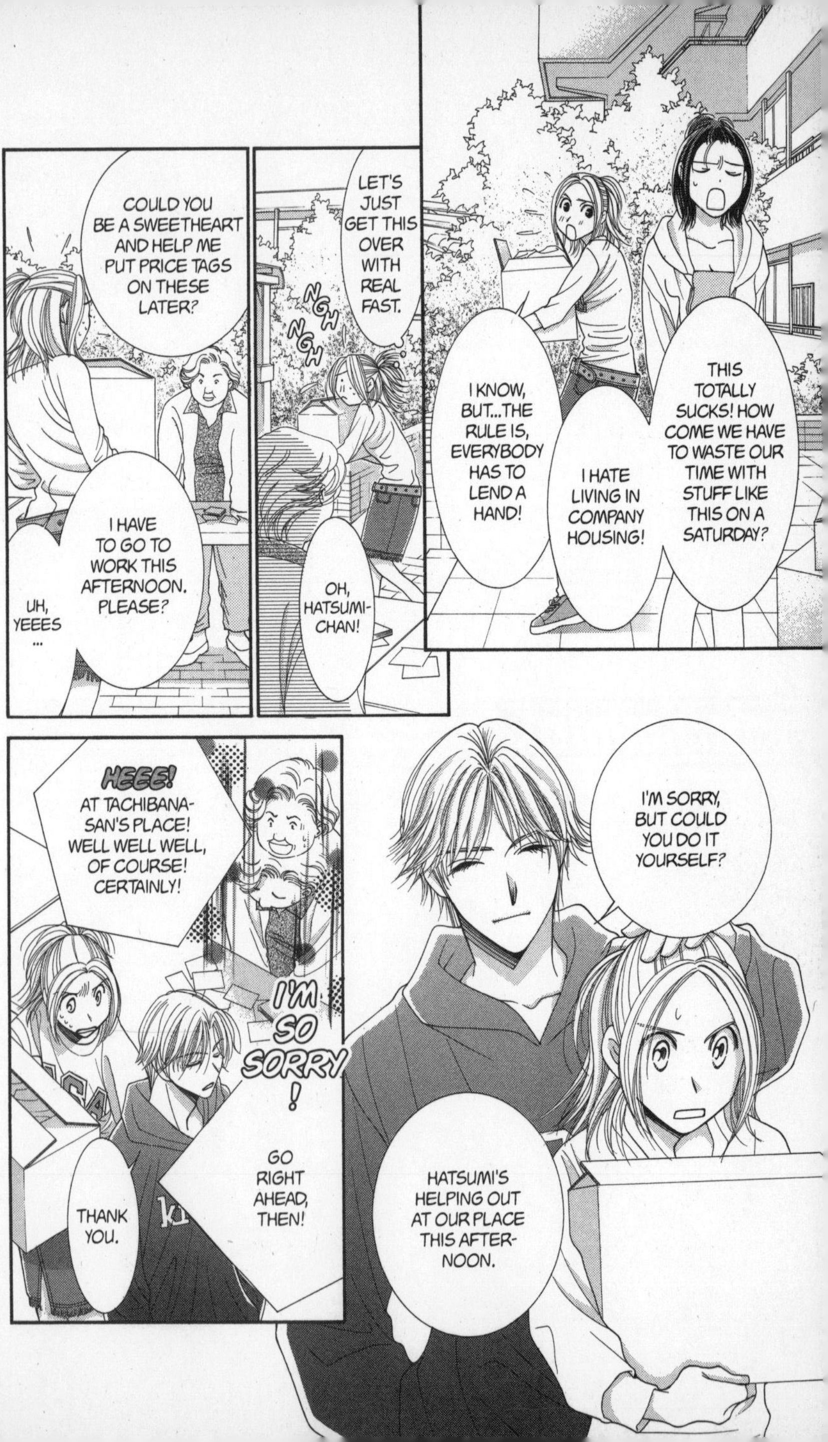
THIS TOTALLY SUCKS! HOW COME WE HAVE TO WASTE OUR TIME WITH STUFF LIKE THIS ON A SATURDAY?
I HATE LIVING IN COMPANY HOUSING!
I KNOW, BUT...THE RULE IS, EVERYBODY HAS TO LEND A HAND!
LET'S JUST GET THIS OVER WITH REAL FAST.
NGH NGH
OH, HATSUMI-CHAN!
COULD YOU BE A SWEETHEART AND HELP ME PUT PRICE TAGS ON THESE LATER?
I HAVE TO GO TO WORK THIS AFTERNOON. PLEASE?
UH, YEEES ...
I'M SORRY, BUT COULD YOU DO IT YOURSELF?
HATSUMI'S HELPING OUT AT OUR PLACE THIS AFTERNOON.
HEEE! AT TACHIBANA-SAN'S PLACE! WELL WELL WELL, OF COURSE! CERTAINLY!
I'M SO SORRY!
GO RIGHT AHEAD, THEN!
THANK YOU.

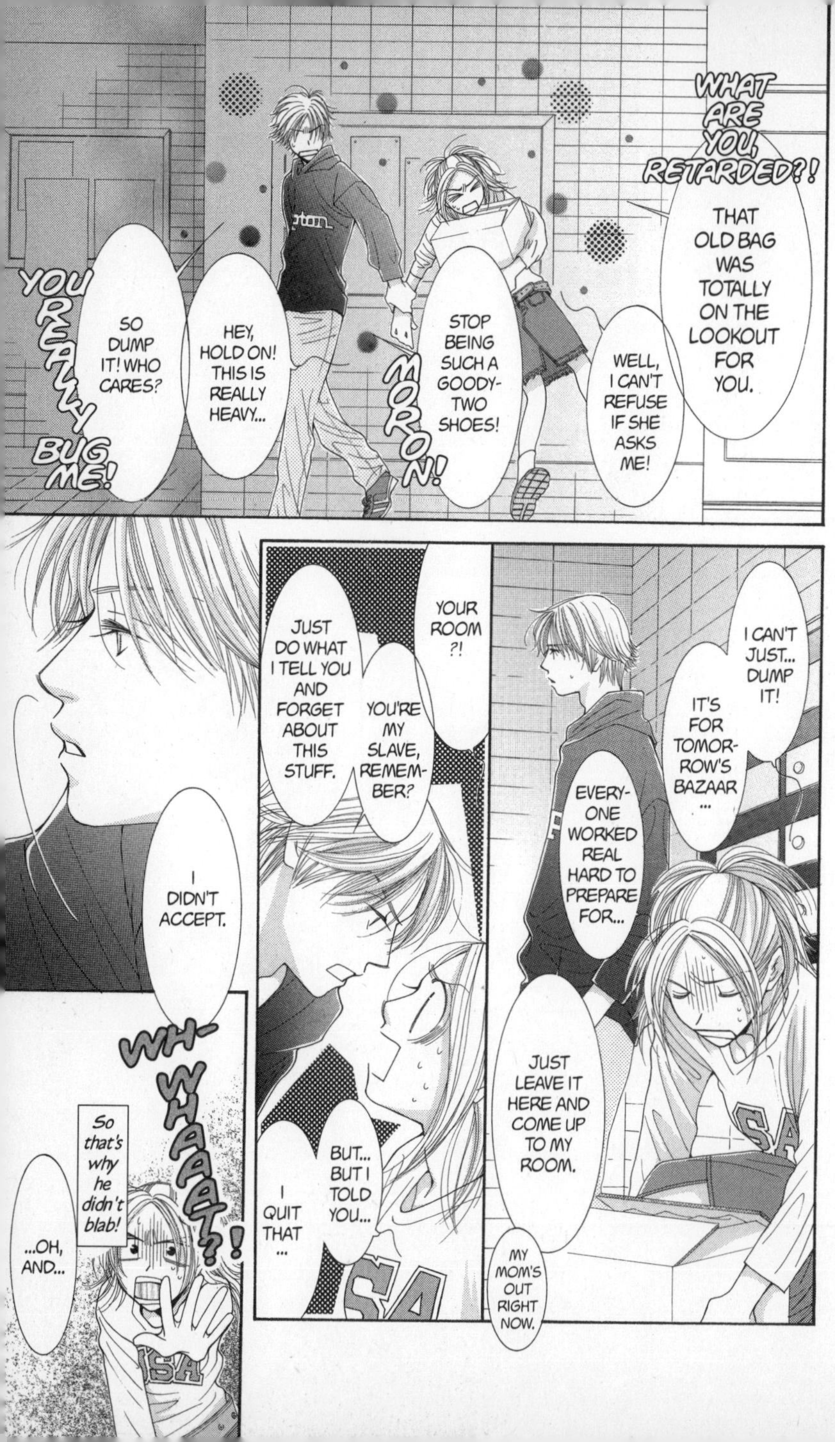
WHAT ARE YOU, RETARDED?!
THAT OLD BAG WAS TOTALLY ON THE LOOKOUT FOR YOU.
WELL, I CAN'T REFUSE IF SHE ASKS ME!
STOP BEING SUCH A GOODY-TWO SHOES!
MORON!
HEY, HOLD ON! THIS IS REALLY HEAVY...
SO DUMP IT! WHO CARES?
YOU REALLY BUG ME!
I CAN'T JUST... DUMP IT!
IT'S FOR TOMOR-ROW'S BAZAAR ...
EVERY-ONE WORKED REAL HARD TO PREPARE FOR...
JUST LEAVE IT HERE AND COME UP TO MY ROOM.
MY MOM'S OUT RIGHT NOW.
YOUR ROOM ?!
YOU'RE MY SLAVE, REMEMBER?
JUST DO WHAT I TELL YOU AND FORGET ABOUT THIS STUFF.
BUT... BUT I TOLD YOU...
I QUIT THAT ...
I DIDN'T ACCEPT.
WH-WHAAAT?!
So that's why he didn't blab!
...OH, AND...

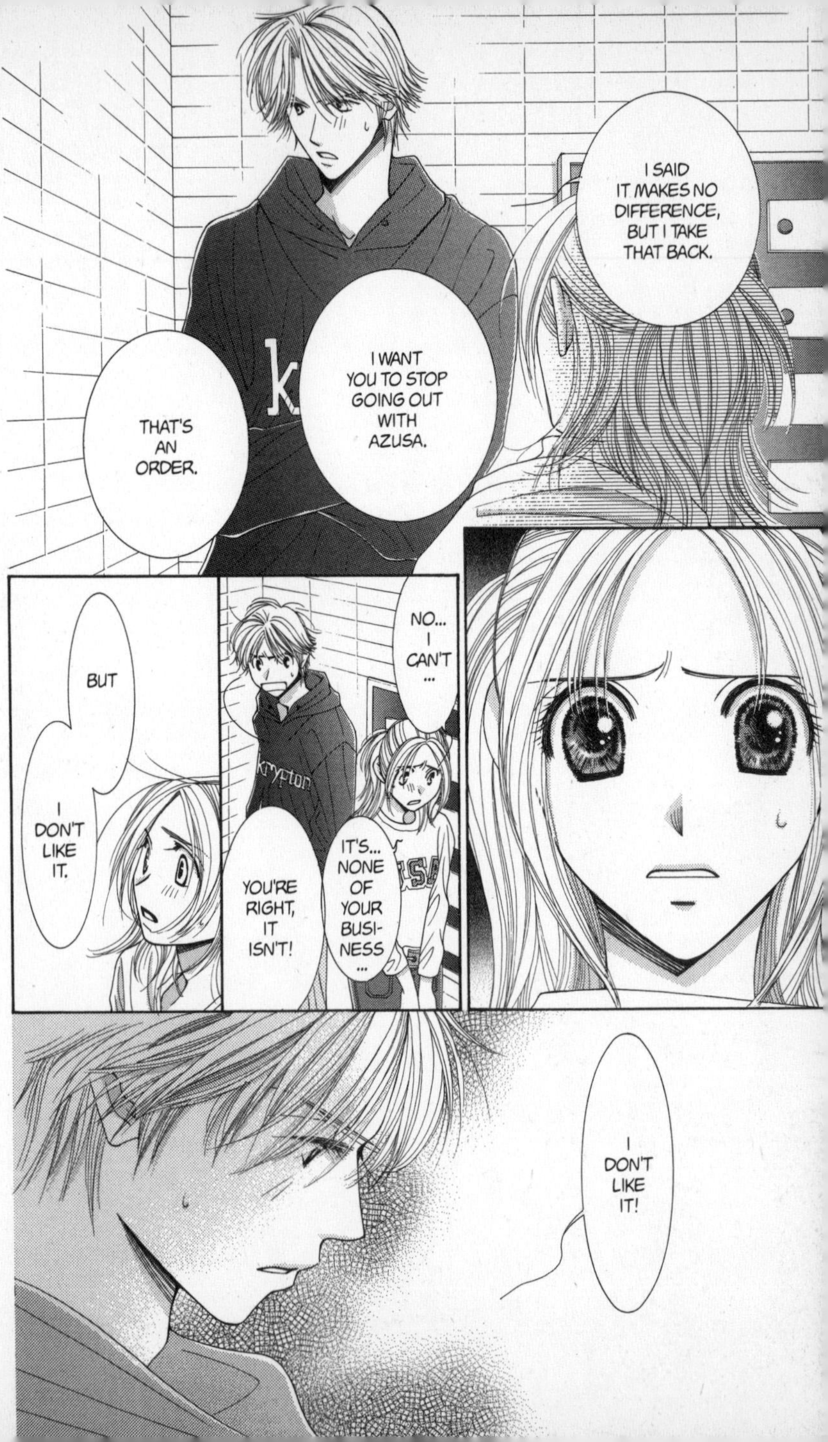
I SAID IT MAKES NO DIFFERENCE, BUT I TAKE THAT BACK.
I WANT YOU TO STOP GOING OUT WITH AZUSA.
THAT'S AN ORDER.
NO... I CAN'T ...
IT'S... NONE OF YOUR BUSINESS ...
YOU'RE RIGHT, IT ISN'T!
BUT
I DON'T LIKE IT.
I DON'T LIKE IT!

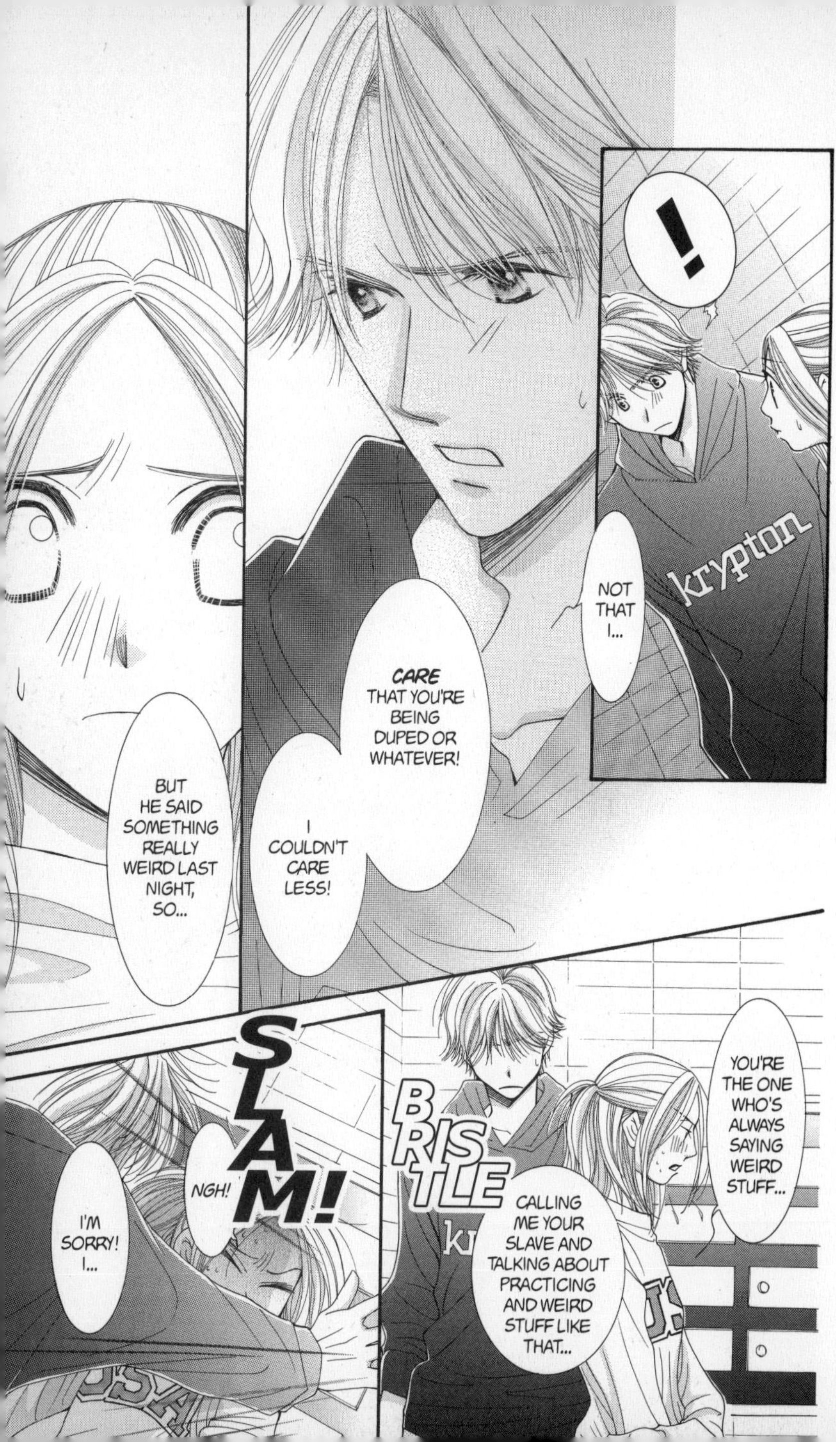
!
NOT THAT I...
CARE THAT YOU'RE BEING DUPED OR WHATEVER!
I COULDN'T CARE LESS!
BUT HE SAID SOMETHING REALLY WEIRD LAST NIGHT, SO...
krypton
YOU'RE THE ONE WHO'S ALWAYS SAYING WEIRD STUFF...
CALLING ME YOUR SLAVE AND TALKING ABOUT PRACTICING AND WEIRD STUFF LIKE THAT...
BRISTLE
SLAM!
NGH!
I'M SORRY! I...

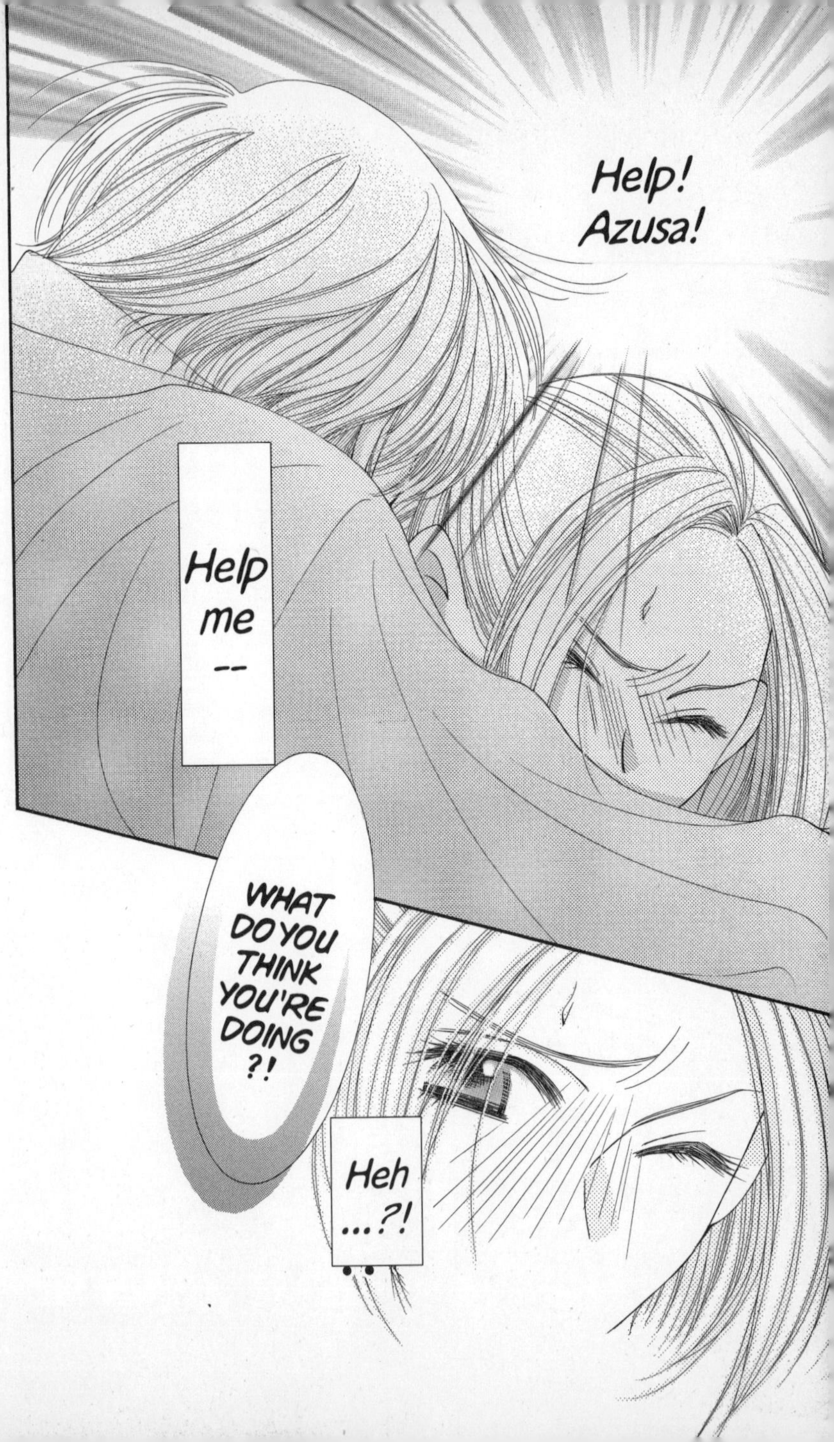
Help! Azusa!
Help me --
WHAT DO YOU THINK YOU'RE DOING ?!
Heh ...?!

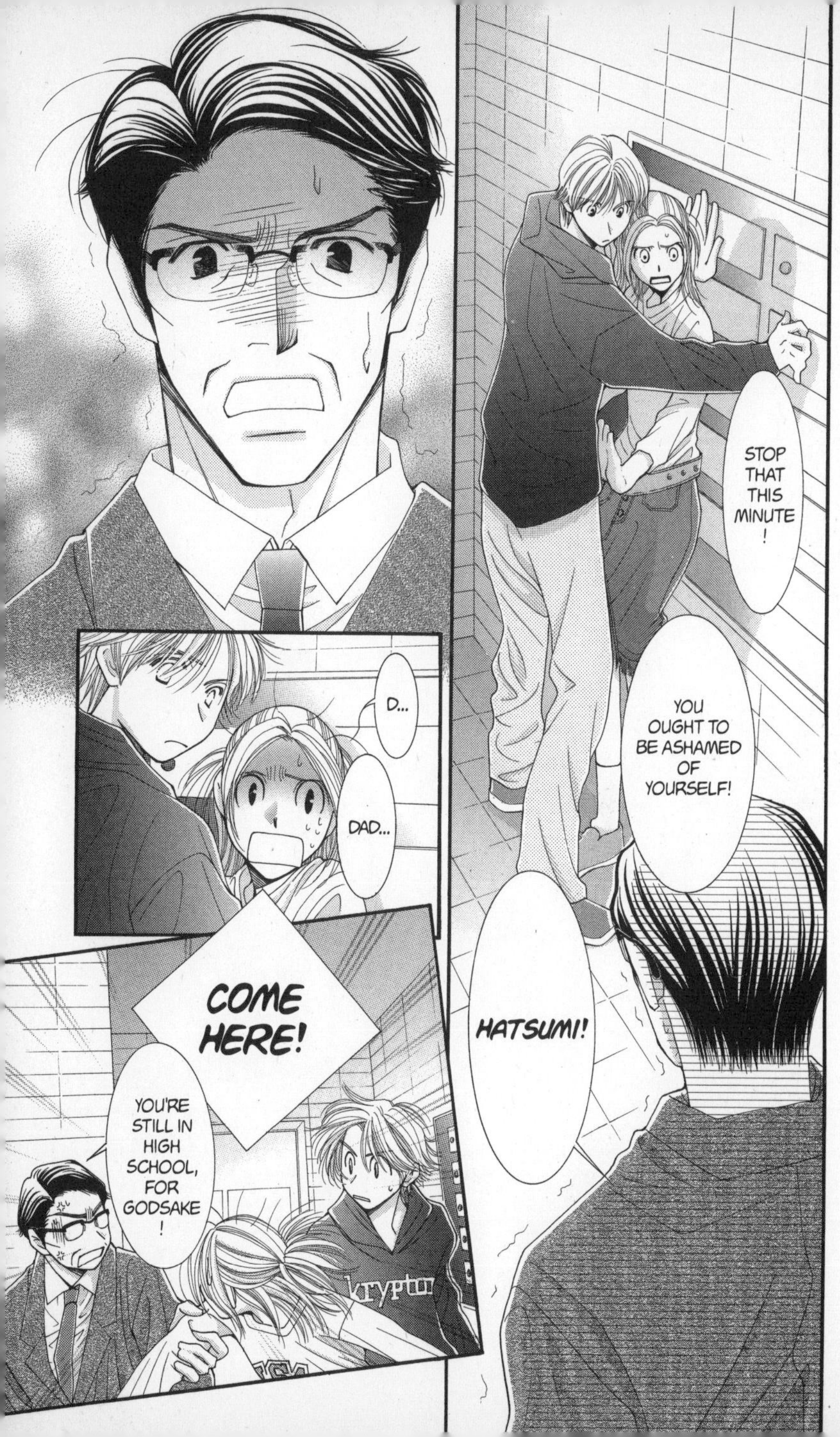
STOP THAT THIS MINUTE!
YOU OUGHT TO BE ASHAMED OF YOURSELF!
HATSUMI!
D...
DAD...
COME HERE!
YOU'RE STILL IN HIGH SCHOOL, FOR GODSAKE!

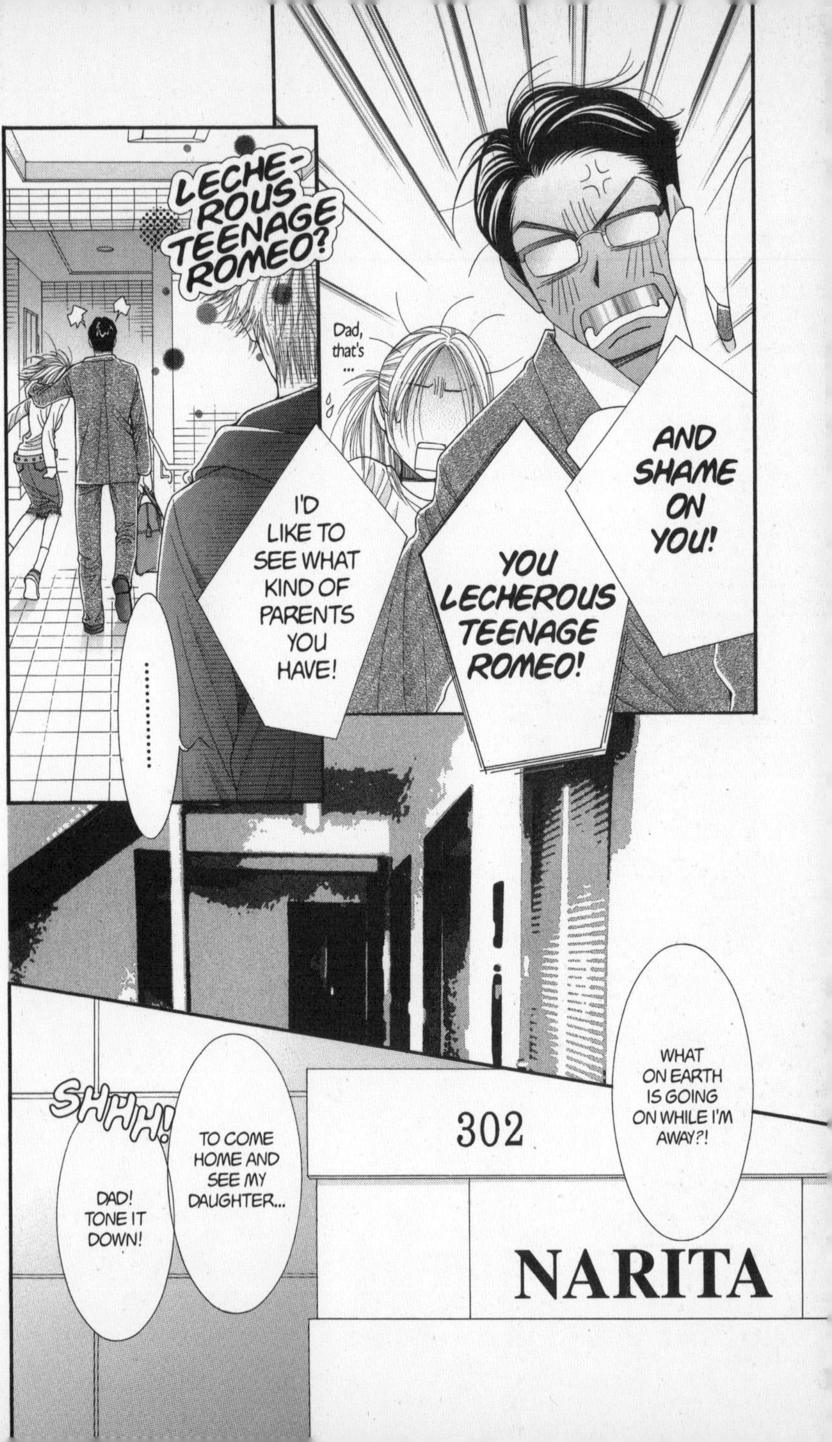
AND SHAME ON YOU!
YOU LECHEROUS TEENAGE ROMEO!
I'D LIKE TO SEE WHAT KIND OF PARENTS YOU HAVE!
Dad, that's ...
LECHE-ROUS TEENAGE ROMEO?
......
WHAT ON EARTH IS GOING ON WHILE I'M AWAY?!
302
NARITA
TO COME HOME AND SEE MY DAUGHTER...
DAD! TONE IT DOWN!
SHHH!

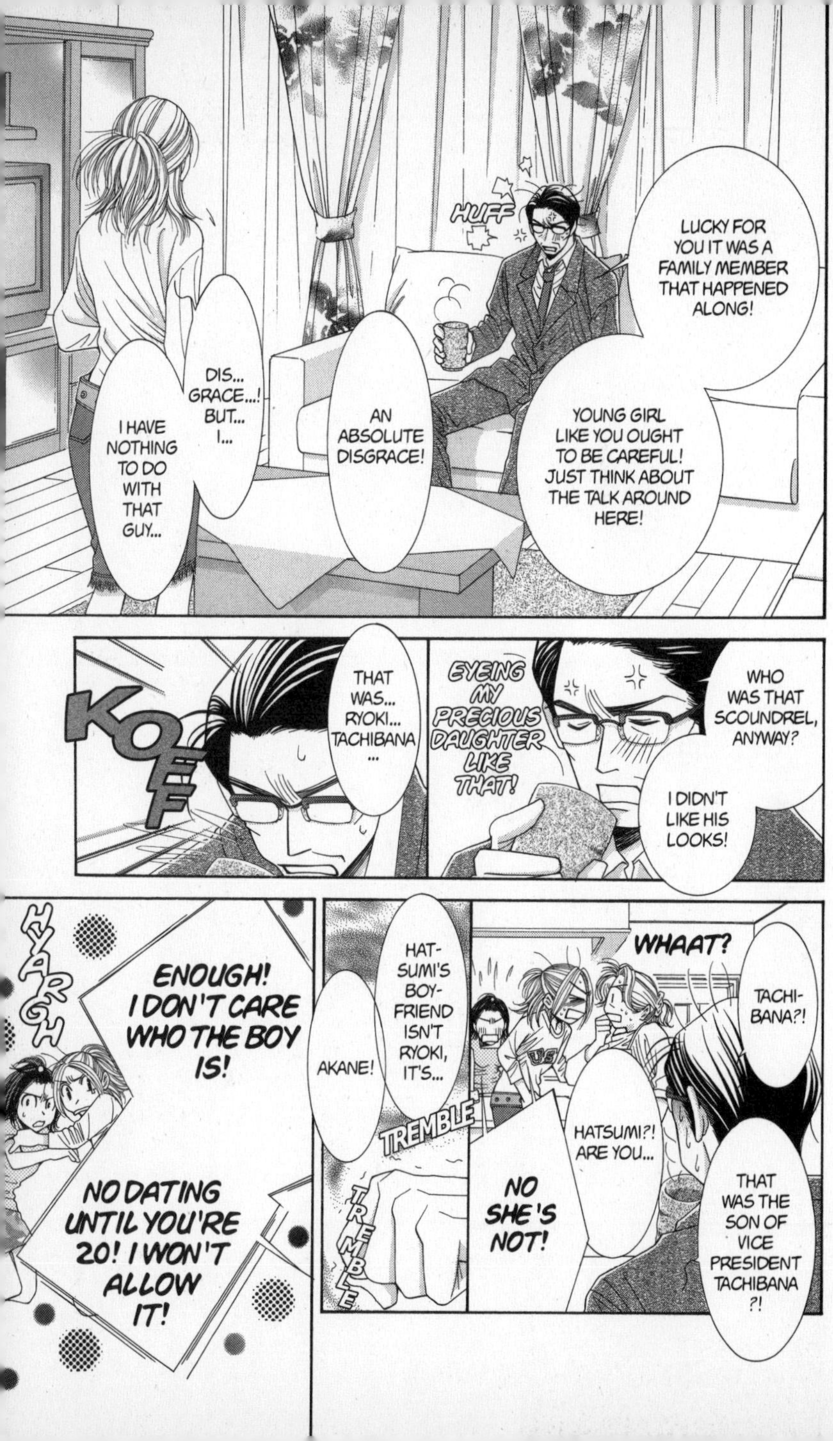
HUFF
LUCKY FOR YOU IT WAS A FAMILY MEMBER THAT HAPPENED ALONG!
YOUNG GIRL LIKE YOU OUGHT TO BE CAREFUL! JUST THINK ABOUT THE TALK AROUND HERE!
AN ABSOLUTE DISGRACE!
DIS... GRACE...! BUT... I...
I HAVE NOTHING TO DO WITH THAT GUY...
WHO WAS THAT SCOUNDREL, ANYWAY?
EYEING MY PRECIOUS DAUGHTER LIKE THAT!
I DIDN'T LIKE HIS LOOKS!
THAT WAS... RYOKI... TACHIBANA ...
KOFF
TACHI-BANA?!
WHAAT?
THAT WAS THE SON OF VICE PRESIDENT TACHIBANA?!
HATSUMI?! ARE YOU...
HAT-SUMI'S BOY-FRIEND ISN'T RYOKI, IT'S...
AKANE!
NO SHE'S NOT!
TREMBLE
TREMBLE
HYARGH
ENOUGH! I DON'T CARE WHO THE BOY IS!
NO DATING UNTIL YOU'RE 20! I WON'T ALLOW IT!

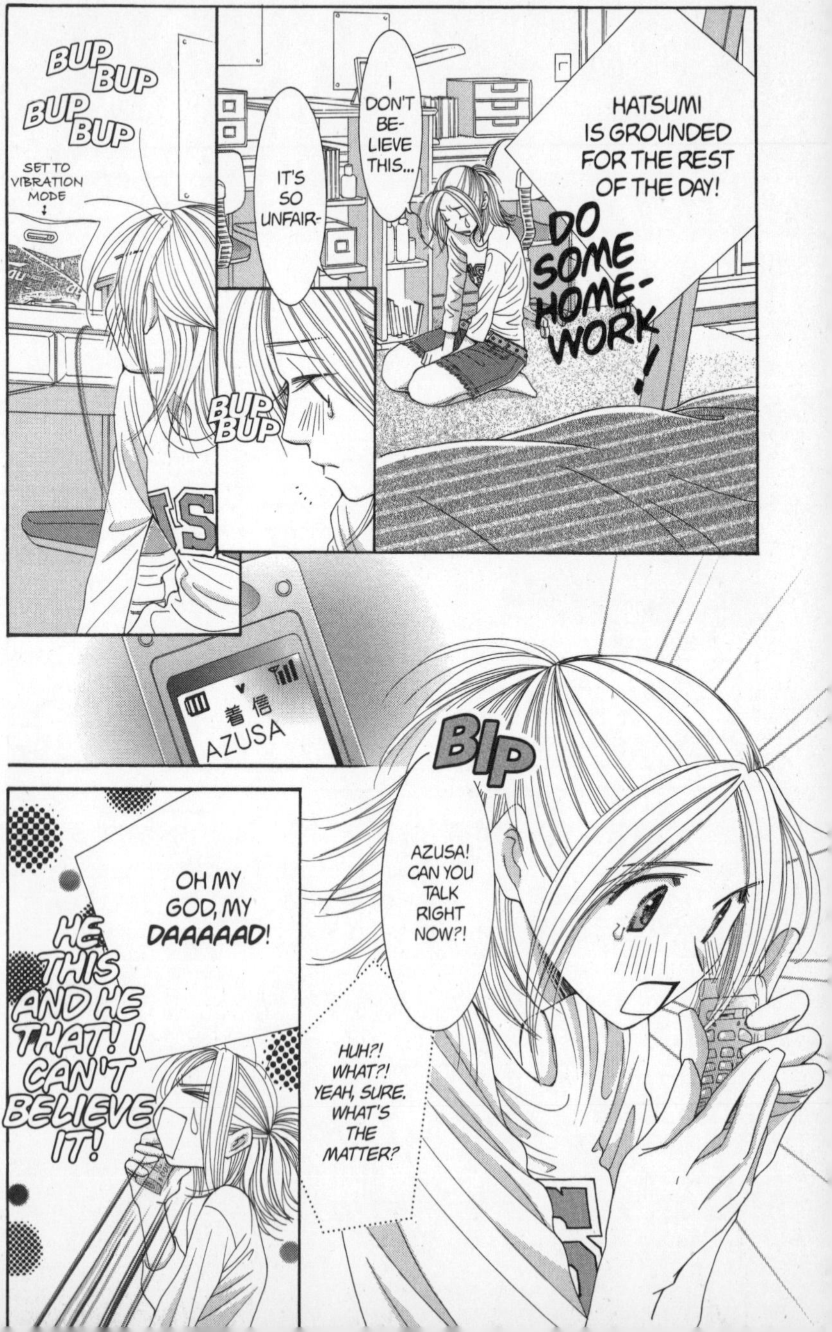
HATSUMI IS GROUNDED FOR THE REST OF THE DAY!
DO SOME HOMEWORK!
I DON'T BELIEVE THIS...
IT'S SO UNFAIR-
BUP BUP
BUP BUP
BUP BUP
SET TO VIBRATION MODE
着信
AZUSA
BIP
AZUSA! CAN YOU TALK RIGHT NOW?!
HUH?! WHAT?! YEAH, SURE. WHAT'S THE MATTER?
OH MY GOD, MY **DAAAAAD**!
HE THIS AND HE THAT! I CAN'T BELIEVE IT!

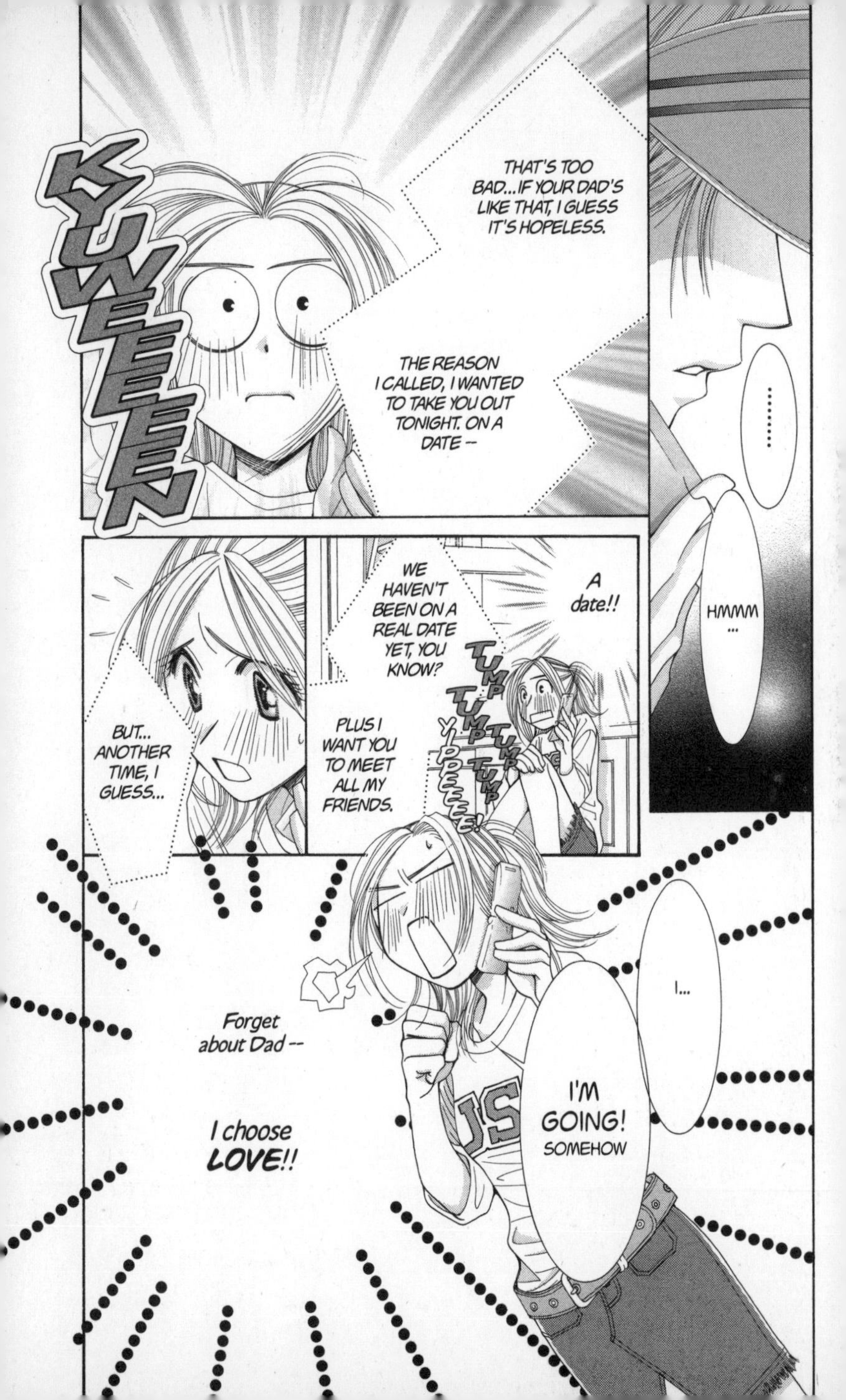
THAT'S TOO BAD...IF YOUR DAD'S LIKE THAT, I GUESS IT'S HOPELESS.
......
HMMM ...
THE REASON I CALLED, I WANTED TO TAKE YOU OUT TONIGHT. ON A DATE --
KYUWEEEEN
A date!!
WE HAVEN'T BEEN ON A REAL DATE YET, YOU KNOW?
PLUS I WANT YOU TO MEET ALL MY FRIENDS.
TUMP TUMP TUMP TUMP
YIPPEEE!
BUT... ANOTHER TIME, I GUESS...
I...
I'M GOING! SOMEHOW
Forget about Dad --
I choose **LOVE!!**

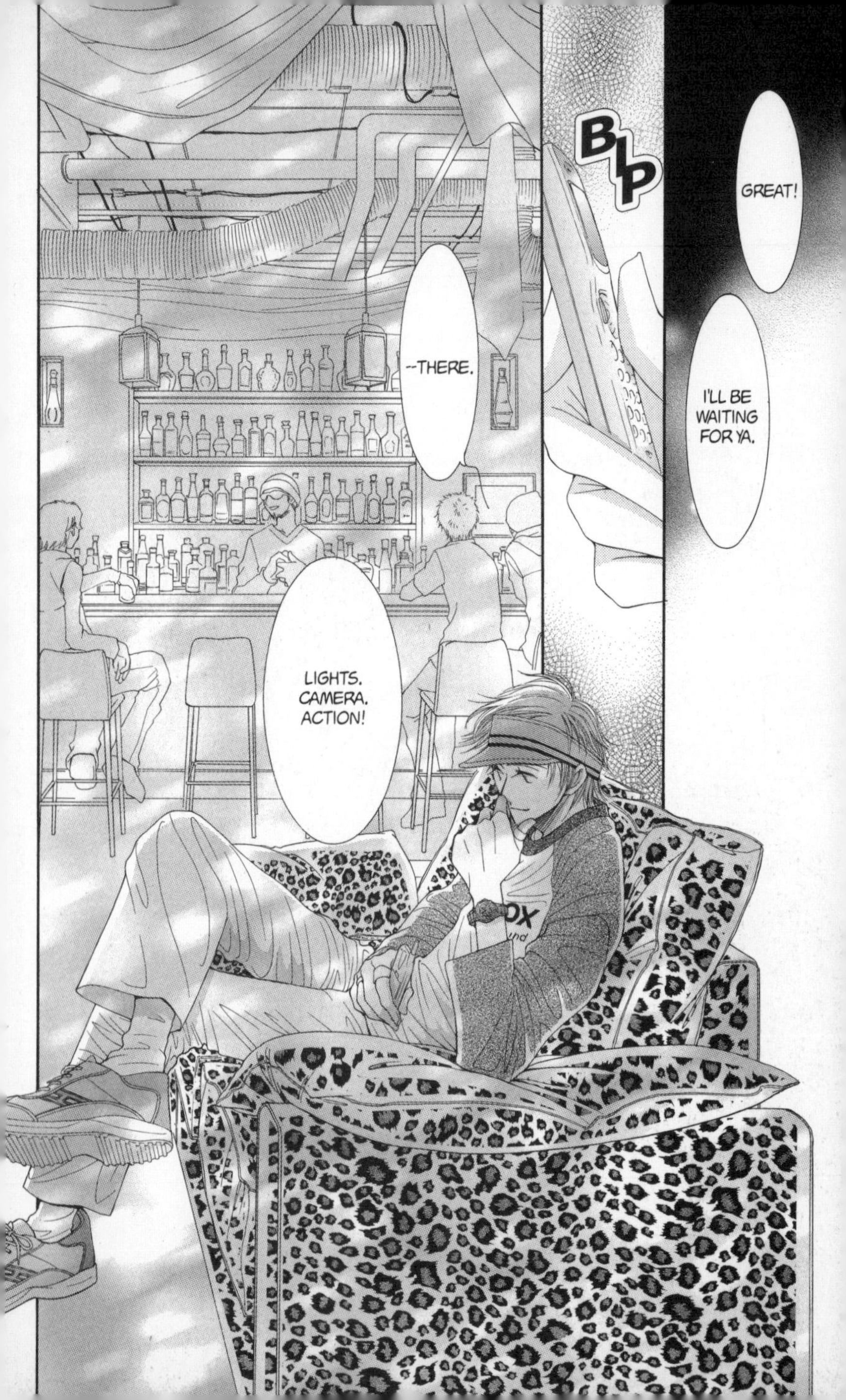
GREAT!
I'LL BE WAITING FOR YA.
BIP
--THERE.
LIGHTS. CAMERA. ACTION!

Chapter 8

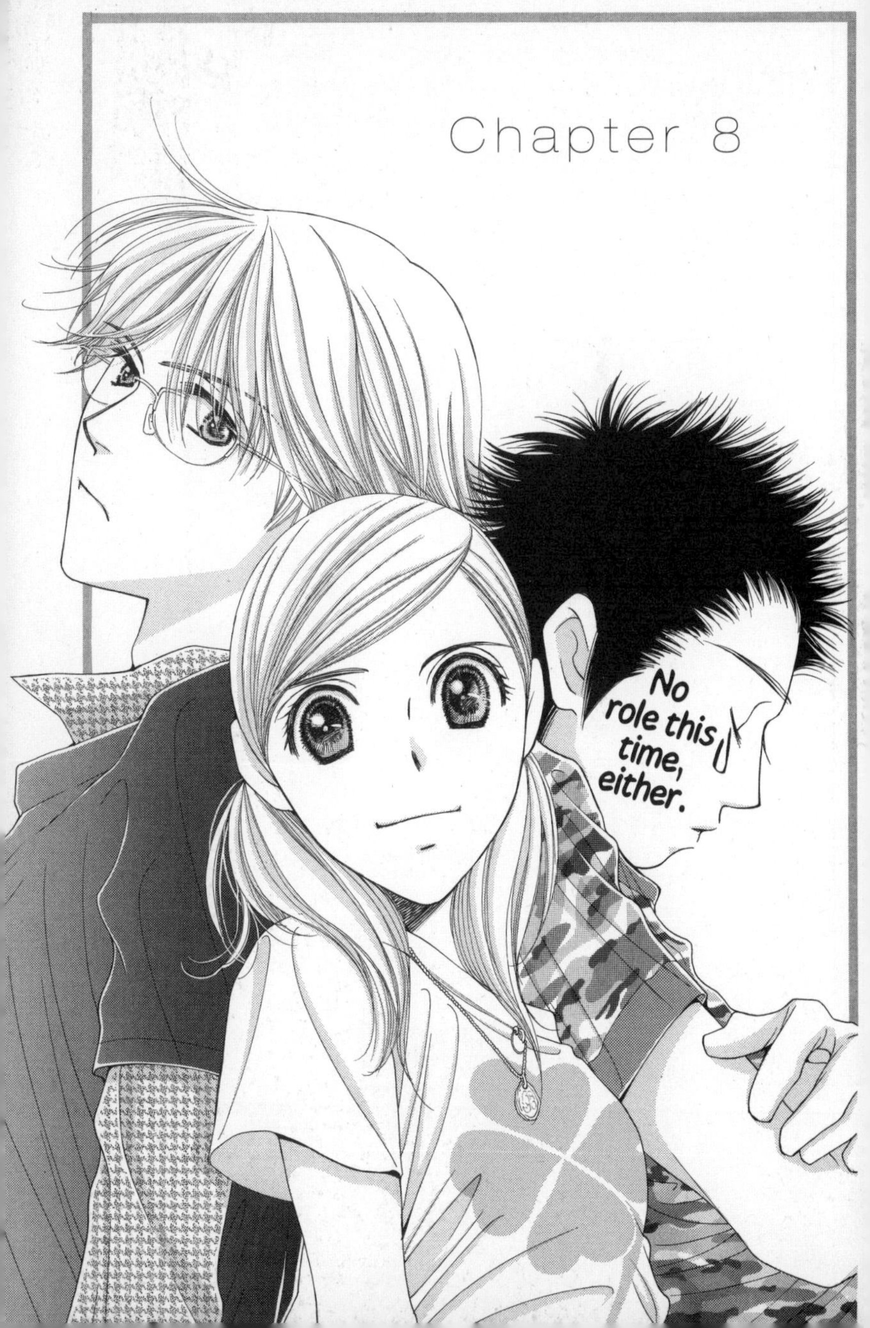
No role this time, either.

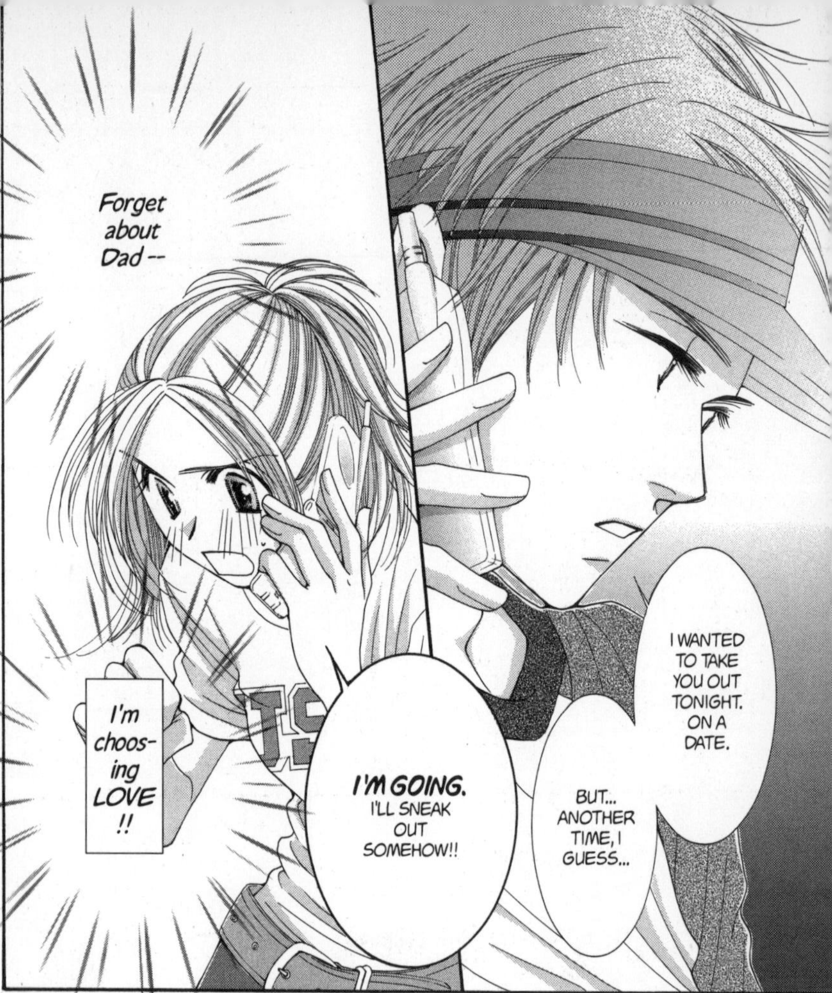
I WANTED TO TAKE YOU OUT TONIGHT. ON A DATE.
BUT... ANOTHER TIME, I GUESS...
Forget about Dad --
I'M GOING. I'LL SNEAK OUT SOMEHOW!!
I'm choosing LOVE !!

hot gimmick

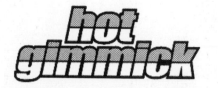

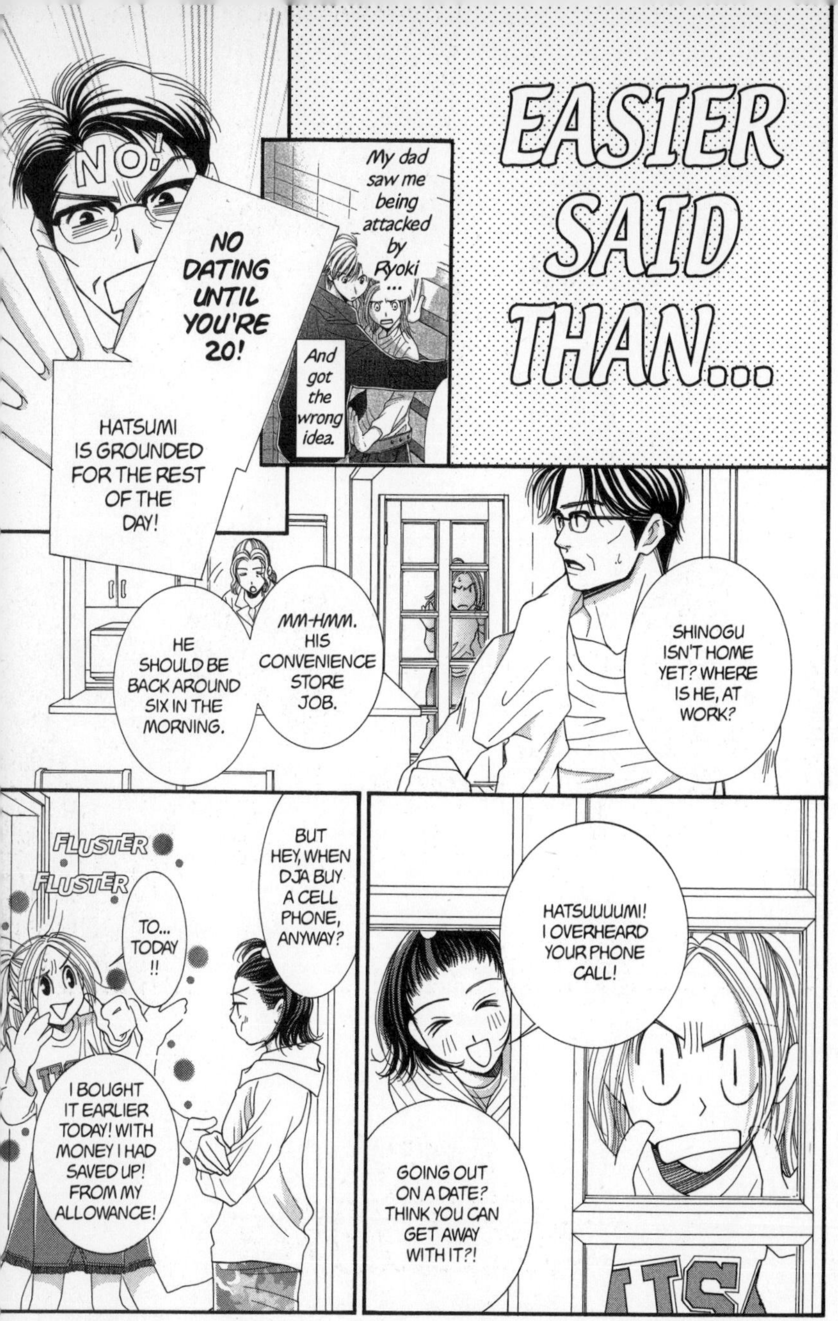
EASIER SAID THAN...
My dad saw me being attacked by Ryoki...
And got the wrong idea.
NO!
NO DATING UNTIL YOU'RE 20!
HATSUMI IS GROUNDED FOR THE REST OF THE DAY!
SHINOGU ISN'T HOME YET? WHERE IS HE, AT WORK?
MM-HMM. HIS CONVENIENCE STORE JOB.
HE SHOULD BE BACK AROUND SIX IN THE MORNING.
HATSUUUUMI! I OVERHEARD YOUR PHONE CALL!
GOING OUT ON A DATE? THINK YOU CAN GET AWAY WITH IT?!
BUT HEY, WHEN DJA BUY A CELL PHONE, ANYWAY?
FLUSTER
FLUSTER
TO... TODAY!!
I BOUGHT IT EARLIER TODAY! WITH MONEY I HAD SAVED UP! FROM MY ALLOWANCE!

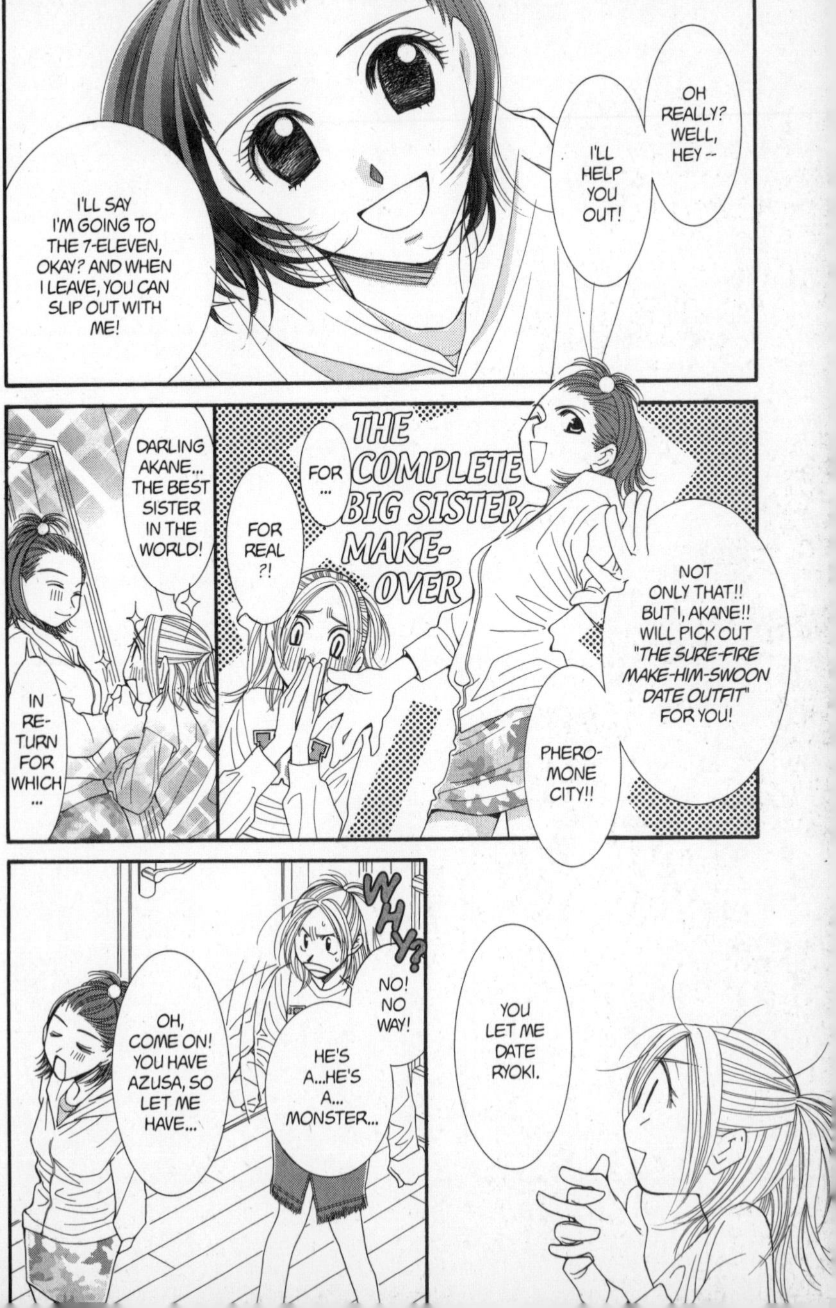
OH REALLY? WELL, HEY --
I'LL HELP YOU OUT!
I'LL SAY I'M GOING TO THE 7-ELEVEN, OKAY? AND WHEN I LEAVE, YOU CAN SLIP OUT WITH ME!
NOT ONLY THAT!! BUT I, AKANE!! WILL PICK OUT "THE SURE-FIRE MAKE-HIM-SWOON DATE OUTFIT" FOR YOU!
PHERO-MONE CITY!!
THE COMPLETE BIG SISTER MAKE-OVER
FOR ...
FOR REAL ?!
DARLING AKANE... THE BEST SISTER IN THE WORLD!
IN RE-TURN FOR WHICH ...
YOU LET ME DATE RYOKI.
WHY?
NO! NO WAY!
HE'S A...HE'S A... MONSTER...
OH, COME ON! YOU HAVE AZUSA, SO LET ME HAVE...

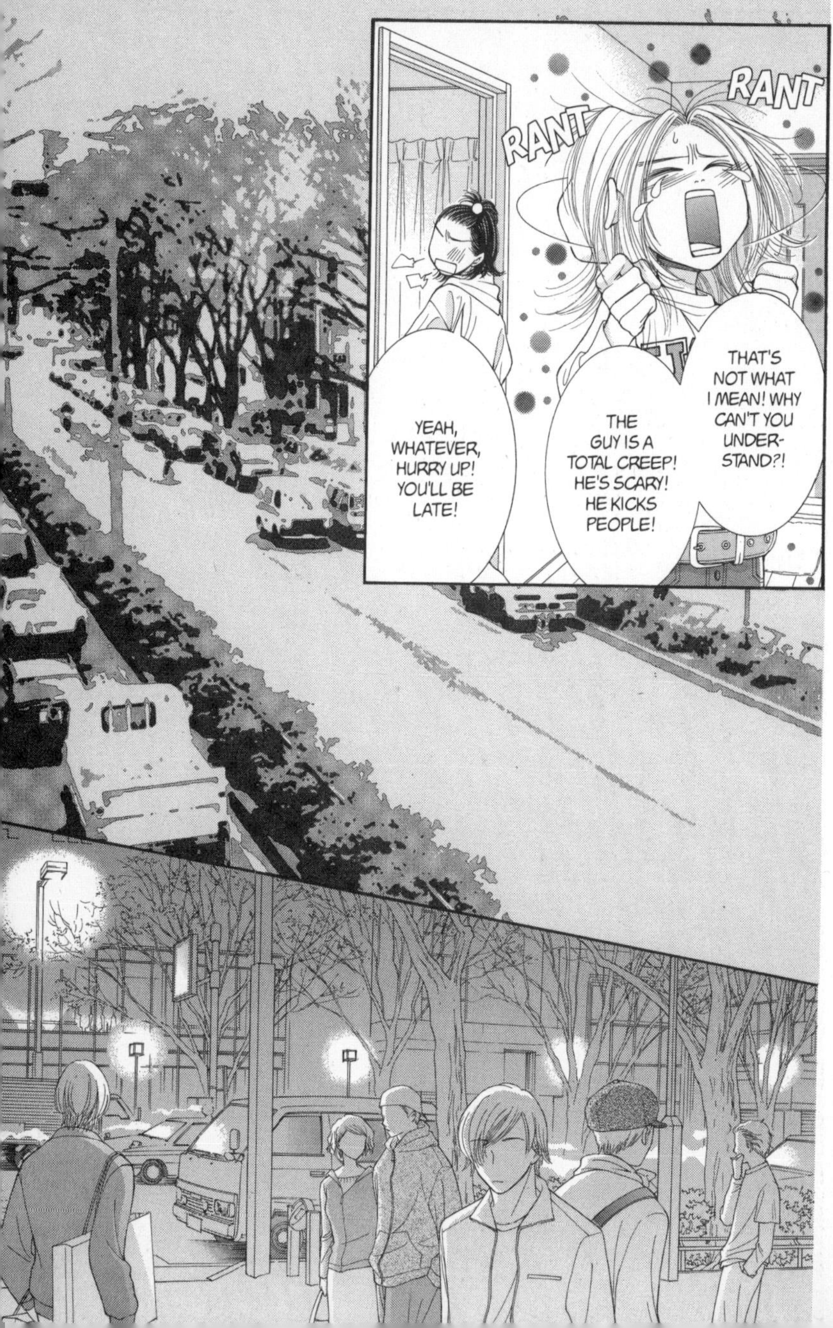
RANT
RANT
THAT'S NOT WHAT I MEAN! WHY CAN'T YOU UNDER-STAND?!
THE GUY IS A TOTAL CREEP! HE'S SCARY! HE KICKS PEOPLE!
YEAH, WHATEVER, HURRY UP! YOU'LL BE LATE!

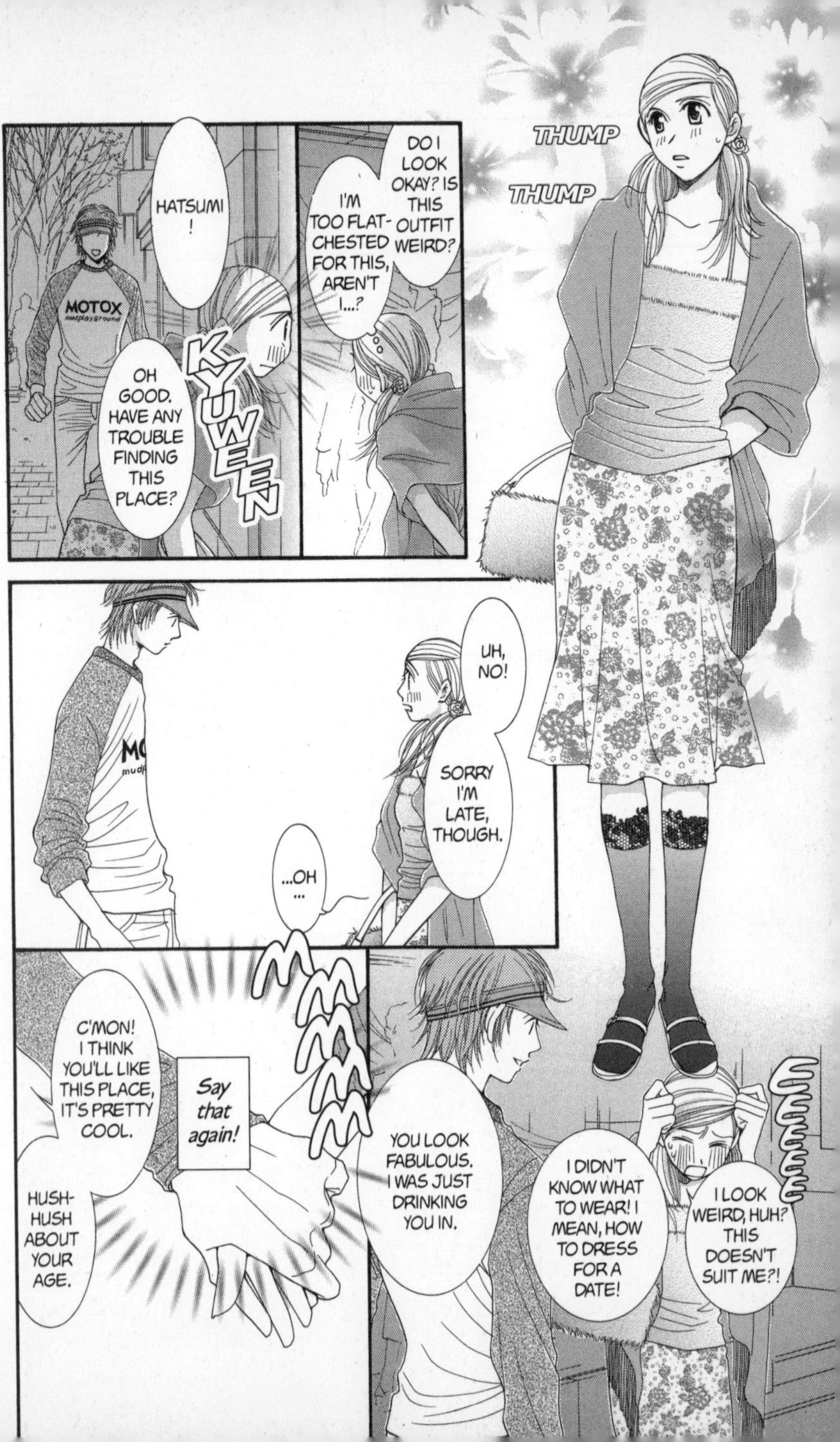
THUMP
THUMP
DO I LOOK OKAY? IS THIS OUTFIT WEIRD?
I'M TOO FLAT-CHESTED FOR THIS, AREN'T I...?
HATSUMI!
KYUWEEN
OH GOOD. HAVE ANY TROUBLE FINDING THIS PLACE?
UH, NO!
SORRY I'M LATE, THOUGH.
...OH...
EEEEE
I LOOK WEIRD, HUH? THIS DOESN'T SUIT ME?!
I DIDN'T KNOW WHAT TO WEAR! I MEAN, HOW TO DRESS FOR A DATE!
YOU LOOK FABULOUS. I WAS JUST DRINKING YOU IN.
MMMMMM
C'MON! I THINK YOU'LL LIKE THIS PLACE, IT'S PRETTY COOL.
Say that again!
HUSH-HUSH ABOUT YOUR AGE.

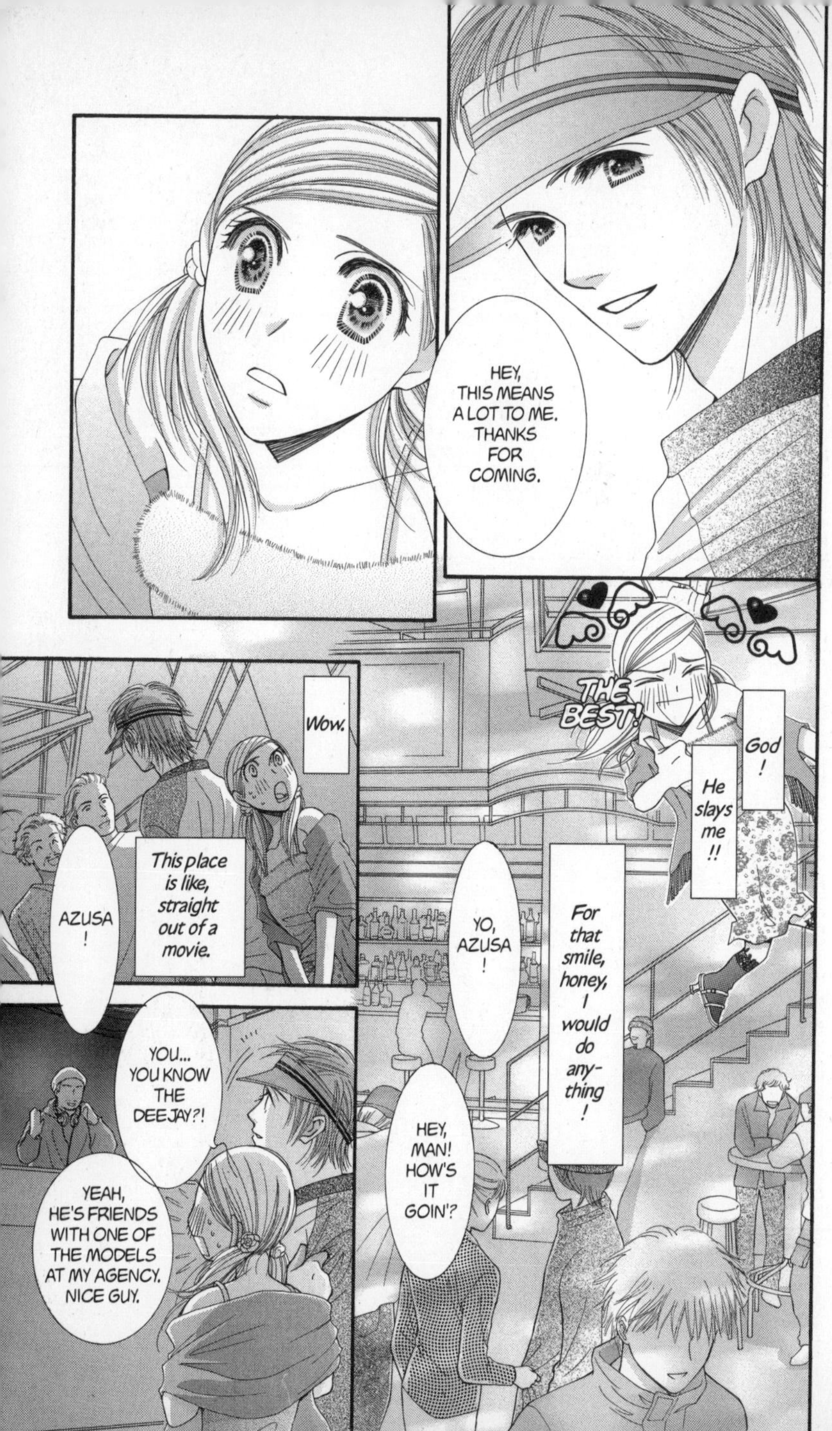
HEY, THIS MEANS A LOT TO ME. THANKS FOR COMING.
THE BEST!
God! He slays me!!
For that smile, honey, I would do any-thing!
YO, AZUSA!
HEY, MAN! HOW'S IT GOIN'?
Wow.
This place is like, straight out of a movie.
AZUSA!
YOU... YOU KNOW THE DEEJAY?!
YEAH, HE'S FRIENDS WITH ONE OF THE MODELS AT MY AGENCY. NICE GUY.

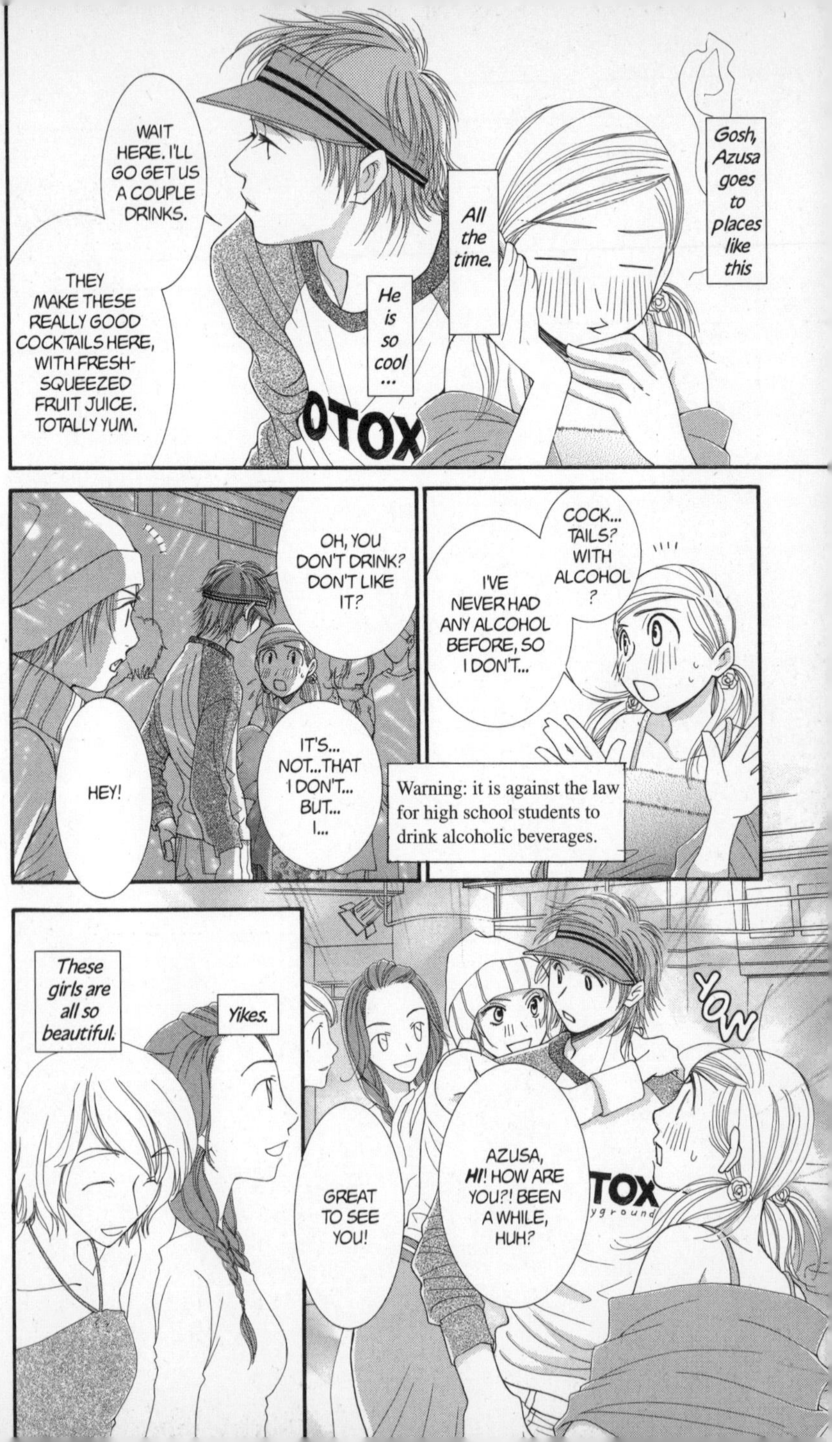
Gosh, Azusa goes to places like this
All the time.
He is so cool...
WAIT HERE. I'LL GO GET US A COUPLE DRINKS.
THEY MAKE THESE REALLY GOOD COCKTAILS HERE, WITH FRESH-SQUEEZED FRUIT JUICE. TOTALLY YUM.
COCK... TAILS? WITH ALCOHOL?
I'VE NEVER HAD ANY ALCOHOL BEFORE, SO I DON'T...
Warning: it is against the law for high school students to drink alcoholic beverages.
OH, YOU DON'T DRINK? DON'T LIKE IT?
IT'S... NOT...THAT I DON'T... BUT... I...
HEY!
YOW
AZUSA, **HI**! HOW ARE YOU?! BEEN A WHILE, HUH?
GREAT TO SEE YOU!
Yikes.
These girls are all so beautiful.

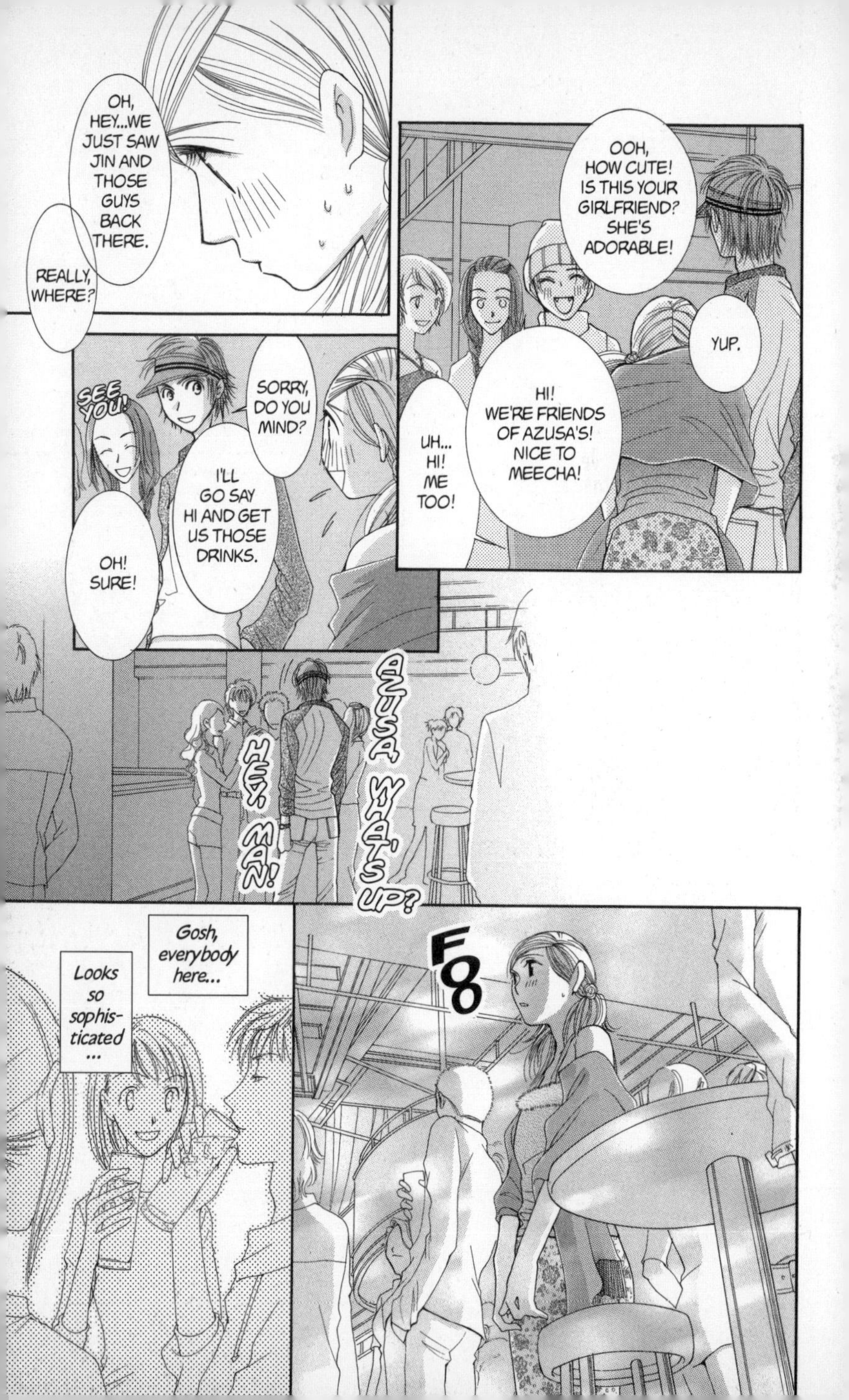
OOH, HOW CUTE! IS THIS YOUR GIRLFRIEND? SHE'S ADORABLE!
YUP.
HI! WE'RE FRIENDS OF AZUSA'S! NICE TO MEECHA!
UH... HI! ME TOO!
OH, HEY...WE JUST SAW JIN AND THOSE GUYS BACK THERE.
REALLY, WHERE?
SORRY, DO YOU MIND?
I'LL GO SAY HI AND GET US THOSE DRINKS.
SEE YOU!
OH! SURE!
AZUSA WHAT'S UP?
HEY, MAN!
F8
Gosh, everybody here...
Looks so sophis-ticated ...

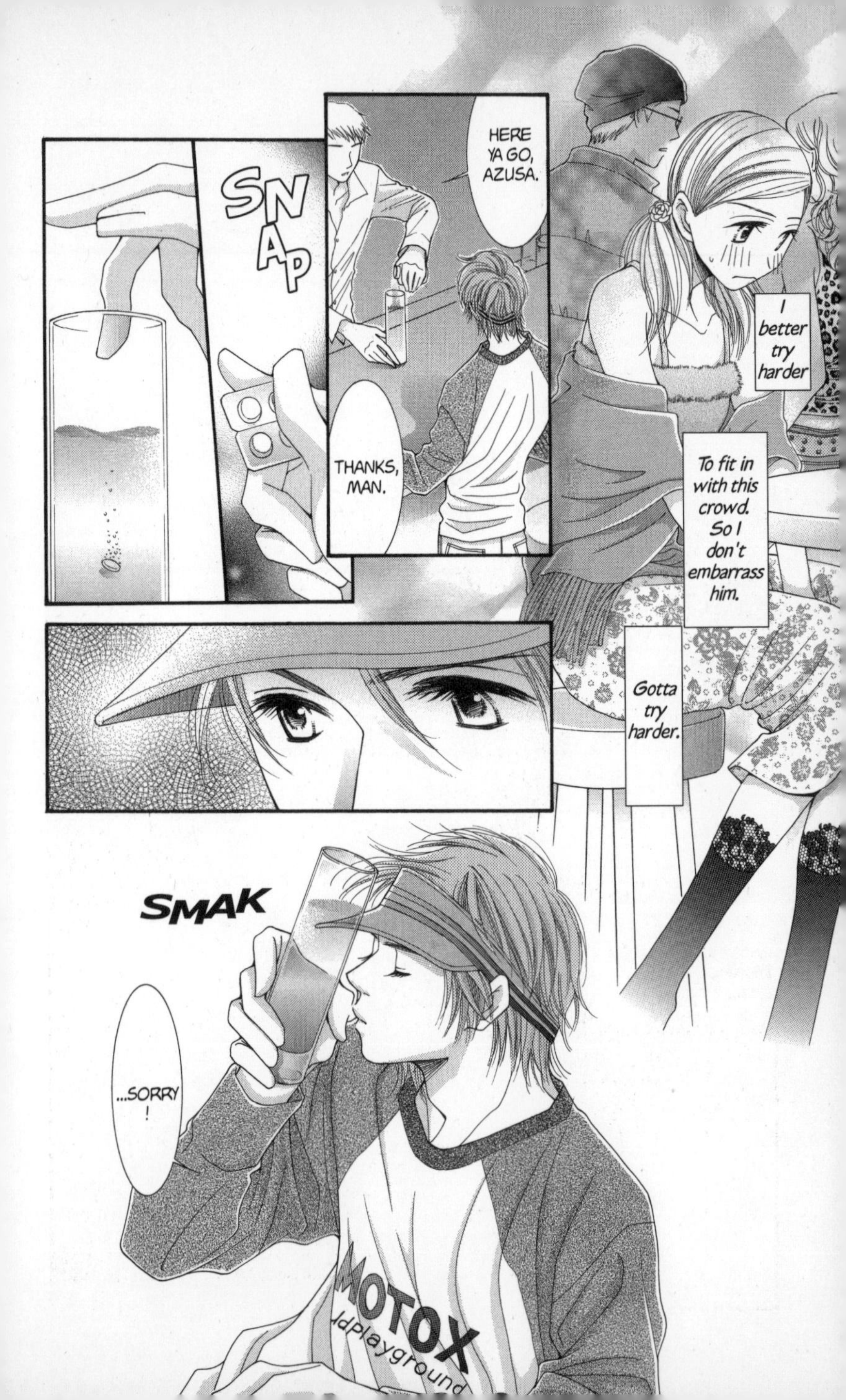
HERE YA GO, AZUSA.
THANKS, MAN.
SNAP
I better try harder
To fit in with this crowd. So I don't embarrass him.
Gotta try harder.
SMAK
...SORRY!
MOTOX

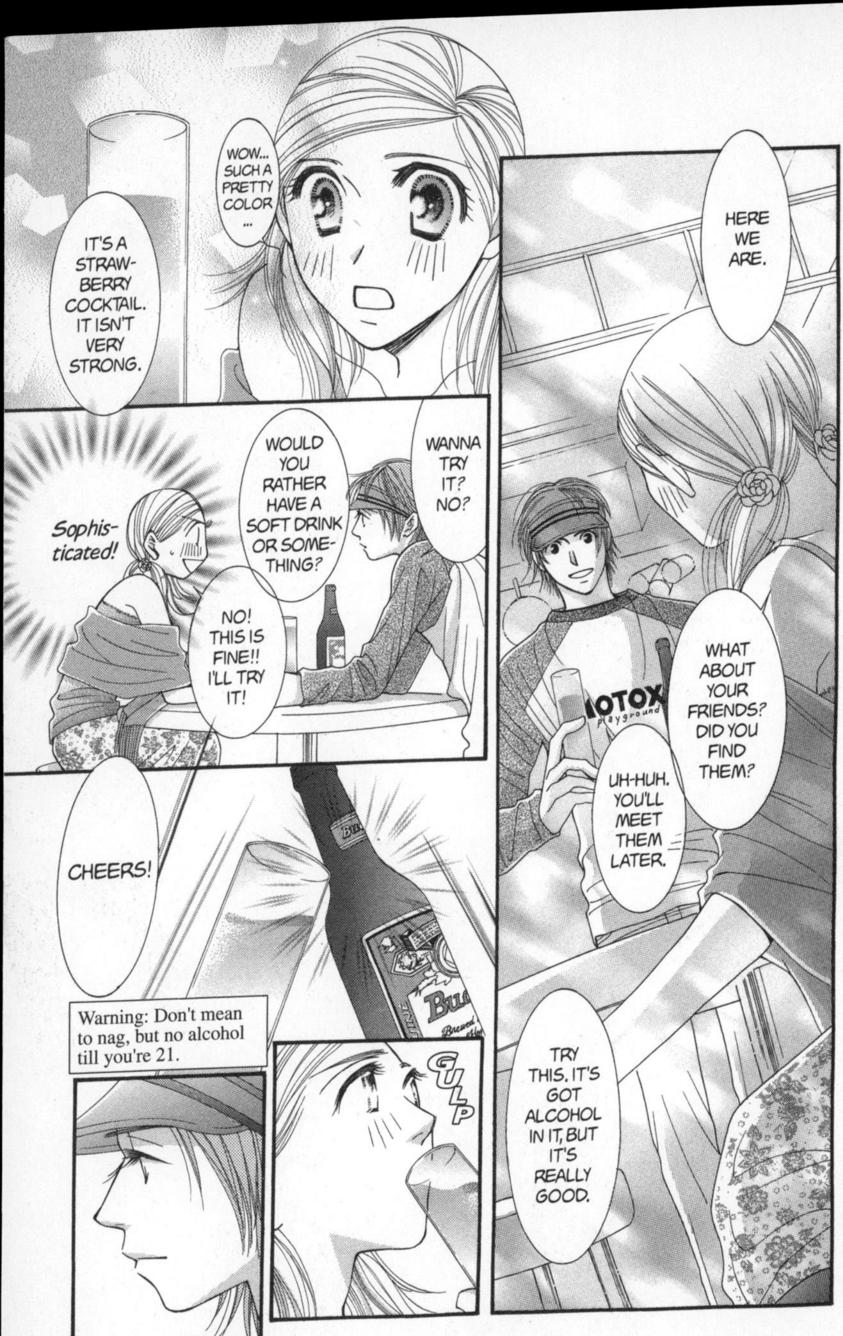
HERE WE ARE.
WHAT ABOUT YOUR FRIENDS? DID YOU FIND THEM?
UH-HUH. YOU'LL MEET THEM LATER.
TRY THIS. IT'S GOT ALCOHOL IN IT, BUT IT'S REALLY GOOD.
WOW... SUCH A PRETTY COLOR ...
IT'S A STRAW-BERRY COCKTAIL. IT ISN'T VERY STRONG.
WANNA TRY IT? NO?
WOULD YOU RATHER HAVE A SOFT DRINK OR SOME-THING?
NO! THIS IS FINE!! I'LL TRY IT!
Sophis-ticated!
CHEERS!
Warning: Don't mean to nag, but no alcohol till you're 21.
GULP

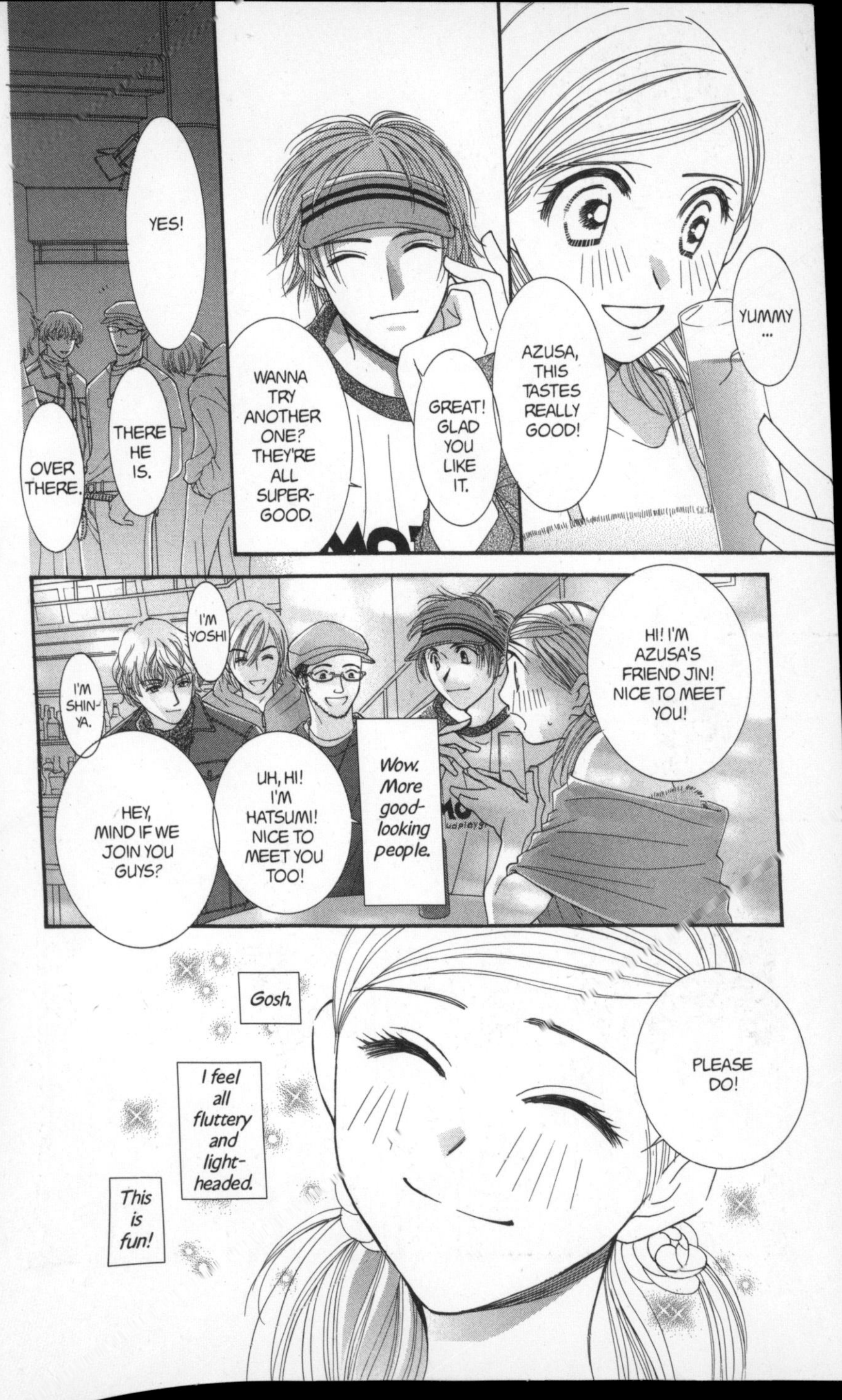

YUMMY ...
AZUSA, THIS TASTES REALLY GOOD!
GREAT! GLAD YOU LIKE IT.
WANNA TRY ANOTHER ONE? THEY'RE ALL SUPER-GOOD.
YES!
THERE HE IS.
OVER THERE.
HI! I'M AZUSA'S FRIEND JIN! NICE TO MEET YOU!
I'M YOSHI
I'M SHIN-YA.
Wow. More good-looking people.
UH, HI! I'M HATSUMI! NICE TO MEET YOU TOO!
HEY, MIND IF WE JOIN YOU GUYS?
PLEASE DO!
Gosh.
I feel all fluttery and light-headed.
This is fun!

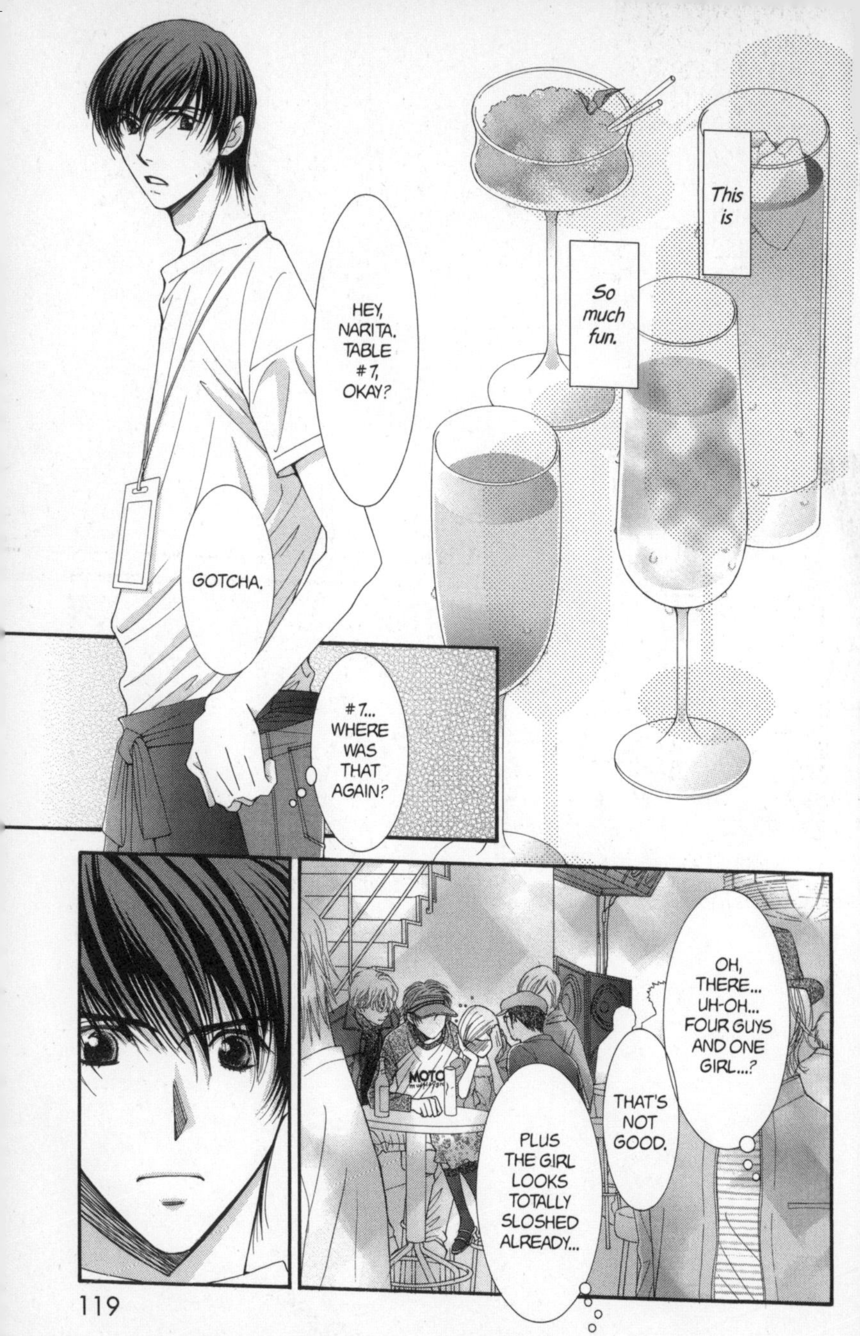
This is
So much fun.
HEY, NARITA. TABLE #7, OKAY?
GOTCHA.
#7... WHERE WAS THAT AGAIN?
OH, THERE... UH-OH... FOUR GUYS AND ONE GIRL...?
THAT'S NOT GOOD.
PLUS THE GIRL LOOKS TOTALLY SLOSHED ALREADY...

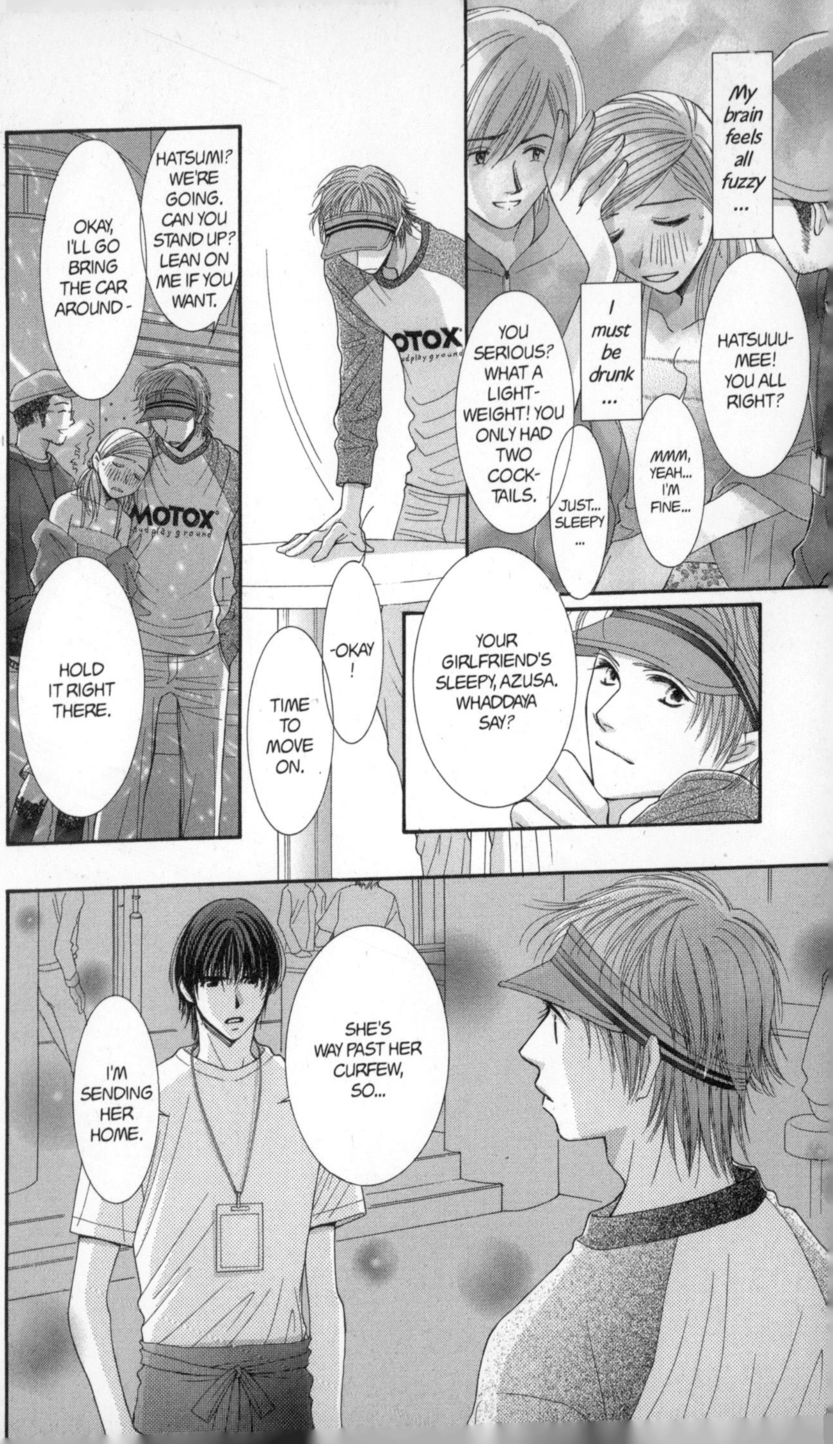

My brain feels all fuzzy ...
HATSUUU-MEE! YOU ALL RIGHT?
MMM, YEAH... I'M FINE...
I must be drunk ...
YOU SERIOUS? WHAT A LIGHT-WEIGHT! YOU ONLY HAD TWO COCK-TAILS.
JUST... SLEEPY ...
MOTOX
YOUR GIRLFRIEND'S SLEEPY, AZUSA. WHADDAYA SAY?
-OKAY!
TIME TO MOVE ON.
HATSUMI? WE'RE GOING. CAN YOU STAND UP? LEAN ON ME IF YOU WANT.
OKAY, I'LL GO BRING THE CAR AROUND -
MOTOX
HOLD IT RIGHT THERE.
SHE'S WAY PAST HER CURFEW, SO...
I'M SENDING HER HOME.

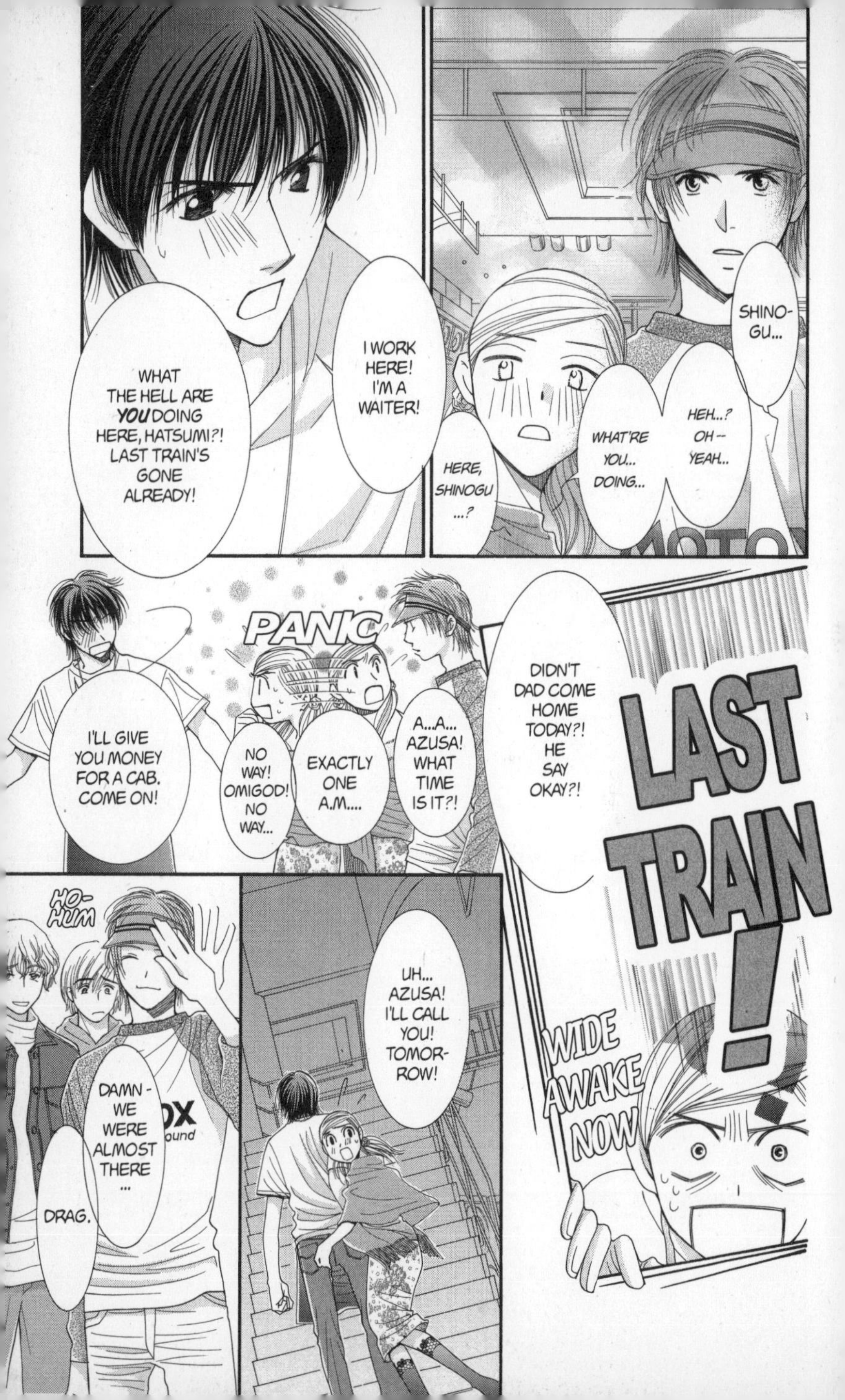
SHINO-GU...
HEH...? OH -- YEAH...
WHAT'RE YOU... DOING...
HERE, SHINOGU ...?
I WORK HERE! I'M A WAITER!
WHAT THE HELL ARE *YOU* DOING HERE, HATSUMI?! LAST TRAIN'S GONE ALREADY!
DIDN'T DAD COME HOME TODAY?! HE SAY OKAY?!
LAST TRAIN!
WIDE AWAKE NOW
PANIC
A...A... AZUSA! WHAT TIME IS IT?!
EXACTLY ONE A.M....
NO WAY! OMIGOD! NO WAY...
I'LL GIVE YOU MONEY FOR A CAB. COME ON!
UH... AZUSA! I'LL CALL YOU! TOMOR-ROW!
HO-HUM
DAMN - WE WERE ALMOST THERE ...
DRAG.

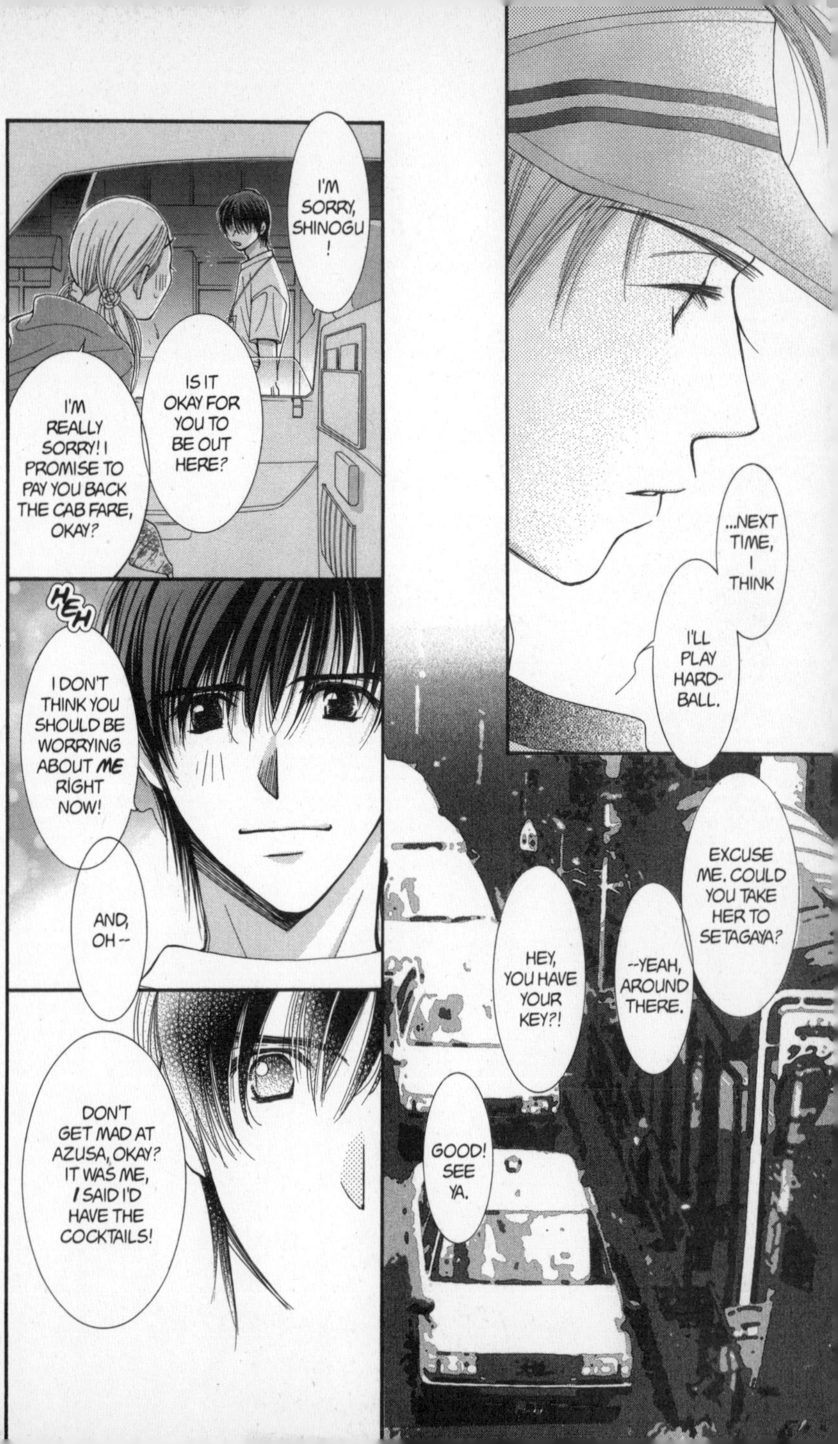
...NEXT TIME, I THINK
I'LL PLAY HARD-BALL.
EXCUSE ME. COULD YOU TAKE HER TO SETAGAYA?
--YEAH, AROUND THERE.
HEY, YOU HAVE YOUR KEY?!
GOOD! SEE YA.
I'M SORRY, SHINOGU!
IS IT OKAY FOR YOU TO BE OUT HERE?
I'M REALLY SORRY! I PROMISE TO PAY YOU BACK THE CAB FARE, OKAY?
HEH
I DON'T THINK YOU SHOULD BE WORRYING ABOUT ME RIGHT NOW!
AND, OH --
DON'T GET MAD AT AZUSA, OKAY? IT WAS ME, I SAID I'D HAVE THE COCKTAILS!

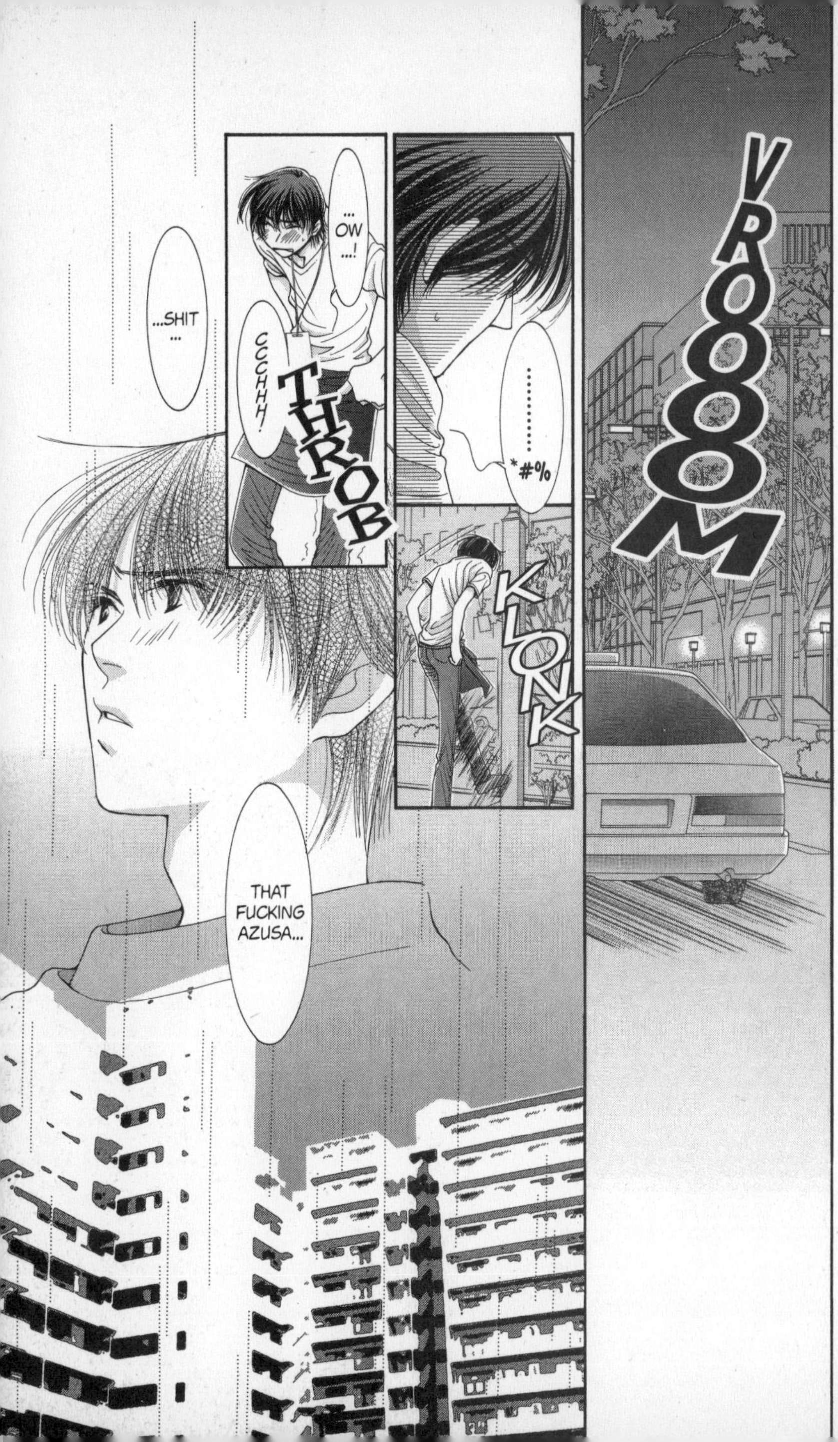

VROOOOM
......
*#%
KLONK
...OW...!
CCCHHH!
THROB
...SHIT...
THAT FUCKING AZUSA...

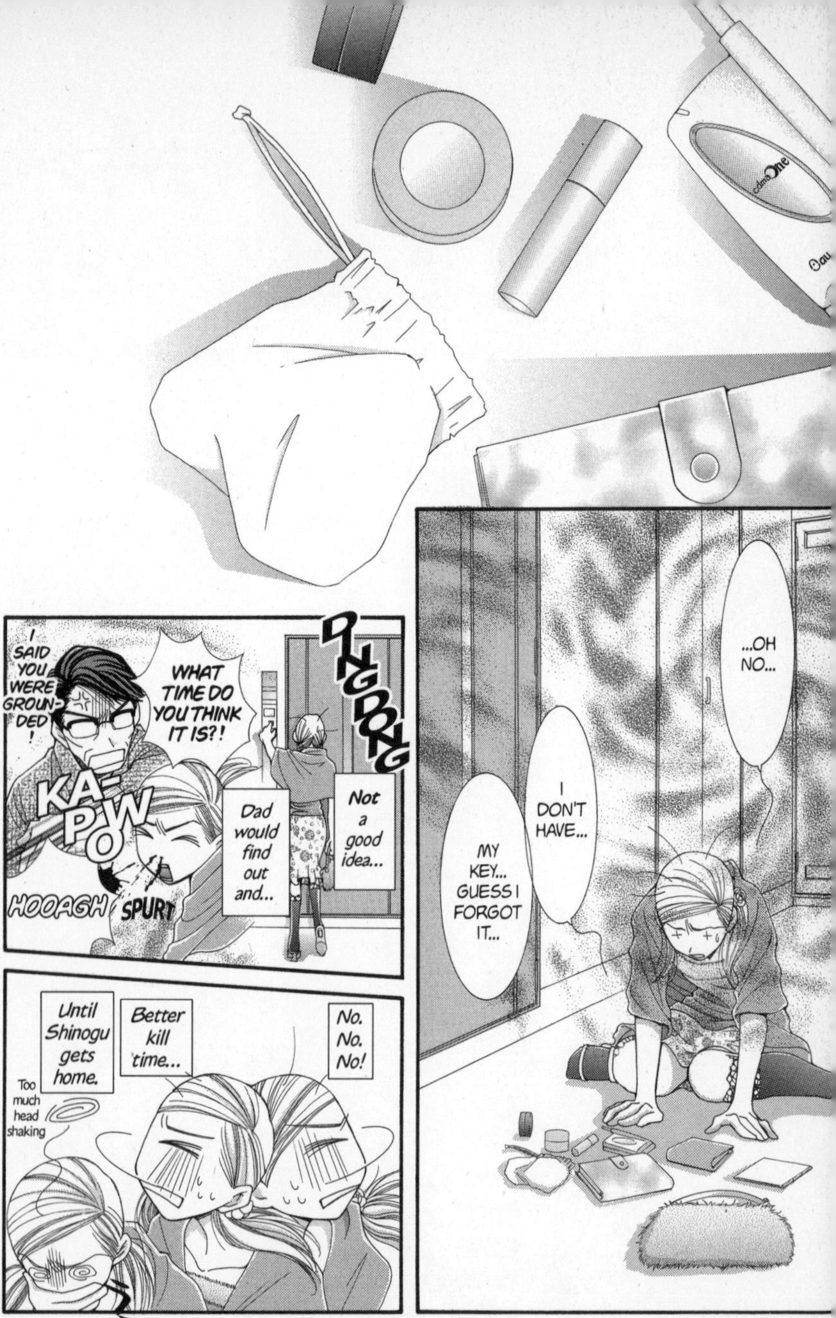
...OH NO...
I DON'T HAVE...
MY KEY... GUESS I FORGOT IT...
DING DONG
Not a good idea...
Dad would find out and...
WHAT TIME DO YOU THINK IT IS?!
I SAID YOU WERE GROUNDED!
KA-POW
SPURT
HOOAGH
No. No. No!
Better kill time...
Until Shinogu gets home.
Too much head shaking

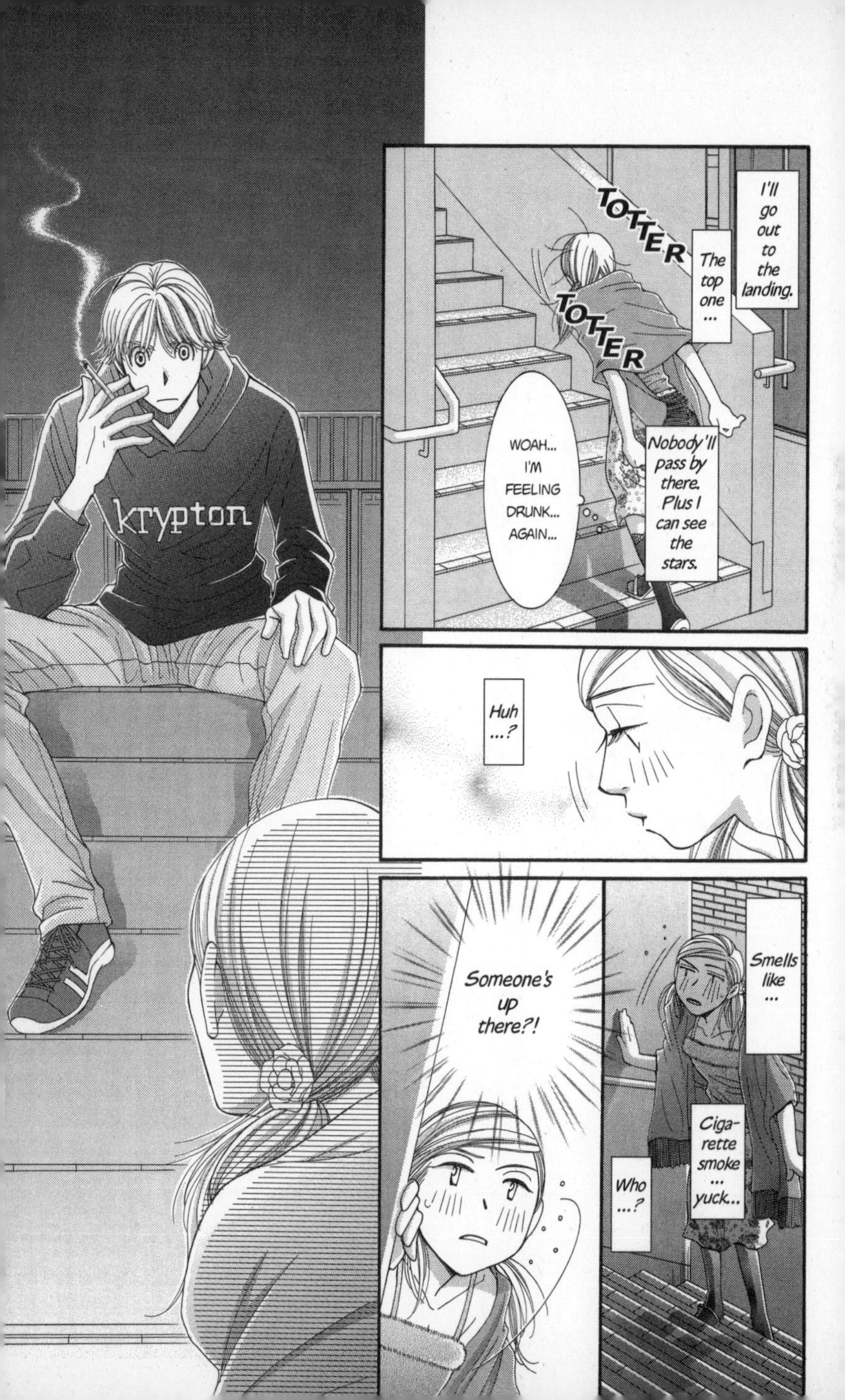
I'll go out to the landing.
The top one ...
TOTTER
TOTTER
Nobody'll pass by there. Plus I can see the stars.
WOAH... I'M FEELING DRUNK... AGAIN...
Huh ...?
Smells like ...
Ciga-rette smoke ... yuck...
Who ...?
Someone's up there?!
krypton

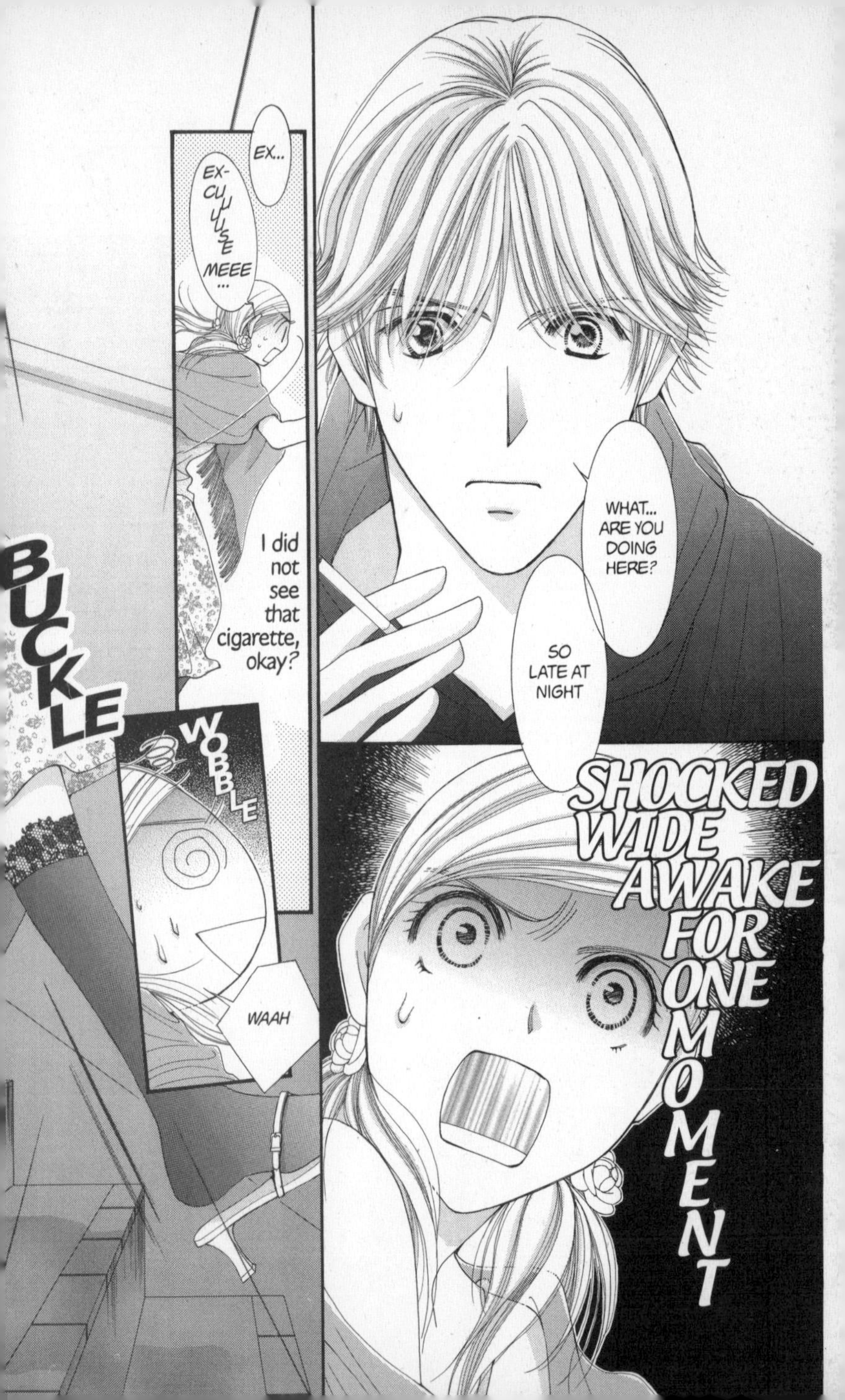
WHAT... ARE YOU DOING HERE?
SO LATE AT NIGHT
EX...
EX-CUUUUSE MEEE...
I did not see that cigarette, okay?
SHOCKED WIDE AWAKE FOR ONE MOMENT
BUCKLE
WOBBLE
WAAH

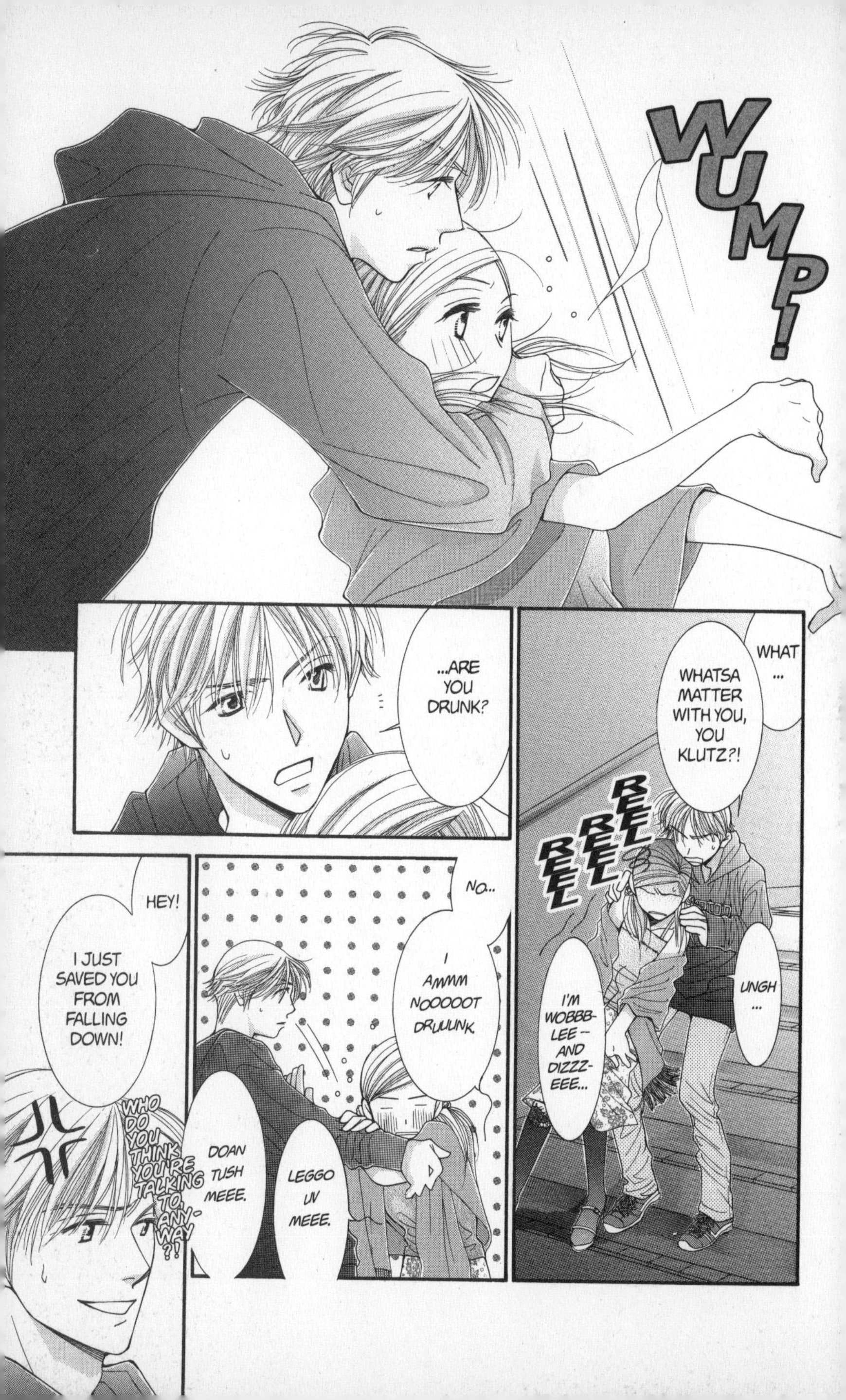
WUMP!
WHAT...
WHATSA MATTER WITH YOU, YOU KLUTZ?!
REEL REEL REEL
UNGH...
I'M WOBBB-LEE--AND DIZZZ-EEE...
...ARE YOU DRUNK?
NO...
I AMMM NOOOOOT DRUUUNK.
LEGGO UV MEEE.
DOAN TUSH MEEE.
HEY!
I JUST SAVED YOU FROM FALLING DOWN!
WHO DO YOU THINK YOU'RE TALKING TO, ANYWAY?!

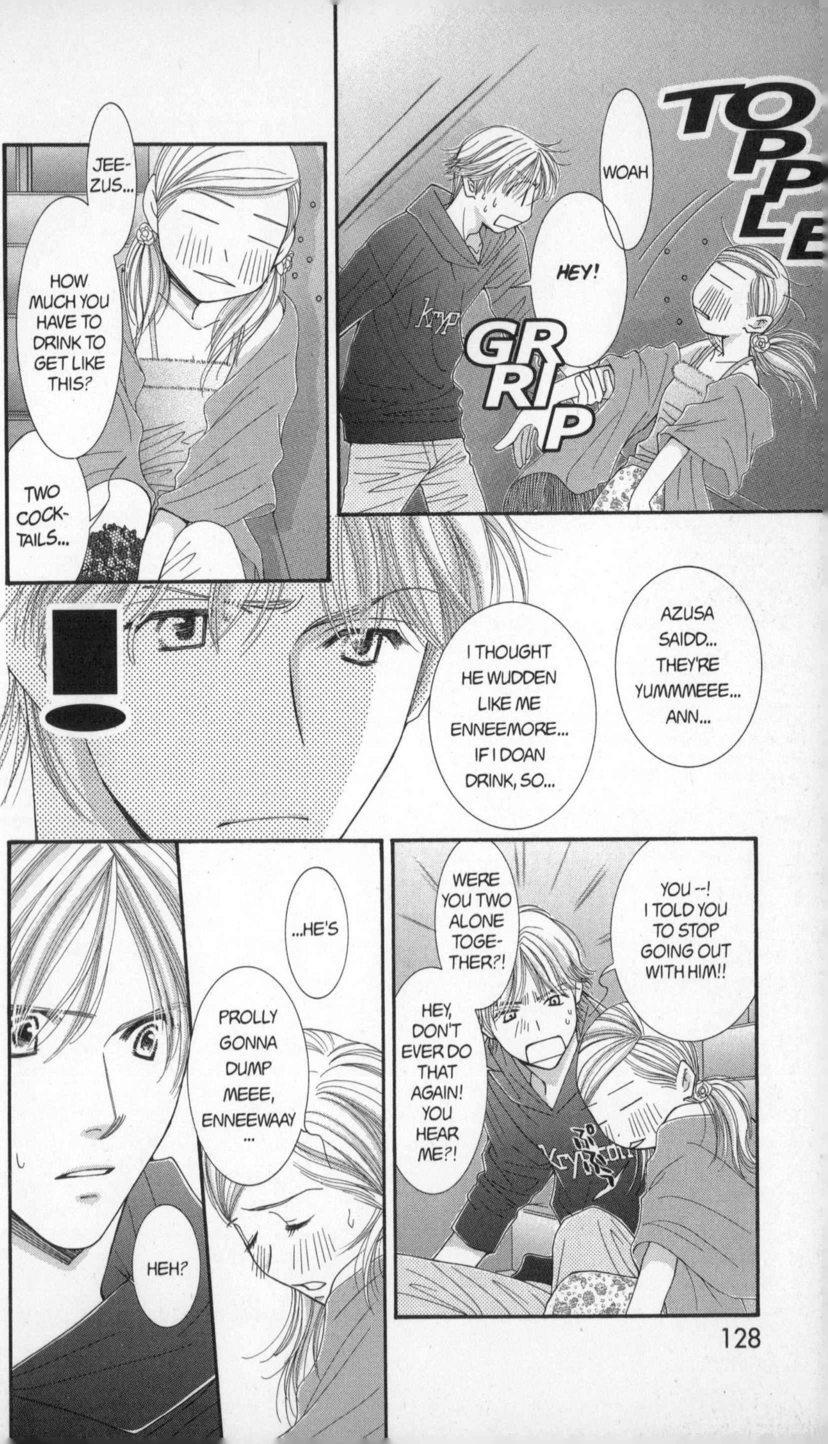
TOPPLE
WOAH
HEY!
GRRIP
JEE-ZUS...
HOW MUCH YOU HAVE TO DRINK TO GET LIKE THIS?
TWO COCK-TAILS...
AZUSA SAIDD... THEY'RE YUMMMEEE... ANN...
I THOUGHT HE WUDDEN LIKE ME ENNEEMORE... IF I DOAN DRINK, SO...
!
YOU --! I TOLD YOU TO STOP GOING OUT WITH HIM!!
WERE YOU TWO ALONE TOGE-THER?!
HEY, DON'T EVER DO THAT AGAIN! YOU HEAR ME?!
...HE'S
PROLLY GONNA DUMP MEEE, ENNEEWAAY ...
HEH?

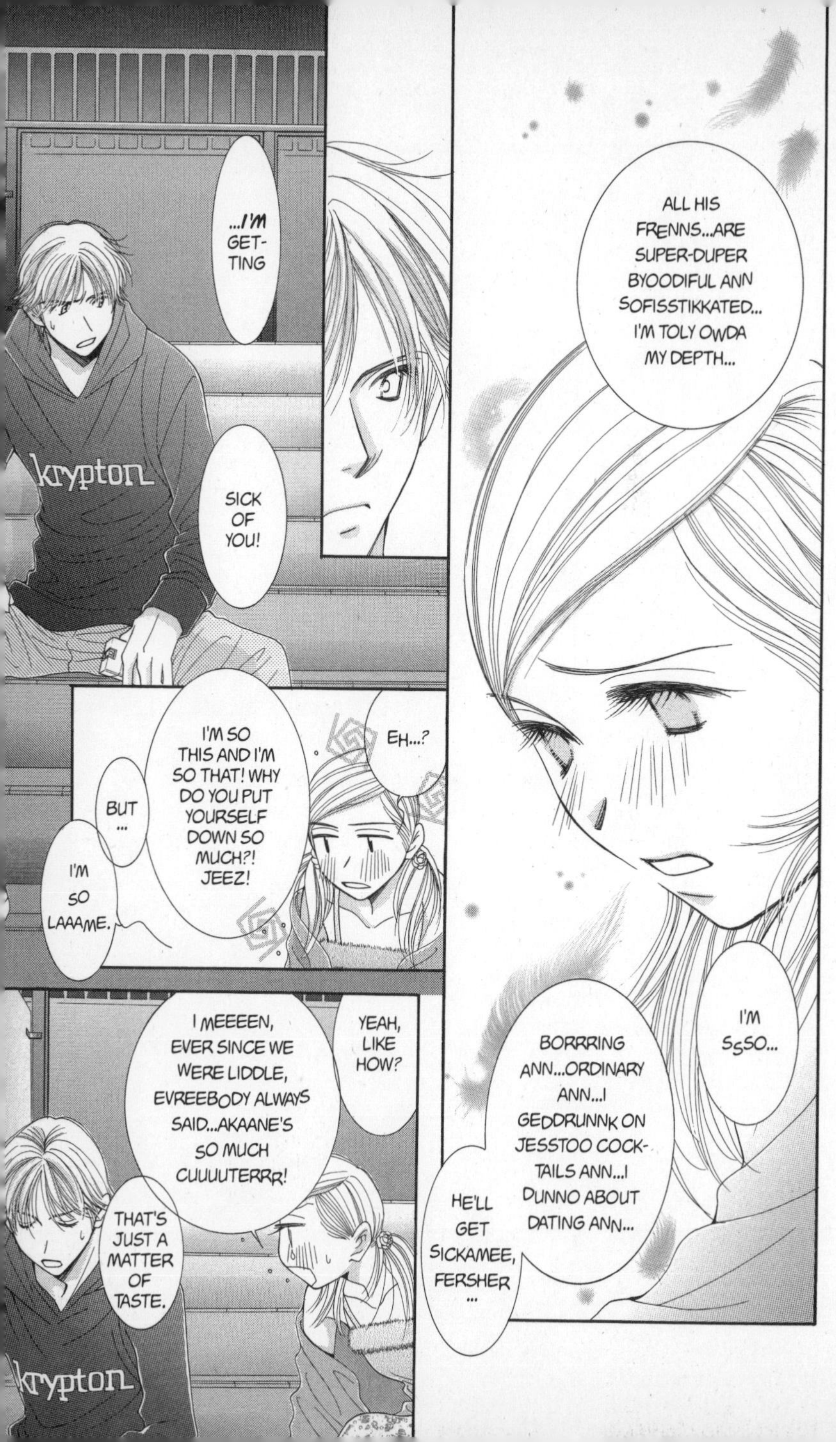
ALL HIS FRENNS...ARE SUPER-DUPER BYOODIFUL ANN SOFISSTIKKATED... I'M TOLY OWDA MY DEPTH...
I'M SSSO...
BORRRING ANN...ORDINARY ANN...I GEDDRUNNK ON JESSTOO COCK-TAILS ANN...I DUNNO ABOUT DATING ANN...
HE'LL GET SICKAMEE, FERSHER ...
...I'M GET-TING
SICK OF YOU!
EH...?
I'M SO THIS AND I'M SO THAT! WHY DO YOU PUT YOURSELF DOWN SO MUCH?! JEEZ!
BUT ...
I'M SO LAAAME.
YEAH, LIKE HOW?
I MEEEEN, EVER SINCE WE WERE LIDDLE, EVREEBODY ALWAYS SAID...AKAANE'S SO MUCH CUUUUTERRR!
THAT'S JUST A MATTER OF TASTE.

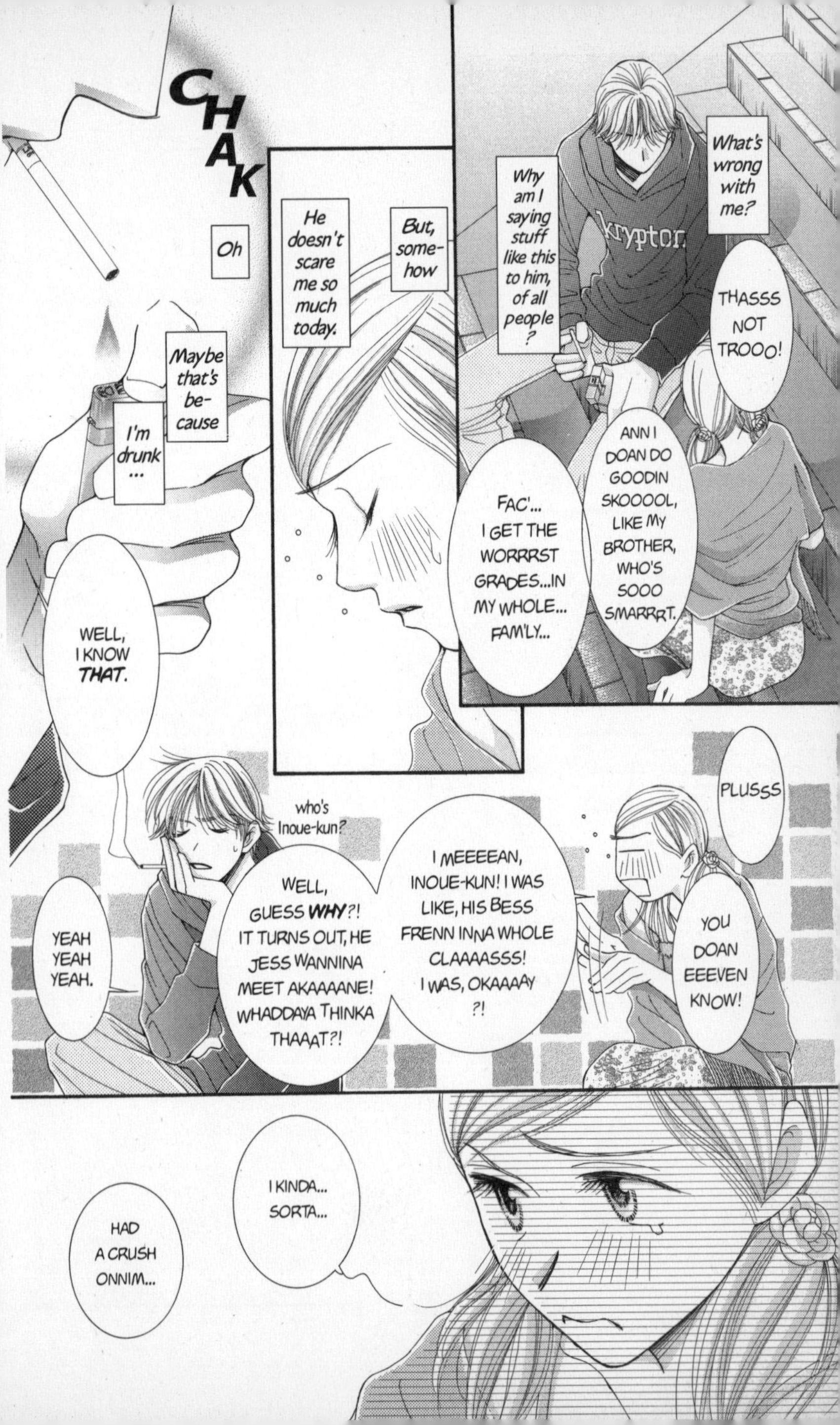
What's wrong with me?
Why am I saying stuff like this to him, of all people?
THASSS NOT TROOO!
ANN I DOAN DO GOODIN SKOOOOL, LIKE MY BROTHER, WHO'S SOOO SMARRRT.
FAC'... I GET THE WORRRST GRADES...IN MY WHOLE... FAM'LY...
But, some-how
He doesn't scare me so much today.
CHAK
Oh
Maybe that's be-cause
I'm drunk...
WELL, I KNOW THAT.
PLUSSS
YOU DOAN EEEVEN KNOW!
I MEEEEAN, INOUE-KUN! I WAS LIKE, HIS BESS FRENN INNA WHOLE CLAAAASSS! I WAS, OKAAAAY ?!
who's Inoue-kun?
WELL, GUESS WHY?! IT TURNS OUT, HE JESS WANNINA MEET AKAAAANE! WHADDAYA THINKA THAAAT?!
YEAH YEAH YEAH.
I KINDA... SORTA...
HAD A CRUSH ONNIM...

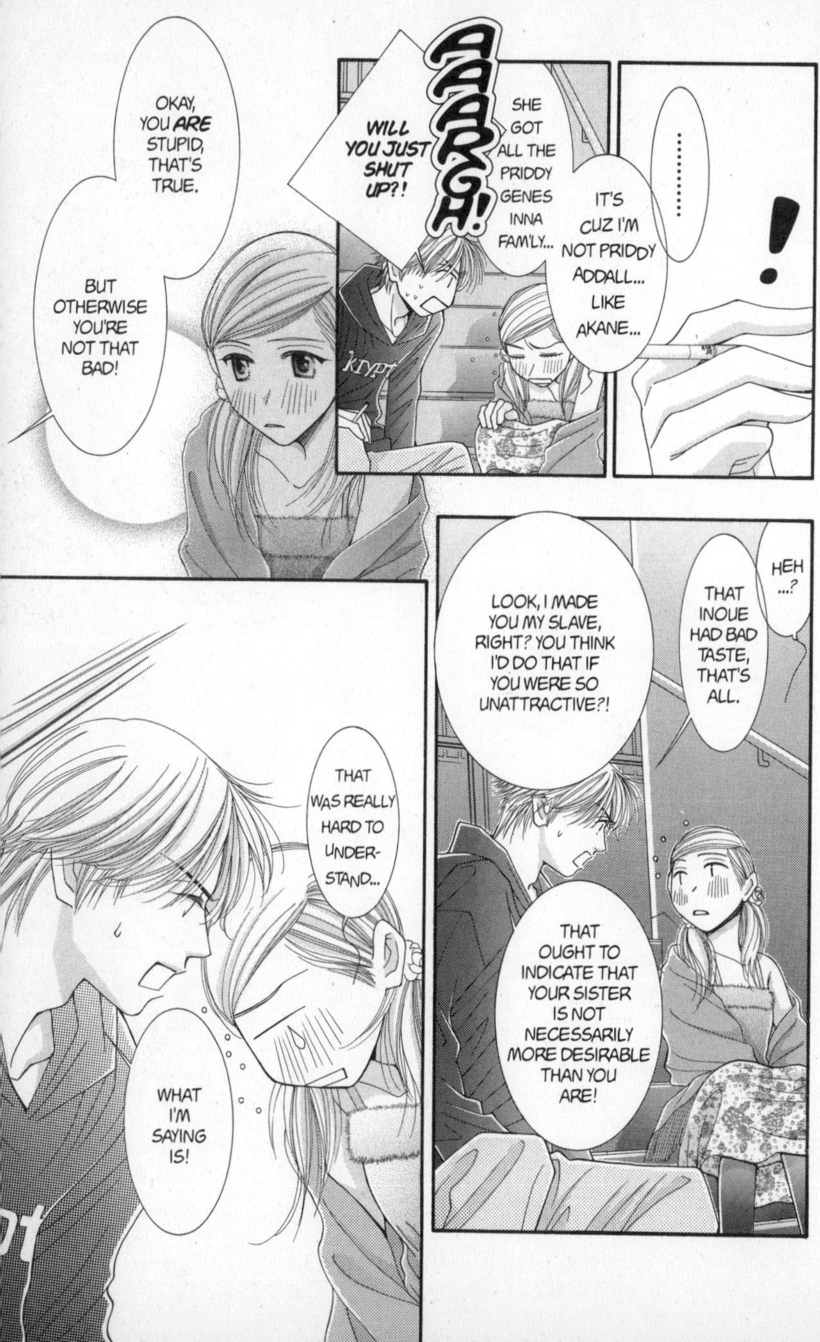
!
......
IT'S CUZ I'M NOT PRIDDY ADDALL... LIKE AKANE...
SHE GOT ALL THE PRIDDY GENES INNA FAM'LY...
AAARGH!
WILL YOU JUST SHUT UP?!
OKAY, YOU ARE STUPID, THAT'S TRUE.
BUT OTHERWISE YOU'RE NOT THAT BAD!
HEH...?
THAT INOUE HAD BAD TASTE, THAT'S ALL.
LOOK, I MADE YOU MY SLAVE, RIGHT? YOU THINK I'D DO THAT IF YOU WERE SO UNATTRACTIVE?!
THAT OUGHT TO INDICATE THAT YOUR SISTER IS NOT NECESSARILY MORE DESIRABLE THAN YOU ARE!
THAT WAS REALLY HARD TO UNDER-STAND...
WHAT I'M SAYING IS!

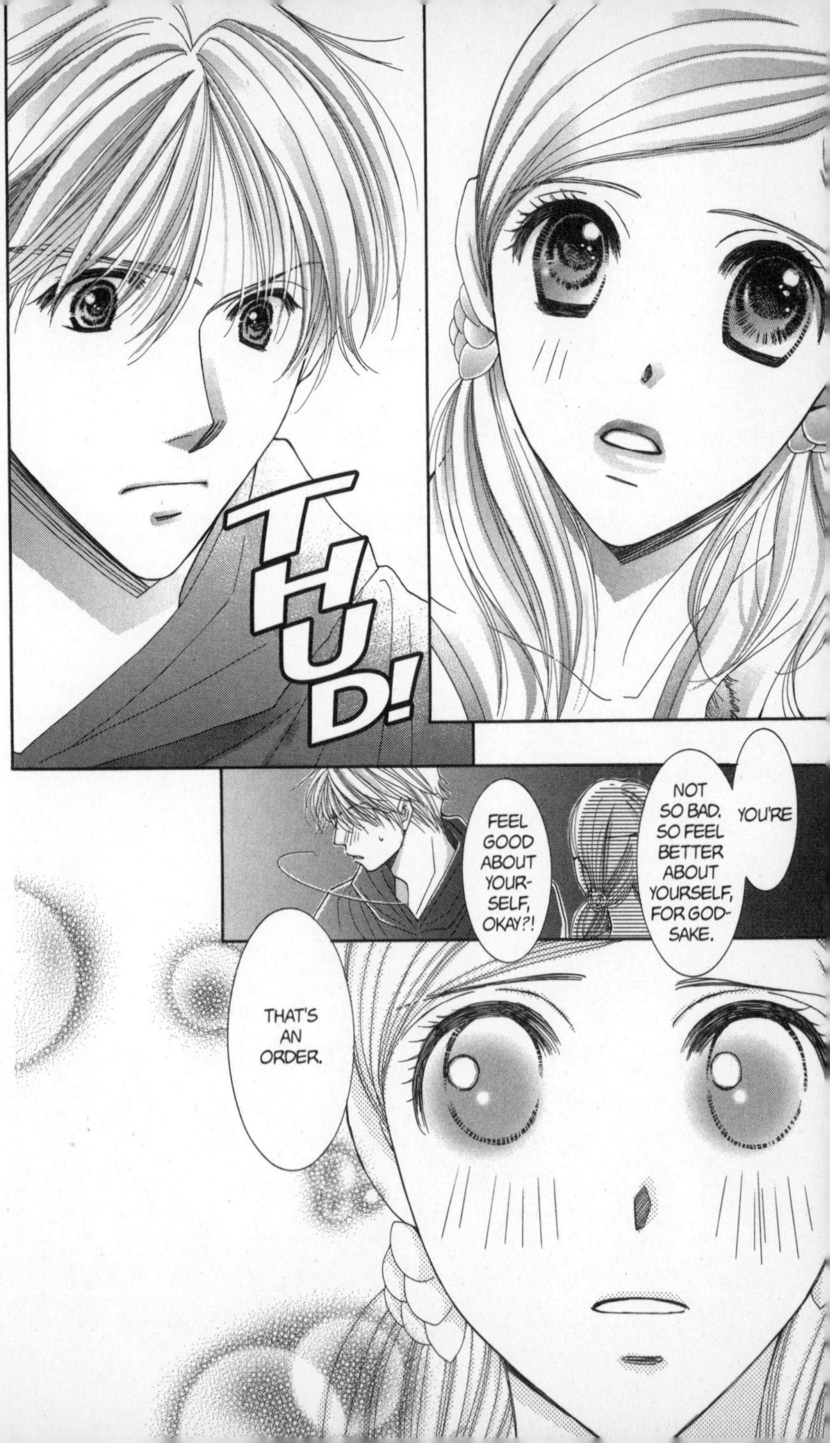
THUD!
YOU'RE
NOT SO BAD. SO FEEL BETTER ABOUT YOURSELF, FOR GOD-SAKE.
FEEL GOOD ABOUT YOUR-SELF, OKAY?!
THAT'S AN ORDER.

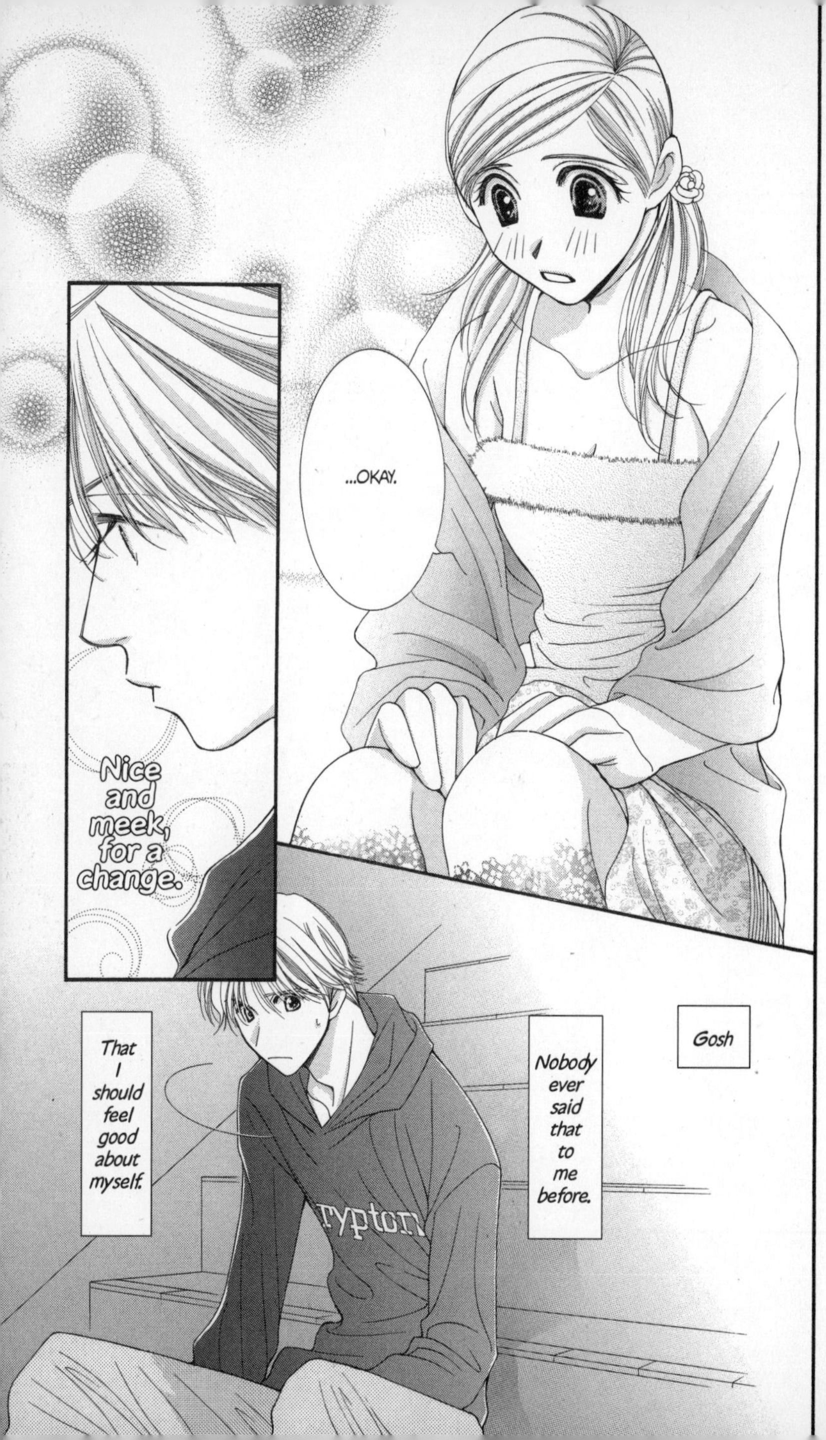
...OKAY.
Nice and meek, for a change.
Gosh
Nobody ever said that to me before.
That I should feel good about myself.

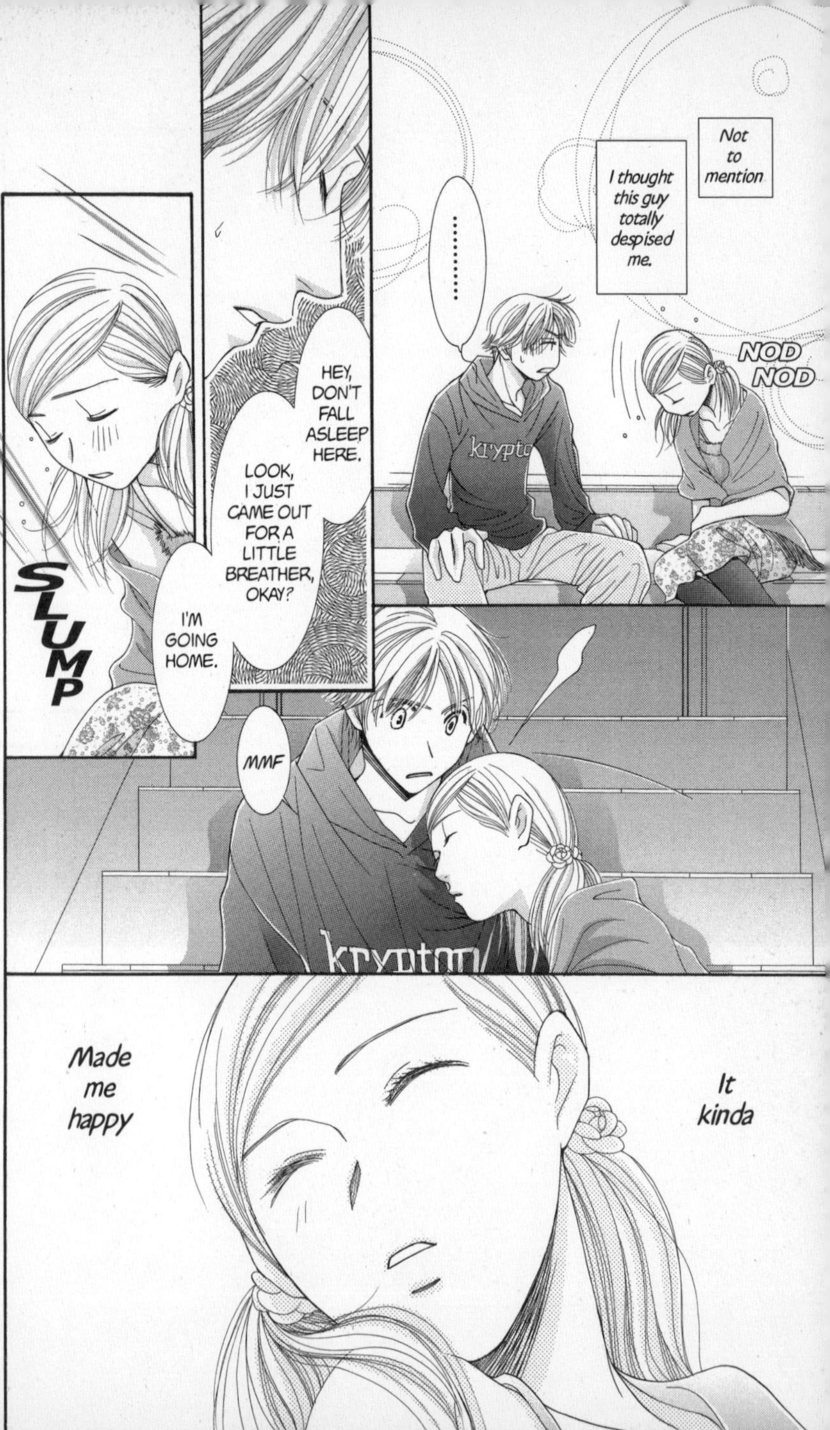

Not to mention
I thought this guy totally despised me.
......
NOD NOD
HEY, DON'T FALL ASLEEP HERE.
LOOK, I JUST CAME OUT FOR A LITTLE BREATHER, OKAY?
I'M GOING HOME.
SLUMP
MMF
It kinda
Made me happy

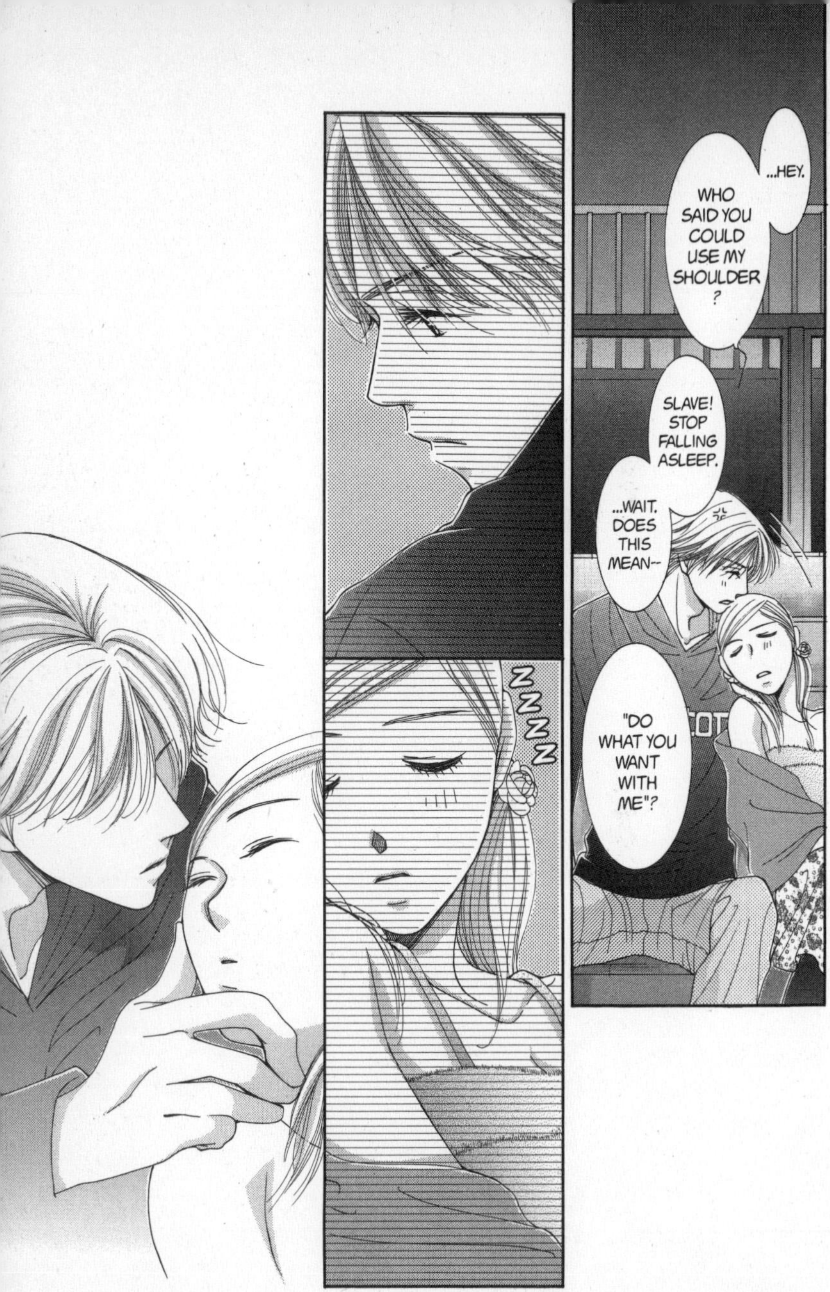
...HEY.
WHO SAID YOU COULD USE MY SHOULDER?
SLAVE! STOP FALLING ASLEEP.
...WAIT. DOES THIS MEAN--
"DO WHAT YOU WANT WITH ME"?
ZZZZ

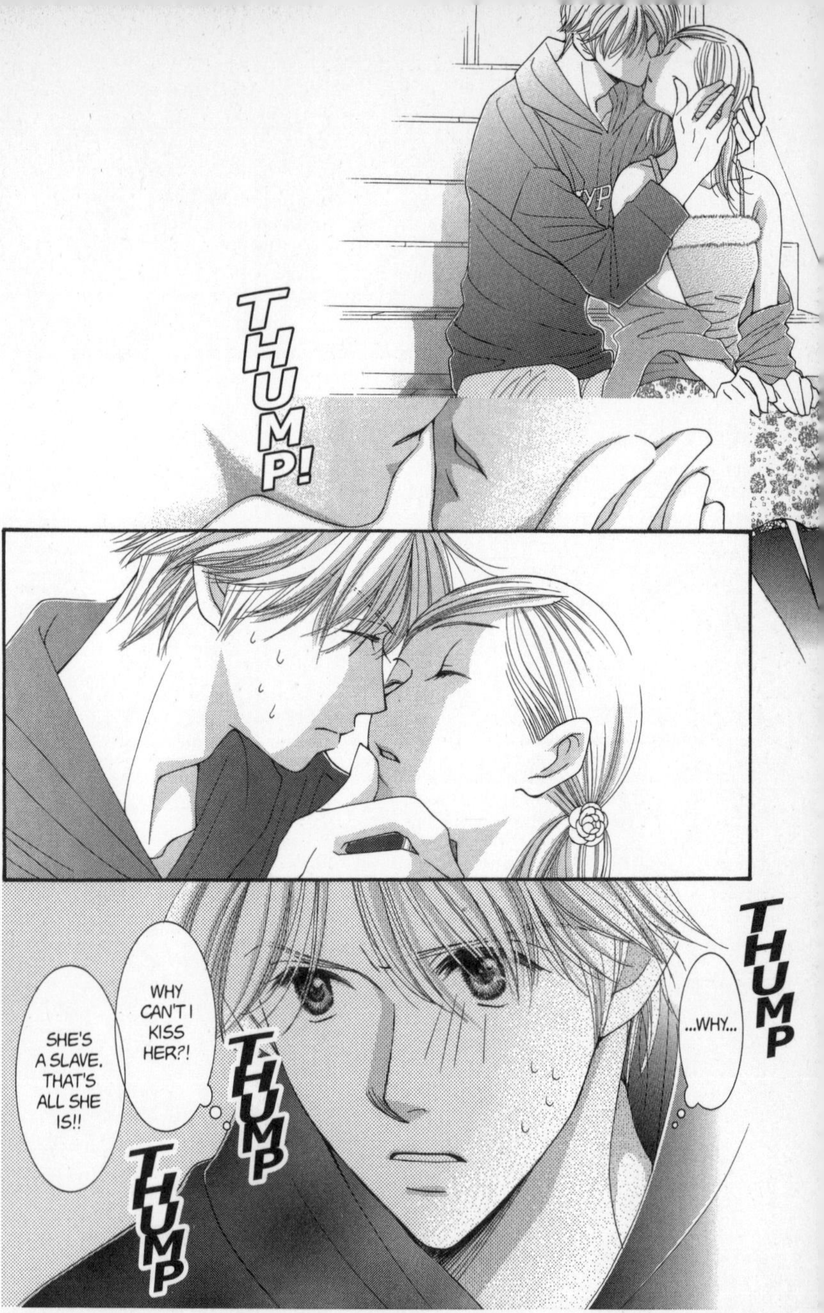
THUMP!
THUMP
...WHY...
THUMP
WHY CAN'T I KISS HER?!
THUMP
SHE'S A SLAVE. THAT'S ALL SHE IS!!

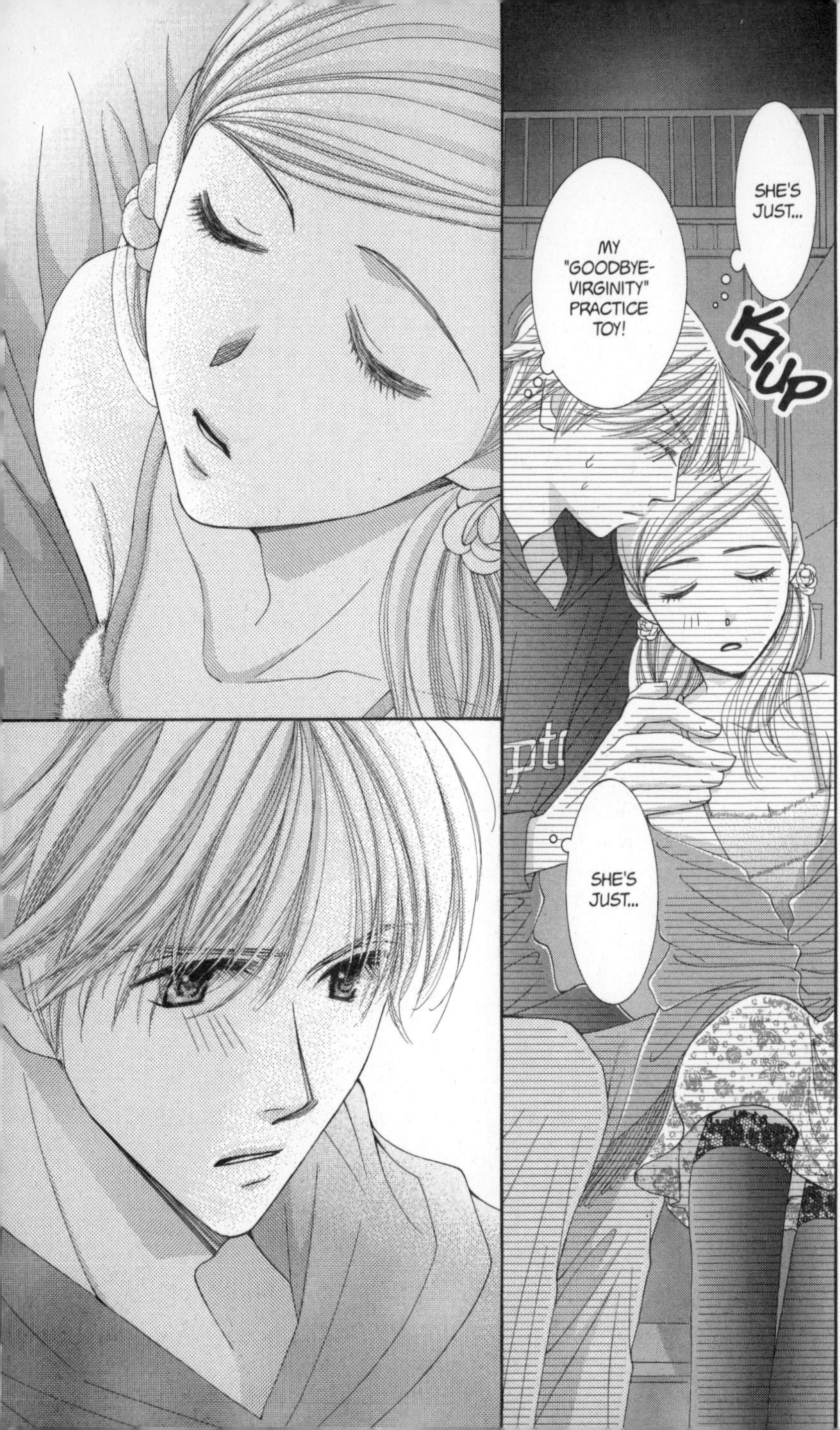
SHE'S JUST...
KAUP
MY "GOODBYE-VIRGINITY" PRACTICE TOY!
SHE'S JUST...

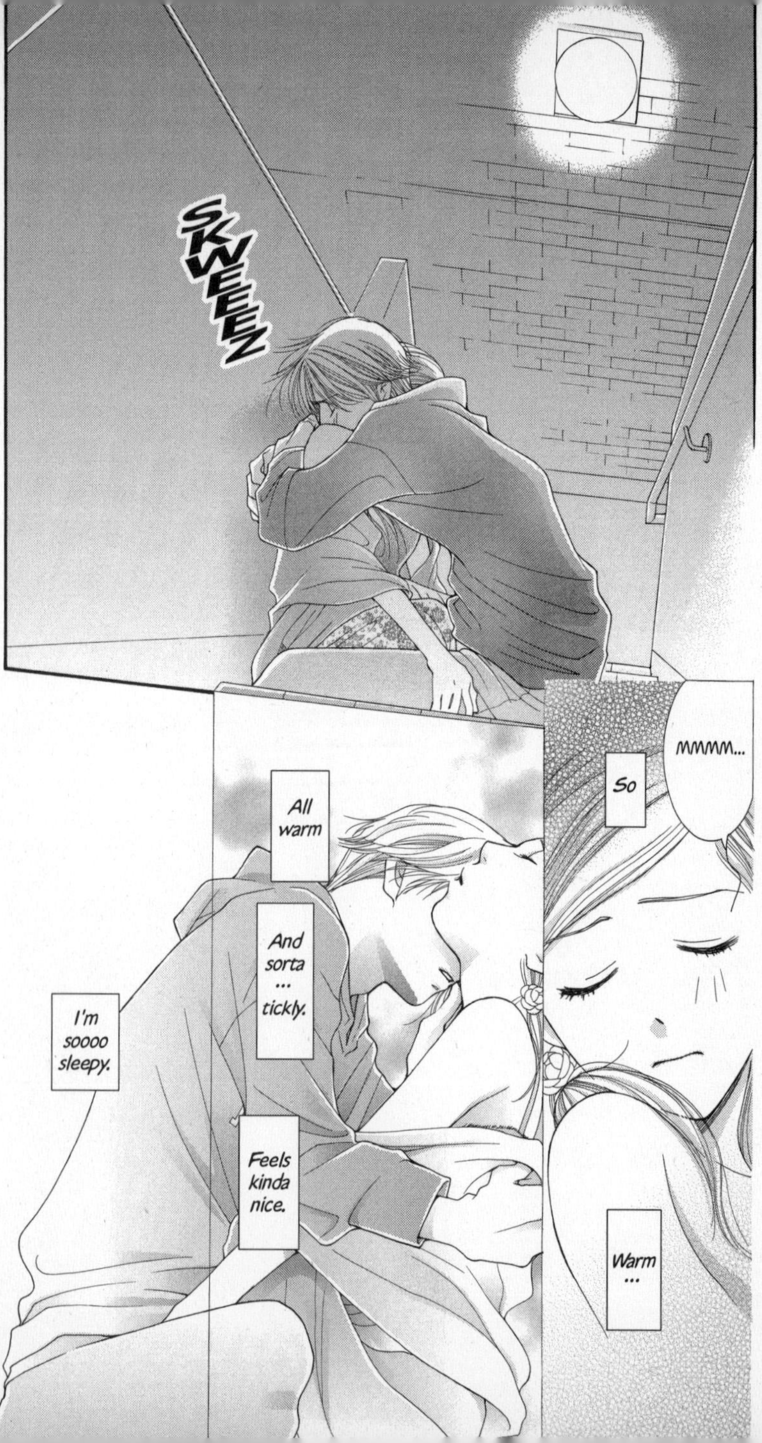
SKWEEEZ
MMMM...
So
Warm
...
All warm
And sorta ... tickly.
Feels kinda nice.
I'm soooo sleepy.

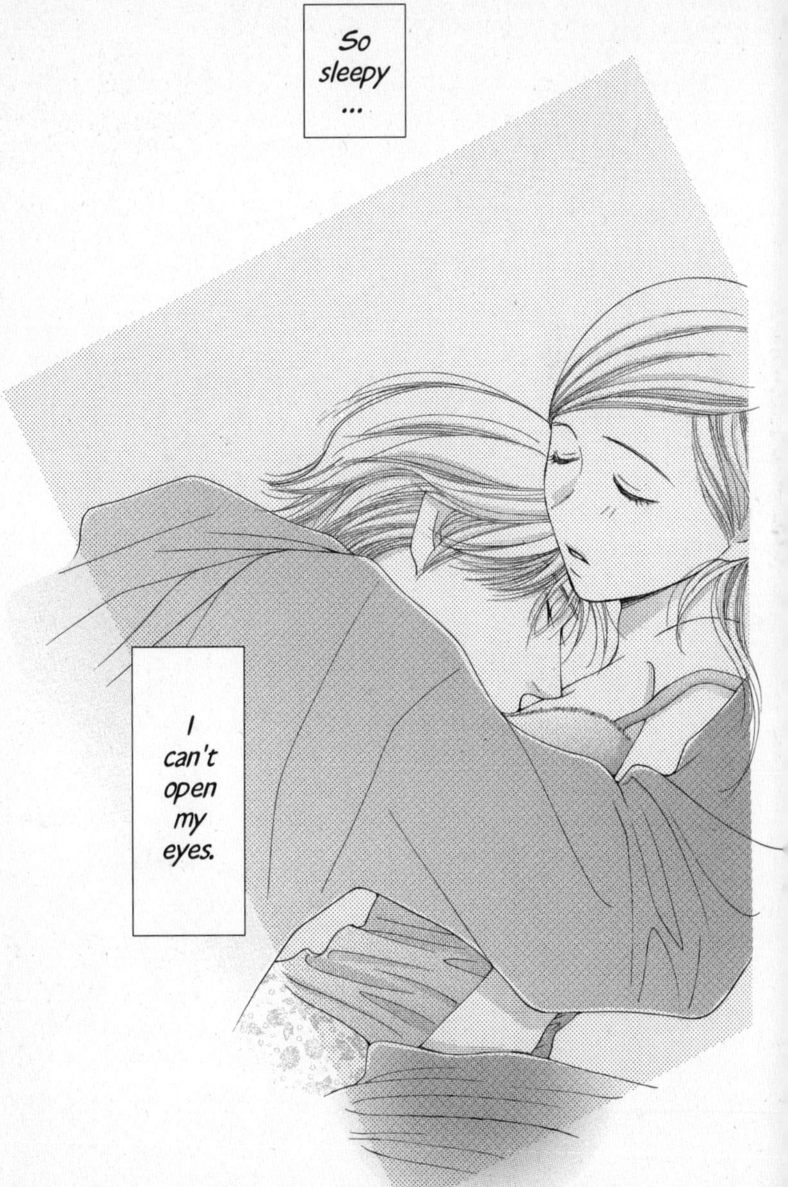
So sleepy ...
I can't open my eyes.

Chapter 9

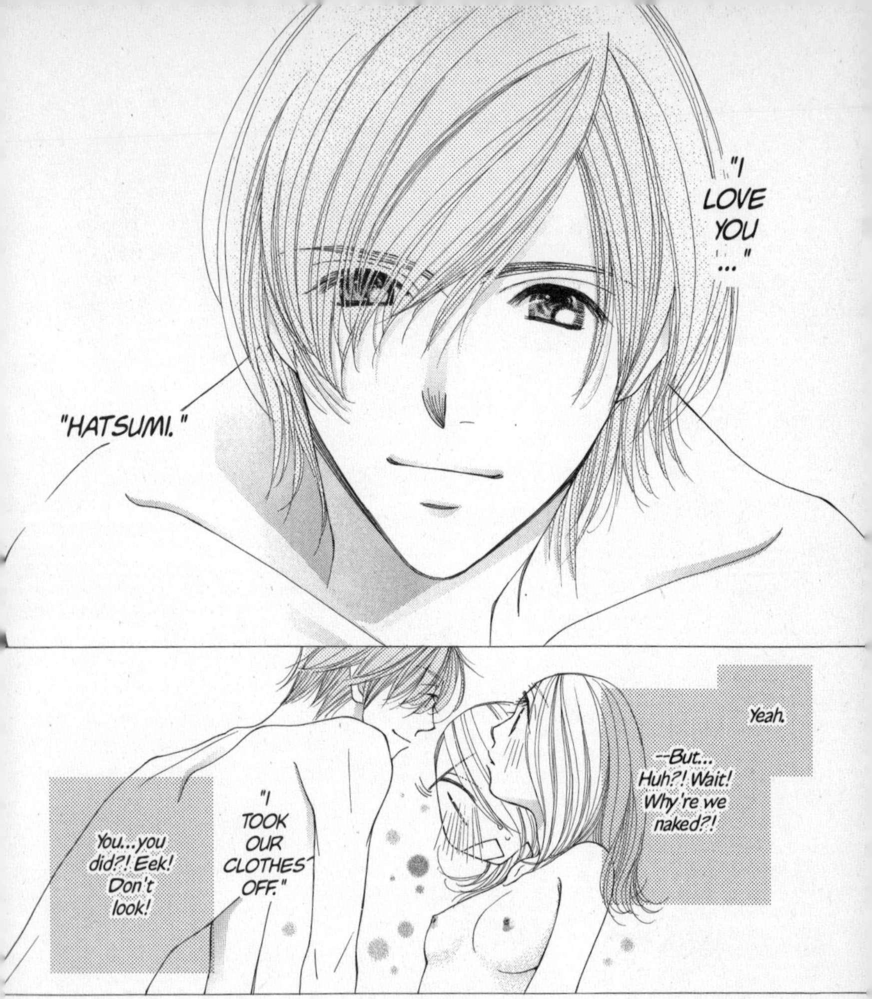
"I LOVE YOU..."
"HATSUMI."
Yeah.
--But... Huh?! Wait! Why're we naked?!
"I TOOK OUR CLOTHES OFF."
You...you did?! Eek! Don't look!

hot gimmick

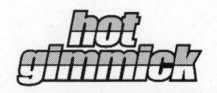

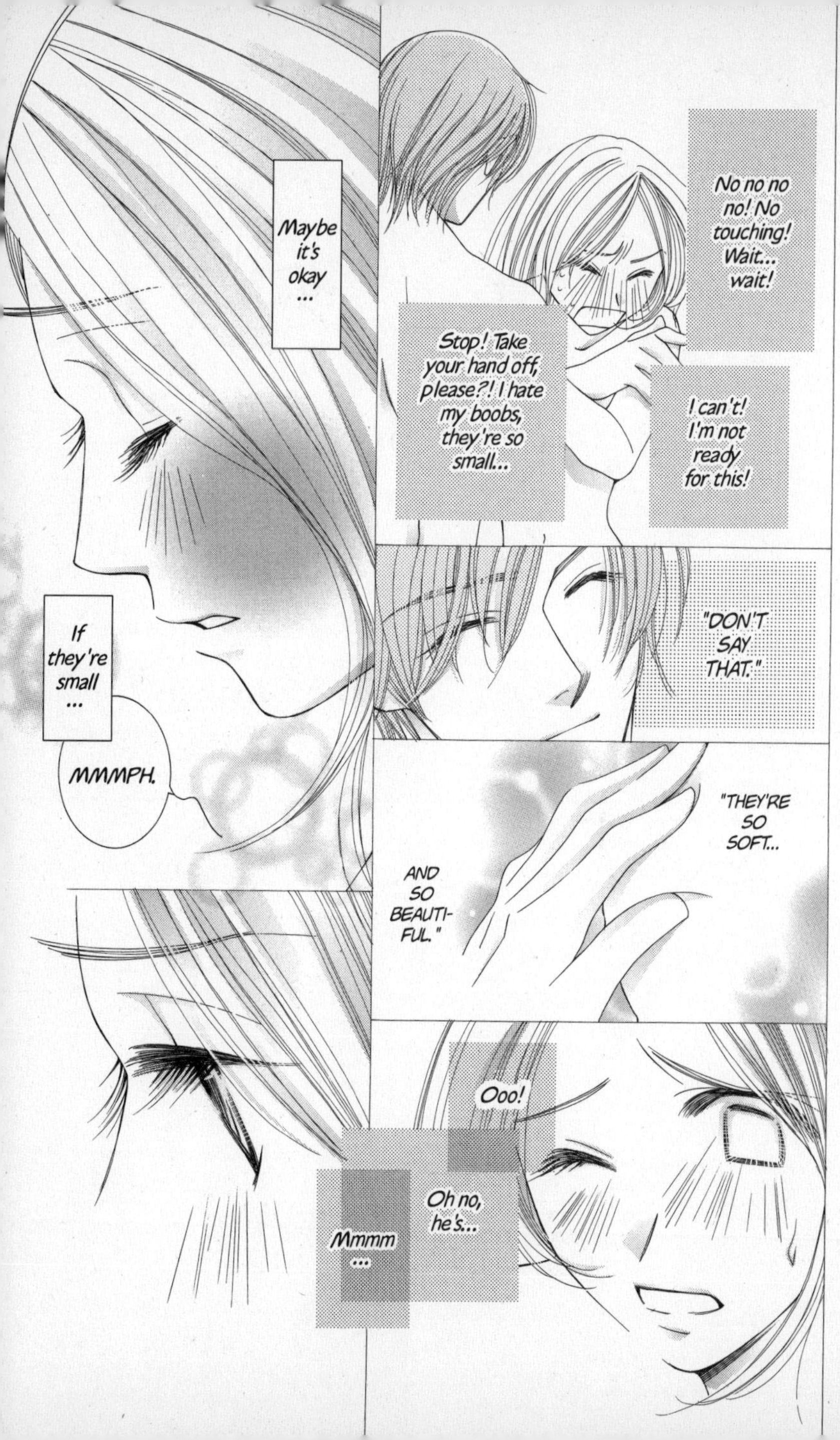
No no no no! No touching! Wait... wait!
Stop! Take your hand off, please?! I hate my boobs, they're so small...
I can't! I'm not ready for this!
"DON'T SAY THAT."
"THEY'RE SO SOFT...
AND SO BEAUTIFUL."
Maybe it's okay...
If they're small...
MMMPH.
Ooo!
Oh no, he's...
Mmmm...

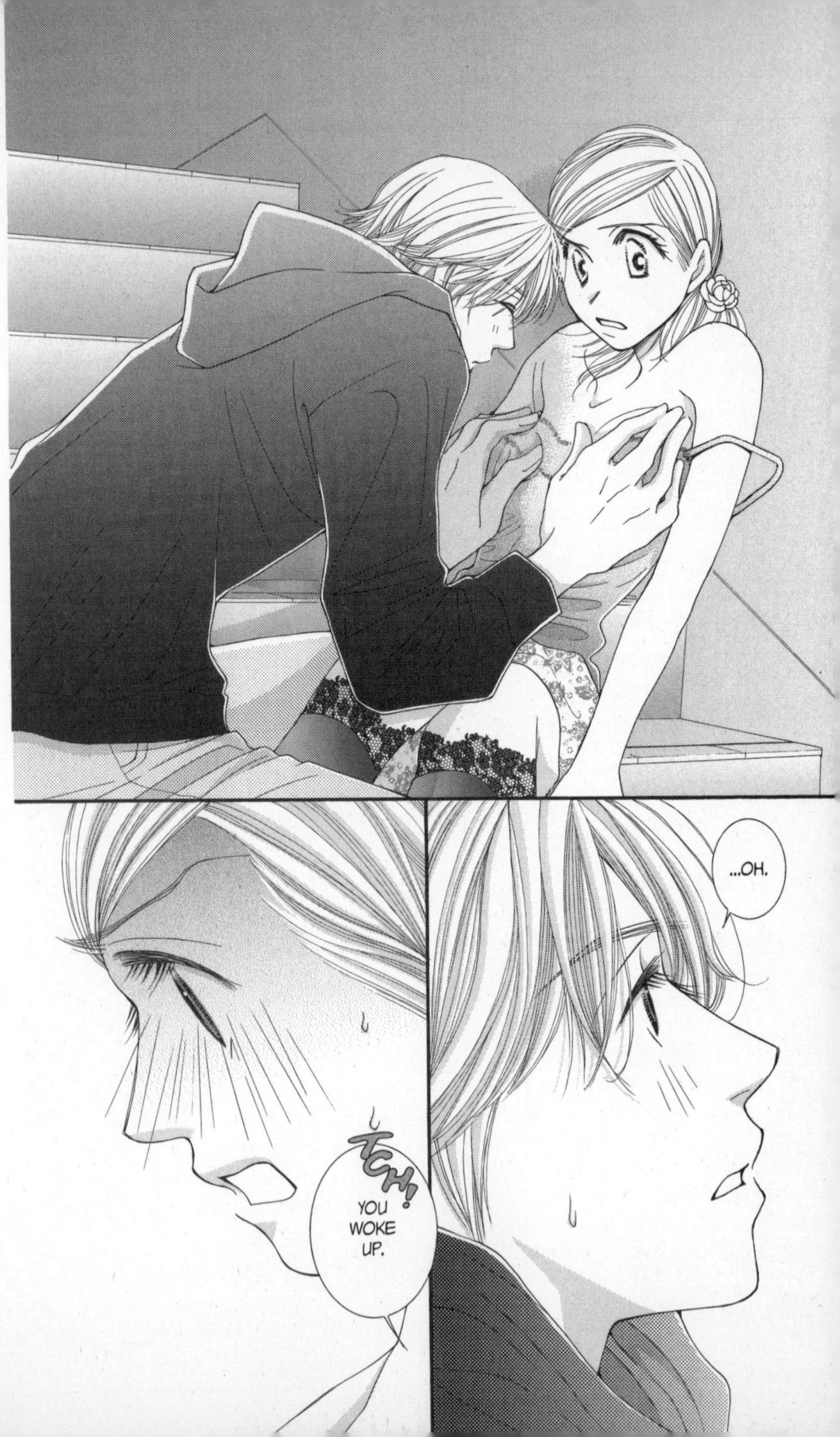
...OH.
TCH!
YOU WOKE UP.

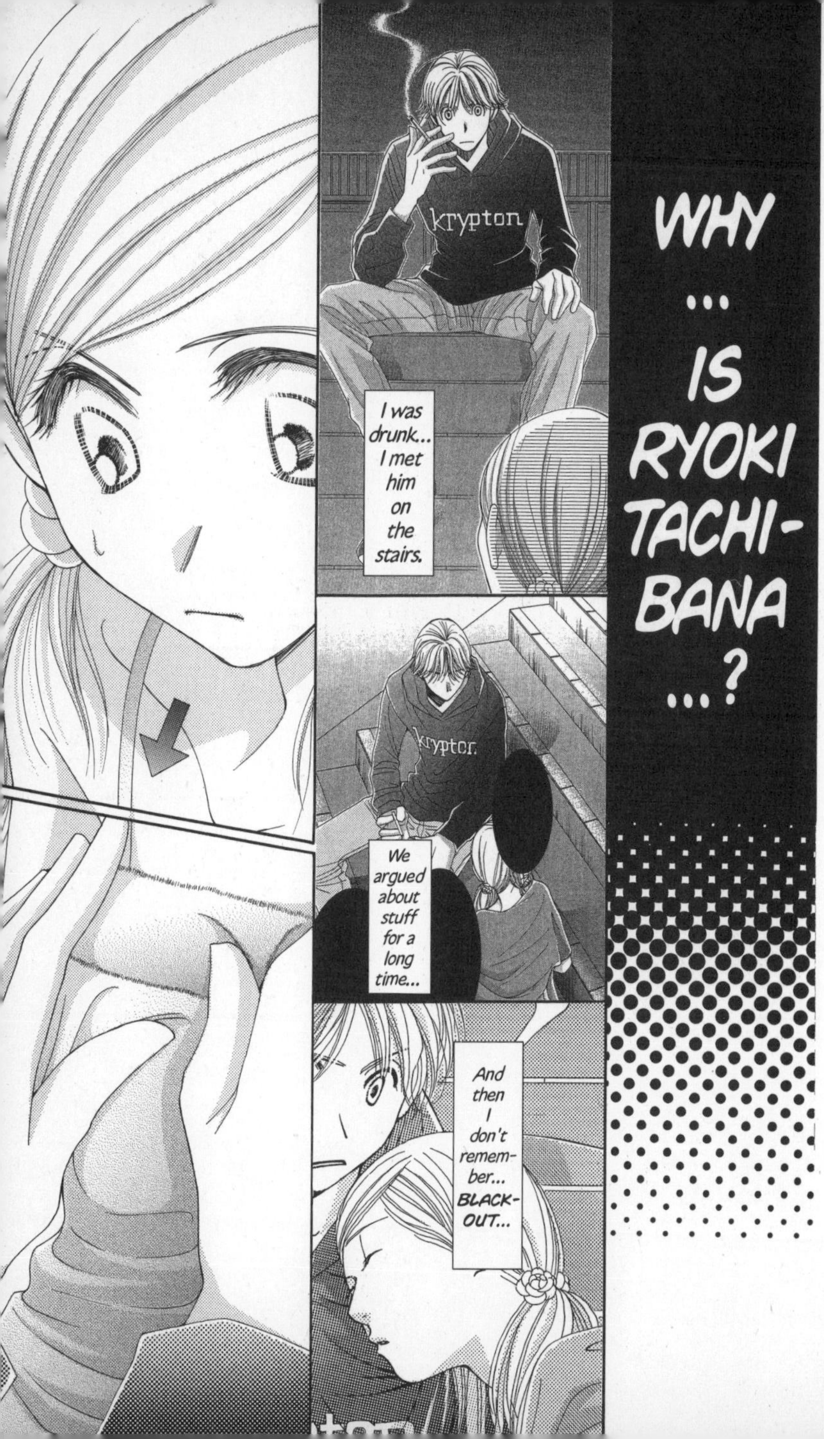
WHY ... IS RYOKI TACHI-BANA ...?
I was drunk... I met him on the stairs.
We argued about stuff for a long time...
And then I don't remem-ber... BLACK-OUT...

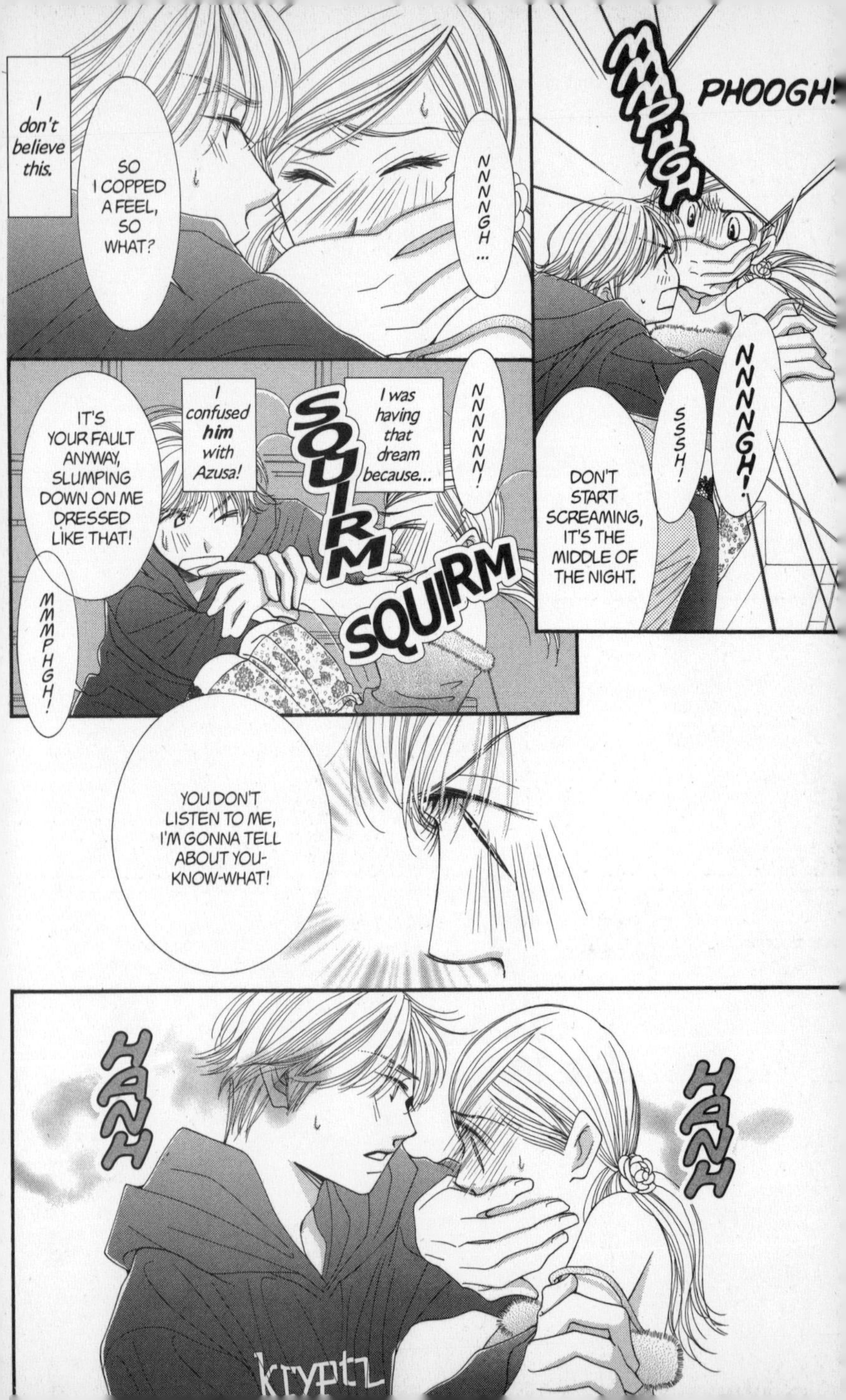

MMPHGH!
PHOOGH!
NNNNGH!
SSSH!
DON'T START SCREAMING, IT'S THE MIDDLE OF THE NIGHT.
NNNNGH...
SO I COPPED A FEEL, SO WHAT?
I don't believe this.
NNNNNN!
I was having that dream because...
SQUIRM
I confused **him** with Azusa!
SQUIRM
IT'S YOUR FAULT ANYWAY, SLUMPING DOWN ON ME DRESSED LIKE THAT!
MMMPHGH!
YOU DON'T LISTEN TO ME, I'M GONNA TELL ABOUT YOU-KNOW-WHAT!
HANH
HANH
kryptz

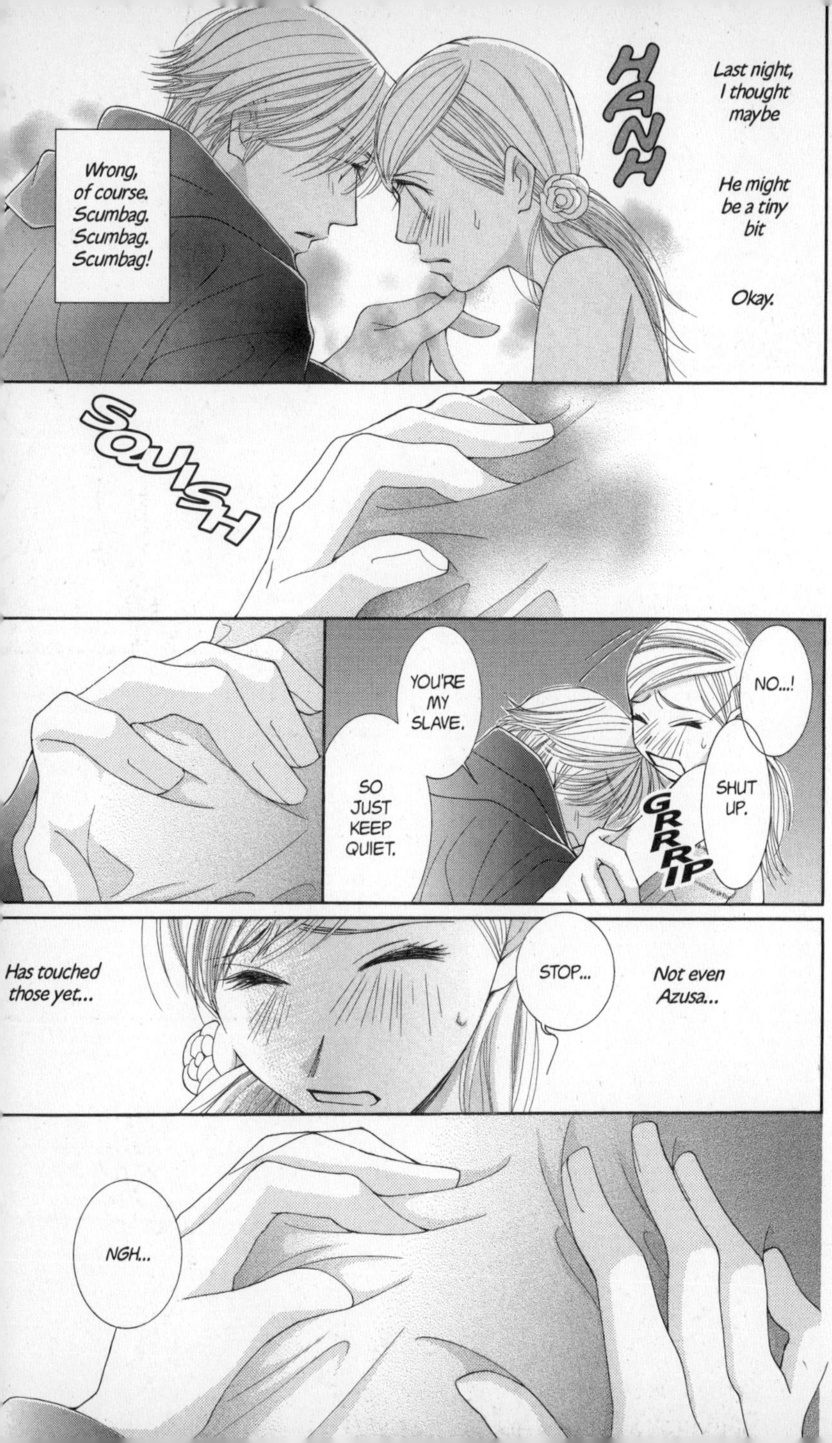
Last night, I thought maybe
He might be a tiny bit
Okay.
HANH
Wrong, of course. Scumbag. Scumbag. Scumbag!
SQUISH
NO...!
SHUT UP.
GRRRIP
YOU'RE MY SLAVE.
SO JUST KEEP QUIET.
Not even Azusa...
STOP...
Has touched those yet...
NGH...

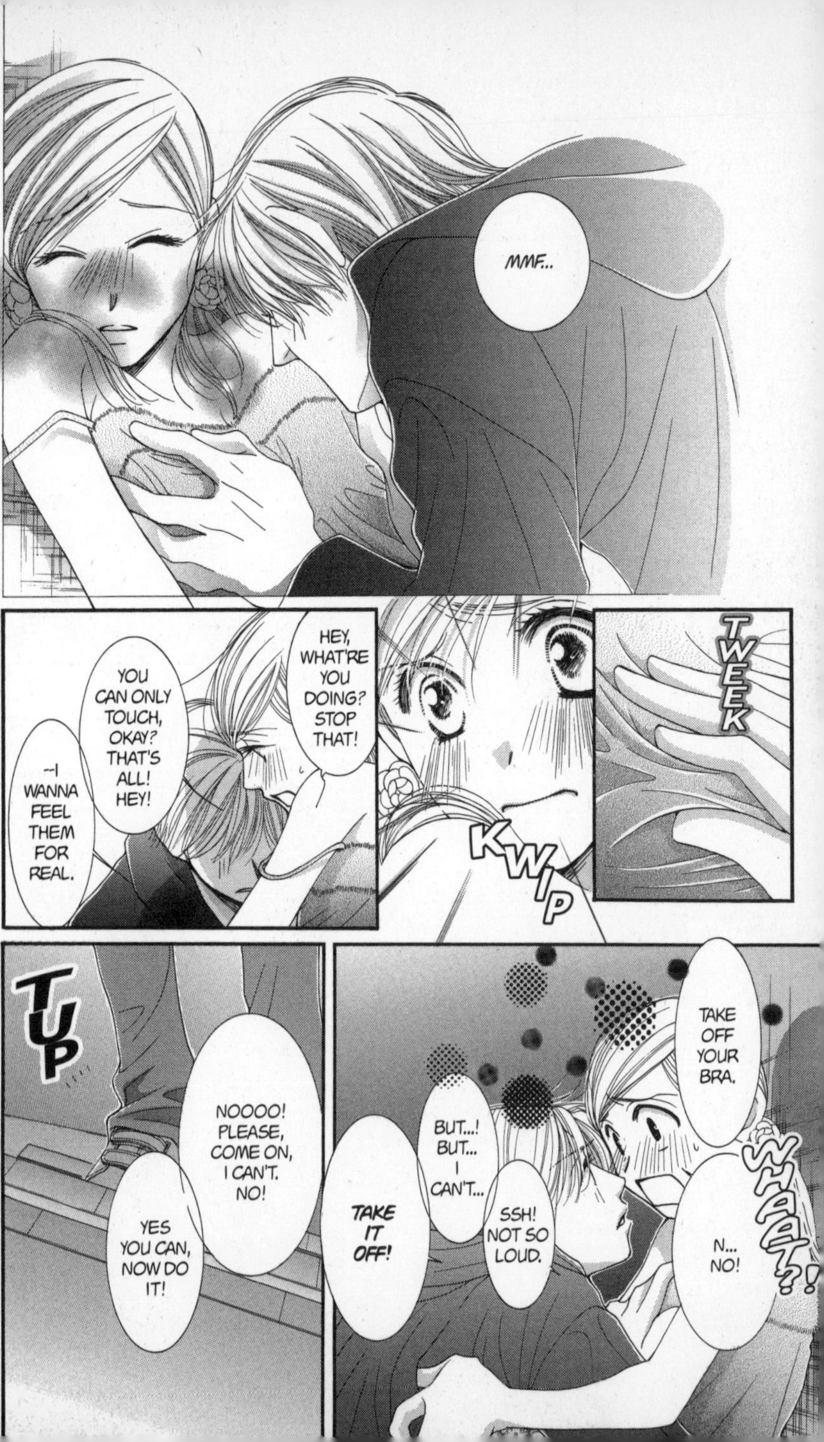

MMF...
TWEEK
KWIP
HEY, WHAT'RE YOU DOING? STOP THAT!
YOU CAN ONLY TOUCH, OKAY? THAT'S ALL! HEY!
--I WANNA FEEL THEM FOR REAL.
TAKE OFF YOUR BRA.
WHAT?!
N... NO!
SSH! NOT SO LOUD.
BUT...! BUT... I CAN'T...
TAKE IT OFF!
TUP
NOOOO! PLEASE, COME ON, I CAN'T. NO!
YES YOU CAN, NOW DO IT!

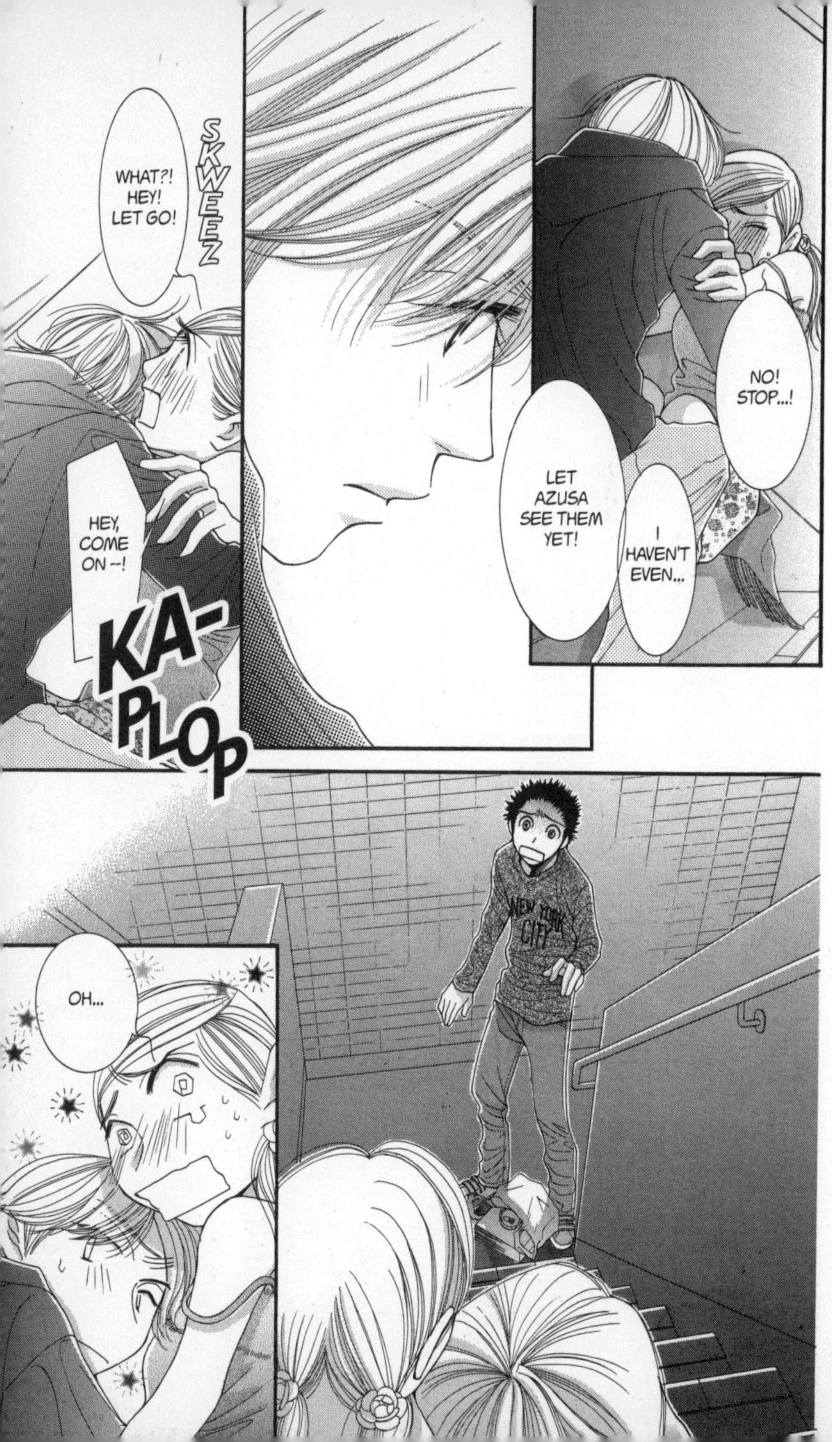
NO! STOP...!
I HAVEN'T EVEN...
LET AZUSA SEE THEM YET!
SKWEEZ
WHAT?! HEY! LET GO!
HEY, COME ON --!
KA-PLOP
OH...

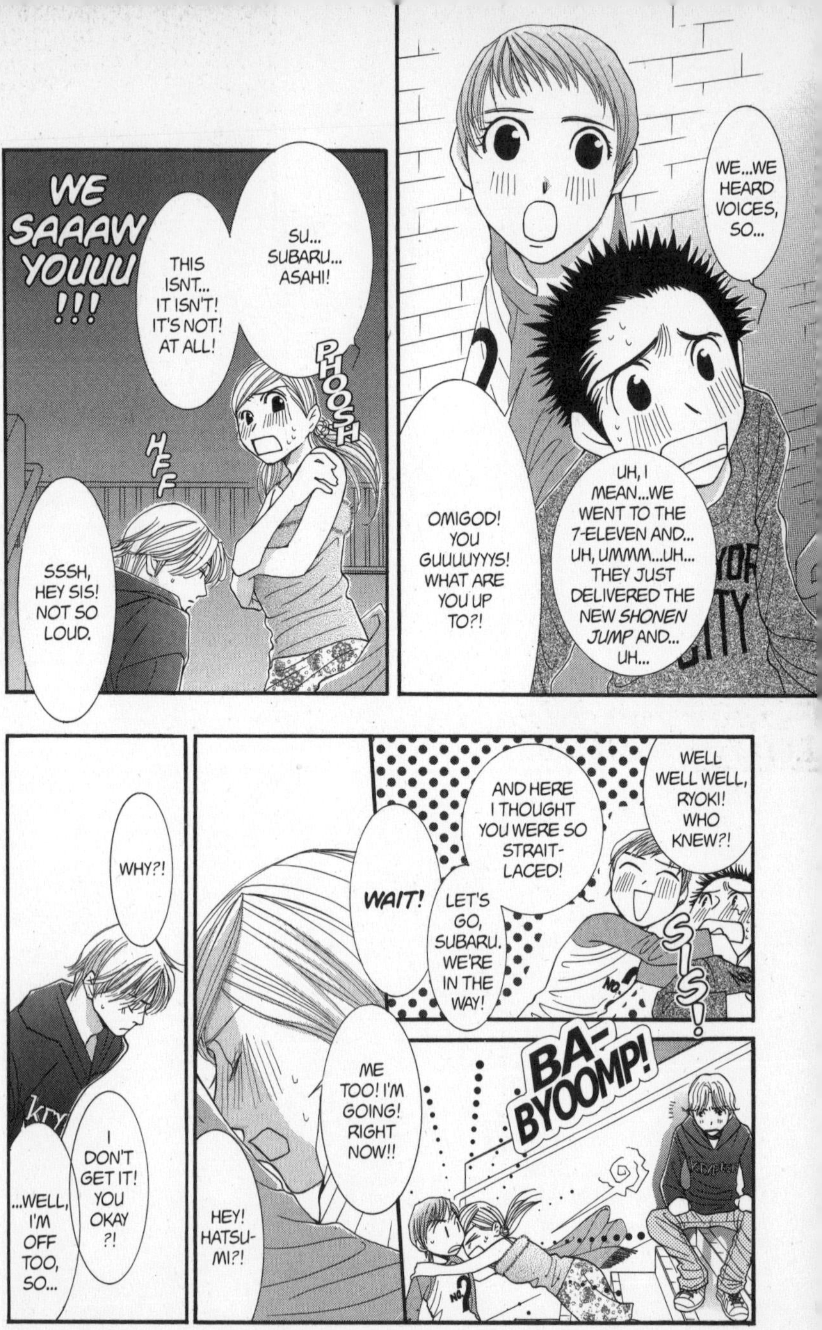
WE...WE HEARD VOICES, SO...
UH, I MEAN...WE WENT TO THE 7-ELEVEN AND... UH, UMMM...UH... THEY JUST DELIVERED THE NEW SHONEN JUMP AND... UH...
OMIGOD! YOU GUUUUYYYS! WHAT ARE YOU UP TO?!
SU... SUBARU... ASAHI!
THIS ISNT... IT ISN'T! IT'S NOT! AT ALL!
WE SAAAW YOUUU !!!
PHOOSH
HFF
SSSH, HEY SIS! NOT SO LOUD.
WELL WELL WELL, RYOKI! WHO KNEW?!
AND HERE I THOUGHT YOU WERE SO STRAIT-LACED!
SIS!
LET'S GO, SUBARU. WE'RE IN THE WAY!
WAIT!
ME TOO! I'M GOING! RIGHT NOW!!
BA-BYOOMP!
HEY! HATSU-MI?!
WHY?!
I DON'T GET IT! YOU OKAY ?!
...WELL, I'M OFF TOO, SO...

hotgimmick

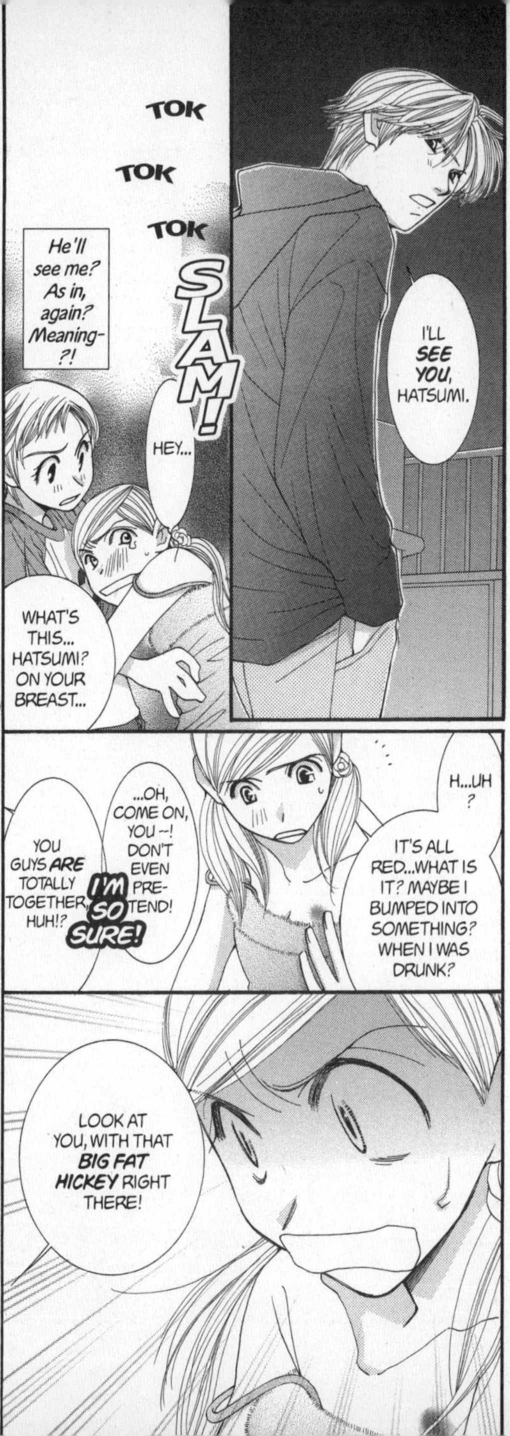

I'LL SEE YOU, HATSUMI.
TOK
TOK
TOK
SLAM!
He'll see me? As in, again? Meaning-?!
HEY...
WHAT'S THIS... HATSUMI? ON YOUR BREAST...
H...UH?
IT'S ALL RED...WHAT IS IT? MAYBE I BUMPED INTO SOMETHING? WHEN I WAS DRUNK?
...OH, COME ON, YOU --! DON'T EVEN PRE-TEND!
I'M SO SURE!
YOU GUYS ARE TOTALLY TOGETHER, HUH!?
LOOK AT YOU, WITH THAT BIG FAT HICKEY RIGHT THERE!

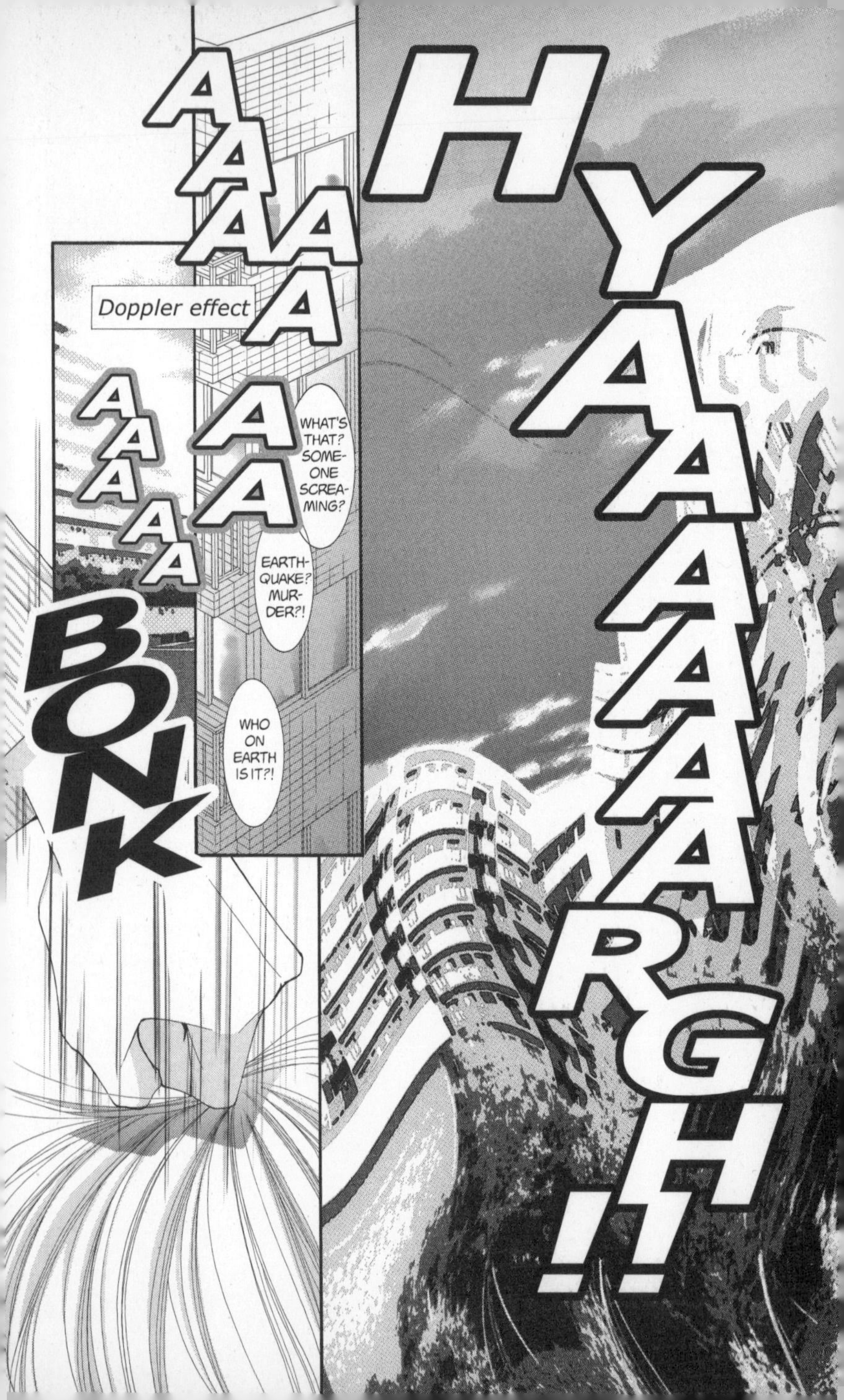
HYAAAAAARGH!!
AAAAAAA
Doppler effect
AAAAA
WHAT'S THAT? SOME-ONE SCREA-MING?
EARTH-QUAKE? MUR-DER?!
WHO ON EARTH IS IT?!
BONK

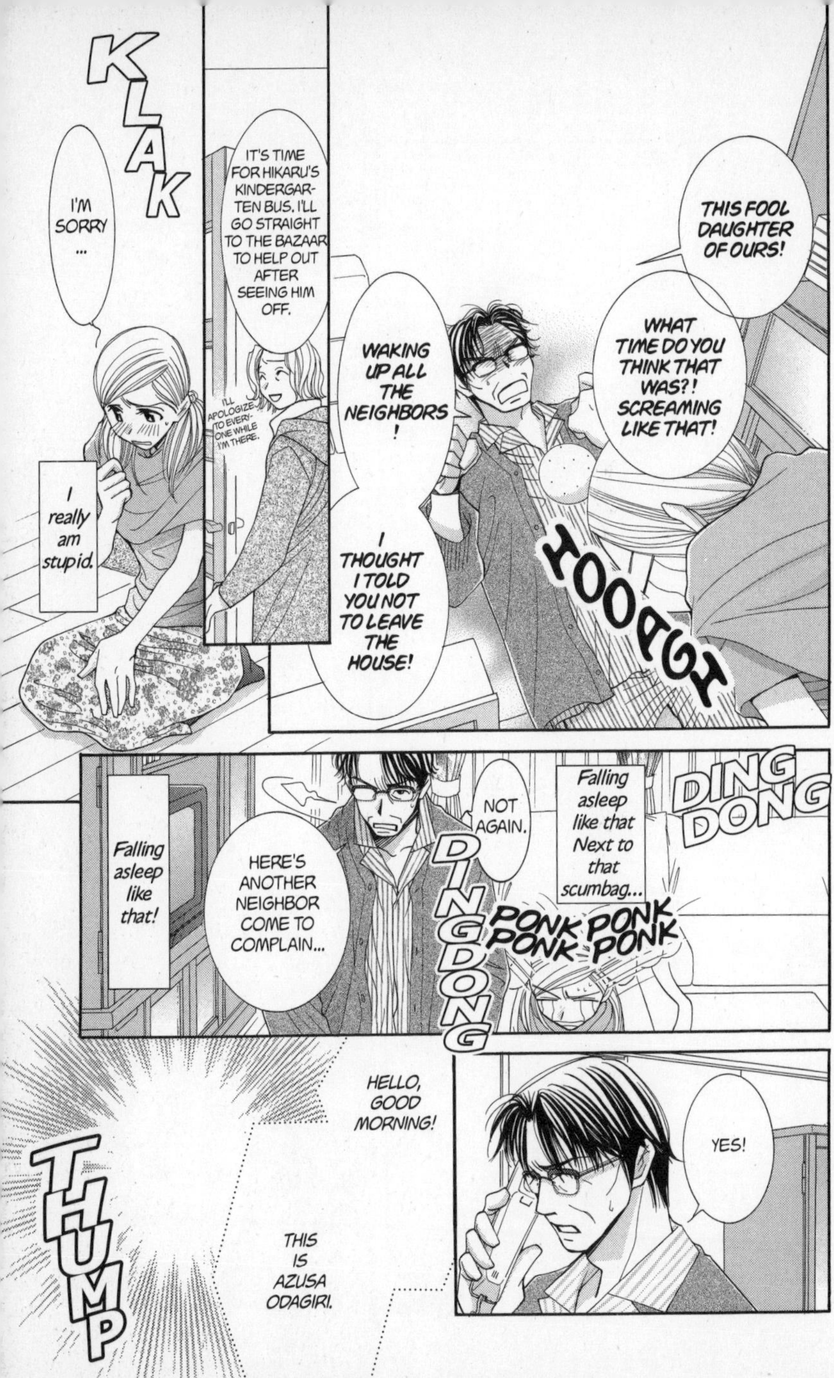
THIS FOOL DAUGHTER OF OURS!
WHAT TIME DO YOU THINK THAT WAS?! SCREAMING LIKE THAT!
WAKING UP ALL THE NEIGHBORS!
I THOUGHT I TOLD YOU NOT TO LEAVE THE HOUSE!
IT'S TIME FOR HIKARU'S KINDERGAR-TEN BUS. I'LL GO STRAIGHT TO THE BAZAAR TO HELP OUT AFTER SEEING HIM OFF.
I'LL APOLOGIZE TO EVERY-ONE WHILE I'M THERE.
KLAK
I'M SORRY...
I really am stupid.
DING DONG
Falling asleep like that Next to that scumbag...
PONK PONK PONK PONK
NOT AGAIN.
DINGDONG
HERE'S ANOTHER NEIGHBOR COME TO COMPLAIN...
Falling asleep like that!
YES!
HELLO, GOOD MORNING!
THIS IS AZUSA ODAGIRI.
THUMP

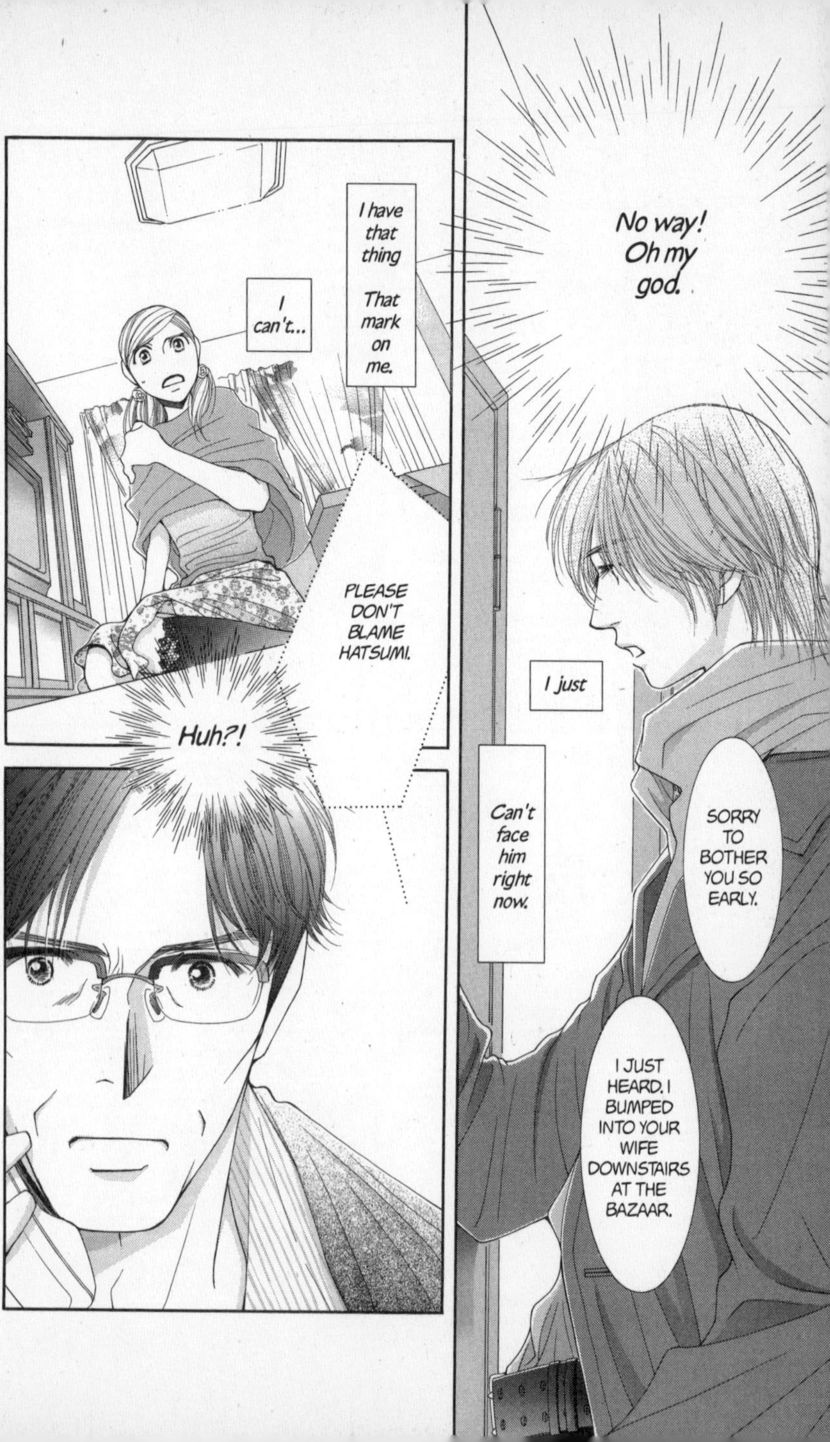
No way! Oh my god.
I just
Can't face him right now.
SORRY TO BOTHER YOU SO EARLY.
I JUST HEARD. I BUMPED INTO YOUR WIFE DOWNSTAIRS AT THE BAZAAR.
I have that thing
That mark on me.
I can't...
PLEASE DON'T BLAME HATSUMI.
Huh?!

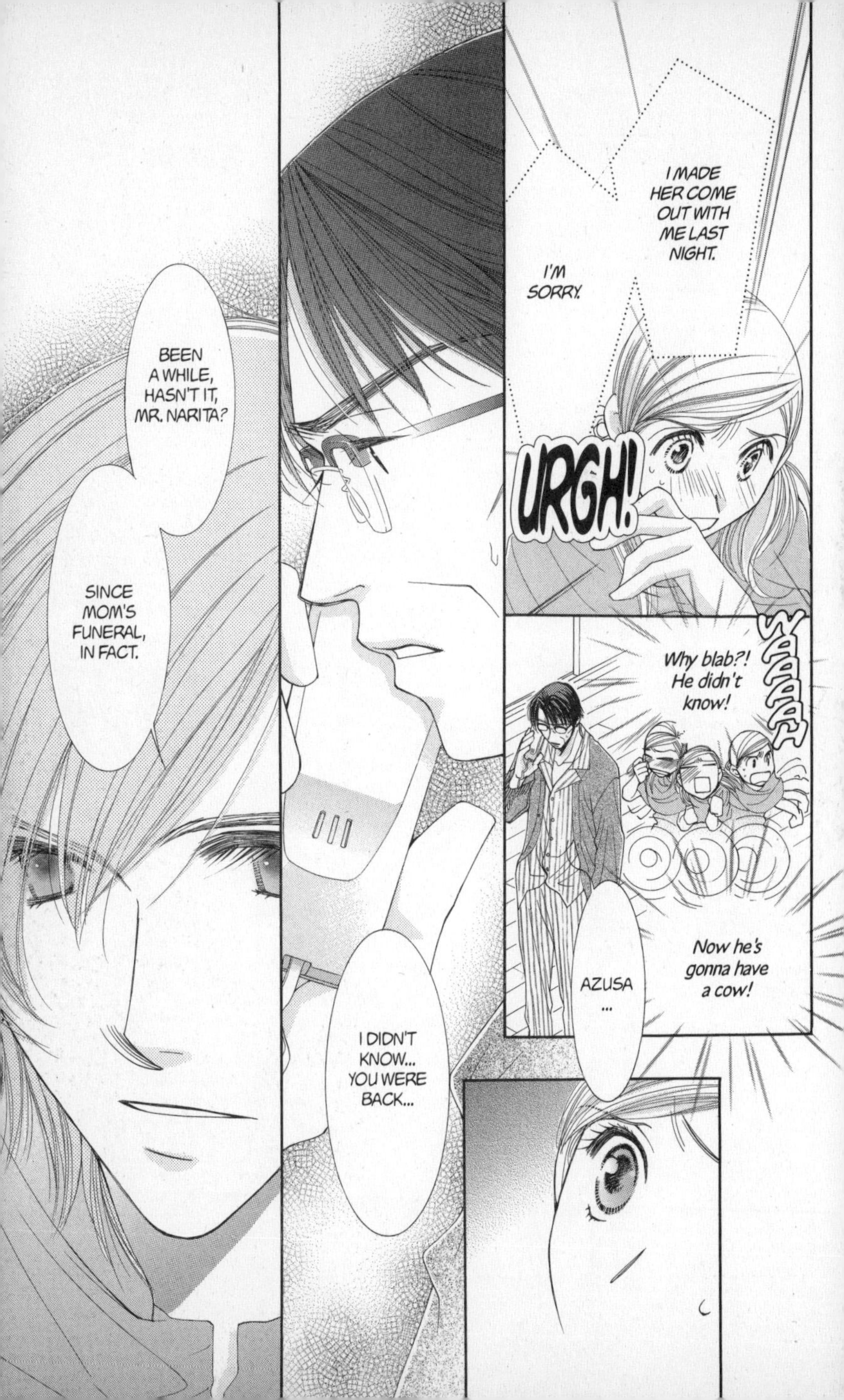
I MADE HER COME OUT WITH ME LAST NIGHT.
I'M SORRY.
URGH!
Why blab?! He didn't know!
Now he's gonna have a cow!
AZUSA ...
I DIDN'T KNOW... YOU WERE BACK...
BEEN A WHILE, HASN'T IT, MR. NARITA?
SINCE MOM'S FUNERAL, IN FACT.

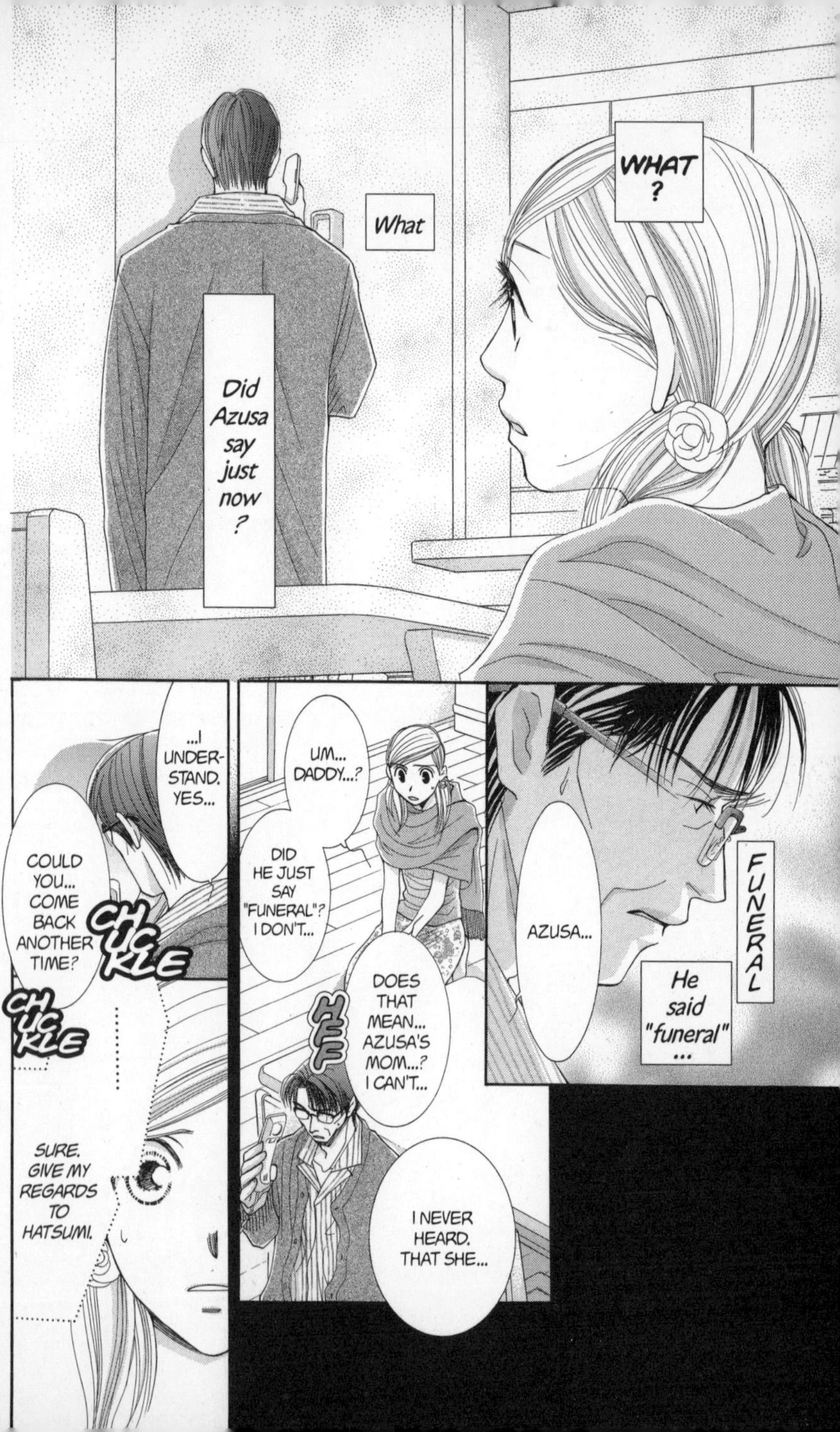
WHAT ?
What
Did Azusa say just now ?
FUNERAL
He said "funeral" ...
AZUSA...
UM... DADDY...?
DID HE JUST SAY "FUNERAL"? I DON'T...
DOES THAT MEAN... AZUSA'S MOM...? I CAN'T...
HEF
I NEVER HEARD. THAT SHE...
...I UNDER-STAND. YES...
COULD YOU... COME BACK ANOTHER TIME?
CHUCKLE
CHUCKLE
SURE. GIVE MY REGARDS TO HATSUMI.

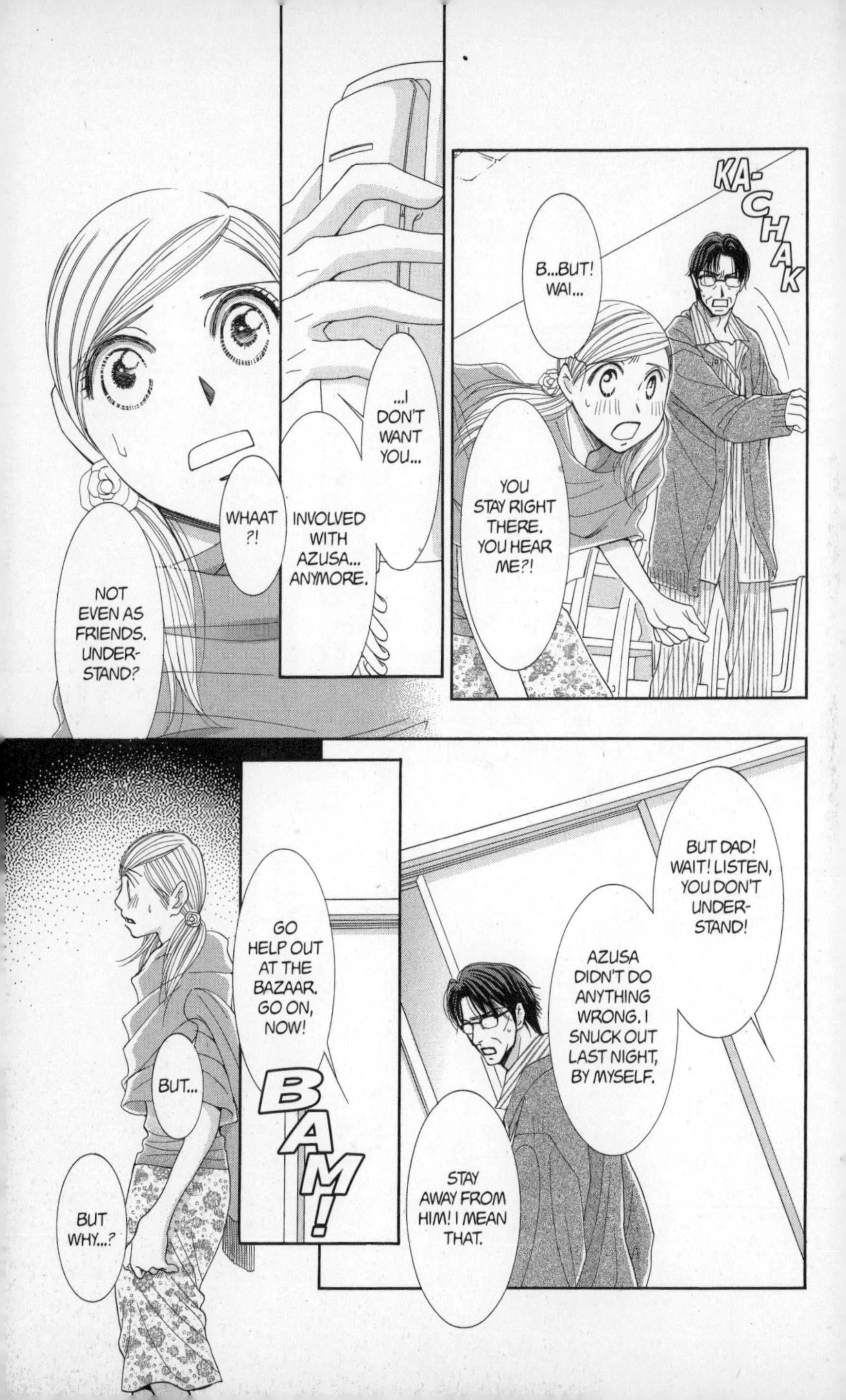
KA-CHAK
B...BUT! WAI...
YOU STAY RIGHT THERE. YOU HEAR ME?!
...I DON'T WANT YOU...
INVOLVED WITH AZUSA... ANYMORE.
WHAAT ?!
NOT EVEN AS FRIENDS. UNDER-STAND?
BUT DAD! WAIT! LISTEN, YOU DON'T UNDER-STAND!
AZUSA DIDN'T DO ANYTHING WRONG. I SNUCK OUT LAST NIGHT, BY MYSELF.
STAY AWAY FROM HIM! I MEAN THAT.
GO HELP OUT AT THE BAZAAR. GO ON, NOW!
BAM!
BUT...
BUT WHY...?

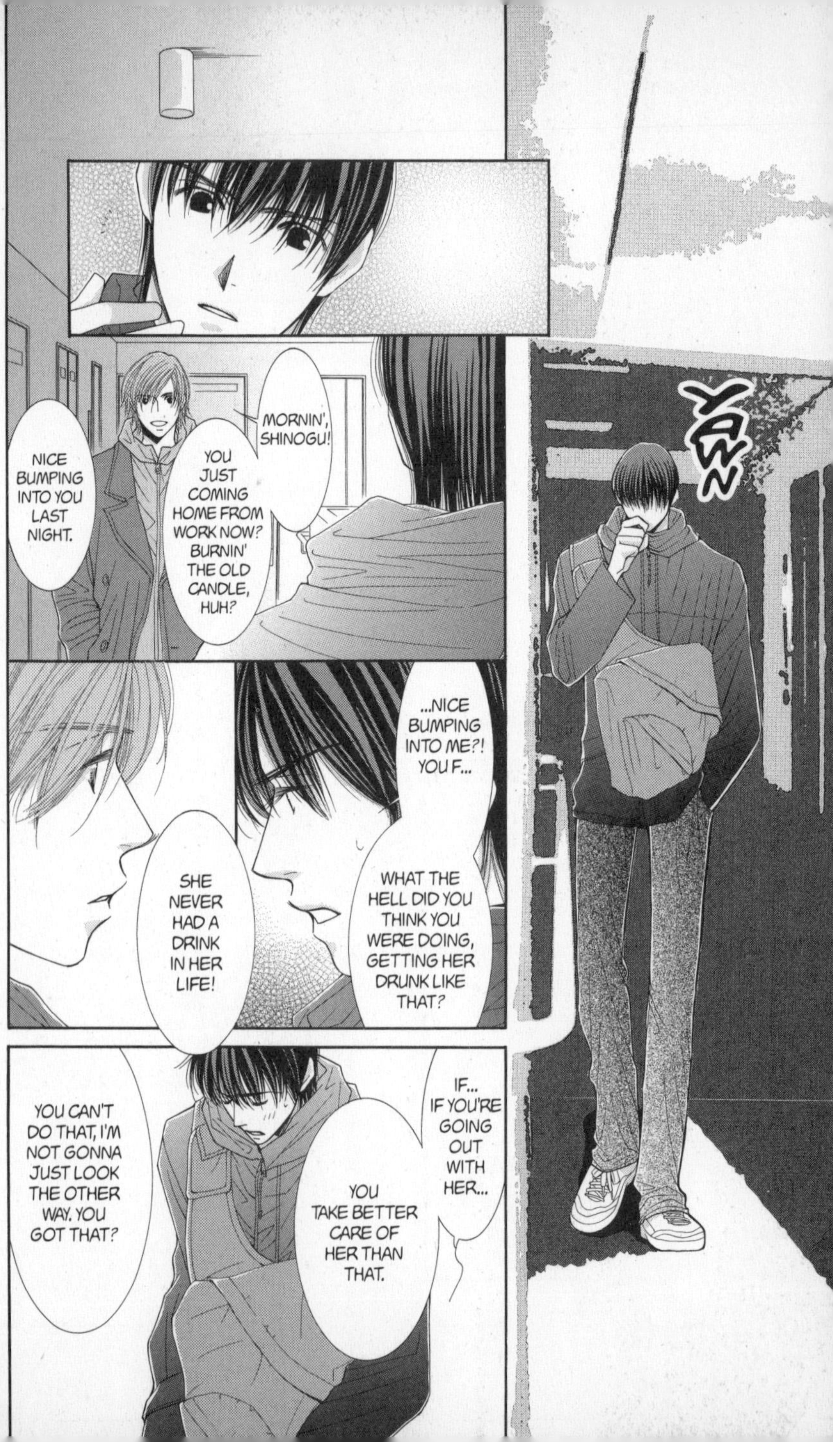
YAWN
MORNIN', SHINOGU!
YOU JUST COMING HOME FROM WORK NOW? BURNIN' THE OLD CANDLE, HUH?
NICE BUMPING INTO YOU LAST NIGHT.
...NICE BUMPING INTO ME?! YOU F...
WHAT THE HELL DID YOU THINK YOU WERE DOING, GETTING HER DRUNK LIKE THAT?
SHE NEVER HAD A DRINK IN HER LIFE!
IF... IF YOU'RE GOING OUT WITH HER...
YOU TAKE BETTER CARE OF HER THAN THAT.
YOU CAN'T DO THAT, I'M NOT GONNA JUST LOOK THE OTHER WAY. YOU GOT THAT?

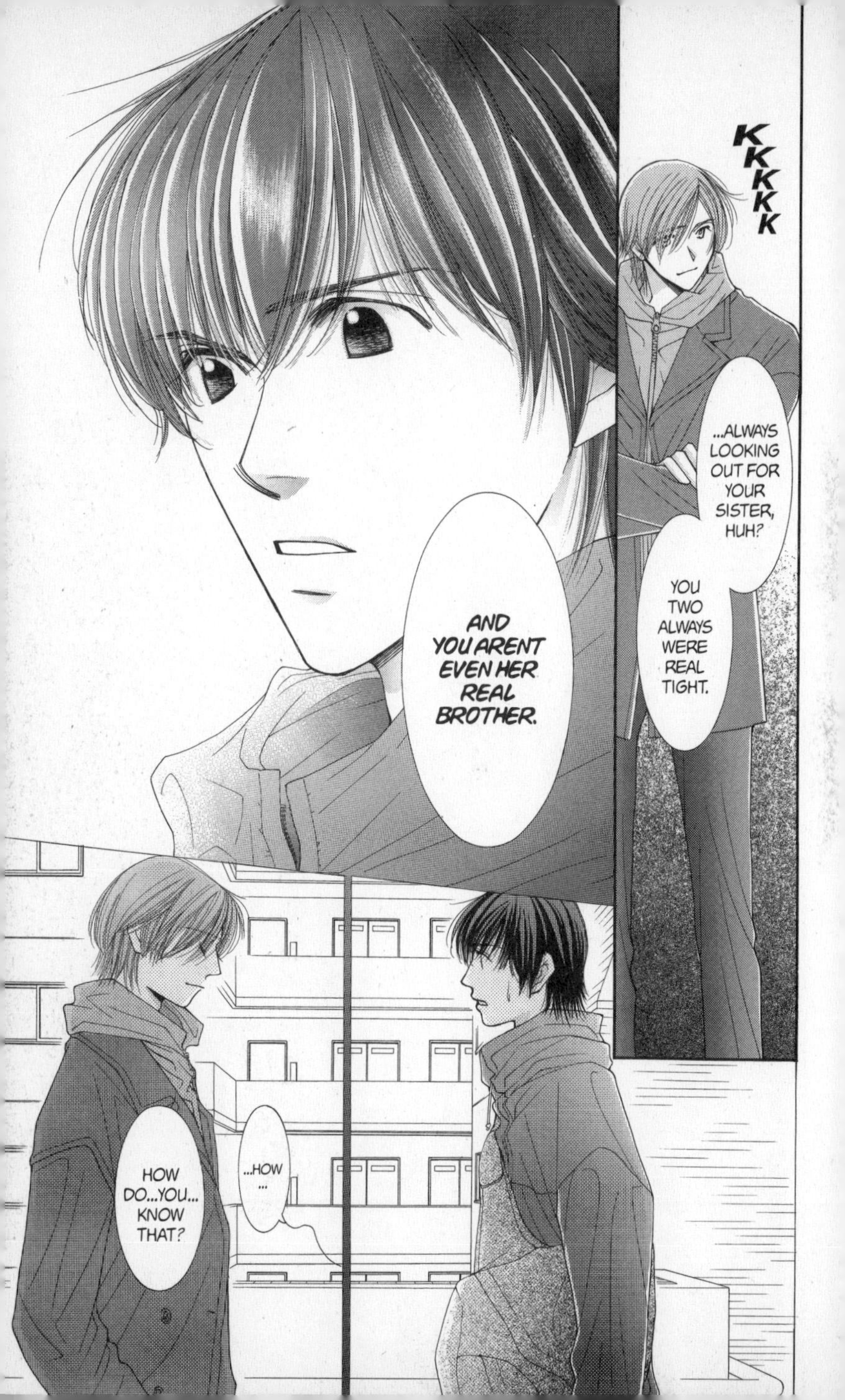
KKKKK
...ALWAYS LOOKING OUT FOR YOUR SISTER, HUH?
YOU TWO ALWAYS WERE REAL TIGHT.
AND YOU ARENT EVEN HER REAL BROTHER.
...HOW ...
HOW DO...YOU... KNOW THAT?

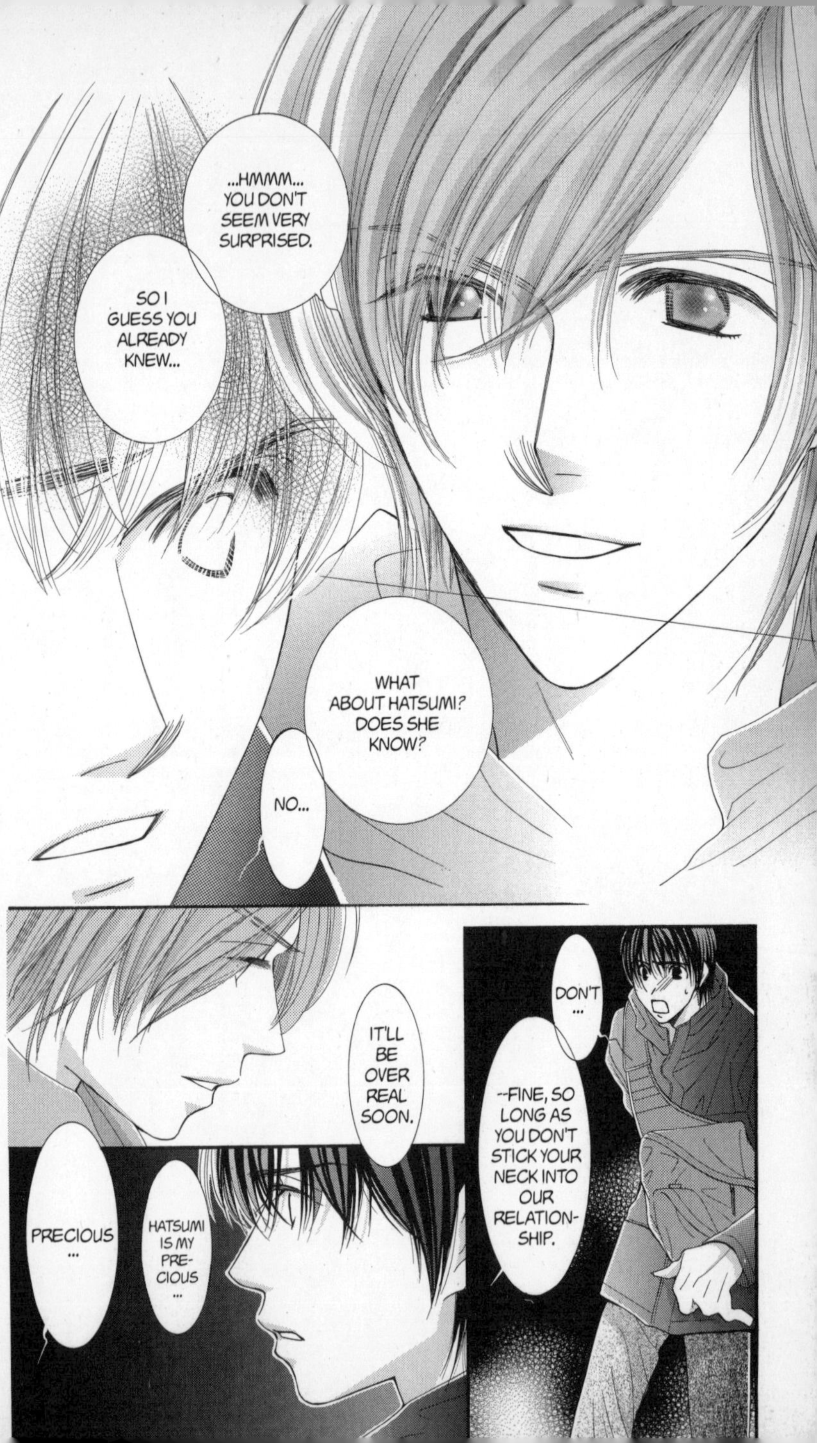
...HMMM... YOU DON'T SEEM VERY SURPRISED.
SO I GUESS YOU ALREADY KNEW...
WHAT ABOUT HATSUMI? DOES SHE KNOW?
NO...
DON'T ...
--FINE, SO LONG AS YOU DON'T STICK YOUR NECK INTO OUR RELATION-SHIP.
IT'LL BE OVER REAL SOON.
HATSUMI IS MY PRE-CIOUS ...
PRECIOUS ...

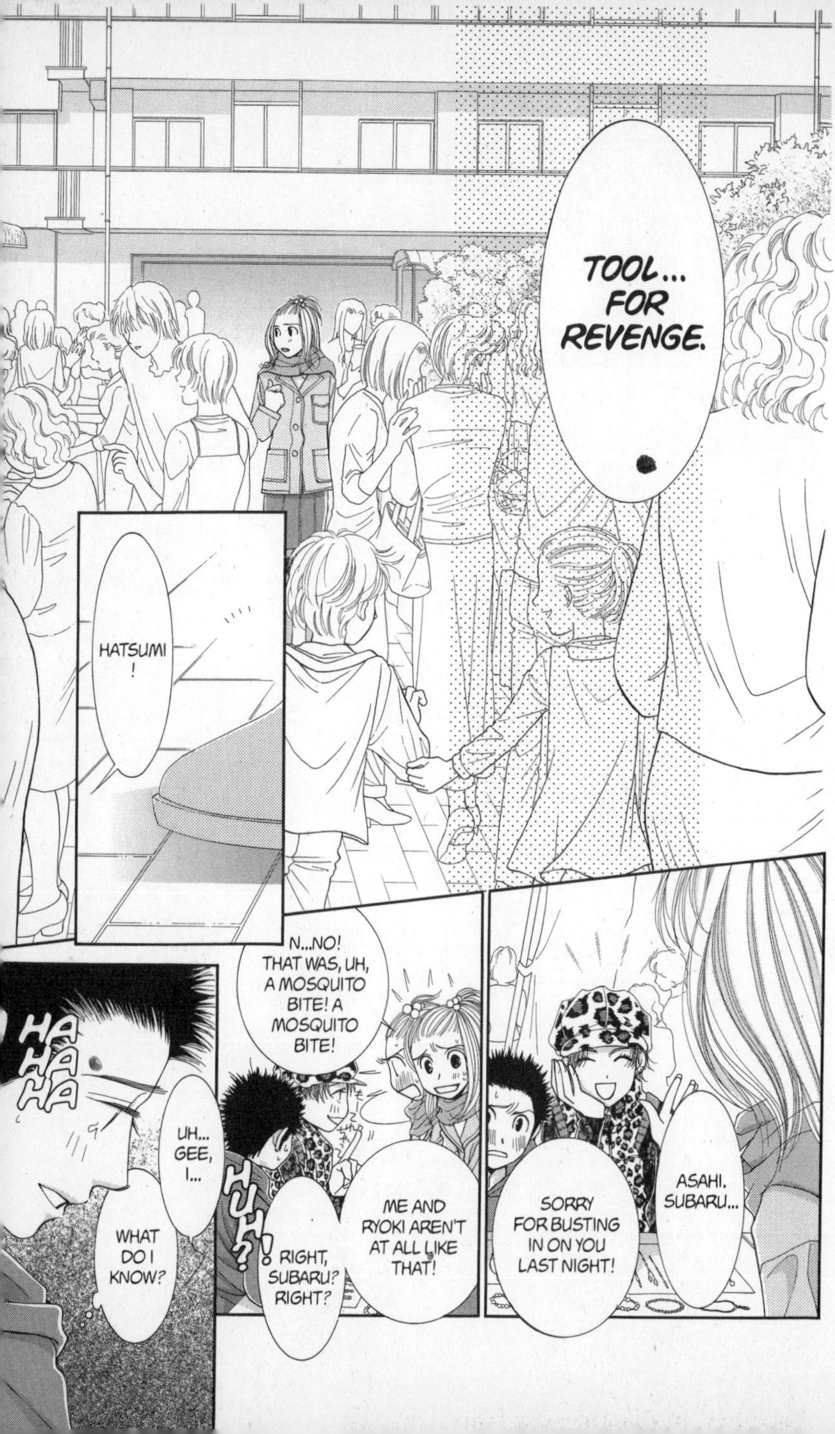
TOOL... FOR REVENGE.
HATSUMI !
ASAHI. SUBARU...
SORRY FOR BUSTING IN ON YOU LAST NIGHT!
N...NO! THAT WAS, UH, A MOSQUITO BITE! A MOSQUITO BITE!
ME AND RYOKI AREN'T AT ALL LIKE THAT!
HUH?!
RIGHT, SUBARU? RIGHT?
HA HA HA
UH... GEE, I...
WHAT DO I KNOW?

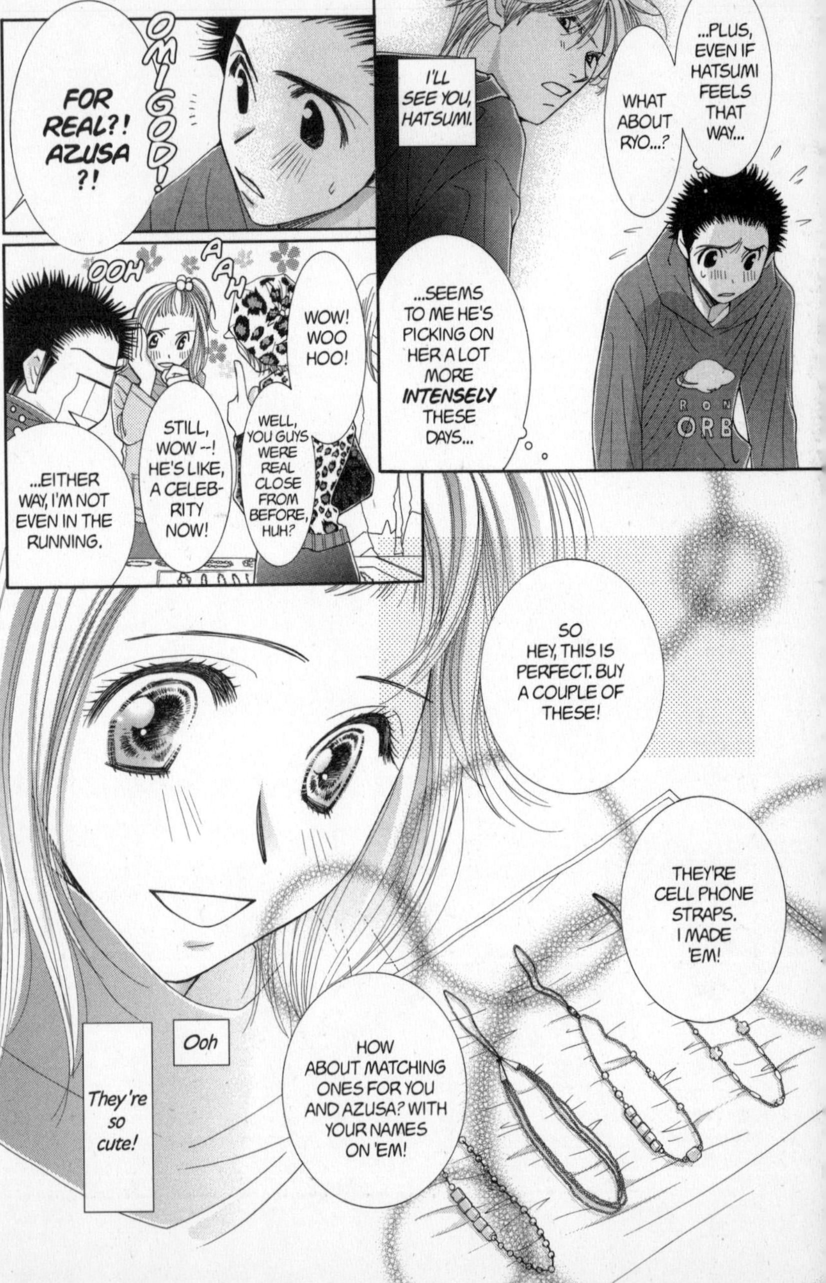
...PLUS, EVEN IF HATSUMI FEELS THAT WAY...
WHAT ABOUT RYO...?
I'LL SEE YOU, HATSUMI.
...SEEMS TO ME HE'S PICKING ON HER A LOT MORE **INTENSELY** THESE DAYS...
OMIGOD!
FOR REAL?! AZUSA?!
WOW! WOO HOO!
AAH
OOH
WELL, YOU GUYS WERE REAL CLOSE FROM BEFORE, HUH?
STILL, WOW --! HE'S LIKE, A CELEBRITY NOW!
...EITHER WAY, I'M NOT EVEN IN THE RUNNING.
SO HEY, THIS IS PERFECT. BUY A COUPLE OF THESE!
THEY'RE CELL PHONE STRAPS. I MADE 'EM!
HOW ABOUT MATCHING ONES FOR YOU AND AZUSA? WITH YOUR NAMES ON 'EM!
Ooh
They're so cute!

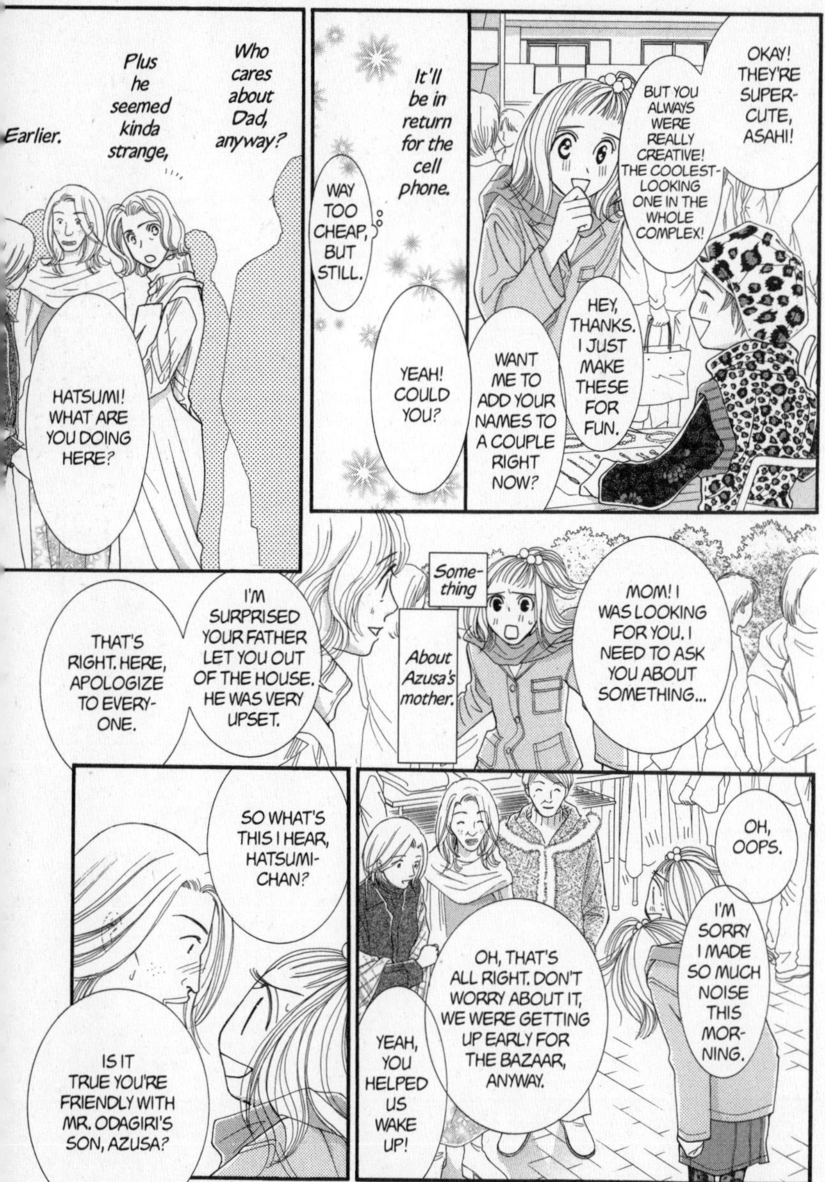
OKAY! THEY'RE SUPER-CUTE, ASAHI!
BUT YOU ALWAYS WERE REALLY CREATIVE! THE COOLEST-LOOKING ONE IN THE WHOLE COMPLEX!
HEY, THANKS. I JUST MAKE THESE FOR FUN.
WANT ME TO ADD YOUR NAMES TO A COUPLE RIGHT NOW?
It'll be in return for the cell phone.
WAY TOO CHEAP, BUT STILL.
YEAH! COULD YOU?
Who cares about Dad, anyway?
Plus he seemed kinda strange,
Earlier.
HATSUMI! WHAT ARE YOU DOING HERE?
MOM! I WAS LOOKING FOR YOU. I NEED TO ASK YOU ABOUT SOMETHING...
Something
About Azusa's mother.
I'M SURPRISED YOUR FATHER LET YOU OUT OF THE HOUSE. HE WAS VERY UPSET.
THAT'S RIGHT. HERE, APOLOGIZE TO EVERY-ONE.
OH, OOPS.
I'M SORRY I MADE SO MUCH NOISE THIS MOR-NING.
OH, THAT'S ALL RIGHT. DON'T WORRY ABOUT IT, WE WERE GETTING UP EARLY FOR THE BAZAAR, ANYWAY.
YEAH, YOU HELPED US WAKE UP!
SO WHAT'S THIS I HEAR, HATSUMI-CHAN?
IS IT TRUE YOU'RE FRIENDLY WITH MR. ODAGIRI'S SON, AZUSA?

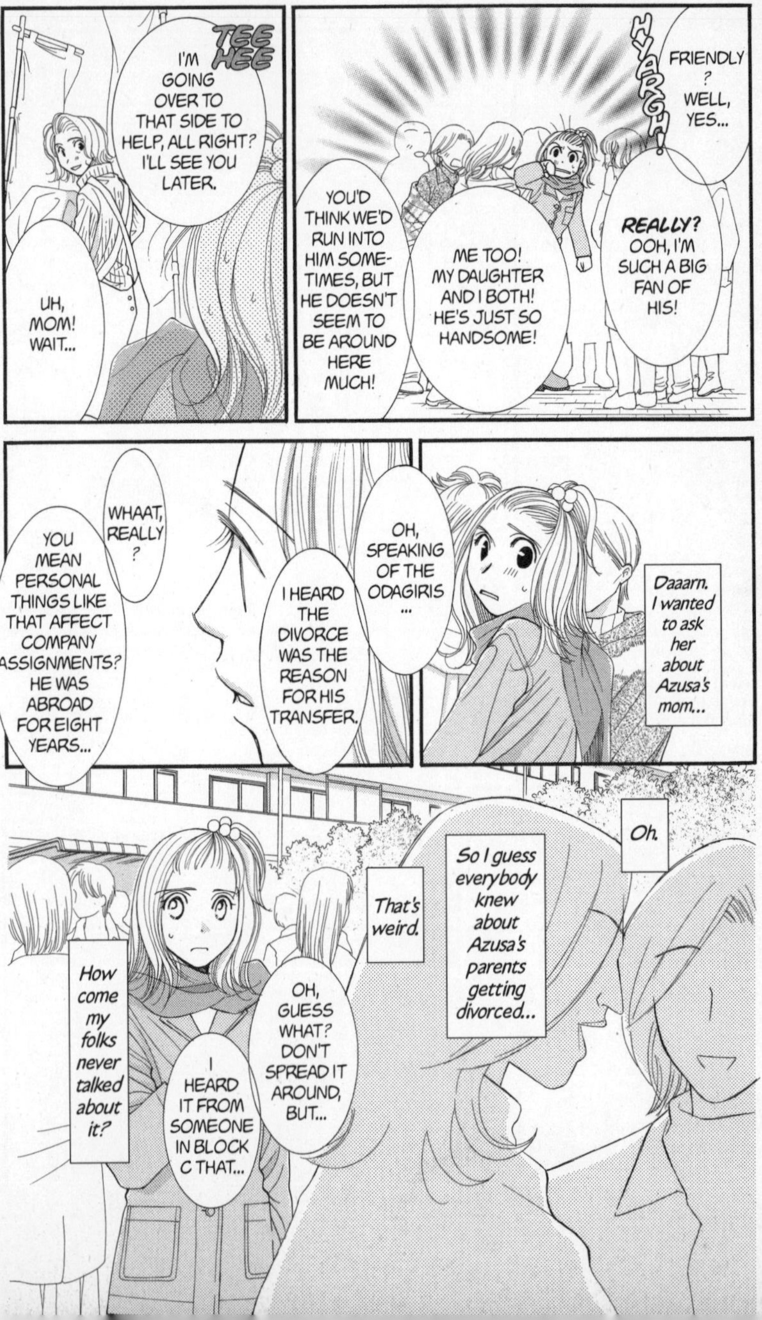

HYARGH!
FRIENDLY? WELL, YES...
REALLY? OOH, I'M SUCH A BIG FAN OF HIS!
ME TOO! MY DAUGHTER AND I BOTH! HE'S JUST SO HANDSOME!
YOU'D THINK WE'D RUN INTO HIM SOMETIMES, BUT HE DOESN'T SEEM TO BE AROUND HERE MUCH!
TEE HEE
I'M GOING OVER TO THAT SIDE TO HELP, ALL RIGHT? I'LL SEE YOU LATER.
UH, MOM! WAIT...
Daaarn. I wanted to ask her about Azusa's mom...
OH, SPEAKING OF THE ODAGIRIS...
I HEARD THE DIVORCE WAS THE REASON FOR HIS TRANSFER.
WHAAT, REALLY?
YOU MEAN PERSONAL THINGS LIKE THAT AFFECT COMPANY ASSIGNMENTS? HE WAS ABROAD FOR EIGHT YEARS...
Oh.
So I guess everybody knew about Azusa's parents getting divorced...
That's weird.
OH, GUESS WHAT? DON'T SPREAD IT AROUND, BUT...
I HEARD IT FROM SOMEONE IN BLOCK C THAT...
How come my folks never talked about it?

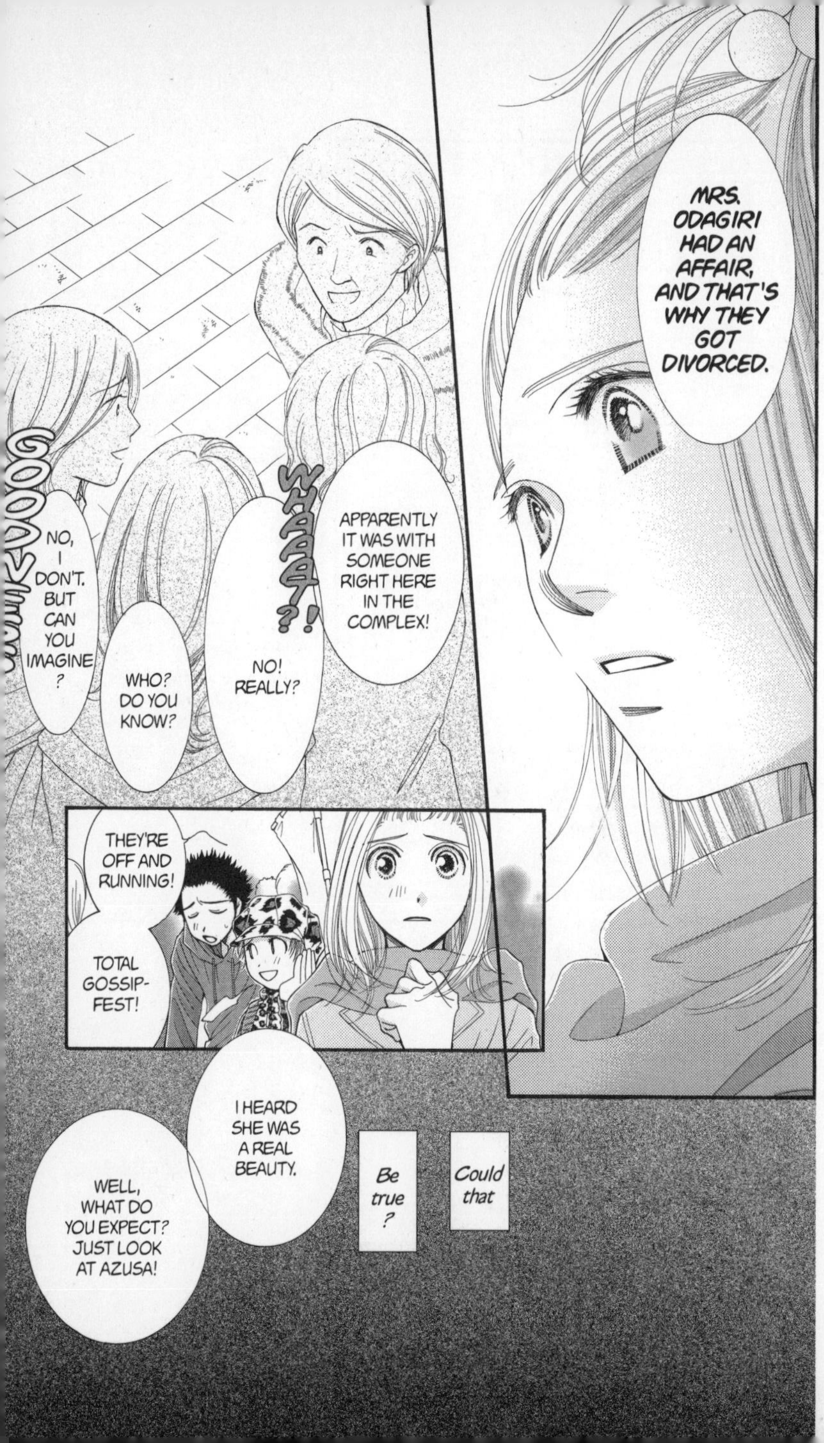
MRS. ODAGIRI HAD AN AFFAIR, AND THAT'S WHY THEY GOT DIVORCED.
APPARENTLY IT WAS WITH SOMEONE RIGHT HERE IN THE COMPLEX!
WHAAA?!
NO! REALLY?
WHO? DO YOU KNOW?
NO, I DON'T. BUT CAN YOU IMAGINE?
THEY'RE OFF AND RUNNING!
TOTAL GOSSIP-FEST!
Could that
Be true?
I HEARD SHE WAS A REAL BEAUTY.
WELL, WHAT DO YOU EXPECT? JUST LOOK AT AZUSA!

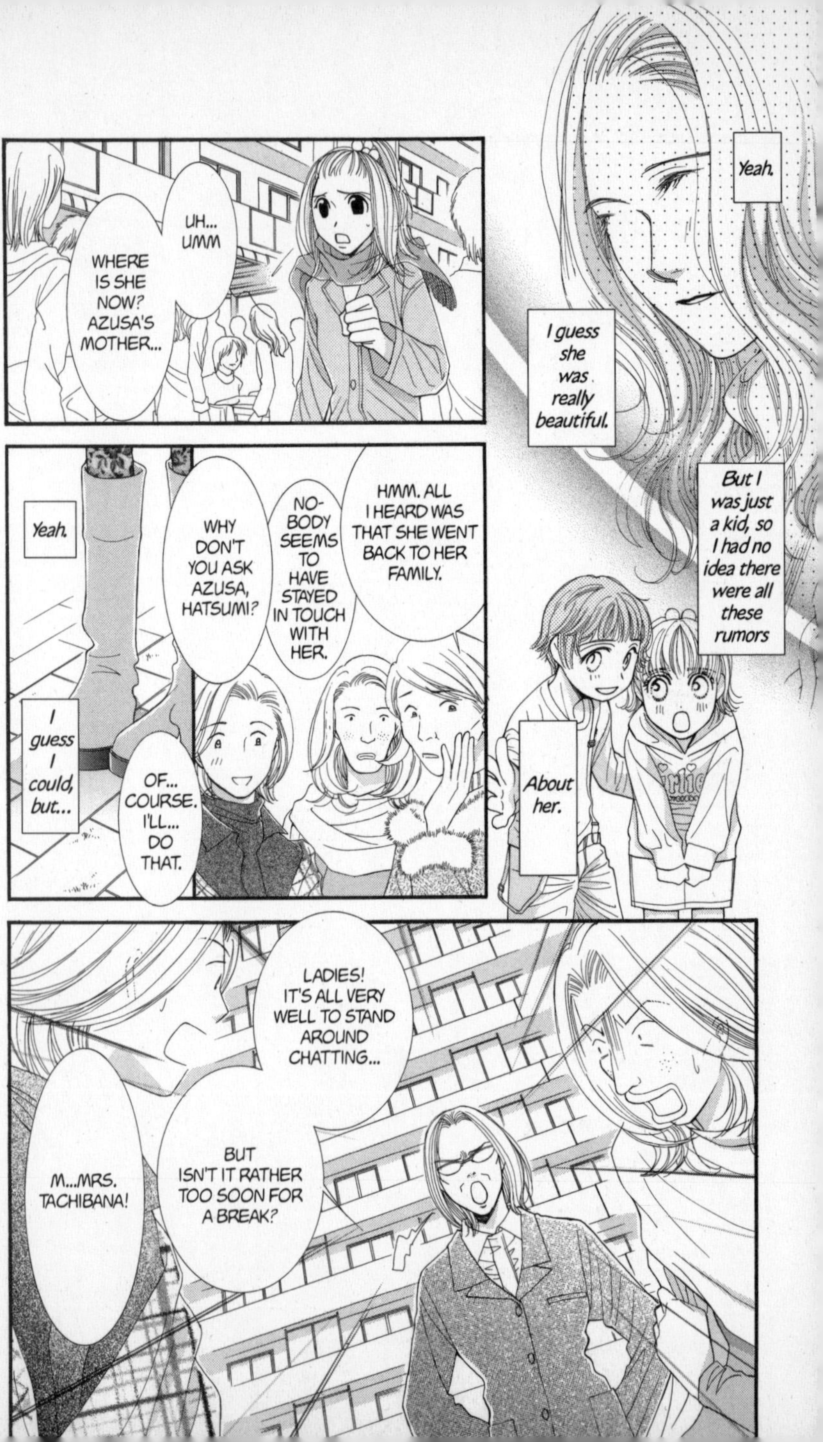
Yeah.
I guess she was really beautiful.
But I was just a kid, so I had no idea there were all these rumors
About her.
UH... UMM
WHERE IS SHE NOW? AZUSA'S MOTHER...
HMM. ALL I HEARD WAS THAT SHE WENT BACK TO HER FAMILY.
NO-BODY SEEMS TO HAVE STAYED IN TOUCH WITH HER.
WHY DON'T YOU ASK AZUSA, HATSUMI?
OF... COURSE. I'LL... DO THAT.
Yeah.
I guess I could, but...
LADIES! IT'S ALL VERY WELL TO STAND AROUND CHATTING...
BUT ISN'T IT RATHER TOO SOON FOR A BREAK?
M...MRS. TACHIBANA!

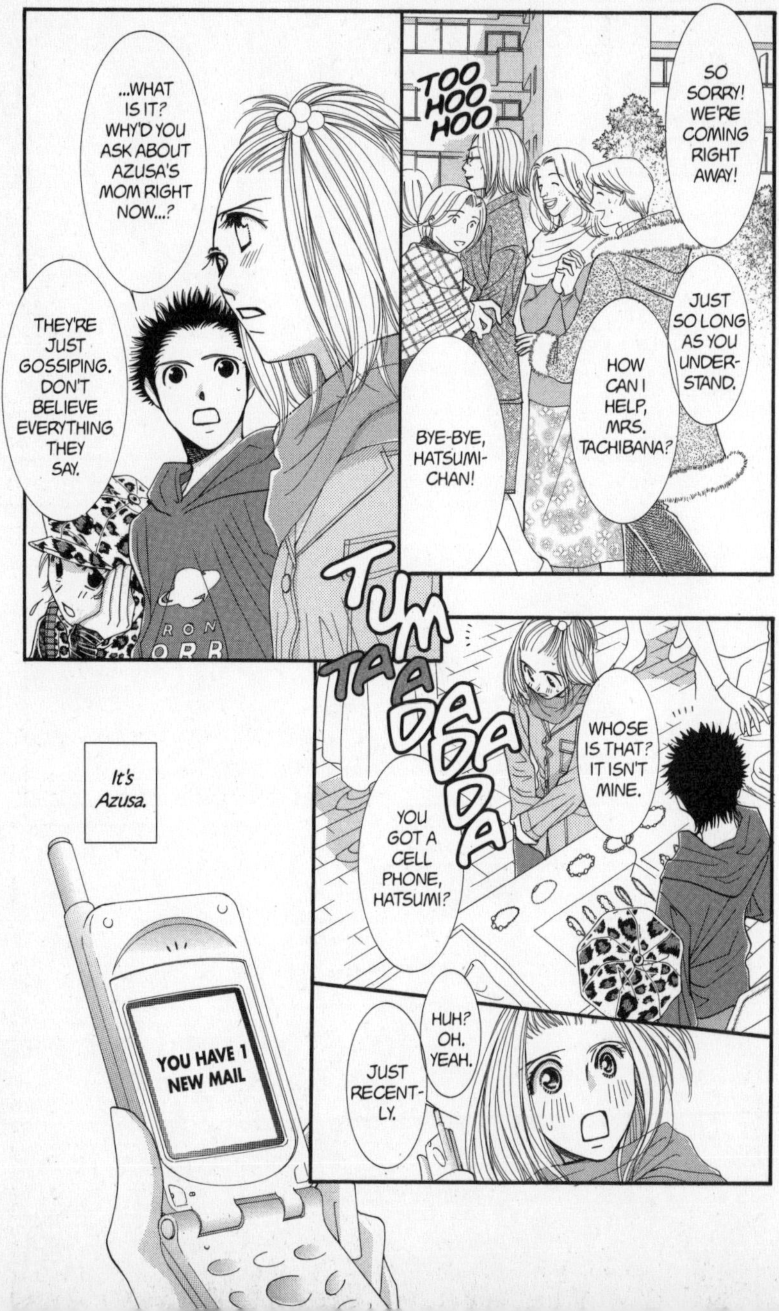

SO SORRY! WE'RE COMING RIGHT AWAY!
TOO HOO HOO
JUST SO LONG AS YOU UNDERSTAND.
HOW CAN I HELP, MRS. TACHIBANA?
BYE-BYE, HATSUMI-CHAN!
...WHAT IS IT? WHY'D YOU ASK ABOUT AZUSA'S MOM RIGHT NOW...?
THEY'RE JUST GOSSIPING. DON'T BELIEVE EVERYTHING THEY SAY.
RON ORB
TUM TA DA DA DA DA
WHOSE IS THAT? IT ISN'T MINE.
YOU GOT A CELL PHONE, HATSUMI?
HUH? OH. YEAH.
JUST RECENT-LY.
It's Azusa.
YOU HAVE 1 NEW MAIL

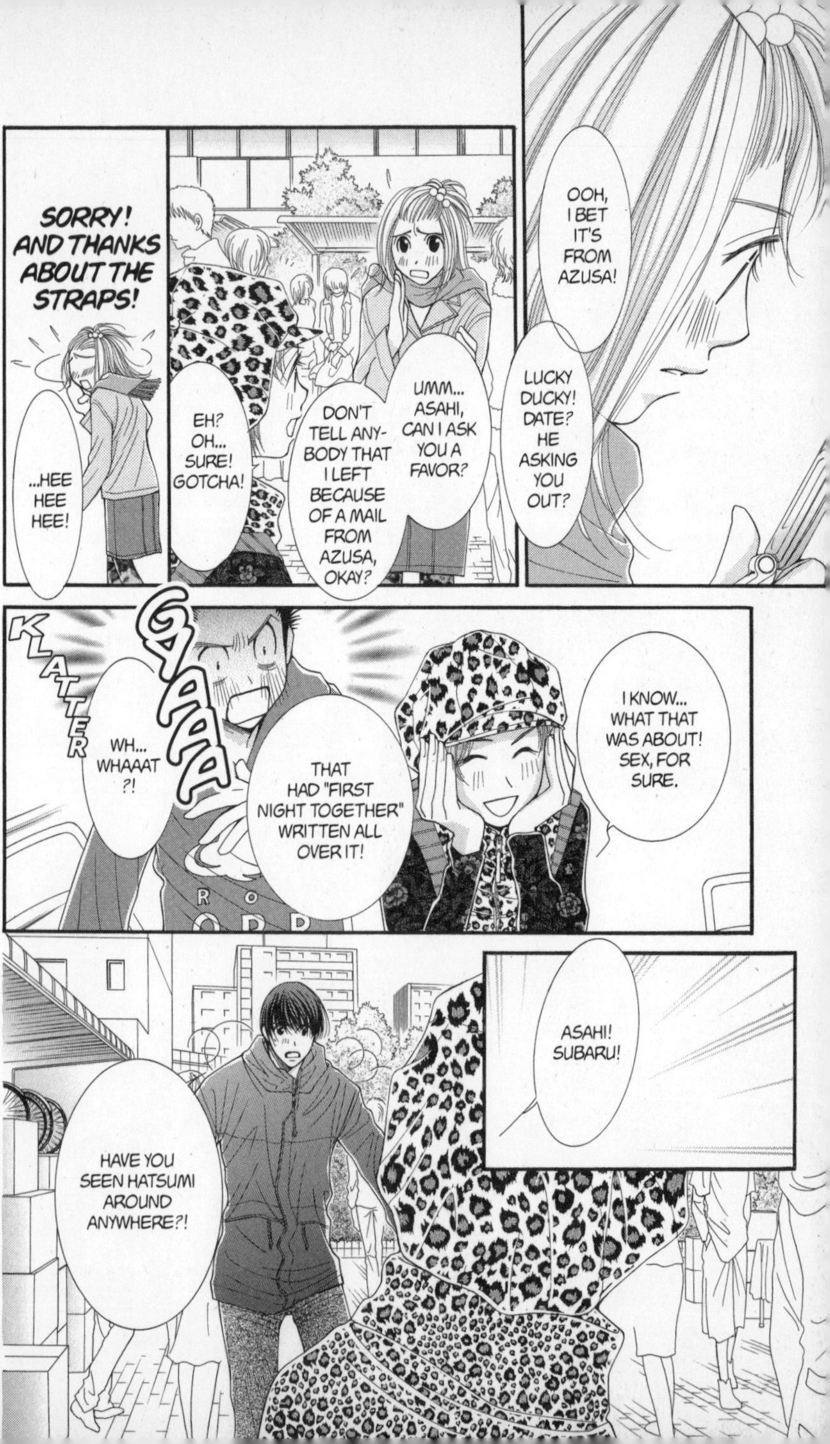
OOH, I BET IT'S FROM AZUSA!
LUCKY DUCKY! DATE? HE ASKING YOU OUT?
UMM... ASAHI, CAN I ASK YOU A FAVOR?
DON'T TELL ANY-BODY THAT I LEFT BECAUSE OF A MAIL FROM AZUSA, OKAY?
EH? OH... SURE! GOTCHA!
SORRY! AND THANKS ABOUT THE STRAPS!
...HEE HEE HEE!
I KNOW... WHAT THAT WAS ABOUT! SEX, FOR SURE.
THAT HAD "FIRST NIGHT TOGETHER" WRITTEN ALL OVER IT!
GAAAA
KLATTER
WH... WHAAAT?!
ASAHI! SUBARU!
HAVE YOU SEEN HATSUMI AROUND ANYWHERE?!

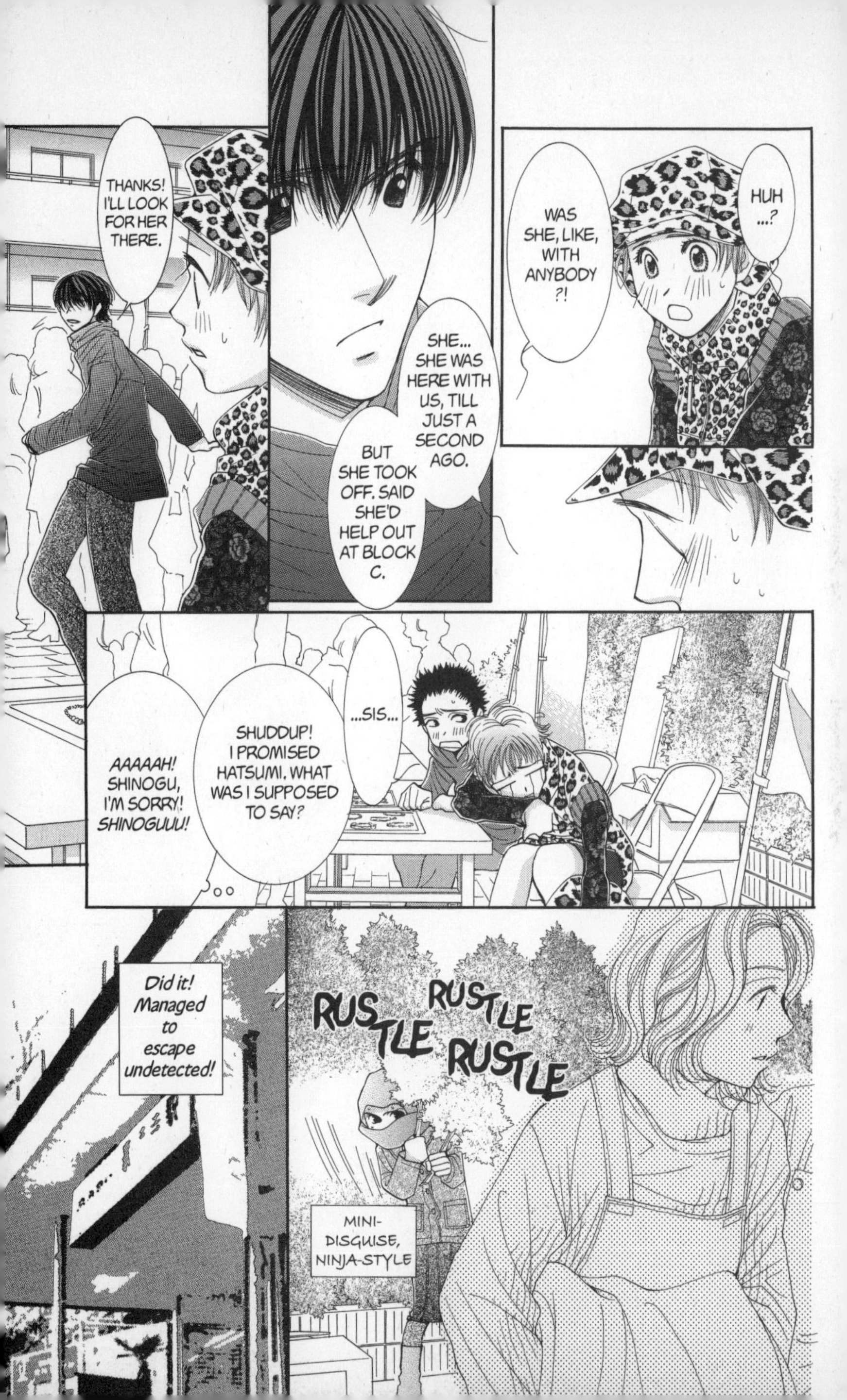
HUH ...?
WAS SHE, LIKE, WITH ANYBODY ?!
SHE... SHE WAS HERE WITH US, TILL JUST A SECOND AGO.
BUT SHE TOOK OFF. SAID SHE'D HELP OUT AT BLOCK C.
THANKS! I'LL LOOK FOR HER THERE.
...SIS...
SHUDDUP! I PROMISED HATSUMI. WHAT WAS I SUPPOSED TO SAY?
AAAAAH! SHINOGU, I'M SORRY! SHINOGUUU!
RUSTLE RUSTLE RUSTLE
MINI-DISGUISE, NINJA-STYLE
Did it! Managed to escape undetected!

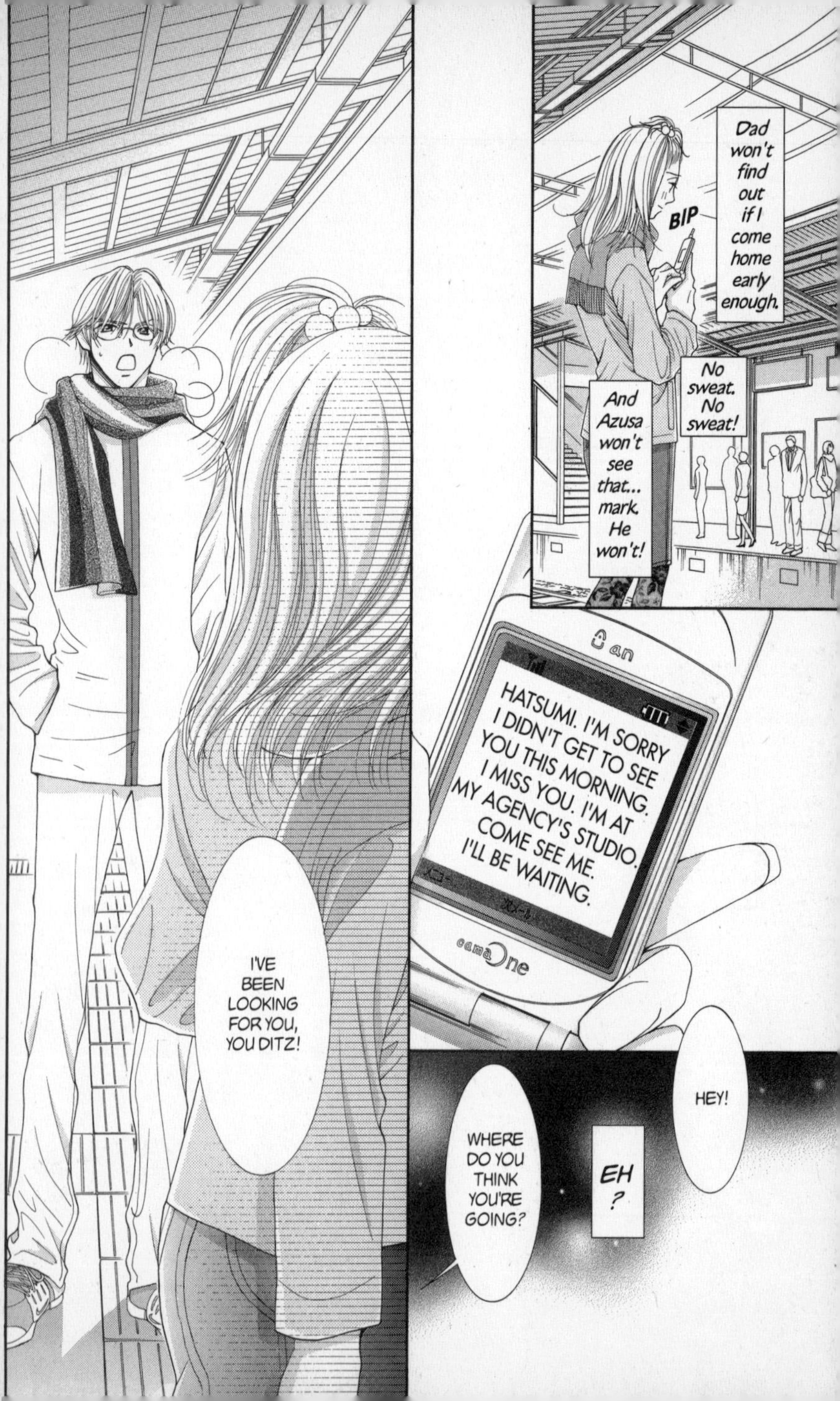
Dad won't find out if I come home early enough.
BIP
No sweat. No sweat!
And Azusa won't see that... mark. He won't!
HATSUMI. I'M SORRY I DIDN'T GET TO SEE YOU THIS MORNING. I MISS YOU. I'M AT MY AGENCY'S STUDIO. COME SEE ME. I'LL BE WAITING.
HEY!
EH ?
WHERE DO YOU THINK YOU'RE GOING?
I'VE BEEN LOOKING FOR YOU, YOU DITZ!

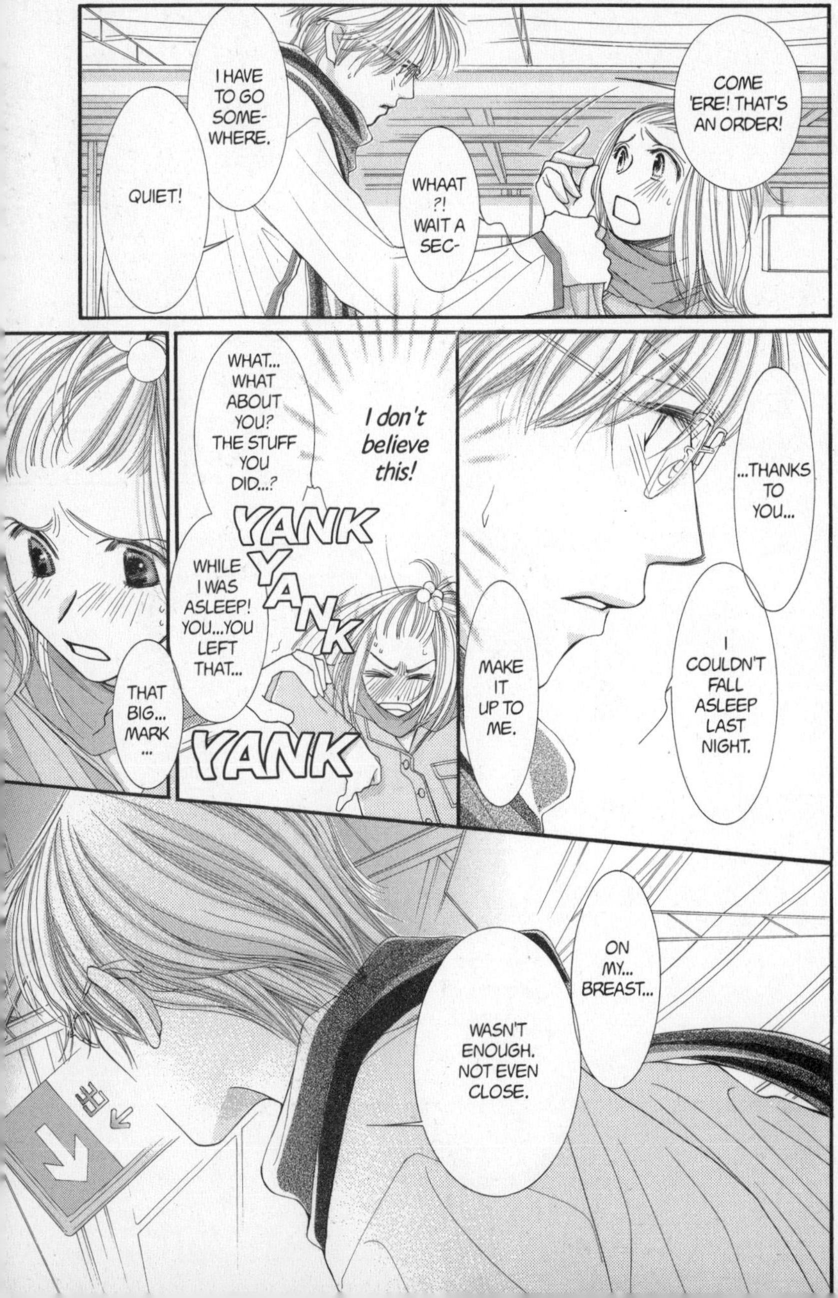
COME 'ERE! THAT'S AN ORDER!
WHAAT?! WAIT A SEC-
I HAVE TO GO SOME-WHERE.
QUIET!
...THANKS TO YOU...
I COULDN'T FALL ASLEEP LAST NIGHT.
MAKE IT UP TO ME.
WHAT... WHAT ABOUT YOU? THE STUFF YOU DID...?
I don't believe this!
YANK
YANK
YANK
WHILE I WAS ASLEEP! YOU...YOU LEFT THAT...
THAT BIG... MARK ...
ON MY... BREAST...
WASN'T ENOUGH. NOT EVEN CLOSE.

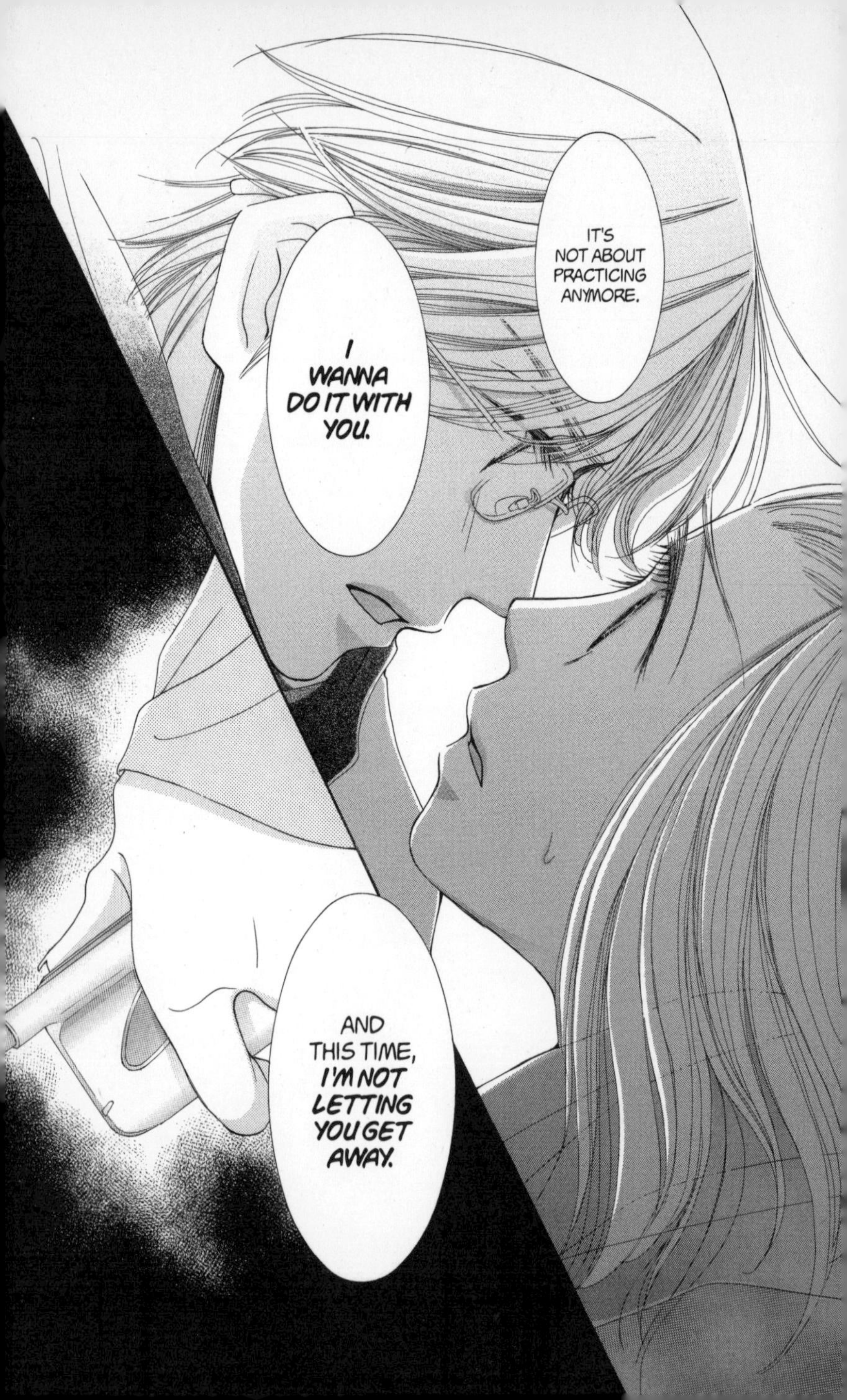
IT'S NOT ABOUT PRACTICING ANYMORE.
I WANNA DO IT WITH YOU.
AND THIS TIME, I'M NOT LETTING YOU GET AWAY.

To be continued

OUR
THREE
CHILDHOOD
BUDDIES.

GIMMICK

Thank you for buying Hot Gimmick Vol. 2.
My name is Miki Aihara.
Here, just for you graphic novel readers, is
more of that extra information that's so hard
to put into the actual story.
Read on!

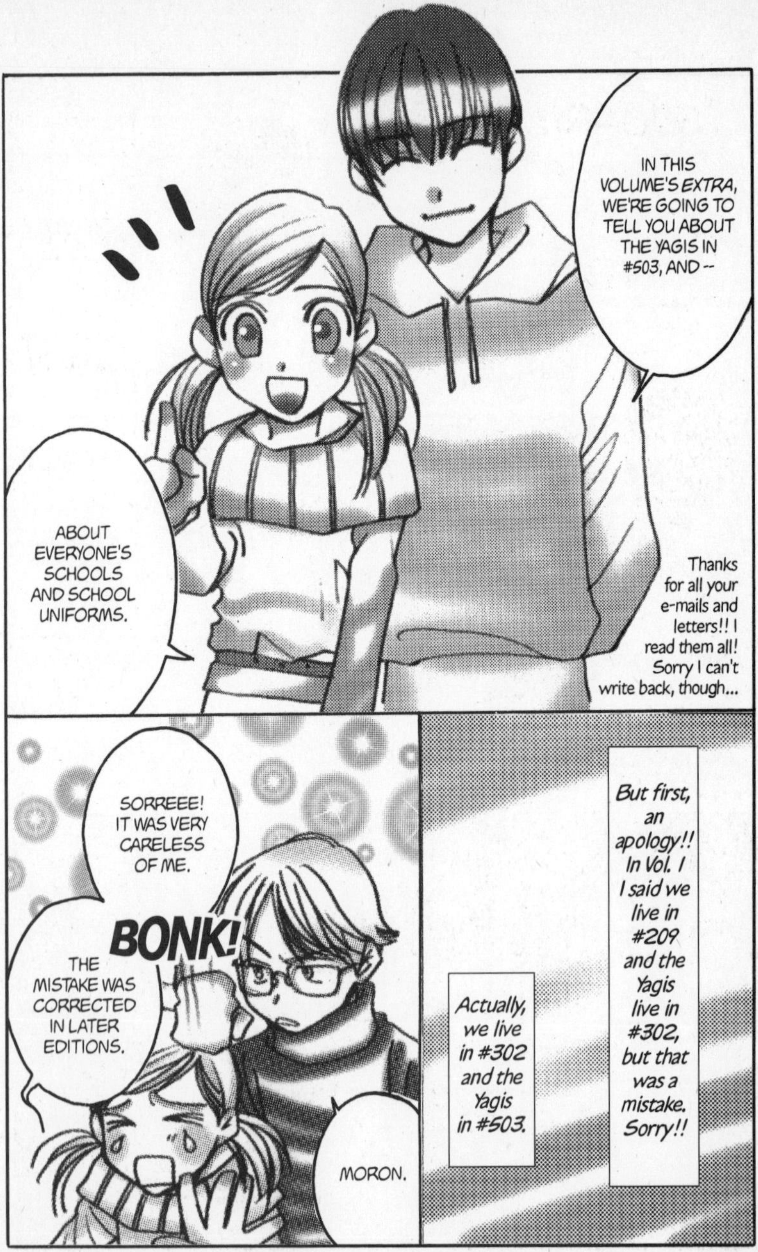
IN THIS VOLUME'S *EXTRA*, WE'RE GOING TO TELL YOU ABOUT THE YAGIS IN #503, AND --
ABOUT EVERYONE'S SCHOOLS AND SCHOOL UNIFORMS.
Thanks for all your e-mails and letters!! I read them all! Sorry I can't write back, though...
But first, an apology!! In Vol. 1 I said we live in #209 and the Yagis live in #302, but that was a mistake. Sorry!!
Actually, we live in #302 and the Yagis in #503.
SORREEE! IT WAS VERY CARELESS OF ME.
BONK!
THE MISTAKE WAS CORRECTED IN LATER EDITIONS.
MORON.

THE YAGI FAMILY

SUBARU (16)

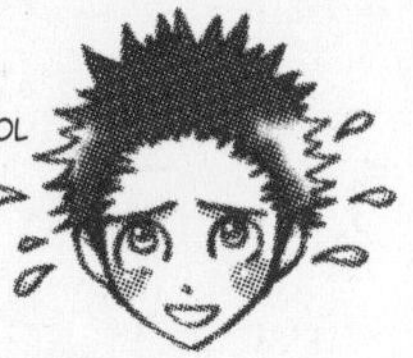

- SECOND-YEAR STUDENT AT TAKAZONO HIGH SCHOOL (CLASS A).
- 165 cm TALL, 45 kg. TOO SKINNY! (AIHARA COMMENT)
- NO CLUB ACTIVITIES OR PART-TIME JOB.
- HOBBIES ARE MAKING AND COLLECTING GUNDAM MODELS AND ACTION FIGURES. ALSO LIKES VIDEO GAMES AND ANIME.
- IN SPITE OF BEING AN OTAKU, LOOKS PRETTY COOL (HAIR, CLOTHES) DUE TO STRICT ATTENTIONS OF FASHIONABLE SISTER.

MRS. YAGI

- HASN'T APPEARED IN THE STORY SO FAR.
- A FLEDGLING TRANSLATOR, SHE'S SORT OF AN "OUTLAW" IN THE COMPANY HOUSING COMPLEX. LONE-WOLF TYPE. BUT GETS ON WELL WITH MRS. NARITA.

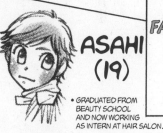

ASAHI (19)

- GRADUATED FROM BEAUTY SCHOOL AND NOW WORKING AS INTERN AT HAIR SALON.
- USES BROTHER'S HEAD FOR PRACTICE AND EXPERIMENTS.
- HAS HAD A SECRET CRUSH ON SHINOGU FOREVER, BUT THINKS HE'S TOO UNATTAINABLE, SO CAN'T TELL HIM.

MR. YAGI

- WENT TO THE SAME UNIVERSITY AS HATSUMI'S DAD, BUT A FEW YEARS BEHIND HIM. A GENTLE SOUL. ALSO HASN'T MADE AN APPEARANCE YET.

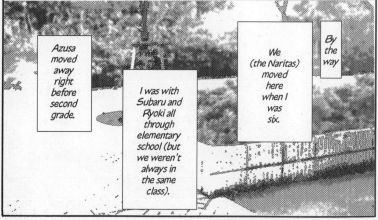

By the way
We (the Naritas) moved here when I was six.
I was with Subaru and Ryoki all through elementary school (but we weren't always in the same class).
Azusa moved away right before second grade.

UNIFORMS

- TAKAZONO HIGH SCHOOL UNIFORM.

  PRIVATE SCHOOL KNOWN FOR ITS "LIBERAL ATMOSPHERE". WHICH IS WHY AZUSA CAN EARN CREDITS WHILE PURSUING A MODELING CAREER.

- BY THE WAY, SHINOGU WENT TO A PUBLIC HIGH SCHOOL. THE UNIFORM WAS THE BASIC BLACK-WITH-GOLD-BUTTONS VARIETY.

  IF ANYBODY WANTS TO SEE IT, SEND ME A REQUEST! (DOUBT ANYBODY WOULD...)

  BROWN JACKET

WHITE UNIFORM WITH BLUE TRIM.

- KAISEI ACADEMY.

  SUPER-ELITE PRIVATE SCHOOL WITH THE COUNTRY'S TOP ADMISSION RATE FOR TODAI. COMPRISES JUNIOR AND SENIOR HIGH SCHOOLS.

  RYOKI IS A STUDENT FROM JUNIOR HIGH. ALL-MALE STUDENT BODY.

  DORMITORY AVAILABLE.

HOT GIMMICK
Vol. 2

Shôjo Edition

STORY & ART BY MIKI AIHARA

ENGLISH ADAPTATION BY POOKIE ROLF

Touch-Up Art & Lettering/Rina Mapa
Design/Izumi Evers
Editor/Alvin Lu

Managing Editor/Annette Roman
Production Manager/Noboru Watanabe
Sr. Director of Licensing and Acquisitions/Rika Inouye
VP of Sales and Marketing/Liza Coppola
Senior VP of Editorial/Hyoe Narita
Publisher/Seiji Horibuchi

Printed in Canada

Published by VIZ, LLC, P.O. Box 77010, San Francisco, CA 94107

Shôjo Edition
10 9 8 7 6 5 4 3 2

First printing, December 2003
Second printing, July 2004

EDITOR'S RECOMMENDATIONS

More manga!
More manga!

If you enjoyed this volume of

Hot Gimmick

then here's some more manga you might be interested in.

HANA-YORI DANGO ©
1992 by Yoko
Kamio/SHUEISHA Inc.

Boys over Flowers by Yoko Kamio: Meet
Makino and Makiko Yuki—cute, popular high
school girls whose lives take a turn for the
worse when a gang of rich boys makes the
whole school pick on them....

© 1996 SAITO
CHIHO/IKUHARA KUNI-
HIKO & BE
PAPAS/Shogakukan, Inc.

Revolutionary Girl Utena by Chiho Saito:
After being saved by a prince, Utena strives
to grow up strong and noble—just like him!
Now she's ready to revolutionize the world, if
only it will lead her to her prince!

© Junko Mizuno 2000

Junko Mizuno's Cinderalla by Junko Mizuno:
The classic fairy tale re-told in psychedelic
colors where Prince Charming is a...
zombie?!

COMPLETE OUR SURVEY AND LET US KNOW WHAT YOU THINK!

☐ Please do NOT send me information about VIZ products, news and events, special offers, or other information.

☐ Please do NOT send me information from VIZ's trusted business partners.

Name: _____

Address: _____

City: _____ **State:** _____ **Zip:** _____

E-mail: _____

☐ Male ☐ Female **Date of Birth** (mm/dd/yyyy): ___ / ___ / _____ (Under 13? Parental consent required)

What race/ethnicity do you consider yourself? (please check one)

☐ Asian/Pacific Islander   ☐ Black/African American   ☐ Hispanic/Latino

☐ Native American/Alaskan Native   ☐ White/Caucasian   ☐ Other: _____

What VIZ product did you purchase? (check all that apply and indicate title purchased)

☐ DVD/VHS _____

☐ Graphic Novel _____

☐ Magazines _____

☐ Merchandise _____

Reason for purchase: (check all that apply)

☐ Special offer   ☐ Favorite title   ☐ Gift

☐ Recommendation   ☐ Other _____

Where did you make your purchase? (please check one)

☐ Comic store   ☐ Bookstore   ☐ Mass/Grocery Store

☐ Newsstand   ☐ Video/Video Game Store   ☐ Other: _____

☐ Online (site: _____)

What other VIZ properties have you purchased/own? _____

_____

How many anime and/or manga titles have you purchased in the last year? How many were VIZ titles? **(please check one from each column)**

ANIME	MANGA	VIZ
☐ None	☐ None	☐ None
☐ 1-4	☐ 1-4	☐ 1-4
☐ 5-10	☐ 5-10	☐ 5-10
☐ 11+	☐ 11+	☐ 11+

I find the pricing of VIZ products to be: **(please check one)**

☐ Cheap ☐ Reasonable ☐ Expensive

What genre of manga and anime would you like to see from VIZ? **(please check two)**

☐ Adventure ☐ Comic Strip ☐ Science Fiction ☐ Fighting

☐ Horror ☐ Romance ☐ Fantasy ☐ Sports

What do you think of VIZ's new look?

☐ Love It ☐ It's OK ☐ Hate It ☐ Didn't Notice ☐ No Opinion

Which do you prefer? **(please check one)**

☐ Reading right-to-left

☐ Reading left-to-right

Which do you prefer? **(please check one)**

☐ Sound effects in English

☐ Sound effects in Japanese with English captions

☐ Sound effects in Japanese only with a glossary at the back

THANK YOU! Please send the completed form to:

NJW Research
42 Catharine St.
Poughkeepsie, NY 12601

All information provided will be used for internal purposes only. We promise not to sell or otherwise divulge your information.